Phil's Favorite 500

Loves of a Moviegoing Lifetime

Phil Berardelli

Mountain Lake Press
Mountain Lake Park, Maryland

Phil's Favorite 500:
Loves of a Moviegoing Lifetime

For my grandchildren – and their children

CONTENTS

3. Award or No Award

11

13

34. Guilty Pleasures

35. Tense, Thrilling or Downright Terrifying

18

Foreword

This is a rookie effort on my part. I hope to make it snappy. Knowing that the author, a personal friend of long standing, has prepared an extended and exceptionally explanatory Introduction, I see no reason to compete.

I recommend diving without further ado into his pool of movie appreciations, 500 titles deep at this point and known familiarly as Phil's Favorites. Having taken the leap, commence to paddle merrily away. You're likely to begin playing cinematic Marco Polo with a film-loving soulmate. Not to mention someone whose enthusiasms can take a turn for the whimsical and debatable. Witness the 50 chapters whose contents can range from a mere handful of movies (and sometimes a single movie) to a veritable bushel, distinguished by headings that range from the catchy ("Flawed But Not Fatally") to the weary ("Last But Not Least…").

I'm not sure the "Last" will have any bearing on this indisputably personal, home-brewed collection, which I regard as one of the most lavishly expansive and browsable books ever published. Or did someone already say that about an edition of the Encyclopedia Britannica long, long ago? For a forecast of how Phil's Favorite 500 will soon be doubling down for your edification and amusement, consult the entry on *Crazy Rich Asians*, the most recent film to make the cut. You'll find it at the end of Chapter 3. Even without a stunning revelation, many entries tend to burst the bounds of "capsule reviews," leaving the book so abundant with references to and discussions of additional movies that The 500 soon swarm their borders and become thousands.

The more the merrier works to Phil's advantage more often than not. Sample his entries on *The Right Stuff* (Chapter 2) or *The Big Lift* (Chapter 23) to appreciate how his fondness for historical lore and production sidelights can enhance your awareness of certain movies; in these cases, an auspicious spectacle that never caught on at the box-office and a topical salute to Air Force valor that has been nearly forgotten.

A happy brainstorm prompts him to draw on *Bringing Up Baby* (Chapter 10, to begin a Cary Grant tribute) to illustrate a witty, easy-to-overlook aspect of trick photography. Phil's interest in the technical side of filmmaking has prepared him to be a guide to assorted tricks of the trade.

Phil also reveals a flair for matchmaking. I wish I'd thought of celebrating Barbara Stanwyck by matching up her great performances as worldly wise sweethearts in *Ball of Fire* and *The Lady Eve* in 1941 (Chapter 15). I laughed out loud at the topic sentence that launches Phil's affable pans of *Earthquake* and *The Towering Inferno* (Chapter 5).

Phil's problematic relationship with the Academy Awards makes an early entrance and should engender solidarity with many readers. Look forward to the entry on *L.A. Confidential* (Chapter 15) for an inspired topper to this enduring estrangement between Academy voters and disillusioned fans.

An admirable use of "the personal angle" pops up in the very first chapter when Phil shares a family anecdote from World War II that elevates his entry for *The Best Years of Our Lives*. Better yet, it suggests a homecoming variation that might have benefitted the movie itself – and could still be irresistible if developed as a mini-series.

At an early stage you realize that these commentaries have merit as casual advice to aspiring filmmakers as well as fondly critical retrospectives. There's a lot of stimulation and disputation waiting to be circulated when Phil's epic reaches a simpatico public, as both ebook and shelftop reference work.

Inevitably, some beloved titles have missed the cut. I plan to lobby for their belated appearance until justice is done. Over the course of the collection, Phil achieves relative parity with the decades stretching from the 1940s to the present. He could use a more generous selection from the 1930s, and silent features have been severely shortchanged. I'm not sure why, because he does a bang-up job on the restoration of Abel Gance's *Napoléon* (Chapter 32, all to itself).

An even roomier Phil's Favorites will be a sturdier treasure house, starting with the addition of Buster Keaton's *The General* and Gance's *La Roue* to the chapter titled "Workin' on the Railroad," way understocked at three paltry titles. Once augmented, the Favorites should decisively reinforce the heading you'll soon encounter in Phil's Introduction.

Repeated browsing and ruminating with the Favorites has persuaded me that the author's phrase "Living in the Real World, Dreaming on the Screen" does sum up this movie fan's commonsensical attachment to the movies. Phil's standpoint is likely to grow on you: a down-to-earth observer and commentator even when confronted by Hollywood's chronic confusion of wayward, mystical and endearing systems of illusion.

Gary Arnold
December 2018

Introduction:
Living in the Real World, Dreaming on the Screen

My first memory having anything to do with movies occurred when I was five years old. It was the beginning of a summer weekend in 1953. My parents had decided to indulge themselves in what was then a popular pastime for families: a night at the local drive-in theater. In those days, a drive-in offered a welcome opportunity for budget-conscious couples to go out for the evening. Paying as little as a dollar per car, they could afford to bring along their young children – in my parents' case, my younger brother David and me. Then, with a little luck, they could enjoy a first-run movie while we kids slipped quietly to sleep in the back seat soon after the cartoons. At least, that was the plan.

From the moment we pulled up to that enormous outdoor screen, I was transfixed. I had never seen anything like its huge white presence, topped by floodlights illuminating the entire parking area between features. The giant images on the screen were overwhelming to me. They seemed to glisten like jewels. On that clear, warm, western Pennsylvania summer night filled with stars, the entire effect was magical.

I don't remember which cartoons played that evening, but I doubt I will ever forget the main attraction. It was the science fiction thriller *It Came from Outer Space*, starring Richard Carlson and Barbara Rush, and directed by Jack Arnold. I didn't know any of that at the time, of course. I also didn't know that the movie, which was showing in a 3-D version in theaters, presented an enlightened science-fiction yarn containing a message of peace and tolerance. Most important, I didn't yet know movies could be quite frightening, particularly to an impressionable young child. I only knew I couldn't get enough of this experience. No way would I join my brother in the back seat. I was determined to stay awake for the duration.

So I watched, wide-eyed, as a giant fireball fell out of the sky and crashed onto a desert landscape. I saw the fireball cool and transform itself into a large, luminous spacecraft with a geometric structure resembling a soccer ball. I saw the inhabitants of a small desert town one by one begin to act strangely and menacingly. Eventually, one of them ran a police roadblock in a pickup truck and ended up crashing and burning to death. Now, 65 years later, I can still envision those flames gutting the truck by the side of the road.

And then I saw ... IT!

Ironic, but the thing that scared me most I remembered the least. It was rather short and octopus-like, with lots of limbs and a big central eye. Other details escaped me, because by that time I *had* joined my brother – but I wasn't sleeping. I was crouching in terror behind the front seat. I had been enjoying the magic of the movies. Now I had been introduced, rather rudely, to their power.

For the next several nights, I had trouble sleeping. My imagination kept producing that THING, either in the dark corners of my bedroom or lurking outside my window. At age five, I had few powers of intellect or analysis. I had been given a raw jolt of terror by something I was years from understanding. Yet as traumatic as this was for a little tyke like me, the experience changed my life. The following week, when my parents started packing the car for another night at the drive-in, I was all for it. The THING still haunted me, but I was ready and willing to face whatever new terrors the giant screen could throw my way. Staying away from the movies never entered my mind. I've been in love with them ever since.

The Perpetual Allure

Read the autobiography of just about anybody connected with the movies, and chances are it likewise begins with some anecdote from their childhood when they saw something on the big screen that dazzled and amazed them – something that left such a strong impression it changed their life. The year before *It Came from Outer Space* scared the bejeebers out of me, Steven Spielberg saw his first movie, Cecil B. DeMille's *The Greatest Show on Earth*. He later said his road to moviemaking probably began with that encounter. Likewise, the past two movie-related books I've read began exactly that way, and the phenomenon is by no means restricted to people who work in the business. Almost everyone I know somehow has been deeply affected by at least one movie, if not in childhood then at some other time in their lives.

What is it that makes movies so fascinating and frequently addictive, luring many of us into a lifelong love affair? Part of it, I'm sure, is the pure enjoyment, the excitement and the vicarious pleasure movies so often provide. Movies help fulfill our desires to visit new places, meet fascinating characters, confront the unfamiliar or unknown. Then, having become acquainted, we enjoy repeating the experiences, as we watch our favorites again and again.

Maybe we love movies so much because they can provide such a strong taste of adventure, particularly when they mix in some mischief and a sense of fun. In their days, *The Adventures of Robin Hood*, *The Crimson Pirate*, *The Magnificent Seven* and the early installments of the James Bond series captivated audiences just as much as the exploits of Indiana Jones and the Skywalker and Avengers clans did decades later.

We often seem to crave a touch of romance and sophistication. Cary Grant's career spanned four decades, and he was just as attractive and popular a leading man with Eva Marie Saint in *North by Northwest* in 1959 and Audrey Hepburn in *Charade* in 1963 as he was with Katharine Hepburn in *Bringing Up Baby* in 1938 and *The Philadelphia Story* in 1940.

At their best, movies offer us a different reality, into which we can willingly escape our day-to-day concerns and, very often, pretend that we're the protagonist. For a couple of hours, we're drawn into sort of a waking dream. Yes, "dream" is an appropriate term here, because so often the movies we come to love work more on emotional and subliminal levels than logically – we *feel* them. We vicariously share the experiences of the characters. We exult at their victories and suffer their defeats. We root for their success against villains or personal demons. And always, in a romantic sense, we hope couples can find each other.

The best movies also provide role models and ideas to help us deal with our own lives. Their characters can present the finest human virtues – courage, honor, compassion, love – in ways so appealing and attractive that we might feel almost compelled to emulate them. Or, more frequently, they present human frailties with which we can personally identify. They become our heroes and heroines, as my dear late friend Sheldon Tromberg used to say, *because of* their faults and *despite* their virtues.

It's fortunate for the movie industry that our society still seems to behave much the way I did, so long ago, after my encounter with *It Came from Outer Space*. Despite unpleasant experiences sometimes, we just can't stay away from the movies. After more than a century, our spirit remains hopeful and our appetite healthy.

So, in that vein…

Here, as promised, are suggestions for your viewing pleasure – my Favorite 500. Some are widely known, while others might be less familiar or even unheard of. But all represent my personal tastes developed during a love affair with movies that has lasted essentially my entire conscious life. I chose each one because, for some reason, it has stuck with me and draws me back every so often – I love watching it. My own preferences notwithstanding, I'm confident that each will offer you something memorable, something striking and entertaining, even if only a flash of brilliance that makes the rest of the attraction worth tolerating, or a useful display of the moviemaking process gone significantly but hilariously wrong.

These are personal picks, so don't expect anything definitive. I confess to their being skewed toward "guy" attractions, but then … well, that's me, though I've also provided plenty of choices for gals, couples, families and kids. Besides, good movies are good movies, no matter your age or gender. I also admit to omitting many titles that are much admired or even beloved by others. Some of them were big, big hits, such as *E.T. the Extra-Terrestrial*, the three *Lord of the Rings* movies, *The Matrix* trilogy, the *Harry Potter* collection, almost all of the *Star Wars* saga, the *Batman* series, the *Spider Man* series, the *Transformers* series, the *X-Men* and *Avengers* series, most of the *Star Trek* movies, *Avatar*, and all of the Pixar and other major computer-animated features, not to mention the multi-billion-dollar juggernaut comprising the Marvel Comics movies, to name a few. They simply didn't do for me what they seemed to do for millions of other moviegoers. I also omitted many titles I highly respect but don't count among my favorites – *To Kill a Mockingbird* and *The Miracle Worker*, or *Kagemusha* and *Ran*, the latter two by the great Japanese director Akira Kurosawa, for instances. My effort here is based entirely on affection and not necessarily on merit.

That said, 500 titles still might seem like a lot. But consider that at last count Hollywood alone was closing in on 50,000 releases. Likewise, Leonard Maltin's perennial movie and video guides have topped 20,000 entries, so my picks here represent a tiny fraction of what's available. By my calculations, I've probably seen more than 5,000 movies over my lifetime and reviewed about 700 during my days as a critic. But just as I don't always like the popular favorites, chances are you won't like all of my choices.

It's natural. I used to attend screenings with my good friend Gary Arnold, former film critic of The Washington Post and, more recently, The Washington Times – and who graciously consented to write this book's Foreword. He and I co-hosted our weekly cable-TV show The Moviegoing Family for five years in the 1980s. Sometimes, we'd sit side by side through the same movie then stand up afterward and give completely opposite reactions. I also can tell you that, at last look, of the 250 most highly rated movies on the Internet Movie Database, my picks appear less than half of the time. On the other hand, 124 of the movies on this list – nearly one-quarter of them – were nominated as Best Picture of the Year by the motion picture academy, and 36 of them won. So, I hope you'll find many to your liking, and maybe you'll even come to regard them as I do as among the cinema's most endearing and enduring treasures.

In agreement or not, we enjoy a tremendous advantage over previous moviegoing generations. Thanks to great new technologies such as DVDs, Blu-rays and digital downloads; resources such as the superior Turner Classic Movies cable channel – a bona-fide national treasure – and the extensive Netflix service as well as Amazon's burgeoning competitive offerings, more and more of these titles, even the oldest and least well-known, are becoming available to watch, rent or purchase, whether in a physical format, a download or streaming. Only a few titles on my list remain unavailable by any means I could find. By sharing my favorites, I hope I might help you discover movies you've never heard of or wouldn't have considered otherwise.

Writing this book, I wanted to create a bridge between myself and succeeding generations – both my own descendants and anyone else in the future who might want to read the capsules. It's a way of conveying the taste and sensibilities of these times on a personal level.

True, you can always opt for the biggest box office draw of the moment or the formulaic attractions, but herein are some fine motion pictures that belong to our cultural heritage, both national and international. I've also included some not-so-fine titles you still might find entertaining, plus some genuine but lovable stinkers. The point is, if you care about the medium, here are 500 opportunities to see why it has captivated me and many others throughout our lifetimes. Maybe give yourself the chance to discover something new that you will grow to love as well. As Ben Kingsley says, portraying French movie pioneer Georges Méliès in the charming *Hugo*, "Come, and dream with me!"

Reading Notes

[B&W] = Shown in black & white

[W] = Shown in a widescreen (also known as "letterbox") format, so look for that version

[3D] = Shown in 3D format (in selected theaters, usually at a premium price)

As some of you might know, this is actually the fifth edition of my compilation – and the first time I've offered the book in print. I started in 2012, and the list quickly grew to more than 600 titles. I've finally decided to pare down my choices to exactly 500 (plus two repeats), and I've once again adjusted the formatting to accommodate the rapid changes and exploding variety of online video content. For example, I originally had included an "[N]" notation with selected titles, signifying Netflix carried them. But I quickly found out that those titles tended to come and go – or they shifted between DVD and instant video – on a regular basis. The same with Amazon's online titles available via its Prime® service. Even the vast IMDB, which once offered a wide variety of easily accessible movie clips, has become more problematic because almost all of them are preceded by ads – most of them lengthy – and even IMDB sometimes shuffles what's available. In short, the changes are happening too rapidly to track. So, for now I'm leaving it to you to search Netflix, Amazon and the other streaming and DVD/Blu-ray services for available titles. There is, however, a new Internet search engine designed specifically to help you with this process. It's called Can I Stream It? and with it you can find every current venue for renting, buying or viewing a given movie, or using a service to stream it via subscription.

Finding Clips and Featurettes

As you also might know, my previous editions were ebook-only, intended that way so I could include live links to videos and online references of interest. But here, in this paperback edition, I can't do likewise (though if you'll permit a shameless self-promotion, please consider getting my ebook edition for that purpose). What I can suggest – and encourage – you to do is search the Internet on your own. The best place to start is YouTube, which has become an immense repository of video references, including clips from and trailers for nearly all of the titles I have listed.

You can do this for all of my categories. For movies, go to the search box at the top of the YouTube homepage. There, type in the movie's title followed by the year of its release. When you enter the information, YouTube will list everything available on that particular day. It's a simple process, though it often will require you to do some scrolling to find a specific video I have recommended. The same for selected movie music soundtracks and related featurettes. What you'll probably encounter over time, however, is that videos are sometimes removed, whether because of copyright issues or other reasons. That's unavoidable. Nevertheless, the YouTube-search approach remains the best available option for viewing clips and excerpts online.

One caution, however. At this writing, YouTube is besieged with what can only be called video spam, at least where movie titles are concerned. When you search for a movie I've recommended, you'll frequently see listings purporting to show you, for free, full-length versions. In reality, they're what has come to be known as "click bait," or invitations to go to other websites or pages, many of which are probably illegitimate. Don't fall for it. You can spot the faux sites by noting the number of views they've received (usually fewer than 1,000) and by their recent posting dates, because YouTube constantly tries to scrub this scourge from its roster. Instead, rent or buy your movie choices from legitimate online retailers – indeed, YouTube and Amazon offer nearly all of my titles for a small fee; likewise

IMDB. You can find other good services as well, and the prices are almost always reasonable.

Titles Included and Not Included

Obviously, with 500 movies to keep track of, and with lots of cross references, I continually risk making things confusing. So, I've employed a simple rule when mentioning other titles within a particular capsule. If I haven't included them on this list of favorites, I parenthetically note their absence; otherwise, you can assume you'll find them elsewhere in the text.

Also, I've employed a style rule for making the movie titles within the list easy to spot: I've italicized them. In cases where I mention stageplays or songs, I've enclosed them in quotes. If it's books, they're underlined. And for TV shows, newspapers and related names, I've just capitalized them. Hope it all makes sense.

1. Some of the Best 'Best Pictures'
(The rest of my choices appear among the 49 other categories)

Beginning in 1928 and every year since, at least during my lifetime, the Academy of Motion Picture Arts and Sciences has picked one movie considered by its members to be the "Best Picture of the Year" – although until 1962 the academy handed out the award under several other names, including (in order) "Outstanding Picture," "Outstanding Production," "Outstanding Motion Picture," and "Best Motion Picture." Whatever the moniker, the public in most cases has agreed with the choices, bestowing each winner with a measure of popular and financial success, and the academy has awarded the producer of each winner with the golden statuette affectionately known as the "Oscar."

But that's the public and the academy. I don't follow conventional wisdom much, and as you'll see in the category after this one, I offer my own list of alternative Best Pictures for many of the years. In the cases below, and 37 in all within these pages, I agree with the academy's choices and recommend these winners.

In general, Best Pictures tend to be directors' movies. That is, with few exceptions, they bear the creative imprint of their directors. That also goes for most of the titles I've listed in the other categories. It takes a superior director – or a director having a superior year – to unify all of a movie's elements into a singular vision. When it works, it can work very well, and sometimes it can even change the way movies are made. Here are 19 of the best of the Best, along with the years of their release and the names of their directors or driving visionaries.

Wings
1928 – Directed by William Wellman

When *The Artist*, a mostly silent movie (not on this list), won the 2011 Best Picture Oscar, it was only the second time that members of the academy chose a non-talkie for the award. *Wings* was the first – and what a way to start the whole process! I'm embarrassed to admit I had never seen more than a few snippets of it until I watched the newly restored version in 2012. Produced by film historian Kevin Brownlow for the 85th anniversary of its release, it premiered at the San Francisco Silent Film Festival in April of that year. No doubt about it, *Wings* is a singular film achievement, one that's unlikely to be duplicated. It's a movie that received more support – logistical and financial – from the U.S. government than any other. Shot entirely at or around Fort Sam Houston in San Antonio, Texas, the production included thousands of soldiers as extras, hundreds of military aircraft, real artillery barrages and astounding aerial sequences. Together, these elements plant *Wings* firmly among the greatest of American cinema's technical achievements. But don't sell the story short, because it's likewise part of the movie's greatness. Basically, it's a wartime love triangle starring the adorable Clara Bow as a smalltown girl, and Charles "Buddy" Rogers and Richard Arlen as her two competing suitors. Arlen had been a pilot in France during World War I, but Rogers had never even been in a plane. I bring this up because many of the aerial shots in the movie were flown – and photographed – by the two actors themselves under the supervision of Wellman, himself a pilot in the war. That meant Rogers needed to learn to fly, and he does it so well that some of his sequences are positively breathtaking. But it's the melodrama that takes things over the top. By the time *Wings* ends, you'll be nearly shattered by what you've just watched. [Trivia notes: 1) Wellman sometimes delayed shooting the aerial sequences for days and days because of the weather. To be more precise, he never wanted clear skies, because he understood to do so would produce only specks on film. He needed clouds to add texture and perspective – and drama – to the images. 2) Though production was completed in 1927, the movie's official release date was 1928, and that's the year in which it qualified for the first Academy Awards] **[B&W] [Silent]**

It Happened One Night [100]
1934 – Directed by Frank Capra

This is the grandparent of all romantic comedies, and it was the movie that established Frank Capra as a major director, Columbia Pictures as a major studio and Clark Gable as a top box-office draw. An enormous crowd-pleaser, it became the runaway hit of 1934 and swept all four major Oscar categories: Best Picture, Best Director, Best Actor and Best Actress – an achievement that remained unmatched for over 40 years. It also won for Best Adapted Screenplay, taken as it was from a short story called "Night Bus to New York." Ellen Andrews (Claudette Colbert), a spoiled and unhappy heiress, escapes the lavish imprisonment of her father's yacht to reunite with the husband she married just to spite her domineering father (Walter Connolly). She is helped in a cross-country chase by Peter Warne (Gable), a wily reporter who has fallen on hard times and needs a blockbuster story to save his career. *It Happened One Night* has been imitated many times, but none of the remakes has ever approached its wit and appeal. Two scenes remain classics: one where Gable proposes to sleep in the same room with Colbert separated only by a blanket folded across a clothesline, and the other where Colbert demonstrates her very effective method of hitchhiking. The sly Connolly is terrific as Ellen's father, and watch for Ward Bond, who played Bert the cop in *It's a Wonderful Life,* and Alan Hale, Sr., whose son played the Skipper on the Gilligan's Island TV series, in minor roles. [Trivia notes: 1) The two scenes where Gable removes his shirt revealing his bare chest practically destroyed the U.S. tee-shirt industry at the time. 2) The scene where Gable munches on a carrot and talks with his mouth full became the inspiration for Bugs Bunny. 3) Capra's Best Director Oscar removed some of the sting he had felt the previous year, when he was nominated for *Lady for a Day* (not on this list). When beloved humorist Will Rogers presented the award, he said, "Come and get it, Frank," at which point Capra stood up and started walking toward the podium – only to suffer the humiliation of discovering that Rogers was referring to Frank Lloyd, who had won for *Cavalcade* (likewise not here). 4) Colbert originally loathed making the movie. When the production wrapped, she reportedly called a friend and said, "I've just made the worst movie of my career!" Part of her distaste was the famous hitchhiking scene, which required her to raise her skirt to attract the attention of a passing motorist (Hale). At first she refused, so Capra proposed using a body double for the shot. That suggestion apparently infuriated Colbert even more, so she did the scene, and from then on she was celebrated for having great legs] **[B&W]**

Mutiny on the Bounty
1935 – Directed by Frank Lloyd

This was Gable's second major starring role and the one where he looks the most handsome and dashing, though he was forced to appear without his signature mustache – a change that annoyed him. The movie is based on the famous true story of a mutiny among the men of the H.M.S. Bounty, a British ship sailing the South Pacific in 1789. Gable plays Fletcher Christian, the second officer, who eventually leads the rebellion against Captain William Bligh. The great Charles Laughton, who suffered constantly from seasickness, plays Bligh. (I'll have more to say about him in other capsules). This is a grand sea adventure, although most of it was shot on MGM back lots and off the California and Mexican coasts. The story was filmed twice more – in 1962 with Marlon Brando and Trevor Howard, and in 1984 with Mel Gibson and Anthony Hopkins, in the Christian and Bligh roles, respectively (and with a lot more Polynesian female flesh exposed, particularly in the Gibson version) – but this production more than holds its own. Yes, Gable is terrific as Christian, but Laughton steals the movie playing Bligh as gloriously sadistic and unrepentant, and Franchot Tone is superb as a conscientious midshipman who resists joining the mutiny but still nearly pays with his life. [Trivia note: If you watch the background extras closely, you

37

might spot two familiar faces: James Cagney and David Niven. Director Lloyd, a personal friend of Cagney's, hired him for a few days to help him earn some needed extra money. And Niven hadn't yet attained enough onscreen experience even for a speaking part] **[B&W]**

The Best Years of Our Lives
1946 – Directed by William Wyler

The great director Billy Wilder (more about him later), who once quipped he could laugh during "Hamlet," marveled at how he found himself bawling shamelessly at one of the earliest scenes in this movie. And legendary actress Bette Davis called it the best movie ever made in Hollywood. Well, not really, but it's justifiably esteemed. The story of three veterans returning home after World War II seemed to resonate with the feelings of the entire country at the time. (It certainly mirrored the experiences of my own parents, Felix Berardelli and Stella Sisco, who met briefly before the U.S. Army Engineers sent him overseas in 1942 and then fell in love during their three years of separation via their letters. They married two months after he returned home in December 1945.) It was a box-office blockbuster in 1946, easily eclipsing *It's a Wonderful Life*. Frankly, the acting is not great in this movie, and some of the dialogue isn't, either. But Wyler managed to transcend those weaknesses and evoke deeply felt sentiments without seeming manipulative or cloying. You really can't help choking back tears and rooting for the three men to resettle and succeed. Most memorable is Harold Russell, who had lost both arms nearly up to his elbows in a training accident. He plays Homer Parrish, a disabled veteran. Not a trained actor, Russell easily matches pros Fredric March, Dana Andrews and Myrna Loy with his screen presence – and Russell won a Best Supporting Actor Oscar along with March for Best Actor. Virginia Mayo is wonderful as a lively and decidedly unsympathetic wife. She gives the movie a lot of its energy. Hugo Friedhofer wrote the deeply emotional music score. [Trivia note: In the scene where Andrews returns to his old drug store, watch for the little girl in the background who follows him

with delight. She's Catherine Wyler, the director's six-year-old daughter, who grew up to make *Directed by William Wyler*, a fine documentary (though not on this list) about her father's career]
[B&W]

Around the World in 80 Days [100]
1956 – Produced by Mike Todd

Officially, the director of this supreme crowd pleaser was Michael Anderson, but its true artistic vision rested with Todd, who introduced the term "cameo performance" to the movies. He persuaded 44 international stars and cinema veterans to appear briefly for very low fees or luxury gifts, just for the fun of participating. The big-screen version of Jules Verne's classic novel stars David Niven in perfect form as the globe-trotting Phileas Fogg, the obsessive and mysterious figure who might have robbed the Bank of England. It's also graced by the gifted Mexican comedian Cantinflas – who at the time, believe it or not, was the richest performer in the world and a legend across the Latin world – as Fogg's manservant Passepartout. And there's the miscast but appealing Shirley MacLaine, at the beginning of her long career (at this writing she's still working) as the Indian princess Aouda. Shot in a 70-millimeter widescreen process called Todd-AO, which Todd pioneered, the location sequences are spectacular, particularly the movie's iconic balloon journey over France, a cross-country train trip through India, and some gorgeous shots on various bodies of water. Tremendously entertaining for all ages, it boasts a lovely, playful score by Victor Young, including the beautiful title number. It's great fun – and be sure to watch the delightful closing-credit sequence by Saul Bass, which reveals the identities of the guest stars. [Trivia notes: 1) Todd holds the unique distinction of producing only one movie over his lifetime but nevertheless turning that movie into a Best Picture winner and a comedy classic. Todd, who had married Elizabeth Taylor, died two years after the movie's release in a plane crash. At the time, he was preparing an epic version of the Don Quixote story. 2) Todd used clever and often outlandish attempts at attracting big stars to play minor roles in the movie. For example, he offered Marlene Dietrich complete editorial control over her scene, meaning if she didn't like the way it turned out she could veto its inclusion. Fortunately, she approved. 3) The cast and crew had originally shot the trans-Atlantic crossing sequence on a studio set, but Todd wasn't satisfied with the result. So, he purchased a boat, refitted it to match its description in the story and had it reshot for real – but mostly in the Pacific off the California coast] [W]

The Bridge on the River Kwai
1957 – Directed by David Lean

The first of five widescreen epics directed by Lean, this tense World War II drama takes place in Burma – although it was shot on the island of Ceylon (now Sri Lanka). Alec Guinness, in an Oscar-winning performance, stars as Colonel Nicholson, the senior British officer in a Japanese prison camp, whose authority is challenged by the commander, played by the fine veteran Japanese actor Sessue Hayakawa. Detailed and authentic looking, the story is largely about the test of wills between the two enemy officers during the construction of a railroad bridge by the British prisoners. One of Lean's greatest movies, winning seven Oscars in all, it features palpably harsh and bleak sequences, one triumphant moment, a nail-biting climax and strong supporting performances by William Holden and Jack Hawkins as well as Hayakawa. [Trivia notes: 1) The story is based on a true World War II prison-camp saga, involving a British colonel named Toosey and a Japanese major who, like Hayakawa's character, was named Saito. The real men, however, developed a strong respect for each other, to the point where Toosey testified on Saito's behalf after the war, saving him from hanging; and Saito made a pilgrimage to Toosey's grave after his British counterpart died. 2) The names of the movie's two screenwriters, Michael Wilson and Carl Foreman, did not appear in the original credits because Hollywood had blacklisted both men several years earlier for being suspected communist sympathizers. The movie's Oscar for Best Adapted Screenplay went to Pierre Boulle, who wrote the source novel – but who did not speak English! The Academy did not correct this wrong until 1984, by which time Wilson and Foreman had died, and Columbia Pictures eventually included their names when the studio issued a restored print of the movie for its 30th anniversary in 1987. 3) The song the Brits whistle in the movie, "The Colonel Bogey March," became a hit in America at the time] **[W]**

Ben-Hur
1959 – Directed by William Wyler
Tied at this writing as the biggest Academy Award winner with 11 Oscars, *Ben-Hur* is not one of the best movies of all time. There are moments during its 212-minutes when it sags into dullness. Nevertheless, it remains a compelling and often powerful story of one (fictional) man's terrible ordeal in biblical times that contains at its centerpiece arguably the greatest action sequence ever presented on the screen, a 9-minute masterpiece. Wyler, helming his still-unparalleled third Best Picture winner, directed Charlton Heston in the role of his career. Heston plays Judah Ben-Hur, a Hebrew nobleman unjustly sent to presumed death as a slave oarsman in the Roman fleet but who survives to wreak revenge on the boyhood friend and ambitious official who betrayed and condemned him. Heston won Best Actor that year, but he was outshone by a trio of supporting cast members: Jack Hawkins as a Roman consul; the great Irish actor Hugh Griffith, who stole the movie – and won his own Oscar – playing an Arab sheikh; and especially Steven Boyd as Messala, Judah's rival and enemy. *Ben-Hur* is most famous, and justifiably so, for its chariot race, nearly a shot-by-shot replica of the 1925 silent version, which Wyler had helped to direct in an uncredited role. The 1959 sequence was supervised by second-unit director Andrew Marton and legendary stuntman Yakima Canutt, whose son was injured while executing a difficult maneuver. It is absolutely riveting to this day in widescreen and color. The movie used no computer-generated horses or effects, or even the old-fashioned rear-projection technique, which was popular at the time, and which filmed actors in a studio against a screen receiving a

41

separate projected image. Instead, co-stars Heston and Boyd, the stuntmen and the camera crew – and the horses – spent days and days – and days! – in the hot sun outside Rome creating the sequence for real, and the effort shows. Take or leave *Ben-Hur* after that, but don't miss the race – it's a moviemaking triumph for all time. With Sam Jaffe as Judah's trusted manservant, Israeli actress Haya Harareet as his love interest, Kathy O'Donnell (who played Wilma in Wyler's *The Best Years of Our Lives*) as his sister, and Martha Scott as his mother. Miklós Rózsa composed the darkly stirring score. [Viewing note: At some point you might want to watch the silent version as well. It's quite good] [Trivia notes: 1) You could argue that William Wyler's talent and achievements easily justified his million-dollar fee for directing *Ben-Hur*, the highest ever at the time. He had directed two previous Best Picture winners, directed more actors and actresses in Oscar-winning roles than anyone else, and his three Best Director Oscars were second only to John Ford's four. 2) Wyler instructed Boyd to play Messala as Judah's jilted gay lover, but the two of them didn't let Heston in on the secret. The result is that certain lines in the movie can bring snickers to those in the know. 3) Wyler gave full credit to Marton and Canutt for creating the spectacular chariot race, a feat he called "one of the greatest cinematic achievements." 4) The story is based on the 19th-century novel by Lew Wallace, who was a general in the Union Army in the Civil War. Its complete title is Ben-Hur: A Tale of the Christ, which is also the title of the silent version. 5) Martha Scott should have won a special award for long-suffering roles, because she also played Heston's mother in *The Ten Commandments,* and in both movies her character doesn't fare well] **[W]**

Tom Jones [100]
1963 – Directed by Tony Richardson
It Happened One Night broke new ground in romantic comedy and movie storytelling in 1934, and *Tom Jones* moved the art form ahead again nearly 30 years later. In fact, its style was far ahead of its time. Based on the Henry Fielding novel, the story

follows the life of Tom (Albert Finney), an abandoned child raised in the household of a generous nobleman (George Devine). He falls in love with his neighbor, Miss Sophie Western (Susannah York), the daughter of the raucous Squire Western (Hugh Griffith, shining again), a man so uninhibited he thinks nothing of jumping his milkmaids out in the open. Though Tom is more genteel about the process, he likewise cannot resist the charms of women, a trait that lands him in trouble time and time again. The movie's a bit bumpy in the early going, but it hits its stride during the fox-hunt sequence, a sprawling, vivacious, sometimes graphic depiction of the custom and the carnage caused to man and beast. It justifies Oscar Wilde's famous description of the practice: the unspeakable in pursuit of the uneatable. After that, it's a rollicking tale, full of cleverness, wit and groundbreaking techniques. Example: At certain points, the actors suddenly turn to the camera and via facial expressions and dialogue they address the audience. Once, Finney even uses his hat to cover the camera lens to preserve a woman's ... ahem, modesty. Tame by today's standards, back then it was considered shocking for its casual treatment of sex and partial nudity. The dining scene between Finney and Joyce Redman – which took hours to shoot and left both actors ill from overeating – is a classic, and John Addison's mischievous score, replete with harpsichord and squeezebox interjections, captures the movie's spirit perfectly. [Caution: sexuality, though as I noted tame by today's standards] [W]

The French Connection
1971 – Directed by William Friedkin
This gritty, realistic police drama boasts two superlative features: Don Ellis's icy-cool score, which sounds grating by itself but fits the movie like a glove, and possibly the greatest car chase ever filmed – a 6-minute knockout of intricate staging, camerawork and editing, and done entirely without optical effects. Based on a true story, Gene Hackman plays Harry "Popeye" Doyle, a New York City detective on the trail of a large heroin shipment from France. He and his partner, "Cloudy"

43

Russo (Roy Scheider, distinctive in an early role), stake out the suspects, but when one of them tries to assassinate Popeye from an apartment rooftop, the chase is on, with the would-be killer attempting to escape aboard one of New York City's elevated trains, and Popeye down on the street in hot pursuit in a commandeered Pontiac GTO in the middle of city traffic. Friedkin mounted his cameras low and on the front of the chase car and transit train, and the effect is electrifying. Even watching on video, you might find yourself holding onto your seat. Veteran Spanish actor Fernando Rey plays the French drug kingpin with a wicked gleam in his eye, and the real Popeye – named Eddie Egan – appears in a cameo as a detective supervisor. [Trivia notes: 1) The shot in the chase scene where the camera appears to collide with the back end of a train actually was filmed backwards, starting out from the point of impact then reverse-printing the individual frames for the movie. Before the days of computer animation this was a common moviemaking trick. 2) The crash between the GTO and another car was a real accident, when an unsuspecting motorist had crossed into the path of the stunt driver. No one was hurt. 3) Rey ended up being cast as the French villain, Chernier, by mistake. Friedkin had seen another actor whom he liked for the role but gave erroneous instructions to his casting director, who invited Rey to America to audition for the movie. By the time Friedkin discovered the error, he had already selected Rey, and neither man ever regretted the mix-up] [Caution: violence, rough language and fleeting sexuality] [W]

Annie Hall
1977 – Edited by Ralph Rosenblum
Woody Allen wrote and directed this classic romantic comedy – one of only four to receive Best Picture – but Rosenblum turned it into an Oscar winner. In his fascinating book on film editing, When the Shooting Stops ... the Cutting Begins, Rosenblum explained how *Annie Hall* started out as a collection of loosely related scenes that was more a personal psychological exploration by Allen than a love story. Only after months of re-

edits and some re-shooting did the story emerge as movie audiences saw it. *Annie Hall* is a flight of fancy, loosely based on the real-life affair between Allen and Keaton (Hall is Keaton's real name). Sometimes sweet and affectionate, sometimes acidly satirical and sometimes laugh-out-loud funny, it was chosen Best Picture in a year that included such crowd-pleasing blockbusters as *Star Wars* and *Close Encounters of the Third Kind*. It is beginning to seem a little dated after four decades, but it remains one of the sharpest American comedies on the screen. Keaton, who won the Best Actress Oscar, is marvelously appealing. Watch for bit parts by future screen stalwarts Jeff Goldblum and Christopher Walken. [Trivia note: As an example of how much guidance Allen needed at the time, he originally wanted to title his movie "Anhedonia," which is the psychological term for people who are unable to experience pleasure] [Caution: language and sexuality] **[W]**

Amadeus
1984 – Directed by Milos Forman
This movie is not a documentary, so don't look for accuracy about the life of perhaps the greatest composer who ever lived. Forman's version of Peter Shaffer's play (Shaffer also wrote the screenplay) was roundly panned by sticklers for veering widely away from the real lives of Wolfgang Amadeus Mozart and Antonio Salieri. Yes, their story is stretched and warped nearly beyond recognition, but that doesn't detract from the movie's dazzling performances of Mozart's best works and its fascinating riff on the natures of genius and mediocrity. An aging Salieri – excellently played by F. Murray Abraham in an Oscar-winning role – receives a mercy visit by a reluctant priest at an asylum after he has unsuccessfully attempted suicide. In telling the priest his story, Salieri becomes the movie's narrator as well as its soul and wit, while Mozart, played by Tom Hulce, remains something of an enigma. The locations (the story is set in Vienna but was shot in Czechoslovakia before it split into the Czech Republic and Slovakia), costumes and other period evocations are flawless, and the music is rapturous, in particular the

performance of Mozart's "Requiem" at the finale. The versatile Jeffrey Jones – best known as Ed Rooney, the sourpuss of a high school principal in *Ferris Bueller's Day Off* (coming in the next compilation) – gives the performance of his career as Emperor Joseph II. Watch also for a young Cynthia Nixon – Miranda in the cable TV series Sex in the City and erstwhile candidate for New York governor – in a minor role. [Caution: language and sexuality] **[W]**

Out of Africa [100]
1985 – Directed by Sydney Pollack

Pollack and screenwriter Kurt Luedtke produced a near-perfect adaptation of the partial autobiography of Karen Blixen (who wrote under the name Isak Dinesin), a Danish baroness who, as she narrates at the beginning of the story, "had a farm in Africa, at the foot of the Ngong Hills" in Kenya starting just before World War I. The movie features an array of superlatives, including David Watkin's breathtaking cinematography, especially the 14-shot, opening title montage. It is among the most beautiful ever filmed, and there has probably never been a sunnier or more verdant landscape in the movies. There's also the stunning 4-minute aerial sequence, as well as John Barry's haunting, exquisite score, his best work of all and possibly the most deeply romantic music ever written for the screen. Then there's Meryl Streep's incredible performance as Blixen. Streep, with 21 Oscar nominations to date and three wins, has earned more than any other actress. Though she didn't win here, I think it's her very best, and her performance easily belongs in the Unforgettable category listed later on. She is well-supported by Klaus Maria Brandauer playing her husband (and, briefly, twin brothers), Michael Kitchen as an ill-fated friend, and Malick Bowens as her wise and steady manservant. Robert Redford, working with Pollack for the sixth time, turns in a surprisingly effective performance as Denys Finch Hatton, the love of Karen's life – although he does so by not even attempting a British accent. Expansive, enrapturing and ultimately heartbreaking, *Out of Africa* envelops you to the point where you will want to

46

reside in it and wish it never would end. Don't miss it, and see it on the biggest screen you can find. [Trivia note: The two lions used in the movie – which appear in four different scenes – were semi-tame and had to be shipped to Africa from the United States because Kenya's laws prohibited all but nature photography of wild animals. And though they appeared to get shot, gored and whipped at various times, neither of them was harmed] [Caution: adult themes and sexuality] **[W]**

Dances with Wolves [100]
1990 – Directed by and starring Kevin Costner
By the late 1980s, Kevin Costner had developed a decent reputation as an actor, having appeared in several fine movies (some of which I've included elsewhere), along with more than a few duds. But nothing he did before would have presaged his extraordinary effort as the director of *Dances with Wolves*, a superior epic western. Based on the novel by Michael Blake – who also wrote the screenplay – Costner stars as Lieutenant John Dunbar, a Civil War veteran who volunteers for a post in a remote part of the nation's western frontier, so he can see it "before it's gone." Reaching his destination, Dunbar finds it inexplicably deserted, and so he resolves to hold the fort, literally, until replacements arrive. Soon he is tormented but then befriended by a tribe of Lakota Sioux, who eventually adopt him as one of their own. Among them, he meets the love of his life, a white woman the Sioux have named Stands with a Fist (Mary McDonnell), who also had been adopted by the tribe, but as a child. The movie is distinguished by having all of its Native American roles played by Native Americans, and screen and TV veterans Graham Greene (as Kicking Bird), Rodney Grant (as Wind in his Hair) and Floyd Red Crow Westerman (as Chief Ten Bears) are particularly memorable, as are Tantoo Cardinal (as Kicking Bird's wife Black Shawl) and Wes Studi as a menacing member of the Pawnee tribe. Alternately joyous and terrifying, as with so many other great epics it's an ultimately heartbreaking story. John Barry's almost painfully beautiful score intensifies the mood – it's every bit as stirring as his music

for *Out of Africa*. [Viewing note: I normally would recommend watching a movie like this on the biggest screen possible – in other words in a theater – and I do here as well. But also consider the longer "Director's Cut," which is available only on DVD or Blu-ray. It provides an emotionally deeper, more effectively detailed version of the story. So, see the theatrical version if you can, but don't pass up a chance to see the longer video version – just try to see it on a large video screen] [Caution: sexuality and graphic violence] **[W]**

Schindler's List
1993 – Directed by Steven Spielberg
Spielberg finally won Best Picture and Best Director Oscars after 19 years of trying with this powerful portrait of one of the most heroic figures of the Holocaust. Based on the historical novel by Thomas Keneally, it's the story of Oscar Schindler (Liam Neeson), a German industrialist who protected and eventually saved hundreds of Jews from the death camps by insisting they were essential for his factory and by bribing Nazi officials into complicity. Shot in black and white except for one symbolic scene, the movie contains moments of extreme emotional intensity. Spielberg's technical crew advanced the ability to portray murder and execution on the screen with horrifying results, and Ralph Fiennes (pronounced RAFE FINE) made his movie debut as the sadistic concentration camp commandant Amon Goeth. It is a vivid, grim portrait of humanity at its worst, yet with a quietly shattering but triumphant resolution. The John Williams score, with a violin solo by virtuoso Itzhak Perlman, is possibly the most exquisitely sad bit of movie music ever written. [Use extreme caution: graphic violence, intense cruelty, full-frontal nudity and sexuality] **[B&W with one brief shot in color] [W]**

Braveheart [100]
1995 – Directed by and starring Mel Gibson
Several times in his career, Mel Gibson (born in the U.S.A. and raised in Australia) has shown he is not only a solid actor but

also an exceptional director. This was the first time. As Kevin Costner had done with *Dances with Wolves* five years earlier, Gibson directed himself in a movie that transcends its star-vehicle genre and becomes an emotionally powerful story extremely well told. Gibson plays William Wallace, a Scotsman who led a rebellion against King Edward I of England in the 14th century and, for a time, held the promise of Scottish independence. As with all Hollywood period epics, this one takes large liberties with history – and Wallace is a most elusive historical figure. But Gibson in the role is tremendously appealing and heroic, and you cannot help but feel for him and grieve with him. With splendid cinematography of the mostly Irish, and some Scottish, locations by John Toll, and a sadly evocative, lyrical score by James Horner – his best of all. The memorable cast includes Brendan Gleeson and David O'Hara as Wallace's trusted lieutenants, veteran TV actor Patrick McGoohan in a gleefully villainous turn as England's King Edward the Longshanks, Ian Bannen as the leprosy-ridden Scottish Lord Robert the Bruce, beautiful Catherine McCormack as Wallace's wife Murron, and gorgeous Sophie Marceau as the daughter-in-law of Longshanks and Wallace's would-be savior. There's also a terrific performance by Angus Macfadyen as the brooding Robert the Bruce the younger, which at times eclipses even Gibson's. Again, don't take this as history. Instead, enjoy it as wishful thinking and exceptional epic moviemaking. [Caution: sexuality and graphically depicted executions and battle scenes] [W]

The English Patient
1996 – Directed by Anthony Minghella
In this wrenchingly sad but enthralling love story, Ralph Fiennes moves seamlessly into a romantic leading role here, projecting fragility and subtlety, where in *Schindler's List* he gave us nonchalantly evil menace. Based on Michael Ondaatje's novel, which in turn is loosely based on a real person, the story follows the last days of a mysterious and badly wounded patient (Fiennes, in heavy prosthetic makeup) who is comforted by a

beautiful nurse (Juliette Binoche) in Italy near the end of World War II. With the aid of exquisite transitions, the patient's story unfolds in flashback, beginning a few years earlier, when he was a mapmaker on a survey of Africa. There, he fell in love with a woman (Kristin Scott Thomas), the wife of a colleague (Colin Firth), and their affair precipitated tragic consequences for both. There is a parallel affair between the nurse and a dashing Indian Sikh who defuses bombs (Naveen Andrews). Often cited as a fine screen romance, the movie runs deeper than that. It is a compelling tale of humans attempting to cling to their humanity while swept into the maelstrom of war. It also boasts Gabriel Yared's score, with its haunting oboe theme, and John Seale's fine cinematography of desert locales, which sometimes approaches the sweep of the great Freddie Young's in *Lawrence of Arabia*. [Trivia note: This movie represents a technical breakthrough of a sort, because the producers created some of the panoramas digitally, and it was the first Oscar-winning movie to have been edited digitally rather than by physically cutting the film] [Caution: violence and sexuality] **[W]**

Shakespeare in Love [100]
1998 – Directed by John Madden
The surprise crowd-pleaser of 1998 upset Steven Spielberg's *Saving Private Ryan* in the Oscar race, largely because of an unprecedented publicity campaign orchestrated by Miramax Pictures, the producer and distributor. *Ryan* is the better movie, but there's no denying this one's appeal. It's the fanciful (meaning entirely fictional) story of Shakespeare (Joseph Fiennes – Ralph's younger brother) as the famous playwright struggling both financially and artistically early in his career. He's writing a play called "Romeo and Ethel, the Pirate's Daughter," which even he knows is going nowhere. Then he meets the love of his life, Lady Viola De Lesseps (Gwyneth Paltrow), and his inspiration suddenly changes. The plot is far too clever to give away, except to say that its telling of the tale of the writing of "Romeo and Juliet," one of the greatest plays in the English language, is so good it doesn't really matter whether it's fictional

50

or not – you'll want to believe it is true. With terrific performances by Fiennes, whose face is wonderfully expressive, Paltrow as "Juliet" in various guises – the best work of her career – and strong support from Colin Firth (playing well against type) as Shakespeare's romantic rival, Geoffrey Rush as a theatre owner, and the incomparable Judi Dench in an Oscar-winning turn as Queen Elizabeth I. Marc Norman and Tom Stoppard wrote the excellent screenplay, and the lush, memorable score is by British composer Stephen Warbeck. [Trivia note: This movie marks the second Best Picture in which Firth's character is cuckolded by characters portrayed by the Fiennes family: Ralph in *The English Patient* and Joseph here] [Caution: sexuality] **[W]**

A Beautiful Mind
2001 – Directed by Ron Howard
Little Ronnie Howard, who began his career in movies in the late 1950s (see *The Music Man*), who became a TV child star in the early '60s, a young adult star in the '70s (see *American Graffiti*), and a fledgling director in the '80s, reaches full maturity here. The story is based on the life of John Nash, a Nobel Prize-winning mathematician who also suffered from raging, delusional schizophrenia. Howard was smart enough to pick the supremely talented Russell Crowe to play Nash in an Oscar-nominated performance, and Crowe – as he had done several times previously – utterly becomes his character. Jennifer Connelly won Best Actress as Nash's long-suffering wife. Sometimes heartbreaking and maybe a little too sentimental at the climax, this is a compelling examination of the tension between genius and insanity that often inhabits great minds. It features fine supporting performances by Christopher Plummer as a psychiatrist and Ed Harris as a mysterious "government" figure. James Horner contributes another excellent score. [Trivia note: As uplifting and inspiring as this story becomes, the real saga of John Nash ended tragically. He and his wife were killed in a taxicab crash in May 2015] [Caution: sexuality and adult language] **[W]**

The King's Speech [100]

2010 – Directed by Tom Hooper

At last! Nearly a decade went by before I agreed with the Academy's choice again. Based on a true story, the title refers to a critical moment in England's history. In September 1939, negotiations between Prime Minister Neville Chamberlain and Adolph Hitler had broken down, and the country found itself at war with Nazi Germany. The people were frightened, and the government was in turmoil. What could be done to bolster the nation for what was coming? The answer: The king, George VI, who had ascended to the throne only three years earlier, needed to rally the citizens of the British Empire with a rousing speech. Except that the king had a problem – a big one: He stuttered, terribly. Actually, that's the movie's climax, not its beginning, and what occurs before it represents one of the most unusual friendships ever presented on the screen. That friendship had begun six years earlier, when the king was still the Duke of York. Magnificently portrayed by Colin Firth, he sought out the services of Lionel Logue, a London speech therapist of questionable credentials played with great relish by Geoffrey Rush. Together and painstakingly, Lionel helps Bertie – the duke's pet name, derived from Albert, his real name – overcome his problem, ascend to the throne and inspire the nation. That's it, but therein lies greatness. The movie is graced with a host of indelible performances, including Michael Gambon as Bertie's father, King George V; Claire Bloom as Queen Mary, his mother; Guy Pearce as Edward, his playboy brother who abdicates his throne to marry his lover from Baltimore; Jennifer Ehle as Lionel's bemused wife; and especially Helena Bonham Carter as the Duchess of York. But the heart of the movie is the priceless interplay between Firth, who deservedly won an Oscar, and Rush, who undeservedly did not. Likewise, I might add, Bonham Carter plays her best role here, and she, too, should have won. Hooper's direction and David Seidler's script, Oscar-winners both, are flawless, and Danny Cohen's muted cinematography fits the mood perfectly. My only, slight, complaint is that Timothy Spall, as Winston Churchill, plays the prime minister as a caricature. Otherwise a fine, fine movie!

Alexandre Desplat contributed the elegant, low-key score. [Trivia notes: 1) When Seidler, who was 74 at the time, accepted his writing Oscar for this movie, he began by saying, "My mother always said she thought I'd be a late bloomer." 2) My quibble with Spall's portrayal stems from my great affection for an HBO movie version of *The Gathering Storm*, based on Churchill's own writing, in which Albert Finney gives a wonderful and highly recommended performance as the old man. 3) Speaking of television, one of these days I'd like to compile a list of my favorite TV programs, and among the very best is a BBC production from 1995 of the Jane Austen novel Pride and Prejudice. In it, Ehle was terrific as Elizabeth Bennett, and Firth immortalized himself in the role of Mr. Darcy. There's a scene in *The King's Speech* that reunites the couple on screen momentarily, and for fans of the miniseries it's a treat. The same for a brief turn by David Bamber, a marvelously versatile actor who played Mr. Collins in the BBC series, as a snooty theater director with no appreciation for Logue's acting ability (I'll mention Bamber's versatility again later in a stunning example). 4) Firth and Pearce appeared together again six years later, though not as brothers, in the biopic *Genius* (not on this list). Firth played legendary book editor Max Perkins, while Pearce played one of his stable of authors, none other than F. Scott Fitzgerald] [Caution: royal profanity] **[W]**

2. They Should Have Been Best Pictures

Setting aside the judgment of the members of the Academy of Motion Picture Arts and Sciences (whom I will never, ever forgive for not awarding – by acclamation – the Best Supporting Actress Oscar to Gloria Stuart for *Titanic*, among many other bum choices), I found these movies to be better, more compelling and more entertaining than their picks for Best Picture. Or, these titles could have been chosen if they hadn't been released in years won by truly deserving competitors. Whichever, I'd stack these 50 titles – my biggest category – against the choices of the academy's membership any day. Some of them rank among the greatest movies ever made.

Foreign Correspondent
1940 – Alfred Hitchcock
The first title in this category is unusual, because it displaces Best Picture winner *Rebecca*, which Hitchcock also directed and was his first American movie. Yet I think Hitch's second American production was the superior choice that year. It's a lively and well-paced tale of Johnny Jones (Joel McCrea), a jaded newspaper reporter whose editor sends him to cover the gathering war clouds in Europe under the pseudonym Huntley Haverstock. In its day, *Foreign Correspondent* was quite daring, because Americans were sharply divided in their opinions about whether the country should become involved in the war in Europe against Germany. Not until after the attack on Pearl Harbor, when Hitler joined the Japanese in an alliance against the United States, did the country finally go to war. So there are villains in the movie, and it's fairly obvious they are German, but they're never named as such. Still, along with the elements that became Hitchcock trademarks – a shocking and expertly staged assassination, clever and witty dialogue, and plot twists galore – there's a fairly strong message about the need for American resolve at a critical time in world history. That's completely evident in the last scene, where Haverstock, broadcasting from a London studio in the middle of an air raid

that has knocked out the power, says "Hello America! Hang onto your lights – they're the only lights left on in the world!" Some things ring true no matter the era. [Trivia notes: 1) Hitchcock shot that dramatic last scene in Hollywood on July 5, 1940, only five days before the Nazis began bombing London. 2) With the war going on in Europe, location shooting became impossible. So, Hitchcock's crew built, among other things, a 10-acre representation of a square in Amsterdam, a 600-foot-long reproduction of London's Waterloo Station, and a life-size replica, complete with interior, of a trans-Atlantic airliner – and a huge water tank to stage the crash scene] **[B&W]**

Citizen Kane
1941 – Orson Welles (Winner: How Green Was My Valley)
One of the two best American movies ever to be denied the Best Picture Oscar, for decades *Citizen Kane* has occupied the all-time Top-10 lists of just about every film critics' organization on Earth. It is a genuine classic, an over-the-top, bravura debut by Welles so full of innovations it has influenced the career of just about every moviemaker who's seen it. Beginning with a brief but now-famous prologue – in which the word "Rosebud" is uttered in a whisper by a pair of lips in ultra-close-up – it documents the rise and fall of fictional newspaper publishing tycoon Charles Foster Kane (played by Welles), whose character is based loosely on real-life tycoon William Randolph Hearst. For that reason, the movie almost didn't get made – because Hearst made so many threats, legal and otherwise, against RKO, the studio of record. Welles, only 25 years old at the time, moves the story along effortlessly. Even this many years after its release, *Citizen Kane* remains full of surprises for first-time viewers, with a razor-sharp, Oscar-winning script by Herman Mankiewicz and with Greg Toland's ground-breaking cinematography. As Welles once said – and demonstrated here – a movie studio is "the best toy train set a boy ever had." I've included three movies on this list that should inspire youngster who dream of making movies. This is the first of the bunch. [Young viewers note: If you watch this movie and learn what

Rosebud turns out to be, you will have taken your first step toward being a cinephile – a real movielover] **[B&W]**

The Third Man [100]
1949 – Carol Reed (<u>Winner</u>: All the King's Men)

Here is Orson Welles again, this time starring in the first Cold War thriller, which Reed brilliantly executes with his screenwriter, the novelist Graham Greene. The title, as you will come to realize, refers to Welles as Harry Lime, the mysterious and thoroughly corrupt character at the story's center, and even though he appears in only three scenes, Welles steals the movie. Joseph Cotton plays Holly Martins, a writer of western novels and friend of Lime's. When Martins travels to Vienna at Lime's invitation and promise of a moneymaking opportunity, he learns upon arrival that Lime has been killed in a traffic accident. That knowledge, and the discovery that many of the city's residents are desperate and therefore dangerous, should alert Martins to leave immediately. Instead, he finds himself falling for Harry's lover, Anna (Alida Valli), and quickly getting himself drawn further and further into the intrigues surrounding his former friend. From the very beginning, though, nothing is what it seems, and by the time the movie is over you still won't be sure what has been going on – but chances are you won't mind the experience one bit. You will rarely encounter snappier movie dialogue, Robert Krasker's Oscar-winning cinematography is brilliant, and the scenes of post-World War II Vienna are fascinating, particularly the climactic chase, which takes place (mostly) down in the city's sewer system. The movie's music and title theme are distinctive and famous, played by Anton Karas on an instrument called a zither. **[B&W]**

Bad Day at Black Rock
1955 – John Sturges (<u>Winner</u>: Marty)

Apologies to my darling Jessie, who loved *Marty*, this was the best movie of that year. *Marty* worked well as a play and as a television drama, but it remained a bit too stagy for the big screen. Despite its hokey title, *Bad Day at Black Rock* is a first-rate

56

attraction. It's a classic stranger-rides-into-town story, because the stranger's arrival challenges or changes the lives of all concerned, and not necessarily for the better. Spencer Tracy is the stranger, John J. Macready, a war veteran with a bum left arm who arrives at a small desert rail stop to deliver something to a resident of the town, a Japanese-American who, he discovers, has disappeared mysteriously. Macready's presence provokes suspicion and eventually exposes the collective guilt of the residents, some of whom react violently but at their peril, because the one-armed stranger can more than handle himself. The strong supporting cast includes Lee Marvin, Dean Jagger, Anne Francis, Walter Brennan, Robert Ryan – and Ernest Borgnine, in the other major role of his Oscar-winning year. Sturges used the Nevada desert locales and the CinemaScope widescreen format to perfection, particularly in the thrilling opening sequence, one of the first ever shot from a helicopter, of the train's arrival. [Trivia notes: 1) Borgnine described the fight his character has with Tracy as being carefully choreographed with the help of a martial arts adviser. But when the time came to shoot it, director Sturges latched the screen door through which Borgnine was supposed to fall. So instead of knocking it open, he plunged through it, making for a more dramatic moment, and fortunately suffering no injury. Meanwhile, Tracy refused to stage the main shots of the fight scene, opting instead for a stunt double. It seems that during the shooting of *Boom Town*, in which his and Clark Gable's characters engaged in a fist fight, Tracy accidentally landed a haymaker on Gable's jaw and knocked out a couple of his teeth. Apparently from then on the great actor feared harming another cast member. 2) During the shoot, Tracy gave a lot of encouragement to Borgnine, a relative unknown at the time. In particular, he encouraged him to go for the title role in another movie that was about to begin production. Borgnine accepted the advice, won the role and received the Best Actor Oscar for *Marty*, – beating out Tracy, who had been nominated for *Bad Day at Black Rock*. 3) Borgnine played a menacing tough here, as he did two years earlier as a sadistic sergeant in *From Here to Eternity*. But in real life, Ernest

Borgnine was a down-to-earth, extremely likable man. A while back, Jeff Krulik, a friend of mine, persuaded Ernie to let him ride along as he traveled in his custom-fitted bus. The result was a delightful video you can find on YouTube] **[W]**

The Spirit of St. Louis [100]
1957 – Billy Wilder

Wilder's glorious telling of one of the most famous feats in aviation history, the lone crossing of the Atlantic Ocean in 1927 by 26-year-old Charles Lindbergh in his single engine aircraft named "The Spirit of St. Louis," is one of the best movies ever made about aviation. It's also a terrific character study. I mention his age because Lindbergh – on whose book of the same name Wilder based his screenplay – is played by 49-year-old James Stewart. Despite that difference, Stewart is perfect simply being himself and not attempting to imitate "Lucky Lindy," as Lindbergh came to be called. Stewart completely embodies his character and personality – his spirit, if you will. The story begins just before the takeoff, from Long Island's Roosevelt Field, on May 20. As Lindbergh tries to grab some last-minute rest, Wilder takes us back to his first days in aviation and his quest to find a plane capable of flying nonstop from New York to Paris. Wilder and screenwriter Charles Lederer continue to use flashbacks intermittently through the movie. Most of the time Wilder also uses a full-size replica of the Spirit for the aerial scenes, and it's thrilling to see it take wing over land and water, particularly in one sweeping shot, as the plane flies low across the harbor in St. Johns, Newfoundland, and out toward the vast and foreboding Atlantic. Out there and through one long, occasionally terrifying night, Lindbergh fought sleep deprivation, darkness and icing of his wings to make it through to the next morning. That flyby scene is one of the greatest in all of cinema, and *The Spirit of St. Louis* is a grand re-creation of one of the most heroic episodes in aviation. Yes, it was extremely courageous of Lindbergh to attempt the first trans-oceanic crossing alone, without a copilot or even a radio (he wanted to spare the weight), and there are several times when he could have been lost along the way. But the most gripping, amazing part of the journey was his landing at Le Bourget field near Paris. There, after flying 3500 miles in 33 hours, with no sleep for nearly three days, Lindbergh managed to put the Spirit down safely, with no communications help from the ground and no runway lights. In my humble opinion, this was the most astounding aviation feat ever, and Wilder and Stewart portray it with great drama – even though you know how the flight ends. This is a dreamy, wonderful movie, and though sordid parts of Lindbergh's personal life have surfaced over the years to tarnish his image, this achievement cannot be diminished. Gorgeously shot in CinemaScope by Robert Burks and J. Peverell Marley, the movie features an appropriately soaring score by Franz Waxman – his best work. [Trivia notes: 1) Lindbergh's May 20 takeoff coincided with Stewart's 19th birthday, and from then on Stewart was enthralled with Lindy's life and had always wanted to portray him. 2) I met and interviewed Lindbergh's daughter, Reeve, on the 75th anniversary of the flight. She had become an author and aviation advocate, and she was a gracious and kind person. Most striking was how much she resembled her father. When she looked at you, it was as though you were looking into his eyes] **[W]**

On the Beach [100]
1959 – Stanley Kramer

Ben-Hur won eleven Oscars that year, but Stanley Kramer did the best work of his career in bringing Nevil Shute's bleak novel to the screen with tremendous poignancy, humanity, romance and even humor. An American submarine arrives in Melbourne, Australia, apparently one of the last places on Earth still harboring survivors after an all-out nuclear exchange between the United States and the Soviet Union renders most of the planet uninhabitable. There the sub's captain, Dwight Towers (Gregory Peck), and crew settle in for their own last days among the Australian people, many of whom still haven't quite accepted their inevitable doom. The fine cast includes Ava Gardner as Moira, a hard-luck spinster and lush who becomes

Peck's love interest. Gardner is riveting, both physically and otherwise, anytime she appears, and this is possibly her best performance. Anthony Perkins, a year before he became the notorious Norman Bates in *Psycho* (not on this list), plays an Aussie navy officer married to newcomer (and Alaska-born) Donna Anderson – a woman on the verge. And of all people, Fred Astaire is wonderful in his first dramatic role as a nuclear scientist drinking himself into oblivion. Devoid of special effects, the movie finds simple but chilling and powerful ways to portray the human species on the edge of extinction. Example: The submarine visits San Francisco and finds the entire city intact and scenic as ever but empty of activity. Another: Near the end, a group of racecar enthusiasts holds a last version of the Grand Prix, and it's rather disturbing to see how such an event might proceed against such a background. Ernest Gold's deceptively moving score takes variation upon variation of the unofficial Australian national song, "Waltzing Matilda," and culminates in a brilliant sequence where a drunken rendition of the tune transforms into an unbearably sad but sweetly sung ballad. Make no mistake, *On the Beach* will shatter you, but you will never regret having seen it. [Trivia note: Peck and Gardner had co-starred twice before, likewise in literary adaptations but in far less affecting stories. The first was *The Great Sinner* in 1949 based on the Dostoyevsky novel The Gambler, and the second three years later in a screen version of Hemingway's The Snows of Kilimanjaro (neither on this list)] **[B&W] [W]**

Spartacus [100]
1960 – Stanley Kubrick (Winner: The Apartment)
An enormous epic and, after *2001: A Space Odyssey*, probably the best movie Stanley Kubrick ever made – although he said afterward he never would work with a Hollywood studio again. Based on a true story of a slave who rose to lead a massive but ill-fated rebellion against the Roman Empire, the movie as usual takes liberties with history – but they are forgivable liberties. The battle sequences are gigantic – set in Italy, they actually were shot in Spain and California – but the intimate moments provide

the movie's emotional power, and they are too numerous to mention or spoil. As Spartacus, Kirk Douglas remains the story's center and heart, and his performance qualifies as Unforgettable (see category elsewhere) from beginning to end. Though the phrase "I'm Spartacus" is now sometimes used in jest, the classic scene where it is repeated still brings tears. The fine supporting cast includes Tony Curtis as a gentle young slave, Laurence Olivier as an effete and ruthless senator, Jean Simmons as the slave woman who bears Spartacus a son, Peter Ustinov as a wily slave dealer, former Olympic athlete Woody Strode as a fellow gladiator, and the great Charles Laughton as a corpulent but crafty senator and rival to Olivier. Simmons, in her best role, was never more beautiful, Ustinov won a Best Supporting Actor Oscar for his witty performance, and Laughton had the time of his life as an unapologetically debauched Roman. The stirring score and tender love theme are by Alex North, and the script is by Dalton Trumbo, who had been blacklisted during the McCarthy era. [Trivia note: In the restored version of the movie, which contains a scenes where the audio recordings had been lost, Anthony Hopkins – at the suggestion of Joan Plowright, Olivier's widow – dubbed an impersonation of the voice of Olivier, who had died some years before] **[W]**

FAIL-SAFE
1964 – Sidney Lumet) (<u>Winner</u>: My Fair Lady)
Though its topic is a nuclear crisis between the United States and the Soviet Union, Lumet's movie is more about the wrenching inner emotions of characters facing a horrific situation. Henry Fonda plays the U.S. president who, from the shelter of the White House bunker, must persuade the Soviet premier that an impending attack on his country by American bombers is a mistake. Meanwhile, military personnel in both countries scramble to intercept the errant, nuclear-armed aircraft. Once the effort begins, the tension is sometimes unbearable, and the climax is literally shattering. Fonda was never better; likewise Dan O'Herlihy as a tormented general, Edward Binns as an aging bomber pilot, Frank Overton as the dour Air Force

Commander, and a young Larry Hagman as an interpreter named Buck. Walter Matthau also appears as an ultra-hawkish national security adviser, and Walter Bernstein wrote the script based on the novel by Eugene Burdick and Harvey Wheeler. Film editor Ralph Rosenblum provided much of the suspense – a feat made even more amazing because 1) almost all of the action takes place indoors, 2) there is no music, and 3) the Defense Department provided no cooperation, so a lot of the aerial sequences had to be improvised. But don't let those limitations deter you – this movie is nail-bitingly tense, and its conclusion will leave you stunned. As a disclaimer among the end credits reads, the Pentagon considered the scenario depicted by the movie impossible. That's probably true, but the movie gives you an unforgettable taste of what might happen if they're wrong. [Trivia note: Rosenblum made some of the aerial sequences seem more frightening by splicing in film negatives of Air Force stock footage, thereby making the aircraft appear bright and otherworldly against a dark sky. He describes more about editing the movie in his fine book When the Shooting Stops ... The Cutting Begins (see Recommended Books)] [B&W] [W]

Funny Girl
1968 – William Wyler (Winner: Oliver!)
Barbra Streisand's first movie remains her best, in which she reprises the role that made her a star on Broadway in the early 1960s, playing 1930s comedienne Fanny Brice. Wyler was near the end of his career here, but he nevertheless retained his master's touch (although Herbert Ross assisted with the musical numbers) and added Streisand to the biggest group of actors and actresses ever to win Oscars under a single director. Several of the Bob Merrill-Jule Styne songs are memorable, including Streisand doing what has become her signature number, "People," and singing a heartbreaking "My Man" for an empty-stage finale. There's also "Don't Rain on My Parade," which she belts out starting in a train station and ending up on the foredeck of a tugboat in the middle of New York harbor, a 3-minute showstopper that contains arguably the two best helicopter shots

ever executed – both accomplished without the benefit of visual effects. Omar Sharif tries gamely to make an impression as Brice's first husband, Nick Arnstein, but Streisand just blows him off the screen. Likewise, Walter Pidgeon as the legendary Broadway impresario Florenz Ziegfeld. This is her movie, and deservedly so. [Trivia notes: 1) Had the academy heeded my advice and awarded Best Picture to *Funny Girl*, it would have added to Wyler's singular achievement in winning more Oscars in this category (three) than any other director. His others were *Mrs. Miniver* in 1942 (not on this list), *The Best Years of Our Lives* and *Ben-Hur*. 2) The comic number "The Swan" performed by Streisand was never performed by Brice; it was written for this movie. 3) Streisand became a voting member of the motion picture academy the year she was nominated. Presumably, she voted for herself as Best Actress, which turned out to be decisive because she ended up tied with Katharine Hepburn, nominated for *The Lion in Winter* (not bad, but not on this list), and the two women shared the Oscar. 4) Also appearing with Pidgeon is Anne Francis, who 12 years earlier had played his daughter in *Forbidden Planet*] **[W]**

Butch Cassidy and the Sundance Kid [100]
1969 – George Roy Hill (<u>Winner</u>: Midnight Cowboy)
This is the first modern buddy movie, and it remains the best, even though it has inspired dozens of imitators in many other genres. Paul Newman, in the first of his three pairings with director Hill, plays Butch, head of the Hole in the Wall gang of robbers and rustlers who hid out in Johnson County, Wyoming, in the late 19th century. Robert Redford is the Kid, who has been carrying the name for quite a while and is beginning to ripen as a gunfighter. Their characters were real, but the story is pretext for William Goldman's hip, Oscar-winning script that plays almost but not everything for deadpan laughs. This perennial audience-pleaser features Conrad Hall's gorgeous, golden-hued photography of Utah and Colorado (but not Wyoming) locales, and Burt Bacharach's contemporary, sometimes completely anachronistic music. The song "Raindrops Keep Falling on My

Head," sung by B.J. Thomas, won the Oscar even though it had nothing to do with the story. It's just that audiences loved the scene with Newman and Katharine Ross looking good riding a bicycle together. The centerpiece sequence is a 30-minute chase across spectacular landscapes, as Butch and Sundance attempt to elude a relentless band of hired lawmen, with one or the other of the two frequently asking, "Who are those guys?" and the chase ending with … well, see the movie. You're likely to love it. [Trivia notes: 1) The photos of Butch, Sundance and Etta (Ross's character) visiting New York City actually were taken on the set of the movie version of the musical *Hello Dolly!* which was being shot at the same time. Parts of those shots were then inserted into archival photos of the city. 2) Redford ended up loving Utah so much he eventually settled there, founded the Sundance Institute for aspiring moviemakers and began the annual Sundance Film Festival as a showcase for new talent] [Caution: violence, language and mildly implied sexuality] **[W]**

Fiddler on the Roof [100]
1971 – Norman Jewison
If this movie doesn't grab you within the opening six minutes and hold you from there on, then you're a hard case indeed. It certainly clutched me that quickly when I first saw it, more than 10 years after its release. At the time, I knew very little about it; only that Gary Arnold had praised its re-release in a capsule review in The Washington Post. Gary described it as Jewison's "glorious" version of the Broadway musical, and that's a perfect adjective. The story of Tevye (TEV-yah), a humble milkman in the Jewish village of Anetevka, Russia, sometime around the turn of the 20th century, was immortalized on the Broadway stage by the great Zero Mostel, and in countless performances elsewhere. Here, the role is played wonderfully by the Israeli actor Topol, who was only 35 at the time. Tevye has five daughters and, according to tradition, those daughters are not destined to marry well, because the family's poverty will not support enough of a dowry to attract worthy suitors. Tradition – which is the movie's theme and the title of its sublime opening

64

number – turns out to be a blessing and curse for Tevye, as he struggles between his devotion to his faith and his love for his daughters, each of whom forces him to confront ever-more-unconventional matches. Often funny, always touching and ultimately heartbreaking – as so many great movies are, *Fiddler on the Roof* artfully depicts Jewish peasant life in Russia during the period and contains disturbing incidents of anti-Semitism and foreshadows of the Holocaust. As Gary also said in his review, the movie develops an overwhelming sense of pathos. But it's also indeed a glorious musical, with many memorable songs, including the already-mentioned "Tradition" as well as "If I Were a Rich Man." Then there is the beautiful "Sabbath Song," the rousing "To Life," the rapturous "Miracle of Miracles," the heartfelt "Sunrise, Sunset" and "Chavaleh," which is guaranteed to bring any father with daughters to tears. And it's probably the finest portrayal of the themes of home, community, faith, marriage and family ever brought to the screen. It's a universal love story. So, what's with the title? Tevye explains it for you right at the start. [Trivia notes: 1) Jewison got to direct the movie because its producers somehow thought he was Jewish, instead of a Canadian Presbyterian. He eventually confessed that he was "a goy," but he got the job anyway and did it masterfully. 2) Though set in Russia, the movie was shot in Yugoslavia, which two decades later became the scene of a horrible civil war and attempted genocide, as its various ethnic groups – particularly the Serbs and Croats – lashed out at one another after the downfall of both the Soviet Union and the totalitarian government of Marshall Tito] **[W]**

Chinatown
1974 – Roman Polanski
The classic L.A. private eye story with an updated sheen, *Chinatown* is actually more than that. It's one of the best detective movies ever made in any setting. The title is a metaphor for something you can't possibly fathom, and Robert Towne's ultra-cryptic, Oscar-winning script carries that metaphor to perfection. You don't understand this movie, you just have to feel it, and

feel it you do, from the very first, almost painfully high violin strokes that transition into a soft and slow trumpet solo in Jerry Goldsmith's lilting, melancholy score. Jack Nicholson plays Jake Gittes, a cynical Los Angeles private investigator in the 1930s who is at first paid to track the philandering husband of a mysterious woman (Diane Ladd) but then is lured into greater trouble by an even more mysterious woman (Faye Dunaway), whose father, Noah Cross (played with relish by John Huston), is one of the best movie villains ever. Polanski appears in a neat little role as a sadistic hood. Though this was one of Nicholson's early starring roles, it remains one of his best. It was beaten out by *The Godfather Part II*, but in another year it might have swept the top awards. [General note: This movie raises a question that haunts me about many of the titles on my list. At present, Polanski remains under house arrest in Switzerland, awaiting extradition to the United States where he faces unlawful-flight charges resulting from his 1977 conviction of statutory rape for having had sexual relations with a young girl. Though Polanski's case is extreme, many other producers, directors and stars have been involved in rather tawdry activities. Likewise, many movie personalities often spout political views quite different from my own, and some verge into the utterly ridiculous (Sean Penn comes immediately to mind). The question is, should we ignore or criticize their work if we disapprove of their personal behavior? That's everyone's right, of course, but speaking for myself I'd rather let the work stand on its own. Also, if I had to omit movies because the people involved have committed disreputable or offensive acts, I'd end up with quite a short list – and you'd miss out on a whole lot of otherwise fine entertainment] [Caution: graphic violence and sexuality] **[W]**

The Seven-Per-Cent Solution
1976 – Herbert Ross (Winner: Rocky)
You've probably never heard of this fine movie, because it came and went with inexplicable speed. But don't pass it up; though hard to find, it's unique and thoroughly delightful. It's unique

66

because it attempts to fill in a gap in the adventures of Sir Arthur Conan Doyle's legendary Sherlock Holmes, the fictional British detective. Screenwriter Nicholas Meyer imagined that the gap in the timeline was due to a personal problem for Holmes (Nicol Williamson): He had become addicted to a seven-percent solution of cocaine. In this story, Holmes's faithful friend and chronicler, Dr. Watson (Robert Duvall, in an unusual role but thoroughly believable), contrives to lure Holmes to Vienna, Austria, where his addiction can be treated by the equally legendary – though real – psychiatrist Sigmund Freud (Alan Arkin in one of his best roles). Holmes submits to the treatment but in the process becomes entangled in a plot to rescue a beautiful but mysterious kidnapping victim. It's delightful, because as the plot unfolds we're treated to a rousing story with colorful characters and a rather exciting chase sequence involving two trains, a chase which derives some of its ingenuity from the Atlantic crossing in *Around the World in 80 Days*. The superb cast includes Joel Grey as a weasel of an informer, Vanessa Redgrave as the alluring damsel in distress, and Laurence Olivier as Holmes's perennial nemesis Professor Moriarty. [Caution: sexuality] **[W]**

My Brilliant Career
1979 – Australia – Gillian Armstrong (Winner: Kramer versus Kramer)

A beguiling import from Australia and a literary adaptation showcasing two budding stars, both of whom later enjoyed successful American careers. This was the breakthrough movie for Armstrong, whom I consider one of the finest directors in the world and one of the three best women in the craft. Based on the popular first novel by Miles Franklin (whose real name was Stella Maria Sarah Miles Franklin), it's a simple story, beautifully told and gorgeously shot. Judy Davis, 24 at the time and in her first significant role, shines as Sybylla Melvyn, a poor country girl in late-19th-century rural southeastern Australia who aspires to be a writer but whose family and her suitor Harry Beecham (Sam Neill, also in his first notable role) have other plans for her.

The versatile Davis has never been more appealing or looked so good, with her long, reddish hair often appearing radiant when backlit by sunlight. The story moves slowly but draws you in strongly, and it builds to a quiet but exquisitely satisfying conclusion. It's an early feminist tome delivered with a light touch and great humanity. One of its highlights: of all things, a one-on-one pillow fight. [Trivia notes: 1) Franklin's novel created such a sensation in turn-of-the-century Australia (it was published in 1901), and presented her family with so much unwanted celebrity, that she eventually recalled her publishing rights and would not allow the book to be re-released until after her death in 1954. 2) The song "Scenes from Childhood" by Robert Schumann, which Sybylla plays on an out-of-tune piano early in the movie, is the same piece played by Joanne Woodward in the 1968 movie *Rachel, Rachel* (not on this list)] **[W]**

The Big Red One
1980 – Samuel Fuller (Winner: Ordinary People)
In its original form, this was one of my favorite war movies. Highly focused and limited in scale, it was a story told in intimate detail, as though filmed entirely through a telescopic lens. I still feel that way somewhat, but the movie has changed. Now, instead of a trim, 2-hour feature, it has been rereleased with nearly 45 minutes added. It turns out that for nearly 25 years a significant portion of the story remained concealed, the product of studio pressures to keep the running time down to the popular theatrical norm. But in 2004 a dedicated, painstaking effort by film historian and critic Richard Schickel brought the full, 162-minute version to the screen. I retain my judgment about the movie's merits, but I can also see why most of the restored material was originally removed. Loosely based on the real experiences of writer-director Fuller, the title refers to the nickname given to the U.S. Army's famed First Infantry Division. The story follows a battle-hardened, aging sergeant (Lee Marvin, in his career-best performance, which represents yet another ill-conceived oversight by the motion picture academy) whom we meet in a flashback on the last day of World

War I. Then, starting in 1942 and continuing through the end of the war in Europe, the Sergeant – who remains unnamed – shepherds four members of a rifle squad through the disastrous loss in Tunisia's Kasserine Pass (where the U.S. Army, in its first battle with the Germans, suffered 1,800 casualties in one day); in Sicily; on Omaha Beach at D-Day; and across France, Belgium, Germany and into Czechoslovakia. It's an unusual war movie, because it neither glorifies nor condemns war. As the Sergeant and a German officer (a recurring character) both say, separately, "We don't murder our enemies, we kill them." It's more a drama about the relationships of five souls who happen to be thrown together in combat. Robert Carradine, whose character is based on Fuller and who narrates the story, sums things up well at the end when he says the only goal of a soldier is to survive, and that he and his cohorts shared more in common with the German survivors than with their dead comrades. It's a debatable point but a forgivable one, given the compelling nature of the story. With Mark Hamill (Luke Skywalker in the *Star Wars* saga), Bobby DiCicco and Kelly Ward rounding out the quartet of dogfaces – as U.S. soldiers were called at the time. [Trivia notes: 1) Some of the battle scenes were shot in Israel, which created the unusual sight of Israeli men – some wearing yarmulkes underneath their helmets – dressed in German uniforms. 2) Marvin fought in World War II in the Pacific, and he was badly wounded in a way similar to what is portrayed in the movie] [Caution: language, sexuality and some explicit depictions of wartime violence] [W]

Prince of the City
1981 – Sidney Lumet (Winner: Chariots of Fire)
A dark but tremendously absorbing drama, this is nobody's idea of a good time. Still, it's a powerful movie inspired by a true story. Treat Williams, in the role of his career, portrays New York City detective Danny Ciello, based in part on real police detective Robert Leuci, a man whose conscience forces him to turn informant about the rampant corruption that surrounds him within his precinct. Lumet had explored a similar theme

eight years earlier with Al Pacino in *Serpico*, but this is a much more subtle and mature work, the chronicle of a cop who seeks to expose corruption in the city's police department but is somewhat caught up in the corruption himself and therefore tormented by the idea of informing on his friends. Unlike just about every other police movie, this one leads to one of the most remarkably understated but tragic climaxes ever filmed. Jerry Orbach's superb performance as a defiant cop was unjustifiably overlooked by the Academy – yet another flub. [Caution: violence and constant rough language] **[W]**

The Year of Living Dangerously
1982 – Peter Weir (Winner: Gandhi)
Weir's exotic drama is one of the most unusual mainstream movies ever made. Based on the novel by C.J. Koch and set in Indonesia in the mid-1960s, at the time of President Sukarno's downfall, the story follows the exploits of Australian journalist Guy Hamilton (Mel Gibson), who attempts to report on the political upheaval around him, thereby enhancing his reputation. The problem is that doing so endangers his life and the lives of other around him – in one case fatally. Sigourney Weaver (affecting a light British accent) provides Gibson's love interest, and Linda Hunt won an Oscar for her portrayal of Gibson's photographer – a *man* named Billy Kwan who also serves as the movie's narrator. Maurice Jarre provided the synthesized, exotic score, one of his most beautiful. Tense and absorbing, the movie envelops you with an almost-palpable atmosphere of mystery and menace. It's the best of its kind since *The Third Man* but a far more evocative and darker story. [Trivia notes: 1) Given the movie's theme, there was no way the government of President Suharto, who deposed Sukarno, would permit filming in his country, so Manila became the stand-in location, at least temporarily. 2) After a few weeks, the filming in Manila had to be shut down because of death threats against Weir and Gibson, who had been rumored to be making an "anti-Islamic" movie. Final production took place in Sydney. 3) Because of the logistical problems, the movie became one of the

costliest productions in Australian history] [<u>Caution</u>: sexuality and violence] **[W]**

The Right Stuff [100]
1983 – Philip Kaufman (<u>Winner</u>: Terms of Endearment)

The other best American movie (along with *Citizen Kane*) to be denied the Oscar, *The Right Stuff* is a combination of spectacular visuals, skillfully structured story and superb characterizations. Like so many other movies, it plays fast and loose with history – in some cases, very fast and loose. Nevertheless, *The Right Stuff* is dazzling, and even in this age of computer-generated images its visual power is likely to remain undimmed for a long, long time. Kaufman's epic starts at the birth of supersonic aviation in October 1947, when test pilots flew above the high California desert – which they called "The Dome of the World" – attempting to break the sound barrier in experimental aircraft that crashed with alarming frequency. Based on Tom Wolfe's outstanding book of the same name, the title refers to an elusive but undeniable combination of courage and coolness owned by only the best of these men, who literally risked their lives every time they climbed into their planes. This was particularly true of Chuck Yeager – the "Ace of Aces," as the other pilots called him. Sam Shepard plays Yeager (whom I've seen in person) perfectly, displaying a manly charm and laconic humor that belie his steely resolve, super-competitiveness and supreme survival instincts in the air. His understated heroism is exemplary. The second act depicts the arrival of America's Mercury astronauts, who were assembled in the late 1950s for NASA's attempts to launch men into space to beat the Russians. Dennis Quaid, Fred Ward, Scott Glenn and Ed Harris each are wonderful as, respectively, astronauts Gordon "Gordo" Cooper, Virgil "Gus" Grissom, Alan Shepard and John Glenn. One of the movie's greatest achievements, however, is the vivid performances by the splendid female cast of Veronica Cartwright, Pamela Reed, Mary Jo Deschanel and Barbara Hershey, playing Betty Grissom, Trudy Cooper, Annie Glenn and Glennis Yeager. They all convey so well the raw fear the real wives of astronauts and test

71

pilots felt as their husbands tempted death on a daily basis. Shot by the great cinematographer Caleb Deschanel, the dramatized scenes display a rich golden tone and match the archival footage seamlessly. Bill Conti adapted Gustav Holst's "The Planets" to provide a rousing, love-of-country score, and a team of film editors expertly handled the visual complexity. In full measures thrilling, funny, harrowing and even touching, *The Right Stuff* recalls another time when America's future and even its existence were not assured, as some volunteered to do symbolic battle at the boundaries of space for the good of their country. In a word, it's unforgettable. [Trivia notes: 1) Despite its multiple settings, including Cape Canaveral, Florida; Washington, D.C., and even Muchea, Australia, Kaufman shot the entire movie in California. 2) In the documentary sequence supposedly showing the astronauts enduring endless challenges to test their fitness for this unusual duty, the goateed Kaufman makes a gratuitous appearance as an astronaut candidate riding a shaking chair with a fried egg slapped over each eye. 3) Two of the three flying sequences with Yeager depict him essentially jumping into an aircraft and taking off without preparation. This never happened. As dangerous as these endeavors were, each was carefully planned to advance the intended feat by small increments. In no way did Yeager commandeer a brand new fighter jet or accept a mission to break the sound barrier without a great deal of authorized preparation. Still, as dramatized, the sequences are thrilling. 4) The fine supporting cast boasts six actors who were already screen veterans or would go on to achieve exceptionally long careers. At this writing, Lance Hendrickson (as astronaut Walter Schirra) remains the champ, holding 235 credits. He's followed by the late Royal Dano (the local clergyman and "death" figure) with 192, Harry Schearer (NASA recruiter) with 164, Veronica Cartwright (Betty Grissom) with 144, William Russ (rival test pilot "Slick" Goodlin) with 134 and David Clennon (Air Force press liaison) with 131] [Caution: rough language and sexual references] **[W]**

A Passage to India [100]
1984 – David Lean

If you choose to see David Lean's adaptation of the E.M. Forster novel about cultural clashes during the British Raj in the 1920s, and come to love it as much as I do, know that it was the only movie made by the great director in nearly 15 years. His previous work, *Ryan's Daughter* (coming in the next compilation) in 1970, was so universally panned that Lean fell into depression and withdrew from moviemaking for nearly a decade and a half. That's a great shame, because this movie, his last, is nearly perfect. It is the story of two women who travel to India from England to see the same man – one's son and the other's fiancé – with tragic results for both. Judy Davis of *My Brilliant Career* plays Adela Quested, the fiancée, and the great Dame Peggy Ashcroft plays the mother (in an Oscar-winning performance). There, they meet a dashing but cynical Englishman (James Fox), a good-hearted but unlucky Indian doctor (Victor Bannerjee) and a mysterious but sometimes annoying Hindu scholar (Alec Guinness in dark makeup and bug-eyed spectacles). Throw in English bigotry, Indian rage and mistaken attempts at cultural understanding, and by the end no one remains unscathed. Yet you hate to see it end, because like Lean's other great movies it draws you in so powerfully you feel psychically a part of the story and do not wish to let go of the characters or the setting it has introduced. And the end sequence is among the most beautiful and beguiling in all of cinema. Also like Lean's best, *A Passage to India* demands to be seen on the biggest screen you can find; with a proper sound system, the better to enjoy Maurice Jarre's exotic orchestral score. [Trivia notes: 1) You wouldn't know it from the magnificent result, but this was a highly troubled production, owing perhaps in part to Lean's long absence from directing. He clashed with the principal cast members and much of the crew on a daily basis, particularly his longtime collaborator Guinness, with whom he developed such a serious rift that neither would speak to the other for the rest of their lives. 2) The "caves" at Murabar do not exist. The company

73

excavated several shallow entrances on a rocky hillside while the interior scenes were shot on studio sets] **[W]**

The Color Purple
1985 – Steven Spielberg

Spielberg's masterful rendering of Alice Walker's bleak and spare novel features many of his signature director's touches, an outstanding cast, beautiful cinematography by Allan Daviau, a finely varied score by Quincy Jones with a pair of memorable songs and a knockout, tear-jerking ending. The story involves Celie (SEE-lee), whom we meet at age 12 (played by Desreta Jackson) and very pregnant. We quickly learn that her father, who also is the father of her child, immediately confiscates the newborn to give her up for adoption – the second time he has done this. When he finally tires of Celie, he offers her to "Mister..." (Danny Glover, in a difficult role), who takes her home to his dirty household and his nasty children. There, she works hard and endures his sexual advances, finding solace only in the temporary asylum he grants to her beloved sister Nettie (Akosua Busia), who begins teaching her to read before Nettie repels one of Mister's advances and ends up banished by him. It is a long and painful ordeal for Celie (played as an adult by Whoopi Goldberg in a terrific screen debut) from utter subservience to self-reliance. Assisting her transformation is Sug (SHOOG) Avery (TV veteran Margaret Avery in a stunning performance) – the woman who begins as Celie's rival but ends up her close and intimate friend – and Sofia (Oprah Winfrey in her own sensational movie debut), a hardheaded woman who won't bend to the will of society or any man. Spielberg's direction is fluid and seamless. Each scene flows perfectly into the next, and several of the sequences are transporting. Perhaps the most memorable is the transition from Jackson to Goldberg in the role of Celie. It's depicted by a printed flier touting Sug's local appearance wafting in the wind and caressing a symbolically important mailbox before winding up stuck to the screen door outside the room where Celie is reading. Someone once said the most intense tears are shed not for sadness and grief but for longing fulfilled, and this movie proves that point. You probably will not be able to resist the sobfest at the finale. My advice is not to try. [Trivia notes: 1) *The Color Purple* suffers from the unfortunate distinction of receiving one of the worst shutouts in motion picture academy history, receiving 11 nominations (but ignoring Spielberg's direction) and winning none. The only other movie so disdained was *The Turning Point* in 1977. 2) Spielberg might seem an unlikely choice to direct this material, but he took on the project at the urging of his friend and the movie's composer, Quincy Jones. At first, Spielberg refused, saying he knew too little about the South and the history of blacks in that region. Jones reportedly replied, "Did you have to be an alien to direct *E.T.*?" Obviously, Jones's argument worked] [Caution: sexuality and language] **[W]**

Witness [100]
1985 – Peter Weir

If there were such a thing as a humane thriller, *Witness* would be it. You could even say it is triumphantly humane, because in this rare case the violence is brought to a halt by moral, not martial, force in a brilliant play on the title. Harrison Ford, in his first and still best mature starring role, plays John Book, a hard-edged Philadelphia police detective who's been assigned to investigate the murder of an informant witnessed by a young Amish boy (Lucas Haas) traveling with his mother (Kelly McGillis). The investigation goes quickly wrong, with Book shot and wounded by one of the murderers – who turn out to be crooked cops. He returns the mother and son to their farm, where he collapses and must be cared for by the family. There, as an alien presence, he interacts with the Amish and begins to be a little captivated by them – particularly Rachel, the boy's mother – and he enjoys a temporary idyllic respite until his dangerous, violent world returns. Beautifully directed by Weir in his first American movie, with another deeply evocative score by Maurice Jarre, *Witness* will captivate you, too. The barn-raising sequence is magical. [Trivia note: Because the Amish shun cameras, no real

Amish appear in the movie] [Caution: violence, strong language, and sexuality] [W]

Hannah and Her Sisters
1986 – Woody Allen (Winner: Platoon)

Platoon (coming in the next compilation) arguably was a worthy Oscar winner, though I didn't include it in the list, but in his half-century of moviemaking this might be Allen's best. It's an affectionate study of three sisters, the men in their lives, and their relationships with one another. The Hannah of the title is played by Mia Farrow, who was paired with Allen in real life at the time (before an infamous affair between Allen and Farrow's adopted daughter Soon-Yi Previn broke them up). Barbara Hershey and Dianne Wiest (who won a Best Supporting Actress Oscar) play her sisters. The men include Michael Caine, who occasionally narrates the story and also won a supporting Oscar for perhaps his best role; Swedish star Max von Sydow and Allen himself. The movie, set as so many of his titles in Manhattan, contains all of the Allen trademarks – the rambling, self-regarding intellectual conversations; the assorted literary and cultural references; the collection of neurotic and depressed characters; the snappy and witty repartee, and the suite of classic love songs from the 1930s and '40s as the soundtrack music – but he weaves them together seamlessly. [Trivia notes: 1) Hannah's apartment, in which many of the scenes take place, was Mia Farrow's real apartment. For some of the production, she reportedly would be feeding or taking care of her children (four of whom appear in the movie) in one part of the apartment while moving to another part to shoot a scene when required. 2) In similar fashion, Hannah's mother in the movie is played by Farrow's real mother Maureen O'Sullivan – Jane in the original *Tarzan* movies] [Caution: language and adult material] [W]

Empire of the Sun [100]
1987 – Steven Spielberg (Winner: The Last Emperor)

I consider this movie, one of Spielberg's least-known, his masterpiece, the most visually poetic *film* – and you know I use that term sparingly – since *Lawrence of Arabia*, and possibly ever. It contains literally stunning images and sequences, not for their scenic beauty but for their emotional impact and Spielberg's genius at composition and at telling stories with pictures. Based on the autobiographical novel by J.G. Ballard, it depicts four years in the life of the 12-year-old son of a British family living in Shanghai before the outbreak of World War II. Spielberg, here at the peak of his talent, devises images and sequences unlike anything else in the movies. Of these there are many, but four stand out as most memorable. One is a caravan of limousines carrying British families across the Japanese-occupied city on the way to a costume party. Another, which follows shortly thereafter, involves the son, Jim (future Oscar-winner Christian Bale in a terrific debut role – he's onscreen nearly the entire time), flying a glider across a field. In yet another, Jim, who is fascinated with aircraft, spots a Japanese Zero on the ground and approaches it. A mechanic is welding part of the fighter, and the sparks create the effect of a shower of stars. As Jim reaches the Zero and touches it almost lovingly, in the background two Japanese pilots stand at attention, silhouetted against the rising sun. And in the fourth and most thrilling scene, American fighter planes attack Suchow, the Japanese air base near the Chinese coast where Jim and many other British nationals are being held for the duration of the war. Done with real P-51 Mustangs plus some large, radio-controlled models, the sequence is likely to take your breath away – it ranks among the greatest moments in cinema. Co-starring John Malkovich as a scheming American living in China, Joe Pantoliano as his weasel of a sidekick, Miranda Richardson as a world-weary aristocrat and Nigel Havers as a doctor who becomes the boy's mentor. Beautifully shot by Alan Daviau, and featuring a majestic score by John Williams, this is a movie that will haunt you long after the fadeout – maybe forever. I will always regard it as Spielberg's finest. [Trivia notes: 1) In a testimony to the director's prowess, Ballard himself once disclosed in an interview that the movie brought out elements of Jim's character – and, by reflection, his own – that even he had not fully understood until he saw the screen version of his novel. 2) Spielberg lucked out by being able to shoot the movie in Shanghai before the city and its skyline underwent a radical transformation, so its streets closely resembled their appearance a half-century earlier when the story took place] [Caution: mild violence but some intense suspense] [W]

The Unbearable Lightness of Being [100]
1988 – Philip Kaufman (Winner: Rain Man)
Kaufman's version of Milan Kundera's cryptic novel is an extremely compelling and hypnotic but ultimately shattering study of three indelible characters: Tomas, a Czech brain surgeon (the incomparable Daniel Day-Lewis); Sabina, a free-spirit artist; and Tereza, a shy and inhibited waif (respectively, Lena Olin and Juliet Binoche, two of the world's most beautiful women). The three are connected by love and friendship, but they eventually become separated in Prague, Czechoslovakia, in 1968, during the Soviet invasion. Day-Lewis plays Tomas (tow-MAHSH), a dashing young surgeon who cannot resist women and whose favorite expression is, "Take off your clothes," uttered with a seductive charm almost unparalleled in cinema. He marries Tereza, who shows up at his apartment one day, but he continues his affair with Sabina, all the while attempting to survive in the new political order. Unfortunately, this brief description does neither the story nor the movie justice. It is better to discover this mesmerizing, sensuous, funny, sad – including a heartbreaking scene involving the euthanasia of a pet – and altogether wonderful movie for yourself. Following up on his magnificent job on *The Right Stuff*, Kaufman triumphs again in an entirely different genre. [Caution: explicit and frequent sexuality] [W]

Glory
1989 – Edward Zwick (Winner: Driving Miss Daisy)
TV director Zwick presents a stirring, perfectly rendered tale based on a true episode of the Civil War, in which the first all-black regiment in the Union Army mounts a heroic but futile

78

assault on Fort Wagner, a Confederate stronghold in South Carolina. The story begins at the battle of Antietam Creek, near Hagerstown, Maryland, in 1862. There, a young army officer, Robert Gould Shaw (Matthew Broderick), is wounded in a way that causes him to consider the rest of his days a gift. Recovering back home in Boston, he is granted the rank of colonel and given charge of the 54th Massachusetts. Assisted by a fellow officer and longtime friend (Cary Elwes), he attempts to train the regiment for combat and to stand by the brave men who enlist – knowing that they will be executed immediately if captured by the Confederate army. Eventually, the story shifts to a small group of soldiers, portrayed by superb trio of actors: Morgan Freeman, Andre Braugher and particularly Denzel Washington, who won a Best Supporting Actor Oscar for his sensational performance as a cocky recruit in a scene in which he speaks not a word. [Trivia note: Broderick might have seemed an unlikely choice to play Shaw, given that Broderick was only 27 when he did the movie. But Shaw was actually a year younger than Broderick when he and his troops attacked Fort Wagner] [Caution: intense battle scenes and graphic violence] [W]

Henry V
1989 – Kenneth Branagh
This might be the best screen version of a Shakespeare play ever produced, and the feat is all the more astounding when you consider that Branagh – who also plays the title role – was only 28 when he directed and wrote the adaptation. His story of Henry, who wages a campaign against France with too few men yet manages to win several great victories, including the Battle of Agincourt, is riveting all the way through. His use of Derek Jacobi as sort of an on-location reporter instead of a stage-right narrator is brilliant, and Branagh's delivery of Henry's speech at Agincourt, which includes the famous phrase, "We few, we happy few," is classic. With Emma Thompson in her first significant role as Katherine, the French princess; Robbie Coltrane as Falstaff; and a bit part by Christian Bale, grown up some from his stunning debut two years earlier in *Empire of the*

Sun. [Viewing note: For those interested in both Shakespeare and the movies, here's a fun exercise: Try reading the play while watching Branagh's version. You'll see how expertly he trimmed and streamlined the dialogue for the screen without disturbing the Bard's narrative thread one bit] **[W]**

Goodfellas
1990 – Martin Scorsese

Where *The Godfather* was mostly darkness and somber mood, Scorsese's version of Nicholas Pileggi's novel contains a surprising amount of wit – though the violence is plentiful and often horrifying. Here is Scorsese at his most assured. His best adult movie is full of energy and chutzpah, portraying a world where people are either totally corrupt or totally helpless, and though just about everything the main characters do is reprehensible – particularly the actions of Joe Pesci as a wiseguy (mob member) with a wicked temper and brutal streak – you usually find yourself siding with them against the law and civilized society. It's the fictionalized autobiography of Henry Hill (Ray Liotta), an Irish kid from Brooklyn who gets taken under the wings of the local Italian mob organization run by Paulie Cicero (Paul Sorvino) and supported by Jimmy Conway (Robert De Niro), Henry's mentor. At first, this association requires Henry only to perform miscellaneous odd jobs for tips – and take occasional beatings from his father. But soon he's drawn into criminal behavior, and by the time he reaches manhood he has done some nasty things, including drug dealing and accessory to murder. Watching all of this from a close vantage point is his Jewish wife, Karen (Lorraine Bracco), who often feels horrified by her husband's antics but also understands it's what maintains their comfortable lifestyle. In some ways, *Goodfellas* is precursor to The Sopranos on television – it even features four of the major actors in that series, including Bracco, plus several bit players – and it's a less-classy successor to *The Godfather*. But in other ways it stands entirely on its own. It's much more complex visually, with rapid-fire editing (by James Kwei and Thelma Schoonmaker) and with several extremely well-staged sequences. One starts with Henry and Karen out on the street, where they descend steps into the basement and large kitchen of a building, walking through a hub of activity then heading upstairs and onto the floor of the Copacabana nightclub, just as the floorshow begins – and Scorsese does the whole thing in one take! As with all gangster movies, this one suffers a procession of violent deaths, and when it's over it offers no heroes – only survivors. [Trivia note: That impressive, one-take scene of Henry and Karen entering the Copacabana happened by accident. At first, the nightclub's management wouldn't allow Scorsese to film the couple using the main entrance. When they agreed to permit the moviemakers to enter the club via the kitchen, Scorsese decided to do it in one take to add dramatic anticipation and serve as a symbolic seduction of Karen by Henry. The extended shot took eight tries] [Caution: lots and lots of graphic violence – including domestic violence – very rough language and sexuality] **[W]**

The Firm [100]
1993 – Sydney Pollack
Once in a while, a screen adaptation actually surpasses a popular novel, and here is one of those times – in this case Pollack's teaming with legendary scriptwriter Robert Towne and several others to refocus and rework the John Grisham bestseller and populate it with an array of outstanding actors: Tom Cruise, Gene Hackman, Ed Harris, Hal Holbrook, Wilford Brimley, Paul Sorvino, David Strathairn, Gary Busey and Holly Hunter, with a breakthrough performance by Jean Tripplehorn. Pollack's direction is just about perfect from beginning to end. It pulls you in from the jazzy opening montage to the finale, which leaves you shaken but relieved. Cruise plays Mitchell McDeere, a star Harvard Law School grad from an impoverished background but with an unlimited future who takes a position with a firm in Memphis, Tennessee, which turns out to represent a Chicago mob family. Intrigued at first by a very generous salary offer and the personal invitation by the firm's head (Holbrook, in a rare villainous role), McDeere quickly becomes trapped in a situation

that threatens to destroy both his marriage and career. Contacted by a wiseacre FBI agent (Harris) and ordered to cooperate with the bureau's investigation, McDeere begins to feel the noose tightening around his neck and that of his wife, Abby (Tripplehorn). The rest of the plot is too good to give away, so just be assured you will be highly entertained, surprised and satisfied by this first-class thriller. Dave Grusin's throbbing piano-jazz score is terrific. [Trivia note: Despite the stellar cast and performances, the only acting nomination went to Hunter for her supporting role, though in some ways it was a tribute because she was onscreen less than 6 minutes] [Caution: sexuality, language, and violence] [W]

The Joy Luck Club
1993 – Wayne Wang
Until this movie, Wang was a little-known director of a half-dozen low-budget stories about Chinese Americans. Here, he joins the big leagues with a beautiful, masterful rendering of the Amy Tan novel. It concerns the relationships of four San Francisco mothers and their daughters. Structured around a longstanding tradition among the mothers to play a monthly game of mahjong, the story jumps back and forth from the mothers and daughters in the present to the past, showing the ordeals of their childhood and youth that formed their characters. The main story focuses on June (Ming Na-Wen), whose mother has just died and who had been scheduled to travel with her mother (the exquisitely beautiful Kieu Chinh) back to China to reunite with the twin daughters the mother was forced to abandon when they were infants. That reunion, and the four separate mother-daughter stories – and mother histories – make for an extremely engrossing and satisfying tale. Even at two-and-a-quarter hours, the movie seems too short. [Trivia note: The four women playing the mothers all boast long acting careers with at least 60 credits each. Tsai Chin, the wry Auntie Lindo, had appeared over a quarter-century earlier as James Bond's seemingly double-dealing lover Ling in the prologue of *You Only Live Twice*. France Nuyen played her first role in 1958

in *South Pacific* (coming in the next compilation) and did a guest-star turn in the original Star Trek TV series. Vietnam-born Kieu Chinh made a splash with her guest portrayal of a Korean noblewoman on a M*A*S*H episode in 1977 as well as many other TV series over the years. And Lisa Lu appeared a quarter-century later as the formidable matriarch of the Singapore family featured in *Crazy Rich Asians*] [Caution: sexuality] **[W]**

Little Women
1994 – Gillian Armstrong (Winner: Forrest Gump)
As I mentioned in the capsule of *My Brilliant Career* (above), I think Armstrong is one fine director. Here, with her version of the Louisa May Alcott children's classic, she achieves something rare: a popular young girl's story that appeals to both genders and all ages. It follows several years in the lives of the four March sisters during and after the Civil War through the eyes of Jo (Winona Ryder), an aspiring writer (and Alcott's alter ego). It isn't an exact rendering of the novel; it's more of a re-imagining with some thematic updates for modern audiences – such as the sense of feminism emerging among the sisters. Geoffrey Simpson's beautiful cinematography gives the movie a feeling of richness (using the landscapes of British Columbia as substitutes for 19th-century Massachusetts) usually reserved for British television productions. [Trivia note: The story had been produced in several earlier versions – this is by far the best] **[W]**

Apollo 13 [100]
1995 – Ron Howard
"Houston, we have a problem." That famous line (which actually is misquoted) begins a faithful, harrowing and ultimately thrilling account of the biggest near-disaster in the U.S. space program. Launched on April 11, 1970, at 13:13 Eastern Time, Apollo 13 would have been the third mission to land astronauts on the Moon. But an explosion aboard the spacecraft sent NASA's engineers at mission control in Houston scrambling to solve problems no one had ever anticipated – such as how to provide oxygen to the three crew members for five days in the

83

landing vehicle, which had not been designed for sustained life support – in order to bring them all home safely. The movie features a superb cast, including Gary Sinise as astronaut Ken Mattingly, who was bumped from the mission because of an impending case of measles but ended up providing critical information that saved the lives of his comrades; Tom Hanks, Bill Paxton and Kevin Bacon as, respectively, Apollo 13 commander Jim Lovell and crewmembers Fred Haise and Jack Swigert. Kathleen Quinlan plays Jim's steadfast wife, Marilyn, and Ed Harris turns in an outstanding performance as the single-minded mission controller Gene Kranz. Likewise, the effects are first-rate and completely convincing. The liftoff sequence, involving the launch of the giant Saturn V rocket, which stood taller than the Statue of Liberty, is breathtaking. To lend authenticity to the scenes aboard the spacecraft, Howard and his cast and crew took more than a dozen flights in the "Vomit Comet." It's a Boeing KC-135 transport that flies astronaut training missions in high, gentle arcs designed to provide short periods of weightlessness – and severe nausea is often the result. James Horner provided the magnificent score. And the story, based on Jim Lovell's memoir Lost Moon, about how mission control managed to stave off one unprecedented emergency after another, marks one of NASA's greatest achievements, helped along by several seemingly miraculous developments. As Kranz says at one point, "I believe this will be our finest hour." It's always a testimonial to a movie if it can maintain your interest and suspense even when you know how it will end. This one does it handily – you'll be gripping your seat and maybe even weeping unashamedly at the climax. [Trivia notes: 1) Jack Swigart's real line, which Lovell partially repeated, is "Okay, Houston, we've had a problem here." 2) Quinlan had worked with Howard 22 years earlier when both were teenagers in the cast of *American Graffiti*, and so did Joe Spano, playing a smalltown hoodlum back then but a dignified NASA official here. 3) Sinise and Hanks likewise had teamed before, the previous year, both winning Oscars in the vastly overrated *Forrest Gump*. They are far better in *Apollo 13*. 4) The last line of the movie, a question delivered by Hanks as Lovell, remains sadly unanswered: When will we be returning to the Moon?] **[W]**

Sense and Sensibility
1995 – Ang Lee
Aside from a gorgeous, six-episode BBC television production of Pride and Prejudice, this is the best rendering ever of a Jane Austen novel, made so partly by Lee's precise direction but mainly by Emma Thompson's wise and thoroughly witty screenplay and her extremely appealing performance in the lead role. Thompson plays Eleanor Dashwood, oldest daughter of a family of three sisters and a widowed mother, all of whom must adjust to diminished circumstances following the death of the husband and father (Tom Wilkinson). As in all of Austen's novels, the story ostensibly concerns the conflict between the rules of 18th-century British society and the individuals who must live by them, but it also probes deeply into matters of the human heart, with a beauty and grace that are rapturous. The topflight cast includes Hugh Grant and Alan Rickman as suitors of the Dashwood sisters, and Kate Winslet as Eleanor's younger sibling Marianne. Every one of the other supporting players is excellent as well. And even if the story were a dud – which it decidedly is not – the sumptuous scenery alone would make the movie worth watching. Oh, England, thou art a beautiful land! [Trivia note: Thompson's Oscar-winning script nearly became an early casualty of the emerging personal-computer age. Before she could complete it, her computer crashed, and it took her friend, veteran actor Stephen Fry, who was an early geek, seven hours to retrieve the file] **[W]**

Saving Private Ryan [100]
1998 – Steven Spielberg
Spielberg lost the 1998 Oscar race to *Shakespeare in Love*, which is a fine movie, but this is by far the better title. It's an extremely harrowing and stirring fictionalization of the events surrounding the Normandy invasion by the U.S. Army and its allies in World

War II on D-Day, June 6, 1944. The story involves a special mission to rescue the sole surviving brother of a family that had already lost three siblings in combat. Tom Hanks, in his best role, plays John Miller, a captain leading the squad charged with saving Private Ryan. The cast is full of appealing young actors, most at the beginning of their careers – including Matt Damon, Jeremy Davies, Vin Diesel, Ed Byrnes, Giovanni Ribisi, Tom Sizemore and particularly Barry Pepper as a Scripture-quoting marksman. There are also three terrific cameo appearances by Dennis Farina and Ted Danson as company commanders, and Paul Giamatti as a platoon sergeant. Harve Presnell, who starred in stage and screen musicals in the 1950s and '60s, gives a dignified portrayal of General George C. Marshall, the Army Chief of Staff. And every single performance, even the most minor, is nearly perfect. Spielberg stages the Omaha Beach sequence with such intensity it is almost unbearable. But then he tops it with the climactic battle scene, in which Miller leads a small U.S. force attempting to prevent an armored German battalion from crossing a bridge. It's a huge, sprawling set piece and looks, as did the opening battle, very, very real. Just as he did in *Schindler's List*, Spielberg employs the latest moviemaking technology to bring the horrors and violence of warfare vividly to the screen, particularly the portrayal of soldiers being hit with bullets, explosives and fire. It is not at all for the faint of heart – or for children – but it's a powerful portrayal of one of the most famous days in history and its aftermath. Once again, John Williams composed a great anthemic score. I read an online comment recently that summed up the movie's theme exceptionally well: It asks one of the most essential questions of human warfare: How does a man in battle retain his most basic decency? [Trivia note: To lend realism to the Omaha Beach scene, the production cast several dozen amputees, all of whom were fitted with prosthetics that could be separated, thereby portraying the losing of limbs in combat] [Caution: graphic violence and intense battle scenes] **[W]**

Three Kings

1999 – David O. Russell (<u>Winner</u>: American Beauty)

A stunning surprise from newcomer Russell, whose two previous features, *Spanking the Monkey* and *Flirting with Disaster* (neither on this list), showed nothing of the visual brilliance and storytelling flair displayed here. Another fictionalized war story, this time it's the end of the first Gulf War in 1991, just after the surrender of Saddam Hussein's forces to the multinational coalition led by the U.S. Army. This is a far smaller movie than *Saving Private Ryan*, but Russell shows some amazing directorial prowess, and he elicits maybe the best big-screen performance of George Clooney's career; likewise from Mark Wahlberg. The plot involves an attempt, shortly after Saddam's defeat, to sneak back into Iraq and steal a cache of gold bars, following a map extracted – literally – from an Iraqi prisoner. The story that unfolds is loaded with compelling drama, and *Three Kings* ranks as one of the most unusual war movies ever made, one that should have trounced the despicable *American Beauty* (not here) at the Oscars. [<u>Trivia note</u>: Despite its setting in Iraq, the movie was shot in the deserts of Arizona and New Mexico – but many of the cast members were actual Iraqi refugees] [<u>Caution</u>: graphic violence and brief sexuality] **[W]**

Cast Away

2000 – Robert Zemeckis (<u>Winner</u>: Gladiator)

No question, this is the best movie Zemeckis ever directed. It is light-years better than his deeply flawed *Forrest Gump*, though that movie won Best Picture of 1994. And Tom Hanks, who won his second Best Actor as Forrest, delivers a fine, natural but nuanced performance here, receiving his fifth nomination. He plays Chuck Noland, a plump, prosperous, globe-trotting Federal Express executive whose plane crashes (in a sequence that will terrify you) in the middle of a storm somewhere in the Pacific Ocean. Marooned on an island for four long years and forced to struggle to survive and remain sane, Noland learns, painfully at first, how to live off the land and the sea. He also comes perilously close to despair, however, which threatens to end his life before he can carry out his carefully constructed plan to escape the hazardous reefs that protect and isolate the island. The rest you should discover for yourself. Know, however, that Zemeckis is a master at using digital effects in very effective but extremely subtle ways. Though the movie appears simple – much of it was shot on a small, deserted island that is part of the Republic of Fiji – it's also quite sophisticated visually, with many effects sequences blended seamlessly into the live action; for examples, when Hanks expertly spears a fish, and when a piece of cloth hung on a stick as a banner changes direction in the wind at a critical time. The script, by journalist and TV veteran William Broyles, Jr., skillfully examines the components that make our lives so comfortable and how we might act when they're taken away. Frequent Zemeckis collaborator Alan Silvestri supplied the appropriately haunting score. [Trivia note: Zemeckis suspended production of the movie for a year so Hanks could lose 50 pounds and grow a beard to portray the supposed effects of his time on the deserted island. In the interim, he directed the unremarkable *What Lies Beneath* (not here)] [Caution: adult material and an intense plane crash] **[W]**

The Bourne Identity
2002 – Doug Liman (Winner: Chicago)
Sometimes, a young and relatively inexperienced director will break through almost immediately with a superior movie, just as Edward Zwick did with the superb *Glory* and David O. Russell did with the stunning *Three Kings*. Here, Liman comes practically from out of nowhere to present a spy thriller that surpasses even the finest of the James Bond series. Loosely based on Robert Ludlum's bestselling novel, Matt Damon plays the title character, a CIA super-agent who suffers from amnesia. Rescued at sea in the middle of a storm, he discovers he has been targeted for assassination – although he has no idea why or by whom. Intense and tight from beginning to end, there's not a single false note in the movie, and Damon is surprisingly riveting as Bourne. The edgy score is by John Powell. For fans of the genre, this is one not to be missed. [Trivia note: The name "Bourne" is based

on a real historical figure, a 19th-century Rhode Island minister who, apparently afflicted with amnesia, left his home and moved to Pennsylvania, where he adopted the name "Brown" and opened a small shop. Then, several months later, he regained his memory and returned to Rhode Island – but he had no recollection of calling himself Brown or why he had moved to Pennsylvania] [Caution: graphic violence and sexuality] **[W]**

Master and Commander: The Far Side of the World
2003 – Peter Weir (Winner: Million Dollar Baby)
Once again, Russell Crowe inhabits a character so thoroughly that you forget all of his wonderful previous performances, and the movie gives a strong sense of what life must have been like for British seamen in the early 19th century. Based on the popular series of novels by Patrick O'Brian, Crowe plays "Lucky Jack" Aubrey, captain of the H.M.S. Surprise, a warship on the trail of the Archeron, a French frigate in Napoléon's navy heading down the South American coast and toward the Pacific. Sailing with Aubrey, and taking medical care of the crew, is ship's surgeon Stephen Maturin (Paul Bettany, one of Crowe's co-stars in *A Beautiful Mind*, in a fine performance of his own), his longtime friend, sometime critic and fellow musician. Their frequent sparring sharpens both the plot and their respective characters. James Cameron used state-of-the-art movie technology to transport his audience inside the fabled and ill-fated luxury liner Titanic by building a one-sided, nearly full-sized replica. Here, Weir goes him one better – using both a real, seagoing vessel and a full-size duplicate housed in the same outdoor facility in Baja California that Cameron employed – to portray life aboard a Royal British Navy ship of the period. Sparing no details (he had the casting director screen thousands of extras from many countries, looking for just the right faces to portray the crew, and he subjected the crewmembers to weeks of intense training in seamanship – including gunnery), Weir provides the most vivid depiction yet of naval life in those days. But as harrowing as some of the sequences are, you might feel the same as the young seaman whom Aubrey employs to play a

desperate and dangerous trick on the Archeron. When the ordeal is over, Aubrey says: "Now, tell me that wasn't fun!" Iva Davies, Christopher Gorden and Richard Tognetti composed the moody, string-heavy score. [Trivia notes: 1) To portray the Surprise at sea, the production company bought the 1757 battle frigate H.M.S. Rose – or rather, a full-size replica built in 1970 from the original plans. 2) Some of the footage used for the ship's passage around Cape Horn, at the southern tip of South America, was taken from the real voyage of a replica of H.M.S. Endeavor, the ship Captain James Cook had used to sail across the Pacific in the 18th century] [Caution: intense battle scenes] **[W]**

Cinderella Man [100]
2005 – Ron Howard (Winner: Crash)
In this stirring movie, based on the life and career of Depression-era boxer James J. Braddock, the "Bulldog of Bergen (New Jersey)," who literally risked his life to support his family, Russell Crowe reaches a point in his career where there might be no more he can do as an actor – because he has mastered the physical limits of the craft. Two years earlier, he thoroughly inhabited the character of Jack Aubrey in *Master and Commander*. Three years before that, he played Nobel Prize-winning mathematician John Nash flawlessly in *A Beautiful Mind*. In 1999, he powerfully portrayed tobacco company scientist and whistleblower Jeffrey Wigand in *The Insider*, and in 1997 he electrified audiences with his portrayal of the rampaging Officer Bud White in *L.A. Confidential*. Here, once again, he doesn't just play Jim Braddock – he *becomes* Braddock, due in part to his year of boxing training (under the tutelage of the legendary Angelo Dundee, who trained Muhammad Ali) and his study of archival footage of the real Braddock. He has altered his speech, mannerisms and even his physical appearance so markedly it is difficult to remember it's Crowe and not the real person. As tremendous as he is, however, the movie's heart belongs to Renée Zellweger as Mae Braddock, Jim's wife. There is a scene in the climactic moments when she does not know how the fight will turn out, and watching her agonize through it is almost

unbearable. The strong supporting cast includes Paul Giamatti in the performance of his career as Joe Gould, Braddock's manager; and Broadway singer and TV actor Craig Bierko in a sensational performance as Max Baer, the heavyweight champion at the time. This is perhaps Ron Howard's best movie, because it thoroughly captivates you from start to tremendously emotional, nail-biting finish. Why the motion picture academy members would not even nominate it as Best Picture, or Crowe and Zellweger as Best Actor and Actress, is both mystifying and disgraceful. At least they nominated Giamatti as Best Supporting Actor – and his peers at the Screen Actors Guild honored him with that award. Shot entirely in Toronto, Canada, it delivers a totally authentic feel for New York City and its surrounding communities in the 1930s. The partly throbbing, mostly lilting score is by Thomas Newman, who had composed similarly fine scores for *The Shawshank Redemption* and *The Green Mile*. [Trivia notes: 1) The movie's one flaw – not insubstantial – is that it takes gross liberties with the character of Baer, whose life in many ways was as interesting and heroic as Braddock's. But then, Bierko was so good playing Baer that someone should have done another boxing story with him reprising the role. It wouldn't have been Howard, however. He infuriated Baer's family with his depiction of Max. 2) I mentioned that Crowe had mastered the physical limits of his craft. As it turned out, that's an understatement. Early in his boxing training, Crowe had badly injured his shoulder. He nevertheless portrayed Braddock so convincingly despite his frequent pain and physician-imposed rest periods] [Caution: boxing violence and a little rough language] [W]

Munich
2005 – Steven Spielberg
Like the director's Oscar-winning *Schindler's List* 12 years earlier, this is not an easy one to watch, but *Munich* is a powerful, compelling piece of moviemaking – though it should not be taken as historically accurate. Cowritten by Tony Kushner, whose stage play "Angels in America" became one of the

greatest miniseries ever televised, the story was inspired by a tragic incident in 1972, when a band of Palestinian terrorists from a group called Black September broke into the Olympic village in Munich, West Germany, and eventually murdered 11 Israeli athletes before a police assault managed to kill them all. In the aftermath, Israeli Prime Minister Golda Meir ordered Mossad, the country's intelligence operation, to hunt down and assassinate 11 members of Black September who planned or ordered the Munich massacre. A Mossad operative (Geoffrey Rush) orders a young specialist named Avner (Eric Bana) to sever all ties with the organization and perform the deeds independently, supported by four other specialists (including one superbly played by Daniel Craig, who in 2006 revitalized the role of James Bond in *Casino Royale*). The movie is unlike anything else Spielberg has done – even *Schindler's List* and *Saving Private Ryan*. Yes, it is gripping and almost continuously harrowing, but there's something deeper going on here. It's as though Spielberg, with Kushner's help, is attempting to probe the soul of Israel and of Jews everywhere, as they remain locked in mortal combat with the Palestinians sworn to eradicate their nation. Nominated for five Academy Awards, including Best Picture and Best Director – but no acting nominations – it became the second Spielberg movie (*The Color Purple* was the first) to be shut out. The movie features one of John Williams's most unusual scores, one that at times mimics the rumblings of a dark engine but at others seems to cry out to the Almighty in grief and sadness. [Trivia note: One of the characters Avner encounters during his mission is Ehud Barak, an Israeli commando who went on to become Israel's prime minister from 1999 to 2001] [Caution: graphic violence and sexuality] **[W]**

United 93
2006 – Paul Greengrass (<u>Winner</u>: The Departed)
Here is yet another example of the motion picture academy showing incredibly bad judgment by not even nominating this towering moviemaking achievement. Greengrass scored an impressive feat in 2004 when he directed *The Bourne Supremacy*,

sequel to the thrilling *Bourne Identity*, which exceeded the suspense and quality of the original. With *United 93*, however, he places himself at the highest plane of the craft, giving us an astounding glimpse at one of the most terrible and tragic events in modern American history. This is a faithful retelling of the fourth commercial airliner that was hijacked on September 11, 2001: United Airlines flight 93 out of Newark and bound for Los Angeles. Except that the plane never made it to its destination – neither the one on its schedule nor the one in the minds of the four al-Qaida fanatics who commandeered it. Instead, an indefinite number of brave passengers fought back, and they forced the plane down in a field near the little town of Shanksville, Pennsylvania, about 75 miles east of Pittsburgh, resulting in the violent deaths of everyone on board. More than any other movie I can think of, this one transports you aboard that plane and gives you a palpable sense of the sequence of emotions those passengers must have felt: surprise, shock, confusion, terror, dread and, finally, anger and selfless determination. The cast includes real military officers and airline crewmembers, performing the same tasks their counterparts did on that horrible day, plus some of the people who actually participated in the event, playing themselves. Chief among them is Ben Sliney, the Federal Aviation Administration national operations manager who gave the unprecedented order to ground every single aircraft that was still in the air over the United States on that terrible, tragic day. This is one of the greatest portrayals of true courage ever filmed, of people who became fully aware of what fate awaited them and yet decided not to go quietly into oblivion. It has moments that are as powerful as the moviegoing experience ever gets. It might be tough to watch, but watching it pales in comparison to what the real people had to endure. [A modest suggestion: Consider visiting the Flight 93 National Memorial, located about 10 miles north of the Somerset exit on the Pennsylvania Turnpike. Spending some time at the crash site allows contemplation of the monstrousness and heroism of this event] [Caution: intense periods of suspense] [W]

The Kite Runner
2007 – Marc Forster (<u>Winner</u>: No Country for Old Men)

It's a sad commentary on the state of the American movie business, in the first decade of the millennium, that this title was ignored by the motion picture academy as a Best Picture nominee. In my opinion, it represents the zenith of modern cinema in terms of mature storytelling. It's far superior to the title that won, and it will haunt you for years to come. Based on Khaled Hosseini's bestselling novel, *The Kite Runner* tells the tale of two Afghan boys growing up in Kabul during the 1970s. Amir is the son of a successful businessman, and Hassan is the son of his servant, though the real nature of their relationship remains hidden for some time. The favorite pastime of the two boys is the popular Kabul sport of kite-fighting, in which youngsters fly kites high over the city and attempt to cut the string of their opponents. The eponymous kite runner is someone who retrieves the downed kite of a friend, as Hassan does for Amir. That act is only one of many that Hassan performs, and yet Amir eventually betrays him cruelly, the consequences of which emerge years later, giving Amir a chance at redemption. Shot in western China, with some scenes in California, the movie approximates life in Kabul, both before and during the rule of the Taliban. [<u>Caution</u>: violence] **[W]**

Defiance
2008 – Edward Zwick (<u>Winner</u>: Slumdog Millionaire)

I bounced back and forth on this one, about whether it belongs in the Unforgettable or Men at War categories. But it's good enough to be here as well. Based on a real episode, it is one of the most unusual, incredible war stories you'll ever see. In some ways it parallels the feat of Oscar Schindler but on a larger scale and in a far more heroic way. In 1941, the four Bielski brothers, members of a Polish-Jewish family – including Alexander, who goes by Zus (ZOOSH) and Tuvia, played by Liev Schreiber and Daniel Craig – flee into a vast birch forest in what is now Belarus after the Nazis murder their parents and most of the people of their village. There and until the war ends, they manage to feed and protect a group that swells to more than 1,200 refugees, even to the point of providing them education and medical care. It's a taut, stark tale of utter desperation and the constant threat of death, unfolding as the Nazis hunt down and murder hundreds of thousands of Eastern European Jews. The most surprising aspect of this movie is Schreiber (who pronounces his first name LEE-ev), who usually plays geeks or wimps. He's absolutely ferocious here, easily dominating the much better-known Craig, who routinely plays tough guys – including the toughest of them all, James Bond. It's particularly true in the climactic scene, when it appears that Tuvia has led everyone to their doom. [Trivia notes: 1) Though the movie emphasizes the roles of Zus and Tuvia, the two other Bielski brothers, Asael and Aron, also protected the refugees. 2) Zwick shot the movie in a Lithuanian forest only about 100 miles from where the real saga took place. 3) Zus and Tuvia, and eventually Aron, moved to New York after the war, where they operated a successful trucking business. 4) As the epilogue to the movie notes, the descendants of the refugees saved by the Bielskis now number in the tens of thousands. 5) Though they have been the subject of several books – and this movie – the brothers never sought recognition for their incredible acts of bravery] [Caution: intense battle scenes and other violence, and fleeting sexuality] **[W]**

Hugo
2011 – Martin Scorsese (Winner: The Artist)
I started this list by raving about *Wings*, the first movie to win an Academy Award, and I referred to *The Artist* (not on this list) because both are silent movies – though the latter does contain a couple of brief sound sequences. I can understand how some people think awarding the top Oscar to *The Artist* in 2011 closed the circle because of that connection. But I would argue that not only is *Hugo* the better movie, but it also does a more effective job of reaching back, in this case to the roots of the movie industry. Indeed, *Hugo* is a love letter to the very first movies, the ones shot on hand-cranked cameras and shown on tiny, dimly lit screens called biographs. Based on the beautifully

illustrated novel by Brian Selznick, it's a fantasy involving an orphaned boy (13-year-old Asa Butterfield) who lives secretly in the attic hollows of a Paris train station in the 1930s. His only connection with his father is his inheritance of a non-functioning automaton, a mechanical man that requires a key to operate. Bright and mechanically talented, Hugo attempts to scavenge parts for the device to make it function, because it seems to be able to create a drawing on paper that he believes will be a message from his father. He progresses steadily, until he runs afoul of a stern shopkeeper (Ben Kingsley) who turns out to possess a marvelous secret of his own. No more details, but know that this is Scorsese's finest and most accessible movie, one displaying beautiful production values, harboring a touching story of loss and redemption, and providing a finale that's the greatest tribute to film since *Cinema Paradiso*. Howard Shore contributed the suitably Francophilic score. [Viewing note: As you might have read in the Introduction, and as you'll see if you browse through these titles, I'm not particularly fond of the moviemaking technique now known as CGI, or computer-generated imagery. That's because in too many cases the effects either overwhelm the story or are poorly conceived so they become obvious and therefore less interesting. But with *Hugo*, Scorsese and his production team have mounted some beautiful sequences using CGI – so seamlessly blended with the live action that it hardly ever interferes with your suspension of disbelief] [Trivia notes: 1) Scorsese, who's best known for his violence-laden features such as *Taxi Driver* (not on this list) and *Goodfellas*, said he made *Hugo* because his wife asked him to do a movie that for once their young daughter could watch – and their daughter had given Scorsese a copy of the book several years earlier as a birthday present. 2) One of Scorsese's beloved movies from his childhood was *Around the World in 80 Days*, which also happens to be one of my childhood favorites. Its prologue contains excerpts from an early movie that Scorsese features in *Hugo*. **[3D] [W]**

Lincoln

2012 – Steven Spielberg (<u>Winner</u>: Argo)

This is far less lyrical than 1987's *Empire of the Sun*, which I mentioned earlier and which I still consider Spielberg's masterpiece, but *Lincoln* is his most mature effort. It's solid, moving and engrossing, though maybe just a tad PC. It is, as the title makes clear, a portrayal – and a perfectly rendered one by Daniel Day-Lewis – of the 16th President of the United States. Spielberg and screenwriter Tony Kushner chose the climactic event in Lincoln's tortured tenure – enactment of the 13th Amendment to the Constitution, which abolished slavery – as the center of the story. The time is early 1865, Lincoln has begun his second term, the Civil War is wrenching to a close, and he is wrestling with members of his own majority Republican Party to gain enough votes in the House of Representatives to send the measure to the states for ratification (the Senate had already approved the amendment). That wrestling match includes cajoling, persuading, flattering, storytelling, horse-trading and on occasion flashing his towering temper. The reason: Lincoln understands that if the South surrenders before the House passes the amendment, the Confederate states rejoining the Union could block its ratification. Therefore Lincoln must stretch his ethical boundaries to the limit to push Congress to act. In every scene, every shot, Day-Lewis's performance is magnificent. He never falters from rising above mere impersonation. Like Russell Crowe has done so often, he inhabits the character – he *becomes* Lincoln, one of the greatest Americans who ever lived, a man who took upon his shoulders the burden of preserving, literally, the United States of America. I said this is Spielberg's most mature effort. That's because here he restrains his singular talent for telling stories in pictures and instead allows the story to unfold in front of the camera – and Day-Lewis's performance defines it. He makes you believe you're actually in the presence of Abraham Lincoln at a pivotal time in American history. The motion picture academy honored this achievement by awarding Day-Lewis the Best Actor Oscar for an unprecedented third time, but they failed to take it a justifiable step further and instead gave Best Picture to the diverting but ordinary *Argo* (not on this list). [Trivia note: *Lincoln* enjoys the rare distinction of influencing real politics. A few months after its release, the state of Mississippi, rectifying a clerical error, filed its ratification of the 13th Amendment, becoming the 50th state to do so, albeit nearly 150 years after the amendment's passage by Congress] **[W]**

Zero Dark Thirty
2012 – Katherine Bigelow

Here's a positively shameful oversight by the academy in 2012 – a deliberate one, done for purely political reasons. Bigelow had directed a fine, Oscar-winning feature three years earlier in *The Hurt Locker*, which I'll mention later in a different chapter, and which dealt with the extremely dangerous job of disarming bombs in Iraq during the war. Here she chronicles, in surprisingly faithful detail, the decade-long search for Osama bin Laden, the leader of al-Qaida, the Islamic terror group that perpetrated the attacks on the United States on September 11, 2001. Engrossing and tense from beginning to end, *Zero Dark Thirty* (a military term for secret and dangerous predawn missions literally beginning at 12:30 a.m.) portrays a small group of CIA officers who are committed to – and often obsessed with – learning the whereabouts of the most wanted man on Earth. Leading the group is Maya (Jessica Chastain), a feisty, determined intelligence officer whose job is to piece together bits of information about bin Laden's whereabouts. The job is so demanding that she essentially shuts out all other aspects of her life, sharing a tentative friendship only with another officer, Jessica (Jennifer Ehle, in a brief but vivid performance). When Maya finally achieves an intelligence breakthrough – in a combination of dogged tenacity and brilliant analysis – she makes her case to the Director of Central Intelligence (James Gandolfini, in a sharp and witty portrayal of Leon Panetta, the real director at the time). He, in turn, orders the raid, and from there Bigelow stages the assault by a Navy SEAL team on bin Laden's formerly secret hideout in Abbottabad, Pakistan. It's a stunningly realistic recreation of the work of America's best covert fighting force. Why the political short shrift? Because many people in Hollywood – as well as among the American electorate – misguidedly believed that enhanced interrogation techniques used by the CIA, including a method known as waterboarding, constituted torture and therefore should be condemned. Yet this movie clearly shows, accurately, that no permanent harm came to the men subjected to enhanced interrogation. Instead, when they finally divulged the information sought by their captors, they resumed uneventful incarceration, including concessions to their Muslim faith. In fact, the chief recipient of waterboarding, Khalid Sheikh Mohammed – known as the mastermind of the 9/11 attacks – actually thanked his interrogators for subjecting him to it and recommended they waterboard every captured al-Qaida member. [Trivia note: The real name of the character Jennifer Ehle portrays was Jennifer Matthews, whose fate is depicted accurately in the movie] [Caution: violence and rough language] [W]

Saving Mr. Banks
2013 – John Lee Hancock (Winner: 12 Years a Slave)
In 1963, the superb creative talents at Walt Disney Studios were working hard on what in the following year would become one of their most beloved and enduring attractions, *Mary Poppins*, starring Julie Andrews and Dick Van Dyke. Based on a popular series of novels by Pamela "P.L." Travers (the 1930s equivalent of J.K. Rowling and her blockbuster Harry Potter books), *Mary Poppins* told the tale of a mysterious nanny who literally flew in with a change in the wind to care for the two children of a London banker, and the movie did so with great charm and unforgettable songs. *Saving Mr. Banks* dramatizes the process by which Disney himself persuaded Travers to grant him the rights to the Poppins story, and how his people – specifically the songwriting brothers Robert and Richard Sherman – gradually won enough of her approval to present her story on the screen their way, including those songs and occasional animation.

Therein lies a beguiling tale about the clash and eventual uneasy synergy of the moviemakers and the author. I won't tell you more, because it's too precious to give away – particularly the connection between the title of this movie and *Mary Poppins*. I implore you to discover that for yourself, which you will in a beautifully subtle, single line of dialog. The great Emma Thompson plays Travers, and she's terrific. Tom Hanks plays Walter Elias Disney, and he does it well. Of the two, however, Thompson creates the more vivid character by far, even when she's silently sitting there. As for the rest of the movie, the direction by Hancock, who did the roughed-edged but engaging *The Blind Side* (coming in the next compilation) is flawless, and the period transitions are sometimes breathtaking. Disney himself could not have done it better. [Viewing notes: 1) Don't miss the first few minutes of the end credits. 2) If you enjoyed watching the Sherman brothers working on the songs for the movie, consider tracking down *The Boys: The Sherman Brothers Story* (upcoming), a lovely documentary] [Caution: The movie's trailer makes *Saving Mr. Banks* seem like a light comedy. Trust me; it isn't, though it has plenty of humorous moments. It's considerably more – but it isn't for children] **[W]**

American Sniper
2014 – Clint Eastwood (Winner: Birdman)
Two stories to tell here. The first is the movie's story, a true and tragic one, about the life and career of Chris Kyle, a Navy SEAL considered the deadliest sniper America has ever produced. Snipers are real-life equivalents of James Bond, the legendary British secret agent with a license to kill. Snipers act as standoff weapons. They settle in, usually at a high elevation on land or the roof of a building in an urban environment. There, they wait, either for a specific individual or to watch over the mission of troops below. If they spot a target, they can hit it with a rifle shot from up to a mile away. Kyle served four tours of duty during the Iraq War, totaling about a thousand days "in country," as the military terms it. During that time, he was credited with 160 kills. This movie chronicles those tours and some of those kills. It

also covers, intermittently, Kyle's personal life, starting with his boyhood and featuring his courtship of and marriage to Taya Renae. On both fronts, the movie is riveting. Bradley Cooper, an actor whose previous performances hadn't impressed me, creates an immense presence here. He embodies Chris Kyle in a way that even acting giants such as Russell Crowe and Daniel Day-Lewis would envy. As Cooper said after the production wrapped, "I loved every moment of walking in his shoes – every moment of it." Likewise, Sienna Miller as Taya brings a strong and painful humanity to her part – particularly in one phone conversation with her husband that makes you ache in sympathy for her. Together, they're more than terrific; they're maybe the most human couple you've ever seen on the screen. You end up caring so much for both of them that the outcome becomes utterly heartbreaking.

The other story of *American Sniper* is Clint Eastwood's. Directing his 37th movie at age 84, he has joined the rarified company of masters such as Lewis Milestone, Howard Hawks, John Ford, Alfred Hitchcock and William Wyler. They all enjoyed similar longevity at the helm, but their talents seemed to diminish as they reached advanced ages. With Eastwood, if anything his talent has increased. Under his direction the story unfolds seamlessly, the action sequences are sometimes so intense you have to force yourself to watch, and the touches of moviemaking excellence are everywhere. Against even his two Best Picture winners – *Unforgiven* in 1992 and *Million Dollar Baby* in 2004, neither of which made my list – I regard this as Eastwood's masterpiece, a genuinely iconic portrayal of one man going to war, the best movie of its kind since *Sergeant York*, and one of the best American movies ever made. [Trivia note: Cooper's remark above, about loving walking in Kyle's shoes, was literal. Kyle's widow had given him a pair of her husband's shoes, which Cooper used presumably to gain a stronger connection with the role he was playing] [Caution: sexuality, rough language and explicit wartime violence and its aftermath]
[W]

The Imitation Game
2014 – Morton Tyldum

In 1939, at the beginning of World War II in Europe, British intelligence gathered a small group of mathematicians and crossword-puzzle enthusiasts at a nondescript location called Bletchley Park, northwest of London. Their task became to solve one of the most urgent problems confronting the military: breaking the infamous German code machine called Enigma, which at the time was universally used by the Nazis but was believed to be invulnerable. This is the gripping, painfully sad story of that effort and in particular of the central figure of that effort, mathematician and computer pioneer Alan Turing (Benedict Cumberbatch, emerging as one of the greatest actors of his generation). Abrasive and neurotic, Turing angered and frustrated his colleagues, but he eventually solved Enigma in part by building the world's first practical computer, an achievement deemed so secret only a handful of individuals in the British government were informed, and the matter remained supremely classified – it was codenamed "Ultra" – for half a century. Tyldum, who three years earlier had directed the sensational Norwegian thriller *Headhunters*, adopts a restrained but sure hand here. He allows the absorbing drama – and Cumberbatch's brilliant performance – to unfold clearly and methodically but relentlessly. Told in three timelines (chronicling Turing as a schoolboy, his postwar experiences, and of course his effort to crack Enigma), it's a complex and often wrenching story, involving Turing's odd quirks and his homosexuality, which tragically affected both his personal life and his career. Cumberbatch is well-supported by a uniformly excellent cast, particularly Keira Knightley in her best role as a brilliant team member and Turing's possible love interest, Matthew Goode as a grudging colleague, Allen Leech as a friend with his own dark secret, Charles Dance as Turing's disdainful superior, and Mark Strong as a shadowy intelligence presence. Alexandre Desplat contributed a fine, brooding score. [Caution: rough and sexual language and wartime scenes] **[W]**

Creed

2015 – Ryan Coogler (<u>Winner</u>: Spotlight)

In 1976, the story of a sadsack loser of a street tough who salvaged himself and won his self-respect by getting into the ring with the heavyweight boxing champion of the world hit the big screen and earned the Best Picture Oscar. That movie was *Rocky* (not on this list), and its writer-star Sylvester Stallone, who had previously labored in obscurity, began a successful career that has lasted over four decades. Frankly, I didn't care much for *Rocky* or its sequels, and other than his first *Expendables* feature I hadn't been much of a Stallone fan, either. Now, consider me a convert in both categories with *Creed*, the seventh installment in the saga of Rocky Balboa. I'll give you three reasons. First and foremost, Stallone plays the role of his career as the aging – and widowered – Rocky, a shrewd, indelible and hugely touching performance that should have (but didn't) won him Best Supporting Actor in a walk. He was wonderful. Second, Michael B. Jordan in the title role establishes himself as an emerging major talent, probably the best young African American actor since Denzel Washington. And third, Coogler, directing only his second feature, shows a mastery of the medium well beyond his years. Put those three ingredients together – along with fine supporting performances by newcomer Tessa Thompson, TV veteran Phylicia Rashad and real-life champion boxer Tony Bellew – and you've got a superior story of determination and reconciliation, friendship and love. No, I haven't mentioned much about the plot, because I want you to discover *Creed* for yourself. But if you think it's going to be just another punk-from-nowhere-rises-to-become-the-champ story, well, as Rocky Balboa might say, you've got another think comin'! [<u>Trivia notes</u>: 1) Coogler and Jordan tried something unprecedented – and extremely difficult – in this movie by shooting one of the fight scenes without edits. They were successful, but the training and choreography challenges must have been enormous. 2) Stallone inducted Jordan into a dubious tradition among the fighter-actors appearing in the *Rocky* movies by having him take a real punch from Bellew. You can't miss it on the screen] **[W]**

Sully

2016 – Clint Eastwood (<u>Winner</u>: Moonlight)

On January 15, 2009, U.S. Airways Flight 1549, carrying 155 passengers and crew, took off at 3:25 p.m. from New York's La Guardia Airport on a presumed two-hour flight to Charlotte, North Carolina. The flight lasted only about six minutes, half of that brief time subjecting passengers and crew to abject terror, as the pilot, Captain Chesley Sullenberger III, attempted something never-before done successfully: a water landing, in this case on the Hudson River off lower Manhattan. Fortunately for all, Sullenberger performed with nearly miraculous skill. With both engines destroyed by bird strikes at an altitude of 2,800 feet, "Sully," as friends and colleagues called him, made an unprecedented decision. Concluding he couldn't bring the crippled aircraft back to La Guardia, or even land at nearby Teterboro Airport in New Jersey, across the river, Sully headed for the Hudson and a brought the aircraft to rest nearly intact in the frigid water. What happened next, known as "The Miracle on the Hudson," is well documented. Nevertheless, Eastwood has crafted a surprisingly gripping movie and gotten terrific performances from Tom Hanks in the title role and from Aaron Eckhart as Sully's copilot Jeff Skiles, who delivers what is among the best fadeout lines ever. Beyond setting longevity records, the 85-year-old director once again demonstrates that he remains at the peak of his creative powers. It's a meticulous re-creation of the event and a lasting testimony to the skills of not only Sullenberger and Skiles but also of the many Hudson River ferry and Coast Guard personnel who quickly jumped into action to rescue the downed passengers and crew from the aircraft on that frigid January day. As Sully's colleague, Carl Clarke (Brett Rice), tells him, "You know, it's been a while since New York had news this good – especially with an airplane in it." [<u>Trivia note</u>: Laura Linney, who plays Sully's wife Lorraine, played Eastwood's daughter in 1997's *Absolute Power*, and she acted in his 2004 Oscar-winner, *Mystic River* (coming, respectively, in my second and third compilations), both of which he directed] **[W]**

3. Award or No Award

Each of these 19 movies had good enough qualities to earn a Best Picture nomination. Some were nominated, one actually won, and one is a made-for-TV title. But I'm not quibbling that they didn't win or get nominated. They're all richly entertaining crowd pleasers – regardless of how they fared at Oscar time.

The Americanization of Emily
1964 – Arthur Hiller

What starts out as a seeming lightweight service comedy quickly becomes a surprisingly thoughtful riff on the madness of war and the virtue of cowardice, courtesy of the acerbic screenplay by Paddy Chayefsky and a career-best performance by James Garner. Set in England just before D-Day, the invasion of Europe, in June 1944, Garner is Charlie Madison, a "dog-robber," or procurer, for his admiral – a role similar to the one he had played the previous year in *The Great Escape*. Julie Andrews is the eponymous Emily, a British widow in whose family the men all have died in the war and who has now become rather promiscuous because she has grown fearful of commitment – a decidedly different role from her Oscar-winning, prim and proper nanny in *Mary Poppins*, done that same year. Charlie and Emily meet, argue, go to bed, fall in love and then strain to determine whether they're meant to be together despite their differences, or they can't be together because of their differences. They make one of the screen's most unusual but most appealing couples. Garner's *Great Escape* co-star James Coburn shows up here as well, as a fellow officer and ladies' man, and Melvyn Douglas is the dotty admiral. [Trivia note: In one of the most notorious cases of creative differences, screenwriter Chayefsky actually forced the replacement of the legendary William Wyler with Hiller as director] [Caution: sexuality, though mild by today's standards] **[B&W] [W]**

Rosemary's Baby
1968 – Roman Polanski

Quite a daring movie for its time, this horror-thriller based on Ira Levin's bestselling novel is chillingly effective because much of the time it seems so normal – but it's the dark underside of *Barefoot in the Park*. Somehow, you know this attractive young couple isn't destined for happily ever after. Mia Farrow plays Rosemary Woodhouse, just married to Guy Woodhouse (John Cassavetes) and newly settled in a spacious Central Park West apartment in Manhattan in a building with a sordid past. Farrow's Rosemary is a fragile creation, and she elicits strong sympathy in the role, while Cassavetes is creepily appealing as a husband who seems unremarkable but who commits a monumental act of betrayal. The lead characters aside, the movie belongs to Ruth Gordon (who won an Oscar) and Sydney Blackmer as the Woodhouses' aging and suspicious neighbors, Minnie and Roman Castevet. Both screen veterans seem to revel in their glorious but subtle villainy as they relentlessly lure Guy and, especially, Rosemary to infamy. The same for Ralph Bellamy, an actor usually consigned to light comedies in the 1930s. There's evil menace behind his twinkling blue eyes. And watch for a young Charles Grodin in a small part at the beginning of his career. Polish composer and sometime Polanski collaborator Krzysztof Komeda wrote the disturbing, often-dissonant score. [Trivia notes: 1) The Dakota, the real building that houses the Woodhouses' fictional apartment, became notorious 12 years later when John Lennon of the Beatles was murdered outside of the entrance. 2) If you think the voice on the phone of the recently blinded actor sounds familiar, it is. It's Tony Curtis] [Caution: nudity, violence and frightening material] **[W]**

Little Big Man
1970 – Arthur Penn

This one occupies a rare genre: an American tragicomic epic Western. That's about the only way to describe it. Dustin Hoffman plays Jack Crabb, a man who claims to be 121 years old and the last survivor of the Battle of the Little Bighorn in 1876, also known as Custer's Last Stand. A skeptical William Hickey is the historian recording his tales, a mixture of wild exaggeration and obvious truth. Often rousing and funny, it also is painfully sad and leaves you with a palpable sense of melancholy at the end as it depicts – often graphically – some of the most shameful episodes in America's westward expansion. In another year, it could have been a serious Best Picture contender, but everything in 1970 was blown away, and rightfully so, by *Patton*. Hoffman had been nominated for Best Actor the previous year in the unsavory *Midnight Cowboy* (not on this list), but this a far better performance. With Martin Balsam (who co-starred with Hoffman six years later in *All the President's Men*) as a philosophical con artist, Richard Mulligan as an egomaniacal General George Armstrong Custer, Faye Dunaway as a sexually aggressive preacher's wife, and Chief Dan George in a magnificent, sly, Oscar-nominated performance as Crabb's adopted grandfather Old Lodge Skins. Calder Willingham adapted the script from Thomas Berger's novel. The movie was beautifully shot in Panavision by Harry Stradling, Jr., most of it in Alberta, Canada, and in Montana, near the actual site of the battle. [Trivia note: When Hoffman debuted in *The Graduate* three years earlier, his co-star Ann Bancroft played an older woman though Hoffman was only six years younger. Here, Dunaway plays the older woman, but Hoffman was actually the elder, by four years] [Caution: sexuality and graphic violence] [W]

The Turning Point
1977 – Herbert Ross

This captivating drama about the world of ballet features the dancing of the incomparable Mikhail Baryshnikov. Anne

Bancroft and Shirley MacLaine star as lifelong friends and rivals Emma Jacklin and Deedee Rodgers. Emma (Bancroft was 47 at the time) has reached the end of her career, while Deedee had long ago abandoned hers to marry and have children, including her daughter Emelia (real-life novice ballerina Leslie Browne). Deedee accompanies Emelia to New York to dance with Emma's company, leading to wonderful glimpses of dancers at work – and I mean work. Here, you can get a sense of the incredible effort it takes to become a ballet dancer. There are also the inevitable plot twists and turns, and there is a classic, cathartic confrontation scene between the two women that ranks among the best acting either has ever done. The ballet sequences are marvelous. If you've never seen Baryshnikov dance, here's your opportunity. Also marvelous is Martha Scott's witty performance as the company's funding-obsessed director. Obviously, she was wasting her time playing Charlton Heston's long-suffering screen mother in *The Ten Commandments* and *Ben-Hur*. Nominated for 11 Oscars (outrageous there was not one for Scott), but shut out in every category, it's nevertheless a solid piece of entertainment. [Trivia note: Although Martha Scott worked in television for another 13 years, this was her last movie role] [Caution: sexuality and adult language] **[W]**

Heaven Can Wait
1978 – Warren Beatty and Buck Henry
This breezy comedy about immortality offers the notion that the folks who run Heaven can be just as mistake-prone as those who run our earthly institutions. A remake of a 1941 movie called *Here Comes Mr. Jordan* (not a remake of the 1943 movie of the same name – and neither on this list), writers Beatty, Elaine May and the uncredited – and legendary – Robert Towne transposed the story from the world of boxing to professional football. It concerns Joe Pendleton (Beatty), a promising quarterback whose soul is accidentally snatched from his body by a novice angel (Henry), who wishes to spare him the pain and suffering of being hit by a car while training on his bicycle. The problem is, it wasn't Pendleton's time to die, so the only solution, as devised

by head angel Mr. Jordan (James Mason, in one of his most appealing roles), is to insert Joe's soul into the body of a nasty tycoon named Leo Farnsworth who has just died from an attempted murder by his wife (Dyan Cannon) and his personal secretary (Charles Grodin). Joe doesn't like the idea very much because it interferes with his plans to lead the Los Angeles Rams to the Superbowl. But when he crosses paths with a beautiful adversary (Julie Christie, with whom Beatty was romantically involved at the time), he rethinks his options. It's consistently funny and inventive, with some impressive scenes of Beatty quarterbacking the real Rams. But it also suffers from the slight problem of a denouement that's somewhat unsatisfying. Jack Warden does a fine job playing Joe's personal trainer, Max Corkle, whose role in the original movie was handled by the inimitable James Gleason. In *Heaven Can Wait's* best scene, Joe must persuade Max that he's not really dead but only living in Farnsworth's body, and Beatty's and Warden's interactions are heartfelt and endearing. [Trivia notes: 1) In a strange case of life imitating art, the movie depicts the Rams playing the Pittsburgh Steelers in the Superbowl. The very next year, the Rams actually did play the Steelers – but they lost. 2) *Heaven Can Wait* is particularly satisfying because, three years earlier, Beatty, Christie and Warden had co-starred in the dreadful *Shampoo* (goes without saying...)] [Slight caution: a little bit of rough language] **[W]**

Victor/Victoria
1982 – Blake Edwards
A delightful and entertaining comedy from Edwards, whose long career produced many hits but surprisingly few bona fide top-drawer titles as well as many genuinely dreadful attractions. His real-life wife Julie Andrews plays the title character. She received an Oscar nomination for her role of a down-on-her-luck singer who teams with a gay impresario (Robert Preston, also nominated, in one of his best roles) to pull off a ruse on the Paris nightclub scene in the 1920s: Victoria plays a man pretending to be a woman. Clever, funny and sometimes touching, it's a full

109

recovery for Edwards after the wretched *10* in 1980 and *SOB* in 1981 (neither on this list). The movie features strong supporting performances by James Garner (who co-starred with Andrews in *The Americanization of Emily*, mentioned at the beginning of this category) as an American mobster who becomes suspicious of Victor's gender; Alex Karras as his bodyguard and Leslie Ann Warren (likewise Oscar-nominated) as his moll. Great fun! [Trivia notes: 1) Though the score for *Victor/Victoria* was far from his best, Henry Mancini nevertheless won an Oscar for his work here, incredibly only the second such honor he received during nearly four decades of composing for the movies. 2) Preston was one of three actors that year nominated for an Oscar playing a cross-dressing character. The other two were Dustin Hoffman in *Tootsie* and John Lithgow in *The World According to Garp*] [Caution: some adult material] **[W]**

Mrs. Soffel
1984 – Gillian Armstrong
An engrossing story based on a true incident that occurred in Pittsburgh just after the turn of the 20th century. It's about an improbable romance that develops between a convicted murderer (Mel Gibson) and the wife of the warden (Edward Herrmann) who has imprisoned him. Kate Soffel (Diane Keaton) seems at first prim, proper and devoted both to her four children and the spiritual needs of the inmates – though she seems to be recovering from some sort of illness or breakdown. As the story proceeds, we become unsure whether Kate has fully recovered from her affliction, and whether Ed Biddle (Gibson) has truly fallen in love with her or is manipulating her to help him and his brother Jack (Matthew Modine) escape. Armstrong shows her considerable talent for probing the nuances of her characters as she unfolds the drama of the two lovers, each imprisoned – him because of his crime and her because of social expectations. The story caused a scandal at the time, and you can understand why, but that doesn't stop you from sympathizing with Ed and Kate, who struggle tragically to break free of the roles – albeit their own choices – they have been forced to play. Russell Boyd's

muted cinematography evokes the bleak winter landscapes of western Pennsylvania (though some of the movie was shot in Ontario), and Mark Isham's score makes high-octave piano notes the musical equivalent of icicles. [Caution: violence and adult material] **[W]**

Starman
1984 – John Carpenter
By far Carpenter's best movie and among the best performances by Jeff Bridges and Karen Allen, this tale of the friendship and eventual love affair that grows between a lonely widow and a mysterious alien is surprisingly affecting. The premise is that beings from an advanced civilization have intercepted one of NASA's Voyager space probes launched in the 1970s, and they have decoded the message contained in the spacecraft's data bank: a greeting from the people of Earth and an implied invitation to come visit. But things go awry when those same Earthlings attempt to shoot down the spaceship containing the alien ambassador – the Starman (Bridges). After he crash-lands he must attempt to reach his rescue rendezvous point within three days. So he assumes human form and enlists – by force at first – the help of Jenny Hayden, the widow. The two drive cross-country pursued by federal authorities. To say any more would spoil the movie's many surprises. But take my word that Bridges is entirely convincing as the alien, Allen has never been more appealing as Jenny, and Charles Martin Smith adds a strong supporting performance as the government's representative. Touching, funny and sometimes achingly sad, *Starman* remains one of the finest American works of science fiction, and the movie, though growing somewhat dated, remains haunting. [Trivia notes: 1) Bridges partly prepared for his unusual character by studying the head movements of birds. 2) Bridges utters a funny line of dialogue that I used in my book on aggressive driving. After nearly scaring Jenny to death while at the wheel, hurtling through an intersection and barely avoiding being broadsided by a semi-trailer, Starman explains, "I have watched you very carefully. Green light, go. Red light,

stop. Yellow light, go very fast." 3) Carpenter relegated the soundtrack duties here to Jack Nitzsche, but he often shares a distinction in some of his movies with none other than Clint Eastwood: he composes and performs the music] [Caution: language, mild sexuality and some violence] [W]

A Room with a View
1985 – James Ivory
A delightful adaptation of E.M. Forster's novel by the superb moviemaking team of producer Ismail Merchant, director Ivory and screenwriter Ruth Prawer Jhabvala. It's the story of Lucy Honeychurch (Helena Bonham Carter in her fine debut role), a prim young Englishwoman who goes on holiday in Florence, Italy, with her cautious but inept chaperone Charlotte (the great Maggie Smith, who has since reached screen immortality in her role as Violet Crawley, the Dowager Countess of Grantham on the TV series Downton Abbey), and thus begins her "awakening," as they say. She meets an intriguing young Englishman (Julian Sands) who makes her begin to think twice about her rather stiff-lipped fiancé (the normally dashing Daniel Day-Lewis in an early role). Beautifully shot by British cinematographer Tony Pierce-Roberts, it's a sumptuously told story to be savored. Two more fine English actors, Denholm Elliott and future Oscar-winner Judi Dench, round out the superb cast. [Slight caution: The movie contains an extended sequence of full-frontal male nudity, but it's in a perfectly innocuous and humorous context] [W]

Broadcast News
1987 – James L. Brooks
Brooks's next effort after winning Best Picture in 1983 with *Terms of Endearment* (coming in the next compilation) is slightly uneven in places, but when it's good, it's very, very good, and the performances are stellar. It's the story of a TV news team based in Washington, D.C., back when the three broadcast networks – ABC, CBS and NBC – ruled the airwaves. This is a fictional network, of course, but the plot rings true. The story involves the

112

careers and love triangle of a talented and rising but neurotic producer (Holly Hunter, in a sensational last-minute casting insertion), an even more talented field reporter (Albert Brooks, who is thoroughly wonderful and should have taken the Best Supporting Actor Oscar) and an undistinguished but good-looking anchor (William Hurt, in a deceptively sly performance). Brooks's script examines a perennial conflict within the TV news business: which should matter most, searching for the truth, no matter where it leads, or attracting an audience? Given the result of the intervening years, it's an easy guess. Jack Nicholson, who did win the Supporting Actor Oscar for *Terms of Endearment*, has fun here in a small role as a vain network news anchor. (Is there any other kind?) Bill Conti's playful score sets just the right tone. [Caution: language and sexuality] [W]

Enemies: A Love Story
1989 – Paul Mazursky

I almost placed this one in the Should Have Been Best Pictures category, but it doesn't rise to the level of *Glory*. Based on the novel by Isaac Bashevis Singer, this haunting rendition by Mazursky follows the travails of Herman Broder (Ron Silver, in his best role), a Jewish survivor of the Holocaust, and his three loves. It's a thoroughly engrossing mixture of humor and pathos – and all of the characters seem utterly real. The story begins with Herman waking from a nightmare of Nazi soldiers discovering his hiding place and threatening a woman who seems to be connected to him. We then see he is living in postwar Brooklyn, near Coney Island, with that woman, Yadwiga (Margaret Sophie Stein), now his wife but formerly his servant. Herman's first wife, Tamara (Anjelica Huston), was believed killed in a concentration camp. But Tamara suddenly appears alive although crippled by torture, thereby forcing Herman to deal with both women – as well as with Masha (Lena Olin), his fiery mistress and lover. It's a complex tale but well worth following, and it leaves indelible if troubling memories. [Caution: explicit sex scenes] [W]

Impromptu

1991 – James Lapine

A trifle, but a most entertaining one, full of breeziness, pastoral beauty, sophistication and a great deal of humor. Loosely based on the relationship between 19th-century composer Frédéric Chopin (Hugh Grant) and Amantine Aurore Lucile Dupin (Judy Davis) – the Baroness Dudevant, who wrote under the name George Sand – the story concerns an outing to the country estate of the Duke and Duchess D'Antan (Emma Thompson in a delightful early role). Actually, it is the ditzy Duchess's idea to invite the cultured class to her home for a bit of enlightened discussion and perhaps even … um, impromptu performances. From there things grow progressively chaotic, uproarious and entertaining. Mandy Patinkin is wonderful as Alfred de Musset, Sand's volcanic albeit occasional lover. There's this scene with him and Davis and a horse … well, it's too good to spoil. [Caution: language and French pastoral lustfulness] **[W]**

Gettysburg

1993 – Ronald F. Maxwell

Often, a movie that tries too hard to be true to history, particularly in the depiction of great battles, ends up on the stilted or dull side. Not this one. The producers spent nearly 15 years bringing the portrayal of the greatest battle of the Civil War to the screen, and their determination shows in every respect, particularly the performances. The uniformly excellent cast includes Tom Berenger as Confederate General William Longstreet, Sam Elliott as Union Brigadier General John Buford, Jeff Daniels as Union Colonel Joshua Lawrence Chamberlain, and Martin Sheen as Confederate General Robert E. Lee – all of whom you'll watch in great human detail as they portray their real-life counterparts during this monumental conflict, which killed or wounded more than 50,000 Americans over the course of only three days. The movie's scope is monumental as well, at four-and-a-half hours in length, featuring more than 13,000 reenactors and shot almost entirely on the actual sites. You might not know much about the battle of Gettysburg (the locals pronounce it GET-tiss-burg), Pennsylvania, which took place in a blazing-hot July 1863, but after watching this movie you'll know well and unforgettably how it unfolded – almost hour by hour. You can't help but feel the anguish and determination of these men. [Trivia notes: 1) The third-day battle, known as Pickett's Charge, actually was no charge at all. Instead, it involved a footmarch by more than 12,000 men across about a mile of open field, during which so many of them were mowed down by Union artillery and musket fire. 2) The sequences featuring cannon fusillades are thrilling, terrifying even, but they only slightly approximate the real battle, where the Union alone had positioned more than 600 heavy guns on the ridge] [Caution: intense battle scenes] **[W]**

Gosford Park
2001 – Robert Altman
From 2010 and into early 2016, American television audiences madly embraced the unforgettable British series Downton Abbey. That saga, created and written by Julian Fellowes, portrayed the lives of the residents and the servants of a large British estate, starting before the beginning of World War I. *Gosford Park*, also written by Fellowes, is its antecedent – though it's set in November 1932, nearly seven years after the Downton story concludes. Altman's finest movie is a sumptuous and well-crafted whodunit, featuring his trademarks of interwoven, multiple storylines; overlapping, often muffled dialogue; and dark humor, plus a smashing denouement. Lord William McCordle (Michael Gambon) is the tyrannical ruler of the country estate and his family, the possessor of a towering temper, a total lack of sympathy for the plight of relatives and an insatiable desire for his young female employees. So, it comes as little surprise when he eventually turns up dead – murdered by someone either residing in the house or one of the visitors invited to a weekend shooting party – there's a long list of suspects. On top of that, it's an interesting glimpse of British society at the time, and although there are no standout performances, everyone does good work. The exterior location,

115

Syon Park, in Brentford, Middlesex, England, is gorgeous. [Trivia notes: 1) Jeremy Northam, one of the cast members, plays Ivor Novello, a real-life Hollywood actor (born in Wales) and composer of some lovely songs, including "Keep the Home Fires Burning." Another Altmanian trademark: Northam, who has a lovely voice, sings several of Novello's songs acoustically in one scene. 2) Novello went on to become a major star on the British stage, to the point where his early death in 1951 drew a huge crowd of mourners. In 2012, the BBC Proms program dedicated an entire program to his life and career] [Caution: sexuality, violence and rough language – deliberately inserted by Altman to keep the kids away] [W]

The Gathering Storm
2002 – Richard Loncraine

In this elegant and beautifully acted drama, originally produced for the HBO cable network, Albert Finney gives arguably the best portrayal ever of Winston Churchill – and he certainly looks and sounds the part. The story begins in 1934 when most of Europe was in turmoil, Adolph Hitler was on the rise and England had retreated into isolation as its population and economy still ached from the deep wounds of World War I. One man foresaw the growing danger from the maniacal but charismatic German leader, however, and despite his falling fortunes and waning credibility among his peers, Churchill unswervingly labored to warn his country and, eventually, to lead it in a life-or-death struggle against the Nazi war machine. But that would come later. *The Gathering Storm* isn't a long feature. It also doesn't delve deeply into the events of Churchill's life or British history of the time. Instead, it endeavors to paint a vivid portrait of the man's character during one of the most challenging periods of his career, and it does so to near perfection. Finney is wonderful, but the movie is also graced by Vanessa Redgrave's excellent performance as Lady Clementine "Clemmie" Churchill. Had this been a theatrical release, instead of an HBO production, both would have deserved Oscar nominations – the scenes between the two stars are priceless.

116

Peter Hannan's cinematography, Howard Goodall's score, and the landscapes surrounding the Chartwell estate – Churchill's beloved home – contribute to the handsome production. [One complaint: Because of the time constraints, the movie's ending is abrupt and, given what had passed and what lay ahead, it's inappropriately upbeat] [Caution: adult themes and shots of Finney's bare derriere when he stands at the "loo"] [**W**]

Possession
2002 – Neil LaBute
An engrossing literary mystery based on the A.S. Byatt novel, in which the previously unknown romantic entanglement of two 19th-century poets is unearthed by a contemporary couple thrown together by circumstance. Gwyneth Paltrow and Aaron Eckhart are excellent as the sparring pair of researchers, while Jeremy Northam and Jennifer Ehle (Elizabeth Bennett in the marvelous British TV miniseries version of Jane Austen's Pride and Prejudice) play the Victorian lovers with great passion. Director and co-writer LaBute moves effortlessly back and forth between the two stories, sometimes brilliantly including both couples and time periods within the same camera shot via staging sleights of hand. It's an excellent production from beginning to end, with a strong supporting cast, gorgeous cinematography by Jean-Yves Escoffier of the rolling English countryside, and a lovely romantic score by Gabriel Yared, whose Oscar-winning compositions had graced *The English Patient* six years earlier. [Caution: sexuality] [**W**]

Finding Neverland
2004 – Marc Forster
A biographical story and a most charming one, concerning the life of Sir James Matthew Barrie, better known as J.M. Barrie, the creator of Peter Pan. Johnny Depp plays Barrie, and as usual he's captivating. The always-dependable Kate Winslet plays Sylvia Llewelyn Davies, the young mother whose four little boys Barrie befriends, to the detriment of his own marriage. As movies almost always do with biographies, *Finding Neverland* takes

certain liberties with the real story – in some cases great liberties. But like the best movies, the story it does tell will likely enchant you. Basically, Barrie's career as a playwright is flagging, and he's becoming desperate for an inspiration. He finds it one day while sitting on a park bench reading a newspaper and suddenly discovering there's a child hiding on the ground beneath him. From there ... well, you should know the result, but that won't interfere with the pleasure of watching it all unfold. With Julie Christie playing against type as Sylvia's uptight mother, and Dustin Hoffman as Barrie's harried theatrical producer Charles Frohman. [Trivia note: This was the second time Hoffman acted in a movie about Peter Pan. The first had occurred 13 years earlier when he played the title role in Steven Spielberg's *Hook* (not on this list)] **[W]**

Crash
2005 – Paul Haggis
I admire this movie very much – and it is a powerful story – but frankly its Best Picture Oscar was misplaced. It was outclassed by *Munich*, which also was nominated, and particularly by *Cinderella Man*, which was not. Still, it's an intense experience and well worth watching. To its credit, I had rated *Crash* the best picture of the year before I saw the other two. It's a thoughtful, compelling, sometimes shattering exploration of the "crash" of the many cultures that inhabit Los Angeles in the 21st century. The story follows a dozen characters over a 24-hour period near Christmas, beginning with a minor fender-bender and a visit to a crime scene, flashing back to the previous day, and eventually returning to its starting point. The excellent cast includes the always-interesting Don Cheadle as a police detective with family issues. There's Matt Dillon in the performance of his career – and one that should have won him an Oscar – as a ferocious patrol cop. Little-known Michael Pena is stunning as an honest Latino locksmith struggling against bigotry to make a living. And Terrence Howard shines as a successful television director who's tormented by his African American roots. Likewise, Sandra Bullock is unusually compelling as the nervous wife of the city's

district attorney, also played well by Brendan Fraser. Hard-edged, often profane and occasionally shocking, *Crash* exposes the city's dark underbelly, which seethes with ethnic tensions and threatens to boil over at any time. It's an unnerving montage of dramas, with several heart-stopping moments. It's also to the movie's credit that it never flinches from trying to get at emotional truth. No one is who he or she seems to be at first glance. As Dillon's Officer John Ryan says prophetically to his young partner (Ryan Phillippe), in what I hope will become one of the iconic movie lines: "You think you know who you are? You have no idea." [Caution: violence, extremely rough language and sexuality] **[W]**

Crazy Rich Asians
2018 – John M. Chu

This was a last-minute insertion, completed just before I sent off the manuscript to be converted into the various formats, because I had just seen the movie's theatrical release and it delighted me. It's a dazzling display of both contemporary moviemaking and of its subject matter: the opulence of the wealthiest family in one of the great metropolises of the East – they're "crazy rich" in terms of the size of their fortune, not their mental state. More pertinent, it's a fascinating study of cultural conflict disguised as romantic comedy-drama, with story elements borrowed from such diverse other favorites as *The Joy Luck Club*, *Monsoon Wedding*, *My Big Fat Greek Wedding* and even *The Godfather*. Based on Kevin Kwan's bestseller, it follows several hectic and dramatic days in the relationship between a young economics professor at New York University (cute-as-a-button Constance Wu) and someone who seems, by all appearances, to be a nice, middle-class guy (Henry Golding), someone who scrimps on ordering desserts and plays basketball at the local YMCA. When the guy, Nick Young, asks his professor/girlfriend Rachel Chu to join him in attending his best friend's wedding in Singapore and to meet his family there, she assumes they'll pinch pennies to make the trip – her mother packs meals for them in Tupperware containers for the long flight. But Nick shatters Rachel's illusion even before the takeoff when he checks them in for first-class luxury and begins to reveal his background. Then, when they reach their destination, and Rachel visits her old college roommate Peik Lin Goh (sensational newcomer Nora Lum – aka Awkwafina), she learns to her shock about the enormity of Nick's family fortune. Therein begin the conflicts, one involving Nick, his domineering mother Eleanor (Michelle Yeoh, the spectacular older swordfighter in *Crouching Tiger, Hidden Dragon*) and the grandmother and family matriarch Ah Ma (91-year-old veteran actress Lisa Lu); and another involving Eleanor and Ah Ma ganging up against Rachel. Other than that I'll just say the movie is full of dramatic surprises and delights, a host of vivid characters, spectacular set pieces, a soundtrack full of terrific Asian performances of Western songs and a finale staged atop one of the world's most remarkable hotels, the triple-towered, infinity-pool-capped Marina Bay Sands. Oh, and my reference to *The Godfather*? Let's just say that in both circles it's tough to go against the family, though in this case, fortunately, it isn't lethal. [Book note: Which title did I drop to make room for this one? From 1992, *Howards End*, James Ivory's fine adaptation of the E.M. Forster novel, starring Anthony Hopkins, Emma Thompson and Vanessa Redgrave. I'll be including it in my second forthcoming compilation, aptly titled Phil's 2nd Favorite 500] [Trivia note: *Crazy Rich Asians* marks the screen debut of Henry Golding, who had been hosting a TV travel show in Kuala Lumpur, Malaysia] [Caution: language and sexuality] **[W]**

4. Flawed But Not Fatally

My dear late friend Sheldon Tromberg – who first distributed and then wrote, produced and directed movies over a long career (and who was my screenwriting teacher) – used to say every movie is a miracle. He meant moviemaking is a collective, collaborative and risky process; all sorts of things can go wrong at any moment that can damage, interfere with or even destroy the product. It's a little like conception: There might be only one egg involved, but thousands or even millions of sperm compete to be the one to fertilize the ovum – and every sperm is capable of producing a different individual. Likewise, thousands of people write and submit screenplays each year, but only a few hundred are sold, fewer are produced and released, and rare is the one that accomplishes near perfection. So, it's a miracle when anything even reaches the screen, let alone achieves fame and fortune. Here are 23 examples that prove Shelly's point. Starting out, they all seemed to have the right ingredients for success, but for one reason or another they got on the wrong track and, in a couple of cases, a terribly wrong one. Or, they represent moviemakers trying but not quite achieving something important. Nevertheless, all deliver at least partly on your time investment, because geniuses are at work here, and much good material remains.

Hell's Angels
1930 – Howard Hughes
This movie had an unusual history and a most unusual director in the notoriously eccentric Hughes. He had already completed it as a silent feature when the age of "talkies" began, so he went back and re-shot many of the sequences in their entirety,

including some of the most complex aerial battles ever filmed, involving hundreds of real aircraft flying over the Southern California landscape (substituting for England and France). As a result, the movie's $3.8 million cost put it hugely above anything else done at the time. It's a depiction of the flying careers of two competitive British brothers (unknowns Ben Lyon and James Hall) who enter the military at the beginning of World War I. They also share a love interest (Jean Harlow, in her first major role). That's melodramatic pretext, however, for those spectacular aerial shots, one of which Hughes, a skilled pilot, flew himself because his stunt flier had refused. He crashed and broke his foot. There's also a sequence involving a Dirigible bombing raid over London that's done with models but looks amazingly convincing. [Trivia note: Two measures of the degree of Hughes's obsessive nature in making this movie: He shot nearly 250 feet of film for every foot that appeared on screen, and three pilots died during the production] **[B&W – but with hand-colored sequences]**

The Big Trail
1930 – Raoul Walsh

Trust me when I say that some of the movies made during the first few years of the sound era were amazing, and this one's a perfect example. I almost placed Walsh's epic Western in the Should Have Been Best Pictures category, because in many ways it's a knockout. For one thing, the cast was enormous, comprising hundreds if not thousands of extras, including pioneers and Native Americans, not to mention scads of horses, cattle, mules, sheep, goats and dogs. The crew had to be equally large to serve such an endeavor, and the production challenges and stresses must have been extraordinary. Almost the entire movie was shot on location – or, I should say, at 14 separate locations in six states – an achievement matched by few if any titles to this day, particularly on such a scale. Still more: The movie depicts, in painstakingly detailed fashion, the transiting of America by covered-wagon train in the 19th century, from the Mississippi River to Oregon. It includes some incredible sequences, such as the wagon train attempting to ford a dangerous river current, or the settlers lowering their wagons down a steep and very high canyon wall, and of course the ensemble fending off attacks by hordes of marauding "Injuns." Leading the procession is Red Flack (Tyrone Power, Sr.), a hulking menace of a man, who might not be serving the pioneers' best interests. Headed for an inevitable confrontation with Flack is Breck Coleman (John Wayne, in his first significant role), who scouts the trail ahead, makes peace with some of the tribes encountered on the way and keeps a-courtin' the lovely Ruth Cameron (Marguerite Churchill, who looks like she'd be more at home in Manhattan than on the prairie – but then, this was the '30s). The movie packs an amazing wallop for its age and running time of over two hours. As Gary Arnold wrote in his review of the DVD release, "There may never have been a more awesomely scenic and evocative Western in the history of the medium." Why place the movie in the Flawed category? Because its weaknesses are significant. The writing and acting are unrelentingly hokey, even amateurish, and that includes Wayne's performance. The man born Marion Michael Morrison obviously needed a few more years to mature as an actor. That said, don't skip this one. *The Big Trail* is often a thrilling spectacle, and it's a genuine piece of cinema history, made less than a century after people were still crossing the country by "Prairie Schooner" for real. [Trivia notes: 1) This was the only talkie made by Tyrone Power, Sr. After nearly a half-century on stage and in silent movies, he died the following year of a massive heart attack, literally in the arms of his 17-year-old son and future movie star Tyrone Power, Jr. 2) As complicated as the production already was, Walsh also shot it in two versions simultaneously: on 35-millimeter film for standard release and in 70-millimeter for a few selected, large-screen theaters. The latter format proved a distinct advantage, because the newly struck print looks terrific on DVD. 3) This is the first movie in which Wayne appeared using his new stage name] **[B&W] [W – 70mm version only]**

The Greatest Show on Earth
1952 – Cecil B. DeMille

Winner of the Best Picture Oscar and the biggest box office hit of that year, this huge, sprawling epic is something only a director with the experience and talent – and audacity – of DeMille could accomplish. It's a distinctive movie because of its semi-documentary style, using many of the real performers, equipment and animals of the Ringling Brothers/Barnum & Bailey Circus to tell the tale. It's also one of Hollywood's first attempts to counter the growing competition from television by providing lavish spectacles that could not be rivaled on the small screen. As huge as the cast is, it includes only a dozen professional actors, and all of them work much of the time in real circus situations – particularly Cornell Wilde and the marvelous Betty Hutton, who studied trapeze artistry for many weeks before taking on her role. The story is self-evident: the trials, tribulations and triumphs of circus performers. The movie's flawed nature is its attempt to weave in stodgy, clichéd melodrama and romantic conflicts with the much more interesting, straightforward tale of how an army of men and women put a circus show together day after day, for weeks on end, traveling from town to town in the 1950s. It's often dazzling to watch, particularly in Technicolor, and by the end not only do you feel a great sense of respect for the people involved, but you also even care a bit for the suffering the fictional characters must endure. This is particularly true after the trainwreck sequence, which was accomplished via a mix of miniatures and full-scale props, rivaling the twin sequences DeMille had staged for *Union Pacific* in 1939. With Charlton Heston in his first major movie role as the circus manager, Gloria Grahame in a wonderful turn as an elephant performer, Dorothy Lamour as an equestrienne, and James Stewart as Buttons, the clown who harbors a dark secret. [Trivia note: DeMille spent two months traveling with the circus preparing to shoot the movie and developing the script and storylines]

How the West Was Won
1963 – John Ford, Henry Hathaway and others

This update of *The Big Trail* was originally shot in Cinerama, with a production so big and complicated that it required four directors – and four directors of cinematography. The movie tells the epic story of the westward expansion of the United States, from the days of the Erie Canal to the Civil War, to the completion of the Transcontinental Railroad and the eventual ... um, winning of the West. Being a big, *big* movie, the cast is filled with big stars – at least of the male variety – including John Wayne (who had appeared in *The Big Trail* over three decades earlier), James Stewart, Henry Fonda and Gregory Peck; plus venerable character actors Richard Widmark, Robert Preston, Eli Wallach and Walter Brennan. There's also Spencer Tracy, who narrates but does not appear on camera. Notable women stars are represented by Debbie Reynolds and Carol Baker. The story traces the saga of the fictional Prescott family, starting at the Erie Canal in New York and, for unclear reasons, heading down the Ohio River toward Missouri, and then over a long period reaching California via wagon train. There are many, many detours, many awkward melodramatic subplots and a few too many times the actors clumsily play their characters too young or too old. But the movie packs a lot of entertainment value into its 2 hours and 44 minutes – including a dramatic and moving epilogue about the enormous legacy left by those who built this nation. The producers used the hugely complex Cinerama process, which required shooting with three synchronized cameras, to create an ultra-wide presentation. On a curved movie theater screen, the effect was overwhelming, particularly the big set pieces, such as a terrifying buffalo stampede, a breathtaking fight aboard an out-of-control train and a gorgeous aerial panorama during the epilogue. On a video screen, however, the wide, wide format is much less effective, and the two visible lines where the three camera images converge can be distracting. Alfred Newman wrote the powerhouse score. [Trivia notes: 1) In an interview, Debbie Reynolds described the strange process of shooting in Cinerama. She said she had to look in specific directions when appearing onscreen with her co-star Preston – but not at him – so it became quite challenging to interact with any kind of convincing emotion. 2) Speaking of the train fight, one of the stunt men in that sequence was injured so badly during filming that it took him five years to recover] **[W]**

The Graduate
1967 – Mike Nichols
This was the first movie to define the Baby Boomer generation, and the second directing effort by Nichols – who started out doing standup comedy sketches with his partner Elaine May. It's a stylish, wry look at the growing sense of ennui that began to envelop young people during the Sixties, as the war in Vietnam was starting to dominate the nation's attention. Dustin Hoffman, in his first starring role, plays Benjamin Braddock, a recent college grad who returns home to Los Angeles from back East and finds he has absolutely no idea what to do with his life. He is completely disconnected from his parents and their circle of friends. The two exceptions are Mrs. Robinson (Anne Bancroft), the wife of his father's business partner, with whom he has an affair, and Elaine Robinson (Katharine Ross), her daughter, with whom he falls in love. In truth, the movie's sensibilities have become dated and trite over the years – hence its placement in this category – and almost all of its acting is stylized. But Bancroft is wonderful in the role of the desperate housewife of her era. The hip score is by Simon and Garfunkel, and includes the best-known song, "Here's to You, Mrs. Robinson." [Trivia notes: 1) Although Hoffman was playing a 21-year-old, he was 31 at the time, so he actually was a little closer in age to Bancroft – who at 37 was playing older – than to Ross, who was 24 and playing younger. 2) In the scene in the rooming house in Berkeley, where Elaine's screams bring the landlord (Martin Fell) and the other tenants, watch for a small speaking part by the young, future Oscar-winner Richard Dreyfuss – his first] [Caution: language and sexuality – though mild by today's standards] **[W]**

Airport

1970 – George Seaton

You might call this a sequel to *The High and the Mighty* but with a bigger budget and cast. It's the first and best of a series of airline disaster movies produced in the 1970s, and it did well at the box office. Based on Arthur Hailey's bestselling novel, it's the story of ... an airport, specifically, one night at a fictional airport called Lincoln in Chicago (with the outdoor winter scenes shot at Minneapolis-St. Paul International). Like most disaster movies – as pioneered by *The High and the Mighty* and a few other earlier but lesser-known titles – it features an assortment of characters with personal dilemmas of one kind or another. There's the airport manager (Burt Lancaster) who's beset with issues – including a blizzard, a plane stuck in the snow and local residents angry because of takeoff noise – so he must neglect his increasingly bitter wife (Dana Wynter). He's also become interested in his secretary (Jean Seberg). There's the veteran pilot (Dean Martin – yes, Dean Martin, and he's pretty good!) who's having an affair with a beautiful stewardess (Jacqueline Bisset) and has started something he might not have bargained for. There's the gruff, cigar-chomping chief mechanic Joe Petroni (George Kennedy), who routinely does the impossible – and will have to do it big-time before the night is over. Then there are the passengers, including an elderly woman (legendary stage actress Helen Hayes, who won an Oscar for this role), who has become an expert (back before airport security was so strict) at sneaking her way onto flights. And there's her seatmate (Van Heflin), who seems distressed and keeps clinging to his briefcase, while back on the ground his wife (Maureen Stapleton, in a thankless role) is terrified of what he might be plotting. And so on. The technicians at Universal Studios did a masterful job of creating the illusion of an airliner in crisis, using a full-scale cabin set and a real aircraft for some of the scenes, but the movie's major flaw is its plot. Though diverting enough to keep you entertained, it contains so much silly melodrama that it overwhelms the truly engaging and suspenseful part of the story, that of an airliner in trouble, which occurs during the second hour. [Trivia note:

Airport holds a tragic connection with *The High and the Mighty*. As in that movie, the real aircraft used for *Airport*, a Boeing 707 jetliner, crashed years later on a landing approach in Brazil] **[W]**

MASH
1970 – Robert Altman

If you've only seen reruns of the classic television series, don't think you've seen the movie. Altman's first big hit is much edgier and darker than the TV show, as well as sexier and far more profane. Based on the novel by Richard Hooker (whose real name was H. Richard Hornberger), it follows the exploits of the 4077th Mobile Army Surgical Hospital in Korea in 1951 during the war. Donald Sutherland plays Captain Benjamin Franklin "Hawkeye" Pierce, an exceptional surgeon who will not conform to Army discipline. He and fellow doctor "Trapper" John Francis Xavier McIntyre (Elliot Gould) confront their polished-brass nemeses, Majors Frank Burns (Robert Duvall) and Margaret "Hot Lips" O'Houlihan (Sally Kellerman) with hijinks and outright ridicule. Meanwhile they often work desperately to save the lives of the wounded soldiers who arrive, usually by helicopter, from the battlefield – hence the famous opening sequence, which was adapted by the TV series.

*   *   *

If ever there was a miracle movie, it was *MASH*. Except for Altman, no one involved in the production had any idea what was going on. The studio executives at 20th Century Fox kept insisting that all of the graphically bloody operating-room scenes be eliminated, leaving only the slapstick comedy. And almost all of the dialogue was improvised by the actors. In the end, Altman won out. The operating-room gore remained, *MASH* became a smash hit and remains to this day one of the most unusual movies ever made, irrespective of subject. Released during the height of the Vietnam War and the growing antiwar movement, it either inspired or offended audiences, depending on their politics at the time. I placed it in this category because much of it seems dated, and because the whole last half hour is devoted to an idiotic football game. But back then critics regarded it as groundbreaking, with its episodic and often disjointed plot, its characters frequently sounding unintelligible and talking simultaneously – the way people sound in real life – and its total disrespect for the military. Now it retains much less of its power as social satire, but some of the comedic moments remain unique. [Trivia notes: 1) Gary Burghoff, as Corporal Walter "Radar" O'Reilly, is the only actor who appeared in a starring role in both the movie and the TV series. 2) One of the movie's trademarks, the hapless and never-seen public-address announcer, was a last-minute insertion by Altman, who realized he needed the device to tie all of the story's loose ends together – and he was right. I don't know this for certain, and I've never seen it reported, but I suspect Altman got the idea from the 1955 movie *Mister Roberts*, which also featured an anonymous PA voice. 3) Both the movie and the TV show were shot on the same location: the Fox ranch in Culver City, California, which also served as the location for *How Green Was My Valley* (coming in the next compilation) in 1941, John Ford's Oscar-winning tale of a small Welsh coal-mining town. 4) Instead of the title that actually appears in the movie, the Fox publicity people adopted a slightly different spelling, "M*A*S*H," for posters and other materials, and it continued that way during the 12 seasons of the TV series] [Caution: sexuality and those graphic operating-room scenes] **[W]**

Nashville
1975 – Robert Altman
Like *MASH*, this is a most unusual movie, an engrossing, disjointed, impressionistic look at the music culture of Nashville, Tennessee. Maybe Altman should have called it *MASHville*. He had intended the story as a political allegory, but it's a clumsy one – and it often left audiences confused and even angry at its conclusion. The story involves about two days in the lives of 24 characters who either live or work in, or are visiting, country music's capital during America's Bicentennial summer. They include an eminent singing legend (comedian and poet Henry Gibson), an unhappily married couple (Lily Tomlin and Ned

129

Beatty), two rival singing stars (Karen Black and the superb Ronee Blakely, who sings the show-stopping number, "Dues"), a womanizing pop balladeer (Keith Carradine, who won an Oscar for his song, "I'm Easy"), and Barbara Harris as a ditzy country star wannabe who delivers the movie's knockout fadeout number, "It Don't Worry Me." Watch for bit parts by Scott Glenn and Jeff Goldblum at the beginning of their careers, and cameos by Elliott Gould (from Altman's *The Long Goodbye*) and Julie Christie (from his *McCabe and Mrs. Miller* – neither on this list). Here's the thing about Altman: Much of what he does is extremely messy, baffling and ultimately frustrating – BUT – he exhibits flashes of moviemaking brilliance unlike anyone else. Example: To build tension just before the climax, during a song by Blakely, he cuts to a full-screen shot of an American flag flowing languidly in a breeze. That shot, believe it or not, creates one of the most apprehensive moments in all of cinema – it will give you chills. [Trivia notes: 1) Actors loved working with Altman, because he was so open to their improvisations. Here, he allowed them to compose and perform their own songs – and he recorded all their performances live. 2) Altman shot so much footage making *Nashville* he once considered producing a nine-hour version for television on the ABC network, but the project never materialized. 3) As with *MASH*, Altman utilized a dialogue device to link and transition the scenes in *Nashville*. Instead of the anonymous public-address announcer, this time he used the recorded voice (performed by novelist and actor Thomas Hal Phillips, who also wrote the narration) of Hal Philip Walker, a fictional, third-party presidential candidate. His words echo through the streets from loudspeakers atop a festooned cargo van. 4) This movie reunited Christie with her *Doctor Zhivago* co-star Geraldine Chaplin, who plays a ditzy BBC correspondent here. Ten years earlier they had portrayed the lover and wife, respectively, of the title character in David Lean's magnificent epic] [Caution: sexuality and a brief moment of shocking violence] **[W]**

All That Jazz
1979 – Bob Fosse

Fosse's semi-autobiographical movie is clumsy, jerky and hugely self-indulgent, particularly in the last half-hour. But it's also engrossing and frequently funny, and the long early sequence, involving a huge dancing audition performed to George Benson's "On Broadway," is dazzling. Roy Scheider plays Fosse's fictional counterpart, a producer-director named Joe Gideon. His story is of a man on the edge, someone who's simultaneously editing and re-editing a movie, directing a new Broadway show and bedding as many women as possible. All the while, he's keeping himself going with prescription stimulants, alcohol and eye drops, starting each shaky day with the phrase, "It's showtime, folks!" uttered in front of his bathroom mirror and proceeding under the watchful eye of the Angel of Death (Jessica Lange). Despite his shortcomings, Gideon is an appealing character, even to the women he betrays. He delivers a great line to one of his dancers and ex-lovers that I've stolen on occasion for other contexts. "I can't make you a great dancer," he says. "I'm not sure I can even make you a good dancer. But I am sure I can make you a *better* dancer." And Scheider is good enough in the role to make you believe that's what he can do. [Caution: language, sexuality, and a graphic operating-room scene] **[W]**

The World According to Garp
1982 – George Roy Hill

The only John Irving novel that has worked when transformed to the screen, this one does so largely because of its appealing cast, including Glenn Close as Jenny Field, a nurse and pioneering feminist; John Lithgow (in his breakthrough performance) as a former professional football player who has become a transgender; and most of all Robin Williams, who is terrific as the title character. The plot is a product of Irving's, shall we say, unusual imagination. Jenny Field wants a baby but does not want the burden of being married. So she contrives to conceive in a most unconventional way. The product of that union is her son, T.S. Garp, who naturally grows up with his own unique view of the world. It's a rollicking, sometimes outrageous tale, with plot twists that will leave you breathless – although some of them just go too far. Yet, like the opening title sequence (which you must not miss), somewhere inside this strange concoction is a sentimental and appealing heart – but it's due more to the actors, and probably director Hill, than to the source material. [Caution: frank language and abundant sexuality – including a recurring plot point revolving around oral sex gone wrong] **[W]**

Twilight Zone: The Movie
1983 – (Four directors)
Tragedy struck the production of this movie, which was based on the popular TV series of the late '50s and early '60s, when cast members Vic Morrow and two small children were instantly killed by a helicopter crashing on top of them. It's particularly sad in Morrow's case, because he delivered the best performance of his career in the movie's first episode. *TZTM* contains three more main segments, much of it all highly inconsistent, with its weakest, second part directed by none other than Steven Spielberg. Called "Kick the Can" (a remake of an original series episode), it involves a magical visitor to an old folks' home. It's cloying in the extreme and completely forgettable. The third episode, directed by Joe Dante, is quite witty, dealing as it does with a young boy who possesses special and frightening powers (in another remake of an original episode). But the fourth segment literally soars. Directed by George Miller, who is better known for doing the Mad Max thrillers in Australia (none on this list), the story concerns an airline passenger who is terrified of flying (played extremely well by John Lithgow) and has very good reason to be. There's also a funny prologue sequence with Albert Brooks and Dan Aykroyd as two bored buddies driving along a highway at night, and Aykroyd appears again in a gotcha fadeout. [Caution: language] **[W]**

The Cotton Club
1984 – Francis Ford Coppola

In this troubled, uneven, constantly over-budget production, Coppola nevertheless manages to paint a striking and highly stylized portrait of one of Harlem's most famous nightclubs of the 1920s. Richard Gere stars as Dixie Dwyer, a jazz musician who makes a marginal living playing his coronet (basically a four-valved trumpet) at night spots and private parties. Eventually, he's taken under the wing of legendary mobster and Cotton Club owner Owney Madden (Bob Hoskins), who protects him from vicious criminal "Dutch" Schultz (James Remar). Meanwhile, tap dancer Sandman Williams (Gregory Hines) is also hired, along with his brother (Maurice Hines), to perform at the club – a place where African Americans were barred for years from patronizing. The movie loosely follows the sagas of both men and their women, played, respectively and well, by Diane Lane and by Lonette McKee, whose rendition of "Ill Wind" is sensational – amazingly so because although she's singing the song, Coppola keeps her on camera only briefly as part of a montage. In fact, she easily upstages Gere and Hines, displaying a talent and a screen presence that easily should have propelled her to a major career. There's also an amusing subplot involving the friendship between Madden and his partner Frenchy Demange (Fred Gwynne), which gives the movie a much-needed sense of fun – particularly their reunion scene – but again Coppola minimizes their onscreen presence. Not for everyone, and a fanciful bit of cultural history, but the onstage and background musical period recreations are uniformly terrific, including a wonderful impersonation by Larry Marshall of Cab Calloway leading the crowd in his signature number, "Minnie the Moocher." Coppola's at his best when he sticks with them. [Trivia note: Schultz's menacing henchman is played by Julian Beck, a legendary presence in New York avant-garde theater circles in the 1950s and '60s] [Caution: sexuality and graphic violence] **[W]**

The Natural
1984 – Barry Levinson
Oh, what a beautiful movie to savor visually, and what wonderful casting, performances and music – but what a thoroughly dumb story! Based on Bernard Malamud's novel about an aging baseball player with superior talents who seems to come from out of nowhere, *The Natural* suffers from an earnestness and literalness that almost destroy it – but only almost. What's left has strong entertainment value. Robert Redford plays Roy Hobbs, the aforementioned aging player who eventually finds a spot on the roster of the fictional New York Knights and also reunites with his childhood sweetheart, Iris Gaines (Glenn Close). Actually, Redford's performance is the weakest, but several of the supporting players more than make up for him, including Wilford Brimley as the team's manager, Robert Prosky as the literally shady owner, Richard Farnsworth as a seasoned coach and Darren McGavin in an uncredited role as a bookie. Randy Newman composed the nostalgic Americana score, which is much better than the movie deserves; likewise Caleb Deschanel's gorgeous, golden-hued cinematography. But you might have trouble getting through the goofier scenes, such as one in which Roy can't seem to buy a hit – until Iris stands up in the grandstands. With her wide-brimmed hat backlit by the sun, she looks like a leftover from *Angels in the Outfield*. Ouch! [Caution: sexuality] **[W]**

Cocoon
1985 – Ron Howard
Here's another case where fine acting and appealing characters overcome a premise that's iffy at best. Four peaceful, immortal aliens land on Earth to rescue a group of their compatriots who have been hiding on the sea bottom in tiny, cocoon-like chambers that can sustain them for thousands of years if necessary. In the process, they encounter a group of residents at a retirement village in Florida, who discover that the pool the aliens are using to store the cocoons temporarily can be most rejuvenating. As I said, it's iffy. Nevertheless, Howard pulls it off

134

and presents a heartwarming tale with laughs and a vibrant spirit. He succeeds because he assembled a marvelous cast of veteran actors, including real-life couple Hume Cronyn and Jessica Tandy, along with Wilford Brimley, Maureen Stapleton, Don Ameche (in an Oscar-winning role) and Gwen Verdon. There's also Steve Gutenberg, who's pursuing Tahnee Welch (Raquel's daughter) to provide a young but quite unconventional love interest. At one point, Gutenberg spies Welch undressing in her cabin and gets to see much more than he – or we – ever would have expected. [Caution: language and sexuality – but mild versions of both] [W]

Little Shop of Horrors
1986 – Frank Oz

This spotty movie's history is a bit convoluted. It started in 1960 as an ultra-low-budget Roger Corman feature that was shot in three days but turned out to be a cult classic (see Little Gems). Then it moved to the off-Broadway stage as a musical in the early 1980s. And here it's brought back to the screen by director Oz and featuring a strong comedy cast, including Rick Moranis and John Candy of the Second City comedy troupe, and Bill Murray and Steve Martin of NBC's Saturday Night Live, as well as Broadway veteran singer Ellen Greene and versatile moviemaker and actor Christopher Guest in a cameo role. It's the story of Seymour Krelborn (Moranis), a schnook who works in Mushnick's Flower Shop on Skid Row, where he fancies Audrey (Greene, reprising her stage role), the checkout clerk. Eager to impress her, he breeds a strange plant that turns out to be not only conscious but hungry for human blood. Though the plant is a hit with customers, things quickly spiral out of control as it begins to grow bigger and nastier and, from a movie-effects standpoint, more spectacular. For the full-size version, which stands nearly 10 feet tall, the technicians employed an extremely complex set of mechanical controls, and the result is amazing – to this day it's still the most elaborate animatronic device ever attempted. Voiced by Levi Stubbs, the lead singer of the soul group The Four Tops, it's also the cleverest thing in the movie.

Second best is Greene's singing voice, which is stunningly powerful coming from a woman of such slight build. There's also a talented trio of young African American women (Tichina Arnold, Tisha Campbell and Michelle Weeks) employed as a hip update of a Greek chorus. And there's a great homage scene to the 1960 movie, with Murray playing the role of a dental masochist that originally was performed by a young Jack Nicholson. So what's not to like? Of all things, the usually affable Martin is thoroughly nasty – and unfunny – here playing a sadistic dentist named Orin Scrivello, who exhibits the very bad habit of physically abusing Greene and torturing his patients. It's Martin's worst role. Every time he appears he spoils the movie's otherwise tongue-in-cheek mood. There's also a sexually distasteful aspect of the plant. [Caution: language and abusive behavior toward Greene's character – by her boyfriend *and* the plant] **[W]**

The Witches of Eastwick
1987 – George Miller
This darkly comic fantasy about a trio of beautiful witches battling Satan in the midst of a picturesque, modern-day New England town works for a good deal of the time. But eventually it falls deeply into wretched excess. Cher, Michelle Pfeiffer and Susan Sarandon play the witches, and the Prince of Darkness – known as Daryl Van Horne – is personified by none other than Jack Nicholson. But the real star of the movie is Veronica Cartwright, playing the town shrew with such relish that she steals the spotlight from the four co-stars. Her bit of unbridled paranoia is awesome. Nicholson's not bad either, playing his self-described "horny little devil" who, one-by-one, charms and seduces the witchy trio in a variety of witty encounters – one involving cello instruction, another a poolside entreaty and the third ... well, let's say it's the most direct approach of the three. Miller, an Australian who's best-known for his hugely popular Mad Max series of action thrillers (none on this list), shows a deft hand at comedy here, and John Williams contributed the sprightly score. [Caution: language and sexuality] **[W]**

136

Regarding Henry
1991 – Mike Nichols

As with several other titles in this category, *Regarding Henry* requires more suspension of disbelief than usual. Harrison Ford is Henry Turner, successful attorney at law, and Annette Bening is his wife, Sarah. Ruthless and self-absorbed, Henry is shot in a convenience store robbery one night and badly injured. Then he must undergo a long and painful rehabilitation that reveals his mental faculties have become diminished. Yet he finds meaning and happiness in life in the process. Facile and contrived, no doubt, but Ford dons the title character so well that he becomes quite sympathetic, so that – as required for all movies – you do eventually suspend disbelief. Nichols's direction is sharp, and Bening's performance is top-notch. [Trivia note: Parts of this movie were shot on the same scholastic campus as *The World According to Garp*: the Millbrook School in Millbrook, New York. It's in the credits, of course, but I know this because I've been there, visiting a friend who was on the faculty. He told me about one day trying to walk up to Ford, who was relaxing between takes, and being blocked from doing so by the star's personal bodyguard. When he asked me why the interference, I explained that because Ford was shooting a movie, he represented a large financial investment by the studio, and the bodyguard's job was to protect that investment from any and all hazards – including eager fans] **[W]**

The Last of the Mohicans
1992 – Michael Mann

This handsomely mounted, lavishly produced update of the James Fenimore Cooper classic suffers from two serious flaws. The first is an overemphasis on an improbable romance at the expense of a taut and often rousing tale about the emergence of pre-colonial America. The year is 1757, as the movie's prologue states, and England and France are at war for control of the continent. Swept up into that conflict are the two surviving members of the eponymous tribe of Native Americans: Chingachgook (Russell Means), the father; and Uncas (Eric

Schweig), the son. Accompanying them is their adopted son and brother, Nathaniel Poe (Daniel Day-Lewis), aka "Hawkeye," whose nickname derives from his superb ability with a rifle. At first, the trio roams the lush wilderness of what is now upstate New York, killing deer for sustenance and accepting the hospitality of friendly colonials. But their idyllic existence is short-lived when they save a British officer (Steven Waddington) and the two daughters of a British colonel (Jodhi May and Madeleine Stowe) from a marauding cadre of the Huron tribe, who are allied with the French. From there, Hawkeye, Chingachgook and Uncas become the targets of the vengeful Magua (MAHG-why), a Huron who seeks vengeance against the women and their father, Colonel Monro (Maurice Roëves), for what he considers a past injustice. The trio also help to defend Fort William Henry, on the shore of Lake George, which is in the midst of a siege by French troops. It's a massive, visually overwhelming sequence that reportedly took director Mann many nights to film. After that, the plot threads inevitably converge, but as I said they take a backseat to the developing romance between Hawkeye and Cora (Stowe), the colonel's eldest daughter, which eventually pushes much more moving events aside. It's an unnecessary sop to contemporary audiences, and it diminishes the movie's power considerably. A pity, because along with the absorbing story, the entire movie is gorgeously shot by Dante Spinotti – though the locations are in the forests and cliffs of North Carolina, near and on the Biltmore estate in Asheville. And the Scottish-sounding score by Trevor Jones and Randy Edelman is rousing. Oh, the second flaw? The movie utterly wastes the great Wes Studi, who must play Magua as a robotic near-simpleton. He's supposed to be a villain, but his character is an embarrassing throwback to Hollywood's worst portrayals of "Injuns." [Trivia notes: 1) Hawkeye's real name in the novel was Natty Bumppo. The moviemakers changed it to Nathaniel Poe, apparently because they thought audiences would find the name created by Cooper laughable. 2) The French attack on Fort William Henry really took place, though the outcome was somewhat different than how the movie portrays it] [Caution: violence] [W]

Sneakers
1992 – Phil Alden Robinson
A quirky and diverting if contrived caper about the early days of computer piracy by Robinson, who gave us *Field of Dreams* (coming in the next compilation). Robert Redford plays Martin Bishop, a computer whiz who specializes in breaching the security of companies such as banks that pay him to test their defenses. But Marty has been harboring a secret from his partners, including Dan Aykroyd as a conspiracy freak, David Strathairn as a blind audio expert, River Phoenix as a break-in specialist and Sidney Poitier as a former CIA agent afflicted with anger mismanagement. Turns out Marty's been on the run from the feds for years for computing hacking. His secret was safe – until two menacing-looking guys show up purporting to represent the National Security Agency, the NSA, which is the federal government's chief listening entity. That sets in motion a rather convoluted and sometimes stilted plot, but the excellent cast, including Mary McDonnell as Marty's former lover and Ben Kingsley as a former friend, keeps the polemics from dragging it all down too much. James Horner's lively score presages his suite for *A Beautiful Mind*. [Viewing note: Film buffs might notice several scenes derived from other movies such as *Blindfold* (not here) and *Rosemary's Baby*, as well as *Three Days of the Condor* (likewise not here), which also starred Redford] [Caution: language and mild sexuality] [W]

Wolf
1994 – Mike Nichols
This is three-quarters of a fairly engaging and clever story (as written by Jim Harrison and Wesley Strick). Jack Nicholson plays Will Randall, an aging and rather tepid book editor whose wife (Kate Nelligan) is losing interest in him while his career is being usurped by a young and unscrupulous rival (James Spader). All of this is background, however, to the primary

matter, which begins as Will is driving his Volvo alone through a snowstorm at night when he hits an animal. It's a large canine that promptly bites Will as he tries to move it from the roadway. It turns out that the canine is a werewolf, a mythical creature that supposedly bestows superhuman powers on the victims of its bites. That it does, because as Will heals from his wound, he begins to develop extremely acute senses of hearing and smell, new hairs are sprouting from his skin and his physical strength becomes extraordinary. All of this makes for some fascinating and witty sequences, and Nicholson's interactions with Michelle Pfeiffer (one of his co-stars in *The Witches of Eastwick*), his eventual love interest, are razor-sharp. But the movie breaks down utterly when Will turns from a man with wolf-like abilities into a literal werewolf, complete with prosthetics and improbable physical feats. Until then, though, it's an intellectual riff on the tensions between the civilized and natural worlds. The music, which sounds eerily like a John Williams score, is by Ennio Morricone. **[W]**

For Love of the Game
1999 – Sam Raimi

What is it about baseball that prompts some moviemakers to go at least a little bit goofy? Here's the second one of the category. Not nearly as beautiful-looking as *The Natural*, or as flat-out loopy as *Field of Dreams* (coming in the next compilation), it's as earnest as they come in attempting to portray the game realistically and in detail. Nevertheless, it nearly fails at critical moments to deliver a satisfying drama. It's the story of the last game in the 19-year career of Billy Chapel (Kevin Costner, who also starred in *Field of Dreams*, as well as the far superior *Bull Durham*), a sure Hall of Fame starting pitcher for the Detroit Tigers. Here, he's facing the dreaded New York Yankees in a bid to deny them yet another division championship. During the course of the contest, in which the prospect of the ultimate pitching performance – a perfect game – slowly emerges, Billy relives a critical part of his life in flashback; his on-again/off-again romance with Jane Aubrey (Kelly Preston), who earlier that day announced she was leaving New York to take a job in London. In between bouts of reverie, Billy deals one-by-one with the hitters in the Yankee lineup. That's where Costner shines, standing alone on the mound, mentally sizing up each opponent and determining the best pitch to throw. But the movie can't manage to sustain those sequences. Instead, it keeps reverting to Billy's five-year history with Jane – though it produces an unexpected benefit in doing so. Preston, who bounced around in various roles since her ingénue and teen-sexpot days in the '80s, turns in the performance of her career. In fact, she's so appealing she makes you yearn to stay with that part of the story and forget about whether or not Billy goes all nine innings putting goose eggs on the scoreboard. As Billy says to Jane at one point, "Don't go," and you find yourself hoping she won't. That's how appealing she is. [Trivia note: Costner's real parents play Billy's parents – seen both in the stands and in the home movies during the opening sequence] [Caution: language and sexuality] [W]

The Patriot
2000 – Roland Emmerich
Let's start by saying that this movie has very little to do with the American Revolution. Yes, it's set in that period and, yes, it's about rebellion in the American colony of South Carolina. It also features sweeping battle scenes between the American colonial army and the British redcoats. It features General Cornwallis and mentions George Washington. And two of the characters convey echoes of real-life enemies Francis Marion of the rebels and Banastre Tarleton of the British army. But that's where the similarities end. If you want true history you won't find it here. Instead, you'll get a fairly rousing yarn of war, courage and revenge focusing on Benjamin Martin (Mel Gibson) a peaceful, quiet family man, farmer and widower hiding a terrible secret from his past. Early on, he's forced into a deadly confrontation with William Tavington (Jason Isaacs), a murderous British colonel. At first opposed to the war with England, Martin eventually organizes the local militia into a band of guerrilla fighters who must harass the forces of Cornwallis (Tom

141

Wilkinson in a fine performance) until Washington can marshal his troops to march south, and the French Navy can arrive to support the colonists. When the battles are engaged, the scenes and sequences alternate between horrific and thrilling, and the movie contains a surprising amount of humor. Why place it in this category? Because the violence is often gratuitous, the domestic scenes are a bit cloying, and the movie treats slavery, bigotry and romance most simplistically. Why not fatally flawed? It was shot entirely in South Carolina by the great Caleb Deschanel, maybe the best cinematographer ever; the score is by John Williams – 'nuff said; Gibson does a really good job as Martin (though for the $25 million he was paid, he should); and the supporting cast is quite strong, especially Heath Ledger, who's particularly appealing as Martin's eldest son, and the always-dependable Chris Cooper. [Trivia note: As Steven Spielberg had done in *Saving Private Ryan* two years earlier, the producers hired amputees as extras to portray men who lost limbs in battle] [Caution: graphic battle scenes] **[W]**

The Hurt Locker
2009 – Katherine Bigelow

It might seem unusual for me to place a Best Picture winner in this category, but as you've already seen in the case of *Crash*, I often don't agree with the judgment of the Academy. This is not to say *The Hurt Locker* isn't a powerful or effective movie; it is – very. But it suffers from a problem I just couldn't overcome. The story about a U.S. bomb-disposal squad in Baghdad during the Iraq War is as tense as any movie in memory. At each moment – each instant – Staff Sergeant William James (Jeremy Renner) works in proximity to a bomb that could blow him to kingdom come. And the script by Mark Boal, who spent time as a journalist embedded with a disposal unit, offers an increasingly terrifying array of what became known as improvised explosive devices, or IEDs. Though James usually works wearing heavy armor, at one point he encounters a bomb so potentially powerful that he sheds his protective gear to continue in his shirtsleeves. "If I'm going to die, I might as well be comfortable,"

142

he tells one of his unit buddies, who's perched far away but on the lookout for hostile activity. At its core the movie isn't about the war at large – or rather about this particular war. Instead, it's about how war can affect a man so deeply and so tragically that in the end, no matter how horrible the experience, he can't let go of it. In fact the ending, which contains no suspense or violence at all, might be more shocking than everything preceding it. My problem? I think the moviemakers erred significantly when they failed to include a single Iraqi character of note. Yes, it's an age-old shortcoming, the marginalization of ethnic characters – such as American Indians in Westerns – but it severely diminishes the story, and in this day and age it's a serious oversight. In contrast, the sensational *Three Kings*, a much more fanciful story, offered an array of Iraqis – including an insurgent who kidnaps and tortures one of the primary characters – whose humanity was evident. Unfortunately, *The Hurt Locker* gives us no equivalent, and it suffers from that flaw. [Viewing notes: 1) Watch for fleeting roles by Ralph Fiennes and Guy Pearce, each of whom had co-starred, respectively, in previous Best Picture winners *The English Patient* and *The King's Speech*. 2) If you can't seem to get enough of suspenseful bomb-disposal adventures, I recommend tracking down the superlative British television production, Danger UXB, from 1979 starring Anthony Andrews. Originally shown in America on PBS as part of the Masterpiece Theater series, the 13-part drama follows the experiences of a British engineer whose job is to defuse and dispose of unexploded German bombs amid the London cityscape during World War II] [Caution: extremely intense episodes and graphic violence] **[W]**

5. Deliciously Bad

Usually, a bad movie is an unpleasant experience, sometimes painfully so. As my dear, late friend Bob Winner used to say after sitting through a particularly putrid one, "It hurts your head!" Don't believe it? Try watching all of *Quantum of Solace* sometime, or *Ziegfeld Follies* or *Amazon Women on the Moon* (none, thankfully, on this list). But once in a great while, a genuinely awful one can provide a tremendous amount of entertainment, because it makes you howl at its misguided sensibilities or go gleefully wide-eyed at its stupidity. Or, it simply disarms your sense of taste and your critical facility, so you end up surrendering to its unjustifiable charms. It's rare, but it does happen, even to the point where you find yourself revisiting a turkey now and then to repeat the experience. Along those lines, not for your education or edification but purely for guilty pleasure, here are 11 delectable stinkers not to be missed.

The Ten Commandments
1956 – Cecil B. DeMille
This easily qualifies as my favorite bad movie of all time. First, a few facts. Yes, in the Old Testament's Book of Exodus there is a description of Moses, a former prince of Egypt, leading the Hebrews out of bondage under extraordinary circumstances – including crossing the Red Sea with the help of some kind of spectacular divine intervention. And yes, there was a Pharaoh who precipitated these events by his ruthlessness and cruelty – though the Bible doesn't name him. But none of this has anything to do with why the movie is so wonderfully clunky. It's the biggest, grandest, most ridiculous Hollywood biblical epic ever made, and even at nearly four hours it's consistently

entertaining. Moses, as played by Charlton Heston, undergoes an amazing transformation, He starts out as a dashing, appealing, benevolent prince and ends up being maybe the dullest man who ever lived. What does it to him? Could it be the sight of a burning bush and the sound of the *basso profundo* voice of God (actually Heston's own voice, electronically enhanced), who turns out to be even duller than Moses? Or, is it because DeMille's ham-handed direction eventually drains the spirit from everybody in the movie? Whatever the reason, the villains are much more interesting than the heroes. And what villains! Vincent Price as the sneering, sadistic Baka, the master builder; Edward G. Robinson as Dathan, the rodentlike overseer and informant; Anne Baxter as the seductive Nefretiri, princess of Egypt; and of course Yul Brynner as Rameses, whose performance has provided comedic material for years. "So let it be written; so let it be done" is his habitual phrase, although my favorite is, "His god *is* God!" Watch also for Martha Scott in the thankless role as Heston's mother, a role she reprised three years later, suffering even greater misery in *Ben-Hur*. Ridicule aside, the entire sequence of parting the Red Sea remains a stupendous achievement, now over six decades later. Steven Spielberg once called it the greatest special effect in the history of the movies. That's an apt description, particularly because the ingenious moviemakers had such relatively crude tools at their disposal. Then there's Elmer Bernstein's music, a score so majestic it can make you tremble. And whatever the dramatic highlights or lowlights, the cinematography by Loyal Griggs makes every scene – every frame – look grand. Bad, yes, but as this category promises, irresistible; and the line, "Moses, there's a man among the sheep!" alone is priceless. [Trivia notes: 1) As mentioned above, the identity of Pharaoh at the time of Moses remains in doubt. Historians guess it was either Amenhotep II or Thutmose III. As for Rameses, he was real, but his timeframe was about two centuries later. Besides, he ruled Egypt for nearly 70 years – until at least age 90 – longer than any other pharaoh, and he fathered hundreds of children. If Rameses was responsible for the Exodus, he apparently didn't suffer much divine retribution.

2) In deference to the morals of its day, the movie plays a little fast and loose about an uncomfortable fact involving Nefretiri, whose parentage isn't mentioned. That's because in ancient Egypt she would have been Pharaoh's daughter, the biological sister of Rameses and therefore his incestuous mate. 3) The infant Moses is played by Heston's own infant son Fraser, which turned out to be his only onscreen role. He went on to become a successful producer. 4) Although she played Charlton Heston's adoptive mother, Yul Brynner's aunt and Cedric Hardwicke's sister in *The Ten Commandments*, Nina Foch was a year younger than Heston, four years younger than Brynner and 31 years younger than Hardwicke] **[W]**

In Harm's Way
1965 – Otto Preminger

Preminger's World War II epic features a big-name cast and some huge battle scenes, but it never approaches the gripping nature of the best of the genre, such as *From Here to Eternity* and *Tora! Tora! Tora!* Like those two movies, this one deals with the events surrounding and including the Japanese attack on Pearl Harbor, in Honolulu, Hawai`i, on December 7, 1941. And like *From Here to Eternity*, it contains quite a bit of melodrama and romantic subplots. But unlike its counterparts, *In Harm's Way* mostly portrays battles that take place on fictitious Pacific Islands with goofy-sounding names, such as Gavabutu and Toulebonne, and the plot lines are utterly standard and often tedious. It also seems like a mid-sixties movie – full of titillation but not quite moving into explicit territory. The biggest drawback, however, is Preminger's decision to skip authentic wartime footage or shooting more of the scenes aboard real vessels. Instead, he used obvious ship models for the climactic battle sequence and neglected to film any aircraft in his staging the Pearl Harbor attack. It severely diminishes their impact. Despite all this, the cast members – particularly John Wayne, Kirk Douglas, Patricia Neal and Paula Prentiss – turn in some highly watchable performances, especially Douglas, playing a Navy officer tormented by an unhappy marriage. There's an exceptionally good scene where he roughs up Patrick O'Neal, a vain and underhanded aide to Admiral Broderick (Dana Andrews), who's more of a politician than a battle commander. The score by Jerry Goldsmith is nowhere near his best, but it's lively enough to bolster the action and provide a sense of drama. One oddity: The opening credits are nearly non-existent, while the end credits, by Saul Bass, are hugely overblown for what has just transpired. [Trivia notes: 1) The movie's title references a quote by American Revolution naval hero John Paul Jones: "I wish to have no connection with any ship that does not sail fast, for I intend to go in harm's way." 2) Wayne and Neal had co-starred in *Operation Pacific* 14 years earlier and didn't like each other much, but they got along much better here] [Caution: sexuality and wartime violence] **[B&W] [W]**

Ice Station Zebra
1968 – John Sturges
Eccentric billionaire Howard Hughes reportedly considered this his favorite movie, but don't hold that against it. In its dopey and predictable way, it's quite entertaining – and one of the sequences, involving a malfunctioning torpedo tube, is heart-pounding. Also, the depiction of normal submarine operations is fascinating and authentic-feeling, and some of the underwater sequences are excellent. Based on a bestselling thriller by Alistair MacLean, the Cold War plot concerns the errant mission of an early spy satellite. Back then such spacecraft took reconnaissance photos on rolls of film and then ejected canisters that parachuted back to Earth, where either U.S. or Soviet Union operatives would have to retrieve them. But in this story a Russian canister veers off course and ends up near a British polar "weather" station. Soon, contact is lost with the station, and a U.S. Navy submarine is dispatched on a secret mission to investigate and recover the canister. Of course there are many complications, double-crosses, confrontations and crises, but all in all it's not bad fluff – though much of the dialogue is dopey as can be. With Rock Hudson as the stiff and formal submarine commander, former football great Jim Brown as an SOB of a commando,

Patrick McGoohan (star of the British TV series Secret Agent) as an even bigger SOB of a … secret agent, and Ernest Borgnine as a former Russian agent – whose accent borders on the ridiculous – now supposedly working for us. Veteran French composer Michel Legrand contributed the classy score. [Trivia note: How big a fan was Hughes of this movie? Before VCRs and DVDs, there was no way for ordinary people to screen a favorite title unless it was showing at a theater or on TV. So Hughes, living in Las Vegas at the time, bought a local station and ordered it to show *Ice Station Zebra* each late night – more than 100 times in all. Whether Hughes was passionately devoted or weirdly obsessed is speculative. But given everything else now known about him, it's a good guess which] **[W]**

Where Eagles Dare
1968 – Brian G. Hutton
Another Alistair MacLean story, this one's set among the gorgeous peaks of the Bavarian Alps. In World War II, the Nazis have captured an American general who knows the secret plans for the forthcoming invasion of Europe. So British intelligence sends a hand-picked team to the Schloss Adler, the impregnable citadel holding the spy, to rescue or kill him. In charge is Major Jonathan Smith (Richard Burton), an intelligence officer who just might be a double agent. He's accompanied by an American explosives expert, Lieutenant Morris Schaffer (Clint Eastwood), who can also kill coldly and methodically. Then … oh, never mind. It's standard wartime-thriller fare, with double-crosses and triple-crosses galore, and the extended escape becomes more and more preposterous as it unfolds. Still, the landscapes are spectacular, and the assault on the citadel is knuckle-whitening. [Viewing note: If you've seen *The Guns of Navarone*, the best movie version of MacLean's best novel, you'll notice several plot similarities; e.g., the protagonists impersonating Nazis to penetrate a heavily defended German fortress, two characters desperately attempting to clasp hands to prevent one of them falling from a great height, a mellow musical interlude preceding a violent attack, deadly booby traps involving

explosives, et cetera] [Trivia note: In case you're interested, Eastwood's character kills more men here than in any other of his movies] [Caution: violence and vertigo-inducing suspense] **[W]**

Airport 1975
1974 – Jack Smight
The original *Airport* was a clunky but genuinely entertaining big-budget disaster movie based on Arthur Hailey's bestselling novel. This one, adapted from Hailey's sequel, is just plain clunky. It quickly descends into standard fare but still delivers some fun and silly thrills. The plot involves an airliner in jeopardy, of course. This time it's because a small plane (piloted by Dana Andrews, who suffers a fatal heart attack at the controls) has crashed into the cockpit of a giant Boeing 747, blinding the pilot and killing the co-pilot. On top of that, the plane is headed straight for the Rocky Mountains, so if someone doesn't figure out a way to get another pilot aboard the aircraft, it's going to crash into a peak or fall out of the sky. So who's the hero this time? None other than Charlton Heston, aided by George Kennedy, reprising his role as Joe Patroni, the crack aircraft mechanic who saves the day – but not before stewardess Karen Black gets to put on her best terrified face. There's some pretty good aerial footage involving a real 747 flying very low across the mountainous landscape, plus a tense rescue sequence involving a helicopter and a stuntman on a cable, but most of the dialogue will leave you howling. [Viewing note: If you'd like to do an interesting double feature sometime, watch this one first and follow it with *Airplane!* (a fun title and coming in the next compilation), some of whose parodies are strikingly similar] [Trivia note: Martha Scott was a fine actress, but for some reason she kept getting stuck in movies with Heston in thankless roles, playing his long-suffering mother in *The Ten Commandments* and his even more grievously suffering mother in *Ben-Hur*. No suffering here, but she's in an inferior role as a nun] **[W]**

Earthquake (and) The Towering Inferno
1974 – Mark Robson (and) John Guillermin

If you've got a weakness for cheesy disaster movies with big-name casts, they must have heard about you when they made these two. In *Earthquake*, Universal Studios' penny-pinching attempt to portray a catastrophic temblor hitting Los Angeles includes such special effects as shaking the camera, painting the film red to suggest spurting blood and dropping obvious Styrofoam debris onto the extras. One of the most amazing things about *Earthquake*, which lured audiences with a new audio system called "Sensurround" – basically a deep bass signal that produced vibrations you could feel as well as hear – was how truly bad the effects turned out to be. There's not a single "wow" moment in the whole two hours and odd minutes. Here's Charlton Heston again, playing an engineer who's stuck in a troubled marriage with Ava Garner but who falls for young widow Geneviève Bujold. In the middle of working out his feelings, and with another half-dozen subplots in midstream – including a couple of lethal foreshadows – all hell breaks loose. Still, there is a morbid fascination with the whole thing, and Heston's *Airport 1975* buddy George Kennedy provides some good moments as a cranky cop. But it's Walter Matthau (listed as "Walter Matuschanskayasky" – *not* his real name – in the credits) who had the right idea. He plays a drunk who basically slumbers through the whole movie, except in one brief scene when his character is supposed to dance, in which case he's replaced by a hoofing double.

Then there's *The Towering Inferno*, which was jointly produced by 20th-Century Fox and Warner Bros., and stars Paul Newman and Steve McQueen. Here, in a tragically prophetic scenario, a fire breaks out on the 81st floor of the world's tallest building, and the race is on to rescue, among others, the people trapped at a party 50 floors above the fire. Naturally, some will make it and some won't in a cast that includes the venerable William Holden, the even more venerable Fred Astaire (who, amazing as it seems, garnered his only Oscar nomination for this one), and the loosely clothed Faye Dunaway. Actually, this is one of McQueen's best roles, because he acts like he really cares whether those in danger will be rescued. The great John Williams, who was Universal's house composer at the time, provided the completely unremarkable scores for both movies – but at least he had nothing to do with *The Towering Inferno*'s wretched theme song, "We Will Never Pass This Way Again," performed by Maureen McGovern during the party scene. Yes, it won an Oscar for Best Song, but ecch!

Why watch these two clunkers? For one thing, eventually you'll realize they're depicting essentially the same plot formula played out in different scenarios. In *Earthquake*, Heston's an engineer who works on skyscrapers. In the *Towering Inferno*, Paul Newman's an architect who designs skyscrapers. In *Earthquake*, George Kennedy and several of the cast members complain about overly ambitious developers constructing too-tall buildings in quake zones. In *The Towering Inferno* Steve McQueen, as the fire chief of San Francisco (the movie's locale), warns about the dangers of fires in high-rise buildings. In *Earthquake*, Heston's character rails against a developer who won't abide by building-safety codes. In *The Towering Inferno*, Newman's character rails against ... well, you get the idea, and you might even want to watch random pieces of the two movies – particularly during the disaster and rescue sequences – to see if you can figure out which title is which. Both feature scenes where building windows must be broken to solve an emergency. Both contain hair-raising attempts by characters trying to descend damaged stairwells while hanging precariously far above the ground. Both contain climaxes involving torrents of water. And if you watch both, you might never want to get into an elevator again. Which do I rate higher? *The Towering Inferno*, because former Oscar-winner Stirling Silliphant's script is more technically astute than former Oscar-winner Mario Puzo's for *Earthquake* – but it's a small distinction. By the way, remember that hilarious line I mentioned in *The Ten Commandments*? There's something similar at the end of *The Towering Inferno* involving Astaire and a living memento of his lost love. That one I'm not giving away. [<u>Academy Awards note</u>: As mentioned,

Fred Astaire was nominated for an Oscar for his supporting performance in *The Towering Inferno*. Add this insult to the long list of the motion picture academy's everlasting shame in not nominating one of its greatest stars for at least one of his immortal performances over a five-decade-long career. Has there ever been anyone in the history of the movies who gave such pleasure to audiences?] [Caution: hokey violence, mild sexuality and fleeting profanity – in both titles] **[W]**

King Kong (1976)
John Guillermin

"Here's to the big one," says oil company executive Fred Wilson (Charles Grodin) in a toast at the beginning of the movie as he sets sail for a secret island supposedly hiding a major oil field. That's exactly what producer Dino De Laurentiis was hoping this remake of the 1933 classic would do at box offices the year after *Jaws* had posted the biggest box-office grosses to date. Despite its lavish budget, however, and its state-of-the-art movie tricks, the new Kong turns out to be a lumbering dud. But that isn't to say it isn't fun to watch, and it offers two attractive features: Rick Baker's portrayal of the great ape, and yet another fine score by composer John Barry. Jeff Bridges and Jessica Lange (in her debut role) do decently as the romantic couple, but Grodin heavily overplays things, and the script is laughable. There's also the matter of the climax, which takes place at the World Trade Center and at the time was meant to outdo the finale of the original at the Empire State Building. Now, it's one of many movies whose images of the ill-fated towers bring a twinge of sorrow at the real tragedy that took place there on September 11, 2001. [Trivia note: Like many movies depicting jungle or exotic locales, parts of this one were filmed along the magnificent Napali Coast on the Hawai`ian island of Kaua`i] [Caution: violence and fleeting glimpses of Lange's bare torso] **[W]**

Star Trek: The Motion Picture
1979 – Robert Wise

Along with Steven Spielberg's *1941* (coming in a future compilation), the other major cinematic disaster of 1979 was the long-awaited, big-screen version of the legendary TV series, and for two stretches of … oh, five minutes each, it pays off big-time. The rest is a colossal mess, although it can be enjoyed if viewed as sort of an unintentionally gay space opera. William Shatner moves to the big screen in an embarrassingly overblown performance as Captain James T. Kirk. Time and time again he utters such groaners as "Bones, I need you" or, referring to Mr. Spock (Leonard Nimoy), "Bones, I need him – I need him bad!" There's also the scene in which Kirk is reunited with his beloved starship Enterprise, and he stares at its form so longingly you think he's going to either swoon or have an orgasm. And there's a scene where Kirk, ordering Sulu (James Takei) to move the starship out of its dry dock, says dreamily, "Take us out." Et cetera. But let's cut to the chase: Shatner is awful here. What else is wrong? Where to begin? There's the matter of the costumes, which feature something that resembles a device huckstered on late-night TV commercials at the time. Worn on the midsection, it was supposed to promote weight loss – I think they called it a "Tummy Tucker" or "Belly Buster," or something like that. Wise, who directed the sci-fi classic *The Day the Earth Stood Still*, as well as Best-Picture Oscar winners *West Side Story* (not on this list) and *The Sound of Music*, seems to have missed a lot of the shoot here, because most of the time the actors appear listless, confused or ridiculous. <u>Case in point</u>: The ship has just settled back down after a rough ride through a wormhole, but apparently no one told actress Persis Khambatta (playing Ilia, a female alien who apparently can make grown men's knees wobble merely by standing nearby) there was no need to keep bouncing around in her chair. It's true! Those two good parts? There's a nifty but all-too-brief opening sequence featuring the dreaded Klingons, and there's Douglas Trumbull's awesome visualization of the alien spacecraft (a much bigger but grungier version of his optical creations for *Close Encounters of the Third*

153

Kind two years earlier). Also, despite its dopiness, the movie looks consistently grand, Jerry Goldsmith's entirely adequate score lends grace throughout, and Nimoy's portrayal of Spock is dignified as always. [Trivia notes: 1) This fiasco is a remake of an episode of the original TV series called "The Changeling." 2) I attended the world premiere of the movie at the old MacArthur Theater in Washington with Gary Arnold and with Tom Shales, The Washington Post's TV critic. Shatner and the rest of the cast attended as well – none of whom had seen the finished movie. Suffice it to say that the enthusiastic smiles on their faces before the screening had tensed up considerably by the time the show ended] **[W]**

The Final Countdown
1980 – Don Taylor

You might wonder how on earth this movie's premise ever got to the screen without someone in authority saying, "Forget it, this is ridiculous!" The sci-fi, time-travel plot involves the aircraft carrier U.S.S. Nimitz sailing out of Honolulu's Pearl Harbor on a routine patrol in the South Pacific and encountering a strange and intense atmospheric disturbance. It turns out to be a time warp that sends the carrier and its battle group back to – guess when? – Saturday, December 6, 1941. No need to get into the story details further. Instead, consider that the movie contains a scene in which Martin Sheen (who played, among other distinguished roles, Confederate General Robert E. Lee in *Gettysburg*) actually holds his hands over a dog's ears in a bed. Let me repeat that: He's in bed with a dog and he's covering its ears. Kirk Douglas does well as the captain of the Nimitz despite the nonsensical plot, and James Farentino and Katharine Ross aren't bad as, respectively, a naval historian and a pioneering career woman. The best parts involve seeing the real work done by the crew of the Nimitz, plus some terrific aerial sequences showing F-14 Tomcat fighters in action, including dogfighting – and out-flying – World War II-era Japanese warplanes. [Viewing note: If this one doesn't interest you, or even if you do watch it, consider investing some time in the truly riveting PBS documentary series, Carrier, which coincidentally was also shot aboard the Nimitz. Produced in late 2002 when the ship was dispatched to support Operation Iraqi Freedom, it provides a memorable look at the young men and women whose labors keep that awesome warship humming] **[W]**

Independence Day
1996 – Roland Emmerich

Talk about forgetting logic – don't even let it enter your head here! Forget science as well. But if you do, you'll find this special-effects extravaganza entertaining and eminently watchable. Just sit back and enjoy the wild ride for two hours and assorted minutes, and you might even find yourself inexplicably moved from time to time. A gigantic alien craft enters orbit around Earth and releases more than a dozen city-sized spaceships that descend to and float ominously above the world's major metropolises. As the earthlings try to figure out how to react, the aliens attack and, for a while, things look truly hopeless – until one maverick genius figures out their weakness. Enough detail, but let's just say the solution involves a witty and updated if implausible twist on the plot of H.G. Wells's classic novel The War of the Worlds. With Jeff Goldblum as the genius, Judd Hirsch as his wisecracking and excruciatingly stereotypical Jewish father, Will Smith exercising considerable star power as a gutsy Air Force fighter pilot, Randy Quaid as a lunatic-fringe former alien abductee, Bill Pullman as a surprisingly appealing U.S. president, Mary McDonnell in a thankless role as the first lady, and Brent Spiner (Lt. Commander Data on the Star Trek: The Next Generation television series) as a scientist who seems to have been kept under wraps a bit too long. David Arnold supplied the brassy score. [Trivia note: Many of the effects used miniature models and high-speed cameras instead of computer-generated imagery (aka CGI), which has become the industry standard today. In fact, the producers have claimed they used twice as many miniatures in this movie than had ever been used before. **[W]**

6. Breaking In or Breaking Through

Here I offer a quartet of entertaining examples of directors and acting ensembles either at the beginning of their careers or on the brink of stardom.

American Graffiti
1973 – George Lucas

This was one of the first movies to capitalize on Baby Boomer nostalgia. It harkens back to those innocent days when teens hung out at burger joints, listened surreptitiously to rock 'n' roll, and drove endlessly each summer evening along the local commercial strip. The cast includes future Oscar-winner Richard Dreyfuss; future megastar Harrison Ford; future Oscar-winning director Ron Howard; future TV stars Cindy Williams, Suzanne Somers and MacKenzie Phillips; and versatile character actors Charles Martin Smith, Kathleen Quinlan, Candy Clark, Paul Lemat and Joe Spano, most in their debut roles. The plot is simple: Two friends (Howard and Dreyfuss) are planning to leave their small California town for college the next morning, but they want to spend one last night cruising the streets for old times' sake. Of course, things get complicated and don't turn out quite as expected. Lucas grew up in Modesto, California, in the early 1960s, and he based this story on his youth. It's his love letter to a bygone era, featuring 41 songs from the period as background to the action, many of them heard acoustically either on car radios or playing from some vague source on the streets. The formula has been tried many times since – including the epilogue, which oddly lists only what happens to the male characters in the future; not the females – but *American Graffiti* remains the proud original. [Trivia note: The movie might have stayed unreleased in the Universal Studios archive if Francis Ford Coppola – newly flush from his success with *The Godfather* the previous year – had not written a check to cover the $750,000 production cost to guarantee against a loss at the box office. It was a good bet, because *American Graffiti* became one of the biggest hits of the year, and Lucas accrued enough leverage to begin his next project, a space adventure called *Star Wars*] [Caution: mild profanity and a few glimpses of Candy Clark's panties] **[W]**

Breaking Away
1979 – Peter Yates
Cycling enthusiast Steve Tesich wrote this thoroughly delightful tale about coming of age – and aging – in Bloomington, Indiana, in the 1970s. A quartet of young friends (Dennis Christopher, Dennis Quaid, Daniel Stern and Jackie Earl Haley) resolve to resist doing anything their first year out of high school that resembles growing up or acting responsibly. The problem is, they are constantly reminded of their limited opportunities by the kids who attend Indiana University, also located in Bloomington, and they deal with it in different ways. The story centers on David Stoller (Christopher), who dreams of becoming a competitive cyclist and idolizes everything Italian, to the chagrin of his father (Paul Dooley, in a wonderfully cranky performance overlooked at Oscar time), but the approval of his mother (Barbara Barrie, who at least was nominated). It's a simple story told very well, with fine, sympathetic direction by Yates and a soundtrack featuring Felix Mendelssohn's lovely "Italian Symphony" and related melodies. Watch for future screen stalwarts John Ashton and Hart Bochner in minor roles. [Trivia notes: 1) Screenwriter Tesich based Stoller's character on a real resident of Bloomington who was a cycling enthusiast, loved all things Italian and won the "Little 500" race after riding the majority of the laps. 2) Tesich, along with Barrie and Haley in the cast, created a TV series based on the movie. But it lasted only one season] [Caution: mild profanity] **[W]**

157

Diner
1982 – Barry Levinson

This is the best of the bunch. It's a richer and deeper story than *American Graffiti*, with on the whole a more talented director and cast, including future stars (onscreen or TV) Kevin Bacon, Ellen Barkin, Timothy Daly, Steve Gutenberg, Paul Rieser, Daniel Stern and Mickey Rourke in mostly debut roles. Like George Lucas, Levinson based the story on his youth, in this case in Baltimore in the 1950s. Where *Graffiti* had no specific locale as its center, much of *Diner*'s action takes place ... well, in a diner, the Fells Point Diner, which no longer existed in 1982 so it had to be re-created in New Jersey. Another difference is that the main characters are a bit older than their *Graffiti* counterparts. All are either working or in college, and one couple (Barkin and Stern) is married. But that doesn't mean they've got life figured out. In fact, in one late scene, Bacon says to Rourke, "You get the idea that there's stuff goin' on we don't know about?" Indeed, there is. Like *American Graffiti*, the movie features a soundtrack full of great and memorable songs from the period. [Caution: rough language and some sexuality, including a raunchy stunt with a box of popcorn] **[W]**

The Big Chill
1983 – Lawrence Kasdan

This ensemble vehicle frequently veers toward cliché, but it never topples entirely and ends up being quite likable. Seven University of Michigan students from the 1960s reunite on the occasion of the funeral for one of their own, a suicide victim. Five of the friends – a likable but unsatisfied TV star (Tom Berenger), a jaded correspondent for People magazine (Jeff Goldblum), a lawyer with sagging ideals (Mary Kay Place), an unhappily married housewife (JoBeth Williams) and a Vietnam veteran turned drug dealer (William Hurt) – travel to Beaufort, South Carolina, for the event, which has happened at the home of the only two members of the group to have married: the owner of a chain of running-shoe stores (Kevin Kline) and a physician (Glenn Close). Over the course of a weekend, the old

158

friends socialize, argue, engage in some soul-searching – while enjoying a sexual liaison or two – and finally reconnect. Sentimental and often predictable, it still has considerable charm – and it features yet another soundtrack array of songs, this time from the sixties. [Trivia notes: 1) The dead friend, Alex, was supposed to be played by Kevin Costner, but Kasdan eventually edited his part out of the movie. As a consolation, Kasdan gave Costner what became his breakthrough role, as the free-spirited, fast-drawing, straight-shooting Jake in *Silverado*. 2) The house in Beaufort, South Carolina, where most of the movie was shot, became overrun with fans in the ensuing years, to the point where the real owners had to erect extra fencing and warning signs. I know this because Jessie and I visited that house 16 years later. Even on a weekday afternoon, gawkers (including us) were driving by, stopping for a closer look and taking photos. Keep this in mind if anyone ever approaches you about shooting a movie on your property] [Caution: language and sexuality] **[W]**

7. This Is Why They Call Them 'Stars'

Some movies mark the beginning of stardom, and some mark the end of an illustrious career, but these five titles serve as validation of the popularity and durability of their lead performers. The story or direction might be flawed, but as long as these stars populate the screen, you're likely to keep your eyes on it – and them.

Arabesque
1966 – Gregory Peck and Sophia Loren

Three years after he directed the superlative romantic thriller *Charade*, with Cary Grant and Audrey Hepburn, Stanley Donen returned to the genre, bringing along from that production Peter Stone as co-writer, Henry Mancini as composer and Maurice Binder to do the main titles. And for his stars he used Peck and Loren, both at the peak of their popularity and physical appeal. Peck plays Professor David Pollock, (PAW-leck), an archaeologist hired to decipher an inscription on a small piece of parchment, while Loren, as Yasmin Azir, takes on Grant's role as the mysterious character who seems to be helpful but also might be one of the bad guys. Whichever side she's on, though, she's positively luminous, and the interplay between these two glamorous stars more than makes up for the muddled and formulaic plot and climax. It's a trifle, and not nearly as much fun as *Charade*, but it definitely has its moments. [Trivia note: It's common for stars to use stunt doubles in potentially dangerous scenes, and *Arabesque* is no exception. But Gregory Peck's double, Vic Armstrong, is notable because that was his first stunt performance and, as of this writing in 2018, he's still working] [Caution: violence] **[W]**

All the President's Men
1976 – Robert Redford and Dustin Hoffman

Director Alan Pakula's faithful recreation of the bestselling book by Carl Bernstein and Bob Woodward turns Hoffman and Redford into reasonable impersonations of the two Washington Post reporters. The story chronicles their quest to solve a political scandal involving the Nixon Administration in the early seventies – a case of presidential overreach and deception that came to be called Watergate and eventually led to President Richard Nixon's resignation. It begins as a rather shady crew breaks into the Democratic party's national headquarters in the Watergate complex – hence the scandal's moniker. They are caught and arrested, and Woodward (Redford) is assigned to cover their arraignment. He very quickly suspects there might be far more to this "third-rate burglary," as it was called at the time by White House press secretary Ron Zeigler. So the editors at the Post assign him to follow the story. They also pair him with Bernstein (Hoffman), an ambitious but marginal player in the newsroom. From there, the two reporters doggedly strive to crack the case, though their success depends greatly on information from a secret source that Woodward had once cultivated in the administration. The Post editors nickname him "Deep Throat." With Jason Robards, Jr., in an Oscar-winning turn as Post Editor Ben Bradlee, Martin Balsam as Managing Editor Howard Simons, and Jack Warden as Metro Editor Harry Rosenfeld. [Trivia notes: 1) Woodward protected the identity of Deep Throat for three decades, until an aged and ailing Mark Felt spilled the beans that he was the legendary source. Felt, former Deputy Director of the FBI, leaked important and scandalous information to Woodward not entirely out of a sense of patriotism but apparently out of spite, because President Nixon had not chosen him to replace J. Edgar Hoover as director. 2) In his quest for accuracy, Pakula insisted on shooting at real locations whenever possible. So, for the scene in which Woodward and Bernstein visit former Nixon aide Hugh Sloan, Pakula filmed a couple of exterior scenes at Sloan's actual house at the time, which happens to be located in my neighborhood in

McLean, Virginia. A decade later, my parents rented that same house for two years. 3) Redford and Robards had worked together for the first time 16 years earlier when they did a live TV production of Eugene O'Neill's downer of a play, "The Ice Man Cometh." 4) Regarding working together, here's another little bit o' trivia. Hoffman romanced Katharine Ross in *The Graduate* in his first major movie role, while Redford romanced her two years later in *Butch Cassidy and the Sundance Kid*] [Caution: rough language – this was the movie that thoroughly the "F" word into the medium's lexicon] **[W]**

Trading Places
1983 – Eddie Murphy
Technically, Murphy shares top billing with Dan Aykroyd in this frequently crude comedy, just as he did with Nick Nolte in the dreadful *48 Hrs.* (not on this list) the previous year. But he ends up outshining Aykroyd as well as everyone else in the cast. He plays Billy Ray Valentine, a hustler who ekes out a living by conning passersby on the streets of Philadelphia. Aykroyd, meanwhile, is Louis Winthorpe III, the snobby scion of Main Line wealth in the employ of the Dukes brothers (veteran actors Ralph Bellamy and Don Ameche), who are even wealthier commodities traders. Louis lives high and well in his Philadelphia brownstone, tended by his manservant Coleman (Denholm Elliott) and engaged to the beautiful and equally snobby Penelope (Kristin Holby). Then the plot intervenes, and soon Louis ends up penniless and dependent on the largesse of Ophelia (Jamie Lee Curtis), a proverbial hooker with a heart of gold, while Billy Ray takes over Louis's house and Coleman. From there it's a question of who ends up on top, so to speak. The movie, as expected from director John Landis, is sometimes downright offensive. But there's something inarguably appealing about Murphy. No matter what he does, you can never dislike him. Elmer Bernstein's score, the beginning of which uses Mozart's sprightly opera "The Marriage of Figaro," pays subtle homage to some of his previous work. [Trivia note: This movie also features former comedian Al Franken, who

162

became a U.S. senator from Minnesota before being forced to resign in disgrace after a series of sexual mishaps. He's listed in the cast as "Baggage Handler #1."] [Viewing note: I think the moviemakers missed a potential crowd-pleaser by choosing an obvious ending. Without giving away too much, after you see the movie, consider this alternative: a reprise of the Duke's introductory sequence, but with Louis and Billy Ray now replacing *them* – and treating the entire household staff quite differently] [Caution: sexuality and rough language] **[W]**

Beverly Hills Cop
1984 – Eddie Murphy

Murphy, who made his debut as a regular on Saturday Night Live on NBC-TV, becomes a certified star in this one. He plays Axel Foley, a detective from Detroit who drives to Beverly Hills, California, to investigate the murder of his best friend. It's an update on the clash-of-cultures formula, with Murphy mugging for the camera in reaction to some of the flamboyant characters that inhabit this exclusive section of Los Angeles, but he displays genuine appeal with his comic antics, and he's convincing as a serious cop. Director Martin Brest, doing his second feature, exhibits an assurance beyond his experience, and he stages a thrilling chase at the opening involving a double-semi trailer, a city bus, dozens of unfortunate automobiles and one very brave stunt double. John Ashton and Judge Reinhold offer solid comic support as members of the Beverly Hills Police Department assigned to keep Axel in line, Ronnie Cox as a detective captain is a good straight man for Murphy's hijinks, and Harold Faltermeyer's throbbing, synthesized music is contagious. Still, the movie is all Murphy's. [Trivia notes: 1) Brest directed only six features, including *Midnight Run*, one of my favorites – also co-starring John Ashton – but before he had even graduated from the American Film Institute's Center for Advanced Film Study, he wowed movie buffs and critics all over the country with his student production, *Hot Tomorrows*. 2) Playwright and veteran actor Steven Berkoff, the smooth but ruthless villain here, four years later played the ultimate villain, Adolf Hitler, in

163

the sprawling TV epic sequel miniseries War and Remembrance]
[Caution: frequent crude language, sexuality and violence] **[W]**

A Few Good Men
1992 – Jack Nicholson and Tom Cruise
This is a gripping courtroom drama based on Aaron Sorkin's
play (he also wrote the screenplay, with some uncredited help
from William Goldman) about a fictional trial of two U.S.
Marines stationed at Guantanamo Naval Base in Cuba (this was
back in the days when "Gitmo" served only as a base for the
Caribbean area and had not been converted into a detention
center for suspected Islamic terrorists). The Marines (James
Marshall and Wolfgang Bodison) are accused of deliberately
causing the death of a comrade. Set to defend them is Lieutenant
Daniel Kaffee (Cruise), son of a renowned jurist, who has been
living a comfortable life in Washington as a military defense
attorney, priding himself on being able to settle cases without
setting foot in a courtroom. His main quarry is Colonel Nathan
R. Jessup (Nicholson), the base commander, who is suspected of
secretly ordering the accused to conduct a severe hazing that
accidentally resulted in the death. Actually, Cruise and
Nicholson are onscreen together only for a two relatively brief
scenes, but when they are the sparks fly. Say what you want
about Cruise, but there's no doubt he's a major acting talent, and
here he's able to hold his own with one of the biggest stars
Hollywood has ever produced (Nicholson was nominated, for
the 10th time, for Best Supporting Actor for his role), including
giving a witty, dead-on, unscripted impersonation of him. And
speaking of holding one's own, Bodison, playing Lance Corporal
Harold Dawson, contributes a sensational debut. He bests Cruise
nearly every time they appear onscreen together. [Trivia note:
The movie trial is based on a real case that occurred at
Guantanamo] [Caution: rough language and intensity] **[W]**

8. Big Stars, But Have You Seen Them in...?

All 10 of these movies feature actors with big names, but you might not be familiar with the titles. Give them a try, just the same.

Jim Thorpe – All American
1951 – Burt Lancaster

Born in Oklahoma to parents who were both half Native Americans (his father half Irish and his mother half French), Jim Thorpe was thought to be the greatest athlete in the world in the early part of the 20th century. Even as a boy, "Bright Path" – as his Indian name translates – could run like the wind. He once raced home more than 10 miles on foot to beat his father, who was driving a horse-drawn buckboard. Under the guidance of legendary coach Glenn S. "Pop" Warner at the Carlisle Indian Industrial School in Carlisle, Pennsylvania, Thorpe excelled in many sports, particularly football. He also won the pentathlon and decathlon events in the 1912 Olympics in Stockholm, Sweden. But when the Olympic Committee discovered that Thorpe had played semi-professional baseball for two summers – where he wasn't paid a salary but given room, board and expenses – they stripped him of his gold medals and sent him on a steep descent into depression and alcoholism. Few actors at the time possessed the physique and energy to play such a demanding role, but Lancaster accomplished this portrayal with ease. He's entirely convincing as Thorpe, with just a little help from camera tricks and some real newsreel footage, and he's well supported by Charles Bickford as Warner. It's a memorable and moving portrait of a tragic but heroic American story. [Trivia notes: 1) Among Thorpe's unprecedented talents, he also

165

turned out to be a pretty fair ballroom dancer. 2) Despite his travails, Thorpe also seemed to retain a sense of humor. Once, as a professional football player, he encountered an opponent who would resort to gouging and biting during the game. During a timeout, Thorpe reportedly tapped the man on the shoulder and said, "Sir. *I'm* supposed to be the savage here."] **[B&W] [W]**

Trapeze
1956 – Burt Lancaster, Tony Curtis and Gina Lollobrigida
Lancaster spent his early professional days as a circus performer, and it shows here – he looks at home in the rigging, and it lends quite an air of authenticity to the aerial scenes. Though transported to the Big Top, the plot is quite standard: The professional relationship between aging veteran Lancaster and talented upstart Curtis is threatened by their rivalry for the affections of the voluptuous Lollobrigida, who looks as good in a circus costume as anyone I can think of. That said, *Trapeze* is an affecting tale, and Curtis, without extensive training, looks completely believable as a flier. Come to think of it, so does Lollobrigida, and there are plenty of moments where the three stars are actually performing well above the ground. All three also benefited from the direction of Carol Reed, who staged almost every scene as though the love triangle was taking place in the midst of a crowd's worth of activity. [Trivia note: Curtis once credited this movie for planting his career on solid ground and leading to several distinctive dramatic roles, including his runaway prisoner chained to Sidney Poitier in *The Defiant Ones* two years later (not on this list), for which he received an Oscar nomination] **[W]**

The Devil's Disciple
1959 – Burt Lancaster, Kirk Douglas and Laurence Olivier
This screen version of George Bernard Shaw's play remains somewhat stagy, but its three stars manage to give it some pizzazz. Lancaster's role here is much more subdued than in *Trapeze*, but his physique hasn't diminished in the intervening three years. He plays the Reverend Anthony Anderson, a peace-

166

loving man with a beautiful but repressed young wife (Janette Scott) who tries as hard as he can to stay out of a scrap between the cynical and rebellious Dick Dudgeon (Douglas, in the title role) and the British general, "Gentlemanly Johnny" Burgoyne (Olivier), who is determined to hang Dudgeon. Eventually, though, Anderson is drawn into the fray, and the transformation is substantial. Suddenly, you feel as though he could whip the whole British army single-handedly. It's an entertaining trifle, and it's interesting to see Douglas and Olivier spar verbally a year before they do it much more seriously and mortally in *Spartacus*. The director is Guy Hamilton, who did several of the early James Bond movies, including the best of them all, *Goldfinger*. **[B&W] [W]**

The Candidate
1972 – Robert Redford
This political movie, directed by Michael Ritchie and shot in semi-documentary style, has a great punch line, posed in the form of a question – which I won't spoil for you. Redford plays Bill McKay, the son of a former California governor who is persuaded to run for the U.S. Senate by an ambitious campaign manager (Peter Boyle, in his best role). The story follows how the candidate is gradually seasoned, and coarsened, by the political process. In fact, the original premise of the movie was to portray a decent candidate who risks losing his soul to win an election – some things never change. There are several good sequences, including footage of real political figures mixed in with the fictional material. With Melvyn Douglas as the sly old political fox of a father, Don Porter as the stodgy incumbent senator, Allen Garfield as a wisecracking media specialist, and former Redford co-star Natalie Wood playing herself in a cameo. [Trivia note: If Redford ever considered beginning a real political career, he might have felt some encouragement via this movie. Released in California shortly before the presidential primary of that year, Redford's character McKay actually received some write-in votes in the election] [Caution: language] **[W]**

167

Serpico
1973 – Al Pacino

In the late 1960s, NYPD, the New York Police Department, seethed with corruption. Cops took payoffs from gamblers, numbers runners and drug dealers, and sometimes tens of thousands of dollars changed hands. A young officer named Frank Serpico joined the force at the time and carried an unusual trait: honesty. Though quickly shunned by his fellow officers and ultimately betrayed, Serpico managed to pave the way for badly needed departmental investigations and housecleanings. Under Sidney Lumet's assured direction, Pacino took on the title role in between his years as Michael Corleone in *The Godfather* parts I and II, and he delivers a ferocious performance as an entirely different kind of character, painting a stark portrait of a tormented man in an organization full of men who eased their own inner demons with bribes and denial. It's a rough-edged and somewhat episodic story, written by Waldo Salt based on Peter Maas's biography, mixing Serpico's travails on the job with his efforts to get city officials to take on the corruption, his bumpy domestic life – which the movie fictionalizes and compresses, giving him a brief fling with a girlfriend (Cornelia Sharpe) and a deeper relationship with a would-be spouse (Barbara Eda-Young) that ends badly – and his ever-more-flamboyant wardrobe and facial hairstyles. But Pacino is well up to the task, and the movie proves a good prelude to his triumph with Lumet two years later in *Dog Day Afternoon*. [Trivia note: The real Serpico, now in his eighties, has spent decades attempting to help other, honest law-enforcement officers fight corruption in their agencies] [Caution: sexuality and plentiful profanity and violence] **[W]**

Whose Life Is It Anyway?
1981 – Richard Dreyfuss

In some ways, this is a better performance by Dreyfuss than his Oscar-winning turn in *The Goodbye Girl* four years earlier, because it is more assured, mature and affecting. Based on Brian Clark's play (Clark also wrote the script), Dreyfuss plays Ken

Harrison, a successful sculptor who becomes totally paralyzed in an automobile accident. As he begins to come to terms with his disability, he decides it would be better to die than live the rest of his life as a quadriplegic. The problem is, he is still in the hospital, and the staff – particularly Dr. Michael Emerson (John Cassavetes) – refuses to approve his discharge. Therein begins the legal battle for control of Harrison's destiny and a truly thought-provoking examination of the conflicts that arise, both personal and institutional, when an individual attempts to exercise the supreme decision – in Shakespeare's words, to be or not to be. John Badham directed the fine cast, including Christine Lahti as a sympathetic doctor, Bob Balaban as Harrison's lawyer, and Kenneth McMillan as the judge who must hear the case. [Trivia note: My comment about the quality of Dreyfuss's performance is highly ironic, because during the production Dreyfuss was still heavily involved in his drug habit, and he has claimed not even to remember playing the role] [Caution: profanity and nudity] **[W]**

Nothing in Common
1986 – Tom Hanks
Before this movie, Hanks had been associated entirely with TV and screen comedies. Here, he sports some comic moments as well, but his greater distinction is in making a smooth and affecting transition into drama. Hanks plays David Basner, a successful advertising executive in Chicago who's enjoying the good life as a bachelor. That is, until he receives a disruptive phone call from his father, Max (Jackie Gleason, in his second-best movie role), telling David that he and his mother (Eva Marie Saint, also in a fine role) have separated. Therein begins a change in both men that will leave them embattled and scarred but closer and devoted to each other. Hanks handles the dramatic role well – though he does sometimes lapse into Bill Murray territory on the comedic side – presaging his powerful performances in *Saving Private Ryan* and *Cast Away*, which ironically were not the two that earned him Best Actor Oscars. The strong supporting cast includes Sela Ward as a supremely

self-assured executive, Barry Corbin as the client Basner is trying to woo, and Bess Armstrong (who's appealing but can never seem to kiss a man onscreen without humming) as his off-again, on-again love interest. The crisp direction is by Garry Marshall, his best work. Oh, and Gleason's best role? As the pool shark (as in billiards) Minnesota Fats in *The Hustler*, which is not on this list but is a first-rate drama. [Trivia note: Seriously ill during the production, *Nothing in Common* turned out to be Jackie Gleason's last role – he died the following year] [Caution: profanity and sexuality] **[W]**

Peggy Sue Got Married
1986 – Kathleen Turner
This one could also fit in the upcoming category of little-known features by big-name directors, because that task went to none other than Francis Ford Coppola. But it's also appropriate here because it is one of the best things Kathleen Turner ever did. It's a time-travel fantasy, but the time-travel aspect takes a back seat to the fine character study of an unhappily married woman who literally gets a chance to go back 25 years and start over. Turner is supported by a fine cast, including Don Murray and Barbara Harris as her parents, and Hollywood veterans Leon Ames and Maureen O'Sullivan (immortalized as Jane in the *Tarzan* movies of the '30s and '40s) as her grandparents. There are also nice little turns by Helen Hunt, Katherine Hicks, Joan Allen and Jim Carrey at the beginning of their careers, and by Barry Miller as a nerdy classmate. The only wrong note is a blond-dyed Nicolas Cage as her boyfriend/husband, Charlie. Cage, who is Coppola's younger cousin – and who has shown himself to be a fine actor given the right role – is utterly ridiculous here. Along with the popular hits of the period, the soundtrack includes a sweetly sentimental background theme by John Barry, who also composed the moody, sexy score for Turner's smashing debut in *Body Heat*. [Trivia note: There's another Coppola involved in the movie: Sofia, daughter of Francis and future actress-writer-director, playing Peggy Sue's younger sister] **[W]**

Fat Man & Little Boy
1989 – Paul Newman
This fine movie depicts the frantic and super-secret effort of the
U.S. government to build an atomic bomb during World War II.
The title derives from two of the products of that effort. "Fat
Man" was the name of the second bomb, dropped on the
Japanese city of Nagasaki on August 9, 1945, while "Little Boy"
was the first, dropped on Hiroshima on August 6. Newman
plays General Leslie Groves, the man who had supervised
building the Pentagon, headquarters of the Department of
Defense, from 1941 to 1943. We meet him just as that project is
completed and he has been assigned the monumental task of
taking over the bomb effort, code named the Manhattan Project.
His two chief challenges are to build a large research facility at
Los Alamos, New Mexico, and to assemble and command the
team of atomic scientists to produce the weapon. At the head of
that team is Dr. Robert Oppenheimer (Dwight Schultz, in his
best role), a brilliant physicist who commands enough respect in
the scientific community to lead his colleagues in a task that
gives many of them profound reservations. This is a thoughtful,
adult treatment of that episode in history, made memorable by
Newman's terrifically intense performance. There's also a fine
acting job by John Cusack as Michael Merriman, a young and
conscientious but ill-fated member of the scientific team.
Likewise, Bonnie Bedelia, Natasha Richardson and Laura Dern
as, respectively, Oppenheimer's wife and his mistress, and
Merriman's love interest. It's a riveting, wrenching story of
people driven to create a terrible weapon in the hope of ending a
terrible, terrible war. The assured direction is by Roland Joffe.
[Caution: language and mild sexuality] **[W]**

The Insider
1999 – Russell Crowe and Al Pacino
Crowe had made a stunning debut two years earlier in *L.A.
Confidential* as Detective Bud White, but here he elevates himself
to that rarified company of the likes of Robert De Niro and
Daniel Day-Lewis – and in an earlier era, Spencer Tracy – as an

171

actor of tremendous range. Based on a true story, he plays Jeffrey Wigand, a research chemist employed by a major tobacco company who agrees to go public on 60 Minutes, the long-running weekly CBS television show, with one of the industry's dirty little secrets: they are manipulating the effectiveness of nicotine in cigarettes to strengthen their addictive hold on smokers. Crowe is perfectly believable as a good man torn between matters of conscience and the need to feed his family while suffering a shocking smear and intimidation campaign by his former employer and receiving less-than-total support from the network. He expresses every emotional facet of the ordeal that must have beset the real Wigand, and Crowe's acting is even more impressive because, 1) he performs opposite Pacino, who plays 60 Minutes line producer Lowell Bergman, and proves more than a match for his famous and supremely talented co-star; and 2) he plays a man 20 years older and 35 pounds heavier. With solid direction by Michael Mann and capable supporting roles by Diane Venora (who had played Pacino's wife in *Heat* four years earlier – also directed by Mann) as Wigand's on-the-verge wife; Philip Baker Hall as Don Hewitt, the TV show's legendary executive producer; Christopher Plummer as Mike Wallace, the show's imperious and equally legendary co-host; Lindsay Crouse as Bergman's quietly supportive wife; and British actor Michael Gambon as the tobacco company's sleazy CEO. It's first-rate, tense drama. The only notable flaw: a jarring and mostly inappropriate score by Pieter Bourke and Lisa Gerrard. [Trivia note: The story's outcome was more complicated than the movie portrayed. Yes, the class-action lawsuit brought against the four largest U.S. tobacco companies, in which Wigand's testimony played an important part, resulted in a settlement of over $200 billion plus severe restrictions on cigarette advertising. But the settlement also, essentially, protected big tobacco from future litigation, ensured the companies' continued prosperity and passed along the costs of the settlement to existing and future smokers] [Caution: plentiful profanity] **[W]**

9. The Face that Launched a Thousand Sighs

Skinny as a rail her entire adult life, how was it Audrey Hepburn could set so many male hearts aflutter? It was because, among the female stars of cinema, no one had a more beautiful, more appealing face, more sophisticated allure or a more fragile-looking nature. You couldn't help but gaze at her whenever she appeared onscreen. Along with *Charade*, I offer these four titles to support my assertion.

Roman Holiday
1953 – as Princess Ann
Hepburn's debut starring role benefited greatly from William Wyler's masterfully light directorial touch, as well as an uncharacteristically playful performance by Gregory Peck. Wyler overcame her on-camera nervousness by telling Peck to ham it up with her and having the cameras continue to run after he said "cut." The result was he got some wonderful spontaneous moments from the young actress when she thought the staged scene had ended. The motion picture academy agreed and awarded Hepburn an Oscar. Oh, the plot? She's a princess visiting Rome for the first time, and he's a journalist named Joe Bradley who's assigned to cover her. Eddie Albert co-stars as Peck's colleague and drinking buddy, and drinking plays a key part in the gossamer plot. That's enough – enjoy! [Trivia note: Dalton Trumbo wrote the screenplay, but he had been blacklisted for his suspected communist ties, so the credit went to Ian McClellan Hunter. Trumbo finally received credit, posthumously, in 1992] **[B&W]**

Sabrina
1954 – as Sabrina Fairchild

So, how can a movie be a comedy when it contains a scene — and early on, no less – in which the protagonist tries to kill herself by asphyxiation? In Billy Wilder's legendary directorial hands, it can, and the movie's as breezy as a comedy can get. Here, Hepburn is cast opposite an aging Humphrey Bogart and an utterly charming William Holden as, respectively, Linus and David Larrabee, brothers and sons of a Connecticut-based industrial tycoon. Sabrina is the chauffeur's daughter, and therefore she must pine for David from afar – hence the suicide attempt. But when she leaves for Paris and cooking school and then returns, all grown up, sophisticated and beautiful, suddenly both brothers become well aware of her presence. Meanwhile, the story buzzes with subplots involving David's family attempting to forge a financial merger by pushing him into marriage with the daughter (Vera Miles) of a rival financial concern, and Sabrina's shifting affections from David to Linus – and Linus's budding affections for Sabrina. Complicated? No really. As I mentioned, it's breezy and gossamer-light, and once again the young Hepburn benefits from a masterful director in Wilder. How will it turn out? Guess which brother punches the other, and guess which one finally gets Sabrina? I'm not telling. [B&W] [W]

Two for the Road
1967 – as Joanna Wallace

This was the second time Hepburn worked with director Stanley Donen (the first was in *Charade* four years earlier – which I'll get to shortly), and although their effort was not as successful, it still showcased Audrey's onscreen allure. It could be called "Scenes from an American Marriage," in reference to the great Swedish director Ingmar Bergman's episodic portrait of a couple. It follows Joanna and Mark Wallace (Albert Finney, in a much more mature role than in *Tom Jones*) through more than a decade of their relationship. But the story is not told sequentially. Instead, Donen and his editing tandem of Richard Marden and

174

Madeleine Gug (this was her only edit of an English-language movie), jump nimbly from the present to various points in the past to relate the couple's current emotions to past episodes in their lives. Sometimes it's done for laughs and other times for irony and poignancy, such as when a younger Joanna tells Mark that she will always love him, no matter what, and he tells her she may regret becoming involved with him. It isn't a particularly deep story, but it is attractively stylized and involving, the emotions ring true, and Hepburn is as captivating as ever. With William Daniels and Eleanor Bron as the traveling-companion couple from Hell, and a brief appearance by a young Jacqueline Bisset, whose voice was inexplicably dubbed by another actress. Henry Mancini, whom Hepburn once called "the hippest of cats – and most sensitive of composers," supplied the romantic score. **[W]**

Wait Until Dark
1967 – as Suzy Hendrix

Audrey's second screen role of the year was a rare dramatic performance and her only thriller. Based on a hit stage play by Frederick Knott, she plays the blind wife of photographer Sam Hendrix (Efrem Zimbalist, Jr.), who purely by chance becomes the target of three thugs (Richard Crenna, Jack Weston and Alan Arkin) because they suspect she is hiding a cache of heroin somewhere in her basement apartment. The plot involves their attempt to trick her into thinking they are, respectively, an old friend of her husband, a police sergeant and a father-son team (both played by Arkin). But as the story unfolds, her suspicion grows that no one is who he seems to be. Arkin plays the most dangerous of the three, a murderous psychopath named Harry Roat. In fact, he is so creepy I would have classified his performance as Unforgettable had I not created this category for Audrey. The suspense gradually builds to a shattering climax, to the point where movie audiences would shriek in terror and cling to their seats until the resolution. Terence Young, who helmed some of the best of the James Bond movies, directed, and Henry Mancini worked against type to produce the chilling score. [Trivia notes: 1) A lot of movie theaters did something for this movie they hadn't done before or since: They turned off all the house lights during the climactic confrontation between Suzy and Roat, keeping audiences literally in the dark and intensifying the movie's most terrifying moment. 2) Arkin was once asked why his performance as Roat didn't earn an Academy Award nomination. He reportedly replied: "You don't get nominated for being mean to Audrey Hepburn." 3) Hepburn and director Young shared a connection long before this movie. During World War II, as a teenage volunteer nurse, she helped care for him, a wounded British paratrooper, in a Dutch hospital] [Caution: violence, intense moments of suspense and some sexual suggestions] **[W]**

10. The Man from Dream City

That's what Pauline Kael called him in her most famous essay. He never won a competitive Oscar – though he was twice nominated – never appeared in a Best Picture of the Year, and rarely played anyone but himself on the screen. Yet, he drew throngs to his movies as successfully as anyone else in the history of Hollywood – and he did it for over three decades. Cary Grant – born Archibald Alexander Leach in Bristol, England – remains the ultimate movie star, someone who could earn the admiration of other men while winning the hearts of women and make them all laugh in the process. He also remains possibly the handsomest man who ever lived and one of the most dignified. LIFE magazine once called him "the least likely man in the world to get pasted with a custard pie" – except he had no reluctance to allow himself to look ridiculous if it meant getting a laugh. If you don't know much about the man, you can find several interesting documentaries on YouTube about his career. And based on the number of his titles on this list, Cary Grant is my favorite movie star. I've featured him elsewhere in *Destination Tokyo*, *The Bishop's Wife* and *North by Northwest*, and here with a dozen more of his best roles. When Hollywood finally acknowledged his star prowess, presenting him with an honorary Oscar in 1970, he responded with his typical grace and charm. Reciting a list of directors and writers with whom he had worked over the years, he concluded by saying, "Ours is a collaborative medium – we need each other." Classy, always and to the last.

Bringing Up Baby
1938 – as Dr. David Huxley

This is probably the funniest movie Grant ever made, and my dear mother could never watch it without giggling uncontrollably. It isn't quite as rapid-fire as *His Girl Friday* or *Arsenic and Old Lace*, but the laughs come often and out loud. In fact, this movie was credited for necessitating the term "screwball comedy." Huxley's a paleontologist and a nerd, engaged to a staid and proper but uninteresting woman (Virginia Walker). Katharine Hepburn is Susan Vance, a society gadabout and a bit of a ditz, but the moment she lays eyes on Grant she knows she'll snag him somehow – and in short order he knows his life will never be the same. [Trivia notes: 1) The studio effects wizards made it possible for Grant and Hepburn to interact with a leopard (the eponymous "Baby") often without actually having to occupy the set at the same time as the animal, or at the least coexisting via a transparent barrier. For example, skillful process photography created the illusion of Hepburn appearing to drag the cat with a rope. 2) Grant had never done slapstick before and was struggling with the role when director Howard Hawks suggested that he play David Huxley as Harold Lloyd, the nebbish silent movie hero. He did, and it worked. 3) The movie quickly became such a dud at the box office that it threatened the careers of both Hepburn and Hawks. It did not achieve its rightful reputation until many years later] **[B&W]**

His Girl Friday
1940 – as Walter Burns

In Grant's third outing with director Howard Hawks he achieves something unique in all of movies: a veritable flood of dialogue delivered in such rapid-fire fashion that sometimes it takes a few seconds to get the jokes. This is a remake of the Ben Hecht and Charles MacArthur play "The Front Page," except that instead of two newspapermen this story turns one of the characters, Hildy Johnson, into a woman (Rosalind Russell) and places both in the role of ex-spouses. Hildy returns to the newspaper ostensibly to say goodbye and introduce her new fiancé (Ralph Bellamy), but

178

in very short order Walter has pushed her headlong into covering a major story. Grant plays Burns with tremendous energy and humor – it's as though he never takes a breath from the beginning of the movie to the end.

And the dialogue is razor-sharp. <u>Example</u>:
> WALTER
> What do you want, my fingerprints?
> HILDY
> No thanks, I've already got those.

[<u>Trivia note</u>: The reason Howard Hawks turned the character of Hildy into a woman was that during the early stages of developing the script he had a female friend read the part just to help him sharpen the dialogue. Hawks quickly realized the comic and romantic potential of switching Hildy's gender, so he made the change] **[B&W]**

The Philadelphia Story
1940 – as C.K. Dexter Haven
It's a testament to Grant's enduring popularity that he could get away with a scene in this movie that probably would have ruined any other actor. At the opening, he's in the middle of moving out of his home and breaking up his marriage to Tracy Lord (Katharine Hepburn, in her fourth and last pairing with him – they also appeared together in *Holiday* and *Sylvia Scarlett*, neither of which I included on this list). She takes one of his golf clubs and breaks it over her knee then returns to the house. He follows her and taps her on the shoulder, threatening to land a punch on her puss. Instead he grabs her face and shoves her to the floor. It could have appeared brutal and shocking in other contexts, but here it's only funny. It's also to Grant's enormous credit that he allowed co-star James Stewart to steal the movie (and win an Oscar) as gossip magazine reporter Macaulay Connor. Hepburn's quite good, too, and extremely appealing as the rich and spoiled socialite who harbors feelings of uncertainty about her engagement to George Kittredge (John Howard), a

self-made but rather dull tycoon. Based on Philip Barry's play, Donald Ogden Stuart's sparkling script is sophisticated and stylish; Hepburn was never lovelier, and Grant couldn't be better as "Dext," as Tracy calls him. [Trivia note: Grant demanded a $100,000 salary for his secondary role, which was an unprecedented amount at the time. But then he donated all of it to Britain's struggling War Relief program. **[B&W]**

Arsenic and Old Lace
1944 – as Mortimer Brewster

I mentioned earlier that *Bringing Up Baby* was probably Grant's funniest movie, but this one features Grant's single funniest scene. In it, he holds his fiancée (the perky Priscilla Lane) in his arms and keeps his lips locked firmly to hers while running all over the house and trying to keep her from speaking. Why? Well, that's part of the delicious plot, based on Joseph Kesselring's smash Broadway play and brought to the screen with tremendous wit and energy by none other than Frank Capra. Brewster is the nephew of two lovable elder aunts, Abby and Martha (Josephine Hull and Jean Adair), who have developed the quaint but lethal habit of entertaining elderly single gentlemen then poisoning them and burying them in the basement. It's fanciful and a little dated, but Grant's energetic performance is well worth a look, and Raymond Massey (at one point resembling Boris Karloff's monster in *Frankenstein*) and Peter Lorre add a great bit of humorous creepiness. [Trivia note: 1) Grant considered his performance as Mortimer his least favorite because he found it excessive. Capra had promised to rein in the slapstick in the editing room, but he had completed shooting in late 1941. Then, the attack on Pearl Harbor intervened and Capra, who had enlisted in the Army that year, redirected his priorities to the war effort. 2) *Arsenic and Old Lace* features a surprising amount of special effects, such as the distant, cloud-shrouded Manhattan skyline, which comprises elaborate flat cut-outs, and the blizzard of leaves Capra had hauled into the soundstage for some of the exterior scenes] **[B&W]**

Mr. Blandings Builds his Dream House
1948 – as Jim Blandings

This might not be the first movie about the American suburban lifestyle, but it's for certain the best early treatment of the subject. Blandings is a Manhattan advertising executive who shares a cramped apartment with his wife, Muriel (Myrna Loy), his two daughters and a housekeeper. Longing for more space, he decides the family should move to Connecticut, where they will enjoy the country while he commutes to work. The plan seems sound but gets derailed at every turn, from the dilapidated farmhouse they buy (for too much money) to the brand new house they end up building (which also costs too much). It's a light romp but enjoyable and entertaining. [Trivia note: The year after they starred together in this movie, Grant and Loy teamed up again to do a radio-play version of *Mr. Blandings* on the Lux Radio Theater. You can find it, as well as the radio versions of other movies from the 1940s and '50s, on YouTube] **[B&W]**

I Was a Male War Bride
1949 – as Captain Henri Rochard

Oh, how times have changed! Imagine the following scene playing out today. A female character learns that Captain Rochard, a French officer, has had a contentious relationship with U.S. Women's Army Corps (WAC) lieutenant Catherine Gates (Ann Sheridan), to the point where it is rumored he has hit her hard enough to make marks on her. The woman's breathless reply to a colleague: "He can make marks on me anytime – I'll bring the stick!" This was yet another successful comedic collaboration between Grant and director Howard Hawks, using the timeless device of having a man and woman who are destined to fall in love start out as adversaries. But the movie's title gives away the outcome. Loosely based on the autobiography of the real Rochard, the story takes place just after the end of World War II, when Rochard marries Gates and thereby creates a dilemma: How can he accompany her back to America when the laws for war spouses were established

181

exclusively to fit brides? As Rochard must state countless times to military officers and bureaucrats, he is "an alien spouse of female military personnel en route to the United States under Public Law 271 of the Congress." The problem is the categorization gets him nowhere, so the couple must constantly improvise to get 'round the rules – with predictable but hilarious results. For example, picture Grant in a WAC uniform, sporting a long, black wig made of horsehair! [Trivia note: This was the third of four lively comedies starring Grant and directed by Howard Hawks (along with *Bringing Up Baby*, *His Girl Friday* and *Monkey Business*). But it nearly became a tragedy when both Grant and Sheridan became seriously ill in the post-war European environment] **[B&W]**

People Will Talk [100]
1951 – as Dr. 'Noah' Praetorius

This might be one of the odder movies Cary Grant ever did, but in its own way it's wonderful. Based on a German play by Curt Goetz that had been produced the previous year – which explains why Grant's character's real name is Ludwig – he plays a doctor at an unspecified university in the United States (the campus scenes were shot at Princeton, but the rest of the filming obviously took place in California) who attracts the envy and enmity of one of his peers, a weasely fellow named Elwell (Hume Cronyn). Elwell seems obsessed with driving Praetorius out of the faculty by exposing his supposedly shady past. It turns out, however, that Praetorius is a most selfless and noble person, and Grant plays him so well he makes you wish you could be just like him. He is fiercely devoted to his patients – to the point where he might have married one (Jeanne Crain) to save her life. With Finlay Currie as an obsessively loyal sidekick, Walter Slezak as a humorous colleague, Sidney Blackmer as a friendly father-in-law, and the inimitable Margaret Hamilton in a neat cameo role. Joseph L. Mankiewicz directed and wrote the witty, sophisticated script the year after he did *All About Eve* (not on this list), which had won Best Picture. My favorite line (by

Slezak): "The trouble with you, Elwell, is that you've never had a cadaver of your own, much less one that bit your finger." **[B&W]**

Monkey Business
1952 – as Professor Barnaby Fulton
Just for laughs, this movie, the fifth and last teaming of Grant with Howard Hawks – more than with any other director, by the way – has him playing a chemistry researcher who's married to Ginger Rogers and, at a certain point, albeit involuntarily, pursues Marilyn Monroe, who's playing the first of her many roles a stereotypical dumb blonde. The plot, such as it is, involves a chimpanzee in Fulton's laboratory that inadvertently creates a formula that restores youthful appearance and behavior. But it's all an excuse for some really funny hijinks and several racy double entendres, such as this one, delivered by Grant with deadpan perfection: "Miss Laurel was just showing me her acetates." By the way, the real star of the movie is Rogers, who's just as appealing as ever, who turns out to be quite a physical comedienne and can still dance up a storm. [Trivia note: One of the neighborhood kids in the "scalping" scene was six-year-old, frog-voiced George Winslow, who played Grant's son in *Room for One More* that same year and had a role in Monroe's *Gentlemen Prefer Blondes* – not on this list – the following year] **[B&W]**

Room for One More
1952 – as George "Poppy" Rose
I could have slotted this one in either the Extremely Rare or Little Gems categories, both of which you'll see later on, because it 1) has remained out of sight for many years, and 2) is such a sweet little movie, a notable but minor title in Grant's repertoire. But it's too precious to disappear permanently, so sooner or later you're bound to find it. And it rightfully belongs here, with his other works. Grant and Betsy Drake – his real-life wife at the time – play George and Anna Rose, a likewise real-life married couple who served as the inspiration for the story. The Roses, with three natural children, a dog, a promiscuous cat and a

fertile rabbit, nevertheless decide to take in two more kids for foster care: a troubled and abused young teen girl and a foul-tempered boy suffering from the effects of polio. The movie has its comedic moments, but at its core it's a drama about a devoted husband and a compassionate wife, both of whom want to be the best possible parents to all of their children, including two who desperately need a loving home. It might seem dated, but much of it still rings true, and several scenes contain a powerful emotional punch. It was based on George Rose's memoir – and perhaps a dispute within the Rose family estate has kept it out of circulation. Grant is tremendously appealing as Poppy, but Drake anchors the movie. [Trivia note: Warner Brothers eventually changed the title to "The Easy Way," apparently because they didn't want to confuse it with the short-lived TV series that aired 10 years later. **[B&W]**

Operation Petticoat
1959 – as Lt. Commander Matt T. Sherman
A comedy about a pink submarine? Well, yes, and actually the whole plot is about as implausible as the premise, but Grant strikes a fine balance between humor and dignity as the commander of the U.S.S. Sea Tiger. It's December 1941, the start of World War II, and the whole South Pacific is in turmoil. The Japanese are keeping U.S. forces on the run, and the sub's crew is scrounging for parts and repairs and occasionally assisting in emergency evacuations. Sherman's foil is Lt. Nick Holden (Tony Curtis), a conniving, smart-alecky hustler who belongs on a submarine about as much as a screen door. Grant's interplay with Curtis and the rest of the cast is inimitable. Where he was serious and determined in *Destination Tokyo*, here he's mostly exasperated and confused but charming as always – and his expressions of bemusement are perfect. This was the first notable directing effort by Blake Edwards, who went on to fame and fortune with *The Pink Panther* (coming in the next compilation) and other hits. [Trivia note: Curtis once told a remarkable story about this movie. As a boy growing up in Brooklyn, he had seen Grant as a submarine commander in *Destination Tokyo*, and his

184

performance so impressed the young Curtis that he enlisted in the Navy. He also aspired to become a movie star and even to work someday with Grant. More than 15 years later, when he had begun to attain stardom, Curtis found himself cast as Lt. Holden in *Operation Petticoat*, teamed with fellow Universal Studios contract player Jeff Chandler. But the two ended up arguing over who would get top billing, and Chandler eventually left the project. Then the producers asked Curtis whom he would like to see play Sherman. Curtis immediately suggested Grant who, to everyone's surprise, readily accepted, and the dream of the young Bernie Schwartz (Curtis's real name) came true] **[W]**

Charade [100]
1963 – as Peter Joshua and...
As sleek and stylish a murder mystery as you will ever see. Set in Paris, where Audrey Hepburn's shadowy husband has been the victim of foul play, Grant shows up seemingly by accident and befriends and protects the new widow – or is his appearance more than coincidental? For one thing, he keeps going through a series of name changes, beginning with Peter Joshua and continuing ... well, see the movie and find out. Thoroughly entertaining, with a neat title sequence by Saul Bass, supremely suave music by Henry Mancini and gorgeous Paris locales. Hepburn was never lovelier, and Grant displayed his incredible staying power as a romantic lead (he was 59 at the time, while Hepburn was only 33) and his skill as a comedic actor – his mugging during a nightclub game of "pass the orange" is hilarious. The fine supporting cast includes George Kennedy as a menacing one-armed thug, James Coburn as a larcenous Texan, and Walter Matthau in a sly performance as a CIA man who might be hiding something. Stanley Donen directed. [Trivia note: Six years earlier, Grant had turned down a leading role opposite Hepburn in Billy Wilder's *Love in the Afternoon* (coming in the next compilation), citing the wide difference in their ages. Here again, he expressed sensitivity to the age difference, declining to play Hepburn's romantic co-star unless she spent the movie

pursuing him. He thought the idea of someone his age pursuing her would not be proper. So, scriptwriter Peter Stone dispelled any misgivings early on when he gave Audrey's Regina Lampert character the perfectly appropriate line: "Do you know what's wrong with you? Nothing!"] **[W]**

Walk Don't Run
1966 – as Sir William Rutland

If you've seen the delightful wartime comedy *The More the Merrier*, then you'll appreciate this update – which was Grant's last movie – all the more. Instead of housing-short Washington, D.C., during World War II, this one's set in housing-short Tokyo in 1964 during the Olympics. Grant, as Rutland, arrives two days early on a business trip and finds himself without accommodations. Seeking help – and finding none – at the British Embassy, he notices an "Apartment to Share" sign on the staff bulletin board. He capitalizes on the good timing and insinuates himself into a shared living arrangement with the prim and proper Miss Christine Easton (the young and very pretty Samantha Eggar). Then he takes pity on Steve Davis (the young and handsome Jim Hutton), an American Olympian who's also without a roof over his head, and suddenly the apartment's mailbox features three names. From there it's part comedy, part romance and all personality clashes, but the mix is just right. Grant seems to be enjoying his onscreen swan song – he frequently whistles or sings theme songs from his other movies (which must have been ad-libbed) – and the story, cast and glimpses of Tokyo in the 1960s are equally diverting. Quincy Jones provided the sprightly theme song. [Trivia notes: 1) Grant retired from movies after this one because, at 61, he thought he had become too old to play romantic leads, and he didn't think his fans would like to see him in supporting roles – go figure. 2) Watch for the screen debut of George Takei, better known as Lieutenant Sulu, one of the original crew members of the starship Enterprise on the Star Trek TV series and the first six movies] **[W]**

11. Connery, Sean Connery

Thomas Sean Connery, born in 1930 in Edinburgh, Scotland, became rich and famous after uttering three words – "Bond. James Bond." – in 1962 when he began playing British secret agent 007 (popularly known as "Double-O Seven"). But since then, Connery has also proven himself one of the finest and most durable movie actors in the world, a man whose screen presence was often electrifying and, as Gary Arnold once said after meeting him, "just a great guy." Along with *The Hunt for Red October* and a bit part in *The Longest Day*, here are seven showcases of his appeal and talent.

Dr. No
1962 – as James Bond
This movie introduced the character of Agent 007 of the British Secret Service to the world and elevated Connery instantly to the rank of star. Still, this is a much smaller and simpler tale than any of the others in the series – even with its effects-laden finale. Connery is very hard-edged here as Bond. He sleeps with a beautiful Asian woman then coldly turns her over to the police. He waits for an expected assassin to arrive then outwits him and calmly dispatches him. And so on. Most of the story takes place in Jamaica, where some odd goings on threaten a U.S. rocket launch. Eventually the mystery leads Bond to a strange island, where the locals think a dragon prowls, and where he meets the eponymous villain (TV and stage veteran Joseph Wiseman), but not before he also meets his love interest, Honey Ryder (Ursula Andress, who barely spoke English but who introduced American moviegoers to the proper form with which to fill a bikini). We're also introduced to the infamous SPECTRE ("Special Executive Command for Terrorism, Revenge and Extortion"), which would continue to threaten Bond through

three of the next four movies. Series regulars Bernard Lee as "M" and Lois Maxwell as Moneypenny also put in their first appearances. Other frequent contributors included director Terence Young, production designer Ken Adam and screenwriter Richard Maibaum. The one noticeable absence is composer John Barry, who did some work on the movie but had not yet perfected his famous "007" themes or his distinctive orchestrations for the series. [Trivia note: That now-famous introductory sequence at the Baccarat table proved a small challenge when director Terence Young was shooting the movie. At first he had Connery simply state his name, but the effect seemed bland and uninteresting. So they eventually worked out that Connery would say, "Bond," light a cigarette and then say, "James Bond." It worked, and the phrase entered cinema immortality] [Caution: violence and sexuality] **[W]**

From Russia with Love
1963 – as James Bond
Many fans of the series consider this one their sentimental favorite and a significant improvement over *Dr. No*. It's the movie where the familiar elements of the series began appearing, including the famous lusty title sequence, the James Bond theme by John Barry, the stalwart supporting characters of the British Secret Service – branch head "M" (Bernard Lee), his secretary Miss Moneypenny (Lois Maxwell) and master of gadgets "Q" (Desmond Llewelyn) – and Connery's iconic portrayal. Here, the story concerns a plot by SPECTRE to trick Bond and the British Secret Service into stealing a Russian decoding machine called a Lektor, lured by the promise of a beautiful defector (Daniela Bianchi) who works at the Russian Embassy in Istanbul. Unbeknownst to 007, SPECTRE has ordered an exceptional assassin (a bleach-blond Robert Shaw at the beginning of his career) to intercept the Lektor and kill Bond on the westbound Orient Express. Actually, the movie is a little more convoluted than that, but agreeably so. Connery is fully into the character here, and his escapades in Venice, Istanbul and across the Eastern European countryside and the Bosporus are great fun.

Matt Monroe sings the memorable title song. [Viewing note: It's a common practice in movie sequels to economize where possible by re-using footage from previous titles. You can spot two shots from *Dr. No* when Bond arrives in Istanbul: one of his plane touching down and another of the control-tower interior overlooking the airport (with appropriately re-dubbed audio)] [Trivia notes: 1) There's a tragic aspect to the casting of this movie. Veteran Mexican actor Pedro Armendáriz, who plays Bond's Istanbul contact Ali Kerim Bey, was dying of cancer during the filming. His health deteriorated so much that certain scenes had to be rescheduled to accommodate him, and stand-ins (including director Young) had to portray him in long shots. Armendáriz committed suicide shortly after the production completed, fearing that his cancer had reached its end stages. He died four months before the movie was released. 2) Another tragic association: President John F. Kennedy reportedly loved Ian Fleming's novel and eagerly awaited the movie. It was shown to him at the White House on November 20, 1963, two days before Kennedy was assassinated in Dallas] [Caution: violence and sexuality] [W]

Goldfinger [100]
1964 – as James Bond
This is the Bond series at its best. Connery, as Bond, is at the top of his form – he easily qualifies in the Unforgettable category elsewhere – and the movie was a monster hit in its day, now well over half a century ago. Connery exudes such confidence and wit in the role that it never matters what threats are thrown his way – you just know he will find an out, all the while maintaining his poise, nerve, deadpan humor and manly allure. The story involves a plot by a villain named Auric Goldfinger (German actor Gert Fröbe) to manipulate the world's gold supply so he can enrich himself. Bond's job is to stop him, something that proves much more difficult and dangerous than he would have guessed. One big obstacle is Oddjob (Harold Sakata, a native Hawai`ian and a real-life martial-arts expert), Goldfinger's seemingly invincible bodyguard, whose Homburg

189

hat contains a lethal steel brim. Another distraction – albeit temporarily – is Goldfinger's personal pilot, a woman named … ahem, Pussy Galore (Honor Blackman, also a martial-arts expert), who seems more than a match for 007. It's a big, sprawling, scenic, glorious, crowd-pleasing thriller involving a plot to render the U.S. gold bullion reserve at Fort Knox, Kentucky, useless for decades. John Barry's now-famous score is excellent and just keeps getting better over the years, including the title ballad, sung with incredible vocal power by Shirley Bassey, the best of the Bond themes. [Trivia notes: 1) When Oddjob knocks out Bond in front of the refrigerator by thwacking him on the back of the neck, Sakata – who had never done movie stunts before – actually hit Connery hard enough for real to knock him out and give him a sore neck for days. 2) The movie's climax is supposed to take place around Fort Knox, but many of those scenes were shot at Pinewood Studios, outside London – including a full-scale replica of the gold repository building. 3) In fact, Connery and the other principal cast members never set foot in the United States for any of their scenes. The production used clever recreations in England, such as having the actors appear in front of rear-projections of the real locations, creating lookalike sets and employing stand-ins for scenes at a distance] [Caution: violence and sexuality] **[W]**

Thunderball
1965 – as James Bond
This one was a slight comedown from *Goldfinger*, but it still offers some razzle-dazzle sequences, including the eye-popping opening credits by Maurice Binder and the climactic underwater battle involving dozens of divers, both good guys and bad, plus a truly harrowing encounter with a real tiger shark. Here, Bond is sent to the Bahamas to trace a missing NATO aircraft carrying two nuclear warheads that has been hijacked by SPECTRE. There, he meets the usual collection of villains and beauties, including Claudine Auger as Domino, his main romantic interest of the story. Connery is in fine form, as usual (his only misfire in the role of 007 was in the dreadful *Diamonds are Forever–*

absolutely not on this list), but the best aspect of the movie is John Barry's enhanced and expanded score, and pop-singer Tom Jones provided the famous voice for the spectacular theme song. [Viewing note: That opening montage, featuring nude women swimming underwater seemingly pursued by fully wet-suited divers shooting spear guns, poses two problems (or an advantage and a problem, depending on your point of view). First, shown on a video screen, the nudity is much more visible than it was on film in a theater. And second, the connotation of predatory men chasing beautiful but vulnerable women has become dated and distasteful] [Caution: violence and sexuality] [W]

You Only Live Twice
1967 – as James Bond

Connery's fifth outing as 007 takes him to Japan to search for a secret rocket base from which SPECTRE is launching missions to disrupt both the U.S. and Soviet space programs and provoke a war between the two superpowers. The movie boasts several distinctions. There's a nifty helicopter sequence, involving an aerial gun battle between four conventional copters and a tiny but fast gyrocopter nicknamed "Little Nellie." There's Ken Adam's gigantic set depicting a secret launch facility, which is supposed to be located inside a volcano. There's gorgeous cinematography by the great Freddie Young, who shot *Lawrence of Arabia* and *Doctor Zhivago*. And there's yet another beautiful, Asian-themed score by John Barry. I would rank *You Only Live Twice* in a third-place tie with *Thunderball* behind *Goldfinger* and *From Russia with Love* in the series with Connery. My only quibble is the movie asks you to suspend quite a bit of disbelief where Bond's gadgets are concerned, because they seem to turn up out of thin air at the most opportune times (such as a safe-cracking device, rather large suction cups, and a special pack of cigarettes that seems to have survived an underwater swim unscathed). Also, the bad guys have no trouble at all tracking him down wherever he goes. Theme song honors this time went to Nancy Sinatra. [Trivia notes: 1) The concept of a hollow volcano housing a secret SPECTRE base arose after the producers took an aerial tour of Kyushu, the Japanese island where some of the movie locales were shot. The producers commissioned supremely talented production designer Ken Adam to build the volcano's interior – on a set so big it had to be specially constructed outdoors and then enclosed. 2) Speaking of that set, its construction budget was bigger than the entire budget for *Dr. No.* 3) Two of Connery's co-stars, Akiko Wakabayashi and Mie Hama, who play his lovers Aki and Kissy, respectively, eventually switched roles from how they were originally cast – and both actresses' voices were dubbed by others] [Caution: violence and sexuality] [**W**]

The Man Who Would Be King
1975 – as Danny Dravot

My late friend Mike Morrison said, after seeing this movie, "What a great yarn!" How true, and what a great bunch of people making this wonderfully exotic tale, shot among the stunning scenery of the Atlas Mountains of Morocco and the Chamonix region of France. Along with Connery's co-star Michael Caine is Caine's beautiful and rarely seen wife Shakira. There's also Christopher Plummer as Rudyard Kipling, on whose story the movie is based; director John Huston, returning to the helm a year after he played the villainous Noah Cross in *Chinatown*; and 103-year-old Karroom Ben Bouih as a high priest in his one-and-only movie role. Along with Connery's Dravot, Michael Caine plays Peachy Carnehan; both are gadabout soldiers in the British Army in India in the 19th century. Danny and Peachy hatch a plot to rule a primitive sect located deep in the mythical kingdom of Kafiristan, which according to the descriptions in Kipling's story is actually somewhere in present-day eastern Afghanistan. That would explain why Shakira Caine plays a character named Roxanne, the legendary woman whose beauty tempted even Alexander the Great when he tried and failed to conquer western Asia in the fourth century B.C. As with Alexander, the best-laid plans of Peachy and Danny go astray, but watching things unravel provides much of the fun in this truly entertaining – and manly – tale. [Trivia notes: 1) The production's own lengthy history grew legendary over time. Huston had been trying to make the movie for several decades, with each attempt pairing the top male stars of the time. First it was Clark Gable and Humphrey Bogart in the 1940s. Then it was Burt Lancaster and Kirk Douglas (who actually did star together several times) in the '50s, and Paul Newman and Robert Redford in the '60s. Each failed, but then Redford reportedly suggested Connery and Caine, and the movie finally reached the screen. 2) When Karroom Ben Bouih, who had been working as a night watchman before Huston discovered him, saw himself in the movie, he reportedly announced that now he would live forever. Through the treasure that is the cinema, he will!] [Caution: violence and mild sexuality] **[W]**

The Untouchables
1987 – as Officer Jim Malone

Connery won his only Oscar as a hard-bitten veteran Chicago flatfoot who becomes the mentor of Elliott Ness (Kevin Costner), a U.S. Treasury agent charged with bringing notorious Chicago mobster Al Capone (a plump and menacing Robert De Niro) to justice. I've never been a great fan of director Brian De Palma, but he does his best work here, creating a seamless narrative based on the true story of the government versus the Chicago Mob during the days of Prohibition. Andy Garcia and Charles Martin Smith round out the quartet of "untouchables" – meaning they could not be bribed or corrupted. Patricia Clarkson plays Ness's wife, and Billy Drago – a perfectly mild-mannered actor in real life – plays Capone's decidedly creepy henchman Frank Nitti. But Connery provides the movie's heart and soul, and his Oscar was well deserved. His Jim Malone is the proverbial honest cop, a man with a keen wit and a sharp eye for talent and villainy alike. Plus, Connery gets to do something here that his fans would never allow during his days as Agent 007 (forgive the spoiler): a heroic death scene. Ennio Morricone did the distinctive score. [Caution: frequent, graphic violence] **[W]**

12. Gary and Walter

One of the little-remembered but most successful acting partnerships in the movies comprised one of Hollywood's most appealing stars and one of its most skilled and versatile character actors, Gary Cooper and Walter Brennan. The tall, handsome Cooper's glamour and appeal were immortalized in 1927 by Irving Berlin in his song, "Puttin' on the Ritz," even before Cooper had entered the sound era of motion pictures. He went on to captivate audiences as a movie idol for over three decades, until his untimely death from cancer at age 60 in 1961. Brennan held the rare distinction of winning three acting Oscars – an achievement matched only by Daniel Day-Lewis and Jack Nicholson – among his astounding 225 film roles over five decades. These three favorite titles demonstrate the seamlessness with which Cooper and Brennan could adjust their onscreen chemistry, moving from a classic wartime biography to an equally classic true sports story, and concluding with a serious and timeless wartime drama. In the annals of male screen partnerships, others such as Clark Gable and Spencer Tracy, Burt Lancaster and Kirk Douglas, Paul Newman and Robert Redford achieved more fame and box office success. But I will always hold a special fondness for these two great actors who emerged from the silent era.

Sergeant York
1941 – Howard Hawks
Cooper and Brennan team in a great biography of one of the most decorated American heroes of World War I, a man who with eight of his comrades silenced 35 machine guns and captured 132 German soldiers in one battle. Cooper plays Alvin York, a backwoods sharpshooter from Pall Mall, Tennessee, who starts out as a hothead but becomes a man of faith and, in a remarkable way, a pacifist. Brennan plays the Reverend Rosier Pile, York's hometown preacher who helps him in his time of

trouble. Brennan – unnecessarily, I think – sported large dark eyebrows for the role, apparently so he would resemble the real Reverend Pile. Cooper won an Oscar for his performance (and Brennan was nominated), displaying an exaggerated Tennessee twang à la Daniel Boone but also conveying determination and personal courage so strongly that this turned out to be one of his finest roles – also made possible because York himself would not allow a movie to portray his early life and military record unless Cooper played him. [Trivia notes: 1) York resisted all offers to profit from his war record for more than 20 years. But when he finally sold the rights to his story, he used a significant part of the money to found an agricultural institute back home (which today remains in service as a public high school), as well as a Bible study school and a lumber mill. He continued to perform public service for the rest of his life. 2) Joan Leslie, who plays his sweetheart and eventual wife, was only 16 here] **[B&W]**

The Pride of the Yankees
1942 – Sam Wood

Cooper stars in this fictionalized but supremely touching biography of one of baseball's most beloved stars, Lou Gehrig, affectionately known as the "Iron Horse." Gehrig played in 2,130 consecutive games for the New York Yankees, a record that stood for more than half a century, until he succumbed to the effects of amyotrophic lateral sclerosis, a severely debilitating disease that now commonly bears his name. Cooper portrays him as an all-American guy who's a little naïve but plays hard, loves his wife (Theresa Wright) and accepts his progressive and incurable illness with dignity and heroism. He duplicates Gehrig's famous farewell speech at Yankee Stadium – which contains the phrase, "Today, I consider myself the luckiest man on the face of this earth" – with perfect emotional authenticity. Brennan plays Sam Blake, a newspaper reporter who became Gehrig's friend, and the legendary Babe Ruth appears in a brief role as himself. [Trivia note: In order for Cooper, who was right-handed and unfamiliar with baseball, to play the left-handed Gehrig on the field and at bat, he had to wear a uniform with the words and numerals printed backwards. Technicians optically reversed the film in the printing process and, voila! Cooper became a southpaw] **[B&W]**

Task Force
1949 – Delmer Daves

The second superior wartime drama written and directed by Daves (see *Destination Tokyo*) is a dated but faithful and engaging portrait of naval aviation in the years before and during World War II, with both Cooper and Brennan casting off their usual "aw-shucks" mannerisms for more sophisticated roles. In the last of their onscreen collaborations, Cooper plays an aviator who helps to pioneer the dangerous maneuvers of taking off from and landing on an aircraft carrier while at the same time promoting the Navy as an aerial assault force. Eventually he becomes captain of his own carrier, which is beset by attacks from Japanese kamikaze fighters. Brennan likewise plays an aviator who becomes a fleet admiral. A lot of standard melodrama, including a romance between Cooper and Jane Wyatt as husband and wife, but the two acting pals are fine together, and the real footage (the moviemakers used no models or miniatures), featuring both aerial and sea-surface actions – of the battles of the Coral Sea, Midway and Okinawa – is often breathtaking, as is a low-altitude flyover at the end of the movie by a squadron of Grumman F9F Panther jets. [Trivia notes: 1) Wayne Morris, a veteran actor who plays one of Cooper's friends and fellow fliers, a character named McKinney, was an actual fighter pilot during World War II. He shot down a bunch of enemy aircraft and helped sink several ships. 2) The real shots of the heavily damaged carrier at Okinawa are of the U.S.S. Franklin, whose ordeal was much, much worse than depicted in the movie, resulting in the loss of 800 seamen. Yet the carrier escaped sinking via the extraordinarily heroic efforts of her crew and the crews of several other warships that came to her aid. Incredibly and as portrayed, the ship really did manage to make it all the way home from the Pacific Theater to the Brooklyn Navy Yard] **[B&W – with some sequences in color]**

13. His 'Wicked, Wicked Ways'

He is beginning to fade into the mists of time now, but in the 1930s and early 1940s Errol Flynn was one of the biggest stars in Hollywood and one of its most notorious personalities. His ghostwritten memoir, My Wicked, Wicked Ways, detailed his amorous adventures and his bouts with alcohol, which most probably contributed to his early death at age 50. Along with his immortal performance as Sir Robin of Loxley in *The Adventures of Robin Hood*, here are four favorites.

Captain Blood
1935 – as Peter Blood
The plight of an innocent man condemned is an oft-repeated theme in the movies, and this is one of the earliest and still one of the best of the genre. Based on a popular novel by Raphael Sabatini, Peter Blood is an Irish doctor convicted of treason against the English crown because he treated a wounded rebel. Sentenced to hard labor on a Caribbean island in the late 17th century, he eventually escapes and forms a band of pirates that raids British ships, soon making him one of the most wanted men on the high seas. Flynn's first major role made him a star and established lasting relationships with his most frequent onscreen love interest, his onscreen rival and his director – respectively, Olivia de Havilland, Basil Rathbone and Michael Curtiz. It's one of the best swashbucklers of the 1930s, replete with a rousing, call-to-arms score by Erich Wolfgang Korngold, one of the great pioneers of movie music. [Trivia note: Flynn's rivalry with Rathbone was not altogether friendly. During one swordfight scene, Rathbone deliberately wounded Flynn's arm, giving him a permanent scar] **[B&W]**

197

The Charge of the Light Brigade
1936 – as Major Geoffrey Vickers

English poet Alfred Lord Tennyson immortalized this story in a poem he wrote in 1870 about a courageous but ill-fated attack by British cavalry officers during the Battle of Balaclava in the Crimean War in 1856. This is a fictionalized version of that story. In it, Flynn's Major Vickers is an army officer whose life is spared during a massacre of unarmed British men, women and children by rebels in India. Learning that the man who had ordered the murders is being protected by a Russian artillery battery at Balaclava, Vickers forges orders for 600 British cavalrymen – himself included – to charge into what would be certain death. As with so many movies about historical events, it isn't even close to what really happened. Nevertheless, it's a glorious, crazy, thrilling scene that no doubt brought movie audiences to their feet at the time, and it captures the spirit of the line of the Tennyson poem: "Theirs not to reason why, theirs but to do and die." Olivia de Havilland again plays Flynn's love interest, and the movie marks the first significant role for David Niven. [Trivia notes: 1) This movie became notorious because of the large number of horses killed or injured during the famous cavalry charge. This happened because many of them were rigged via the now-disdained practice of trip-wiring, which forces the horses to collapse suddenly, as though they've been shot. In fact, the reported cruelty and indifference to the suffering of the animals by the production led Congress to pass protective legislation. The incident also created a rift between Flynn, a horse lover, and director Michael Curtiz that would last the rest of their lives. 2) The movie was made in California, of course, but if you Google "Valley of Death Balaclava," you can find photographs of the actual scene taken a short time after the battle, including bodies of the dead cavalrymen] **[B&W]**

The Sea Hawk
1940 – as Geoffrey Thorpe

There's more to this story of piracy on the high seas in the 16th century than meets the eye, although even at a superficial level

198

it's a rousing tale. Flynn's second pirate movie, again directed by Michael Curtiz with another splashy score by Erich Korngold, also was an effort to raise British spirits during the first full year of World War II, when Europe seemed completely vulnerable to Hitler's forces. Here, Flynn plays the captain of a sea hawk – ostensibly a British pirate ship plundering the bounty of the empire of King Philip II of Spain but acting as a kind of special operative for Queen Elizabeth I (Flora Robson) as well. Ordered on a secret mission to attack a Spanish stronghold in Panama, Thorpe's plans are uncovered by spies, creating a dangerous situation when he and his crew are trapped in a mosquito-infested Central American swamp (actually, an artificial outdoor set in Laguna Beach, California). Will they live to fight another day? You'll just have to watch and see. [Trivia note: As usual, Olivia de Havilland was recruited to play Flynn's romantic partner, but she had grown tired of the damsel-in-distress roles, so Curtiz cast Brenda Marshall, the future Mrs. William Holden, instead] [B&W]

Gentleman Jim
1942 – as Jim Corbett
Some 40 years before James J. Braddock became the "Cinderella Man" of boxing in America (portrayed by Russell Crowe in the movie I discussed earlier), Jim Corbett charmed the pants off crowds as the most popular fighter in the country and the eventual heavyweight champion. This is a fanciful telling of that story, but Flynn is delightful in the title role, an irrepressible member of a rowdy Irish family living in San Francisco in the late 19th century. Professional boxing was officially banned in the state at the time, but promoters skirted the law by staging fights on barges anchored in the harbor and therefore in federal jurisdiction. That's where Gentleman Jim made his reputation, fighting in matches that could only end in knockouts. His greatest triumph was over the legendary John L. Sullivan (Ward Bond), America's first heavyweight champion, who had held the title for an astounding 10 years. This is not Flynn's best movie, but it's one of his most appealing roles, playing opposite Alexis

Smith as his foil and love interest, and directed this time by Raoul Walsh. The scene after the championship fight, where Sullivan visits Corbett to surrender his belt, is surprisingly touching, as much for Corbett's expression of humility as for Sullivan's graciousness. You wish more professional athletes could demonstrate as much class as these two – but then, this was Hollywood. [Trivia notes: 1) Flynn appeared in every single fight scene in the movie, refusing a stunt double, even after he suffered a mild heart attack during the production. 2) The nickname "Gentleman Jim," given to Corbett by sports reporters, was due to both his outside-the-ring activities, which included acting on the stage and in early films, and to his emphasis on developing refined boxing skills instead of employing brute force and vicious tactics like so many others in the fight game at the time. In terms of his acting, Corbett presaged similar pursuits by heavyweight champion Max Baer four decades later] **[B&W]**

14. Gable and Tracy

During the same period when Errol Flynn reached stardom, standing at the very top of the heap was Clark Gable, who had earned the title "The King" in the 1930s with box office blockbusters *It Happened One Night* and *Mutiny on the Bounty* even before he dominated *Gone with the Wind* – Best Picture Oscar winners all. But some of Gable's best work involved his co-starring with probably the finest natural actor to appear on the screen: Spencer Tracy. No pair of movie sidekicks – with the possible exception of Paul Newman and Robert Redford – ever exuded better chemistry, with Gable playing the scalawag to Tracy's square-jawed straight-shooter. Here they are in action, and what a treat it is to watch them in this trio of titles.

San Francisco
1936

This fine tale of the City by the Bay in the fateful year 1906 stars Gable as Blackie Norton, owner of The Paradise, a gambling and beer hall on the city's notorious Barbary Coast. Among other pursuits, Blackie wants to showcase the beautiful but prim and proper opera singer Mary Blake (Jeannette MacDonald) in a musical revue at his place. But he's opposed by Tracy as Father Tim Mullen, his pal from boyhood, now a crusading reformer. Though not onscreen much, Tracy nevertheless makes a strong impression as the padre, appealing to Mary's better nature while Blackie pulls her in another direction. That's the focus of the story until the morning of April 18, when the catastrophic earthquake strikes, followed by a gigantic fire that sweeps through and destroys the city. The movie features a sharp script by Anita Loos, one of the first women screenwriters to make it big in Hollywood, with outstanding special effects for its day and a terrific performance by MacDonald, who never looked lovelier and was never more appealing or heroic. Her rendition of "Nearer My God to Thee" at the end is sublimely moving, as is Blackie's act of contrition. [Trivia note: Of all the movies on this list, *San Francisco* claims the unique distinction of carrying no directing credit. That's curious, because the director of record is W.S. "Woody" Van Dyke, aka "One-Take Woody," one of the industry's most capable hands at the time, with a career that spanned four decades, beginning in the early silent era and including *Tarzan the Ape Man*. Apparently, a dispute between Van Dyke and MGM caused his name to be removed] **[B&W]**

Test Pilot
1938 – Victor Fleming

The year before he directed Gable in *Gone with the Wind*, and the year after he directed Tracy in *Captains Courageous*, Fleming had the two vying for aerial supremacy in a tale of the brave and sometimes foolhardy men who test and race aircraft. This time Gable is Jim Lane, the best of the best who, too often, gets himself into trouble that requires Gunner Morris (Tracy), his best buddy and stalwart, to come to his rescue. During one predicament, Lane literally drops in on Ann Barton (Myrna Loy), and before she can think twice he marries her and pulls her into the stressful life of a test pilot's wife. Yes, it's frequently formulaic, but the aerial sequences are often thrilling, there's a fine performance by Lionel Barrymore (who also had worked with Tracy and Fleming in *Captains Courageous*), and it's just a pleasure to watch these two actors go toe to toe. Loy called this her favorite performance. [Trivia notes: 1) This was actually Gable and Loy's seventh onscreen pairing, going back to the silent era. Most notably, they played a doctor–nurse couple in *Men in White* in 1933, they teamed the following year in *Manhattan Melodrama*, a crime story featuring Gable in a rare villainous role; and two years after that, in *Wife vs. Secretary* (none on this list), Loy played Gable's wife and Jean Harlow was his … um, secretary. 2) Among the five screenwriters contributing to this title were director and former aviator Howard Hawks, and former military aviator Frank "Spig" Wead, both of whom you'll see associated with several other titles on this list] **[B&W]**

Boom Town

1940 – Jack Conway

The guys saved their best work for their third and last pairing in this hugely entertaining tale of oilmen in the early part of the 20th century. Gable as Big John McMasters and Tracy as Honest John Sand play a pair of two-fisted wildcatters who alternate between being close friends and bitter rivals, and their interplay is among the best ever seen between men on the screen, particularly in their inevitable fight scene. Joining them are Claudette Colbert (who had co-starred with Gable and likewise won an Oscar six years earlier in *It Happened One Night*) as their mutual love interest, the gorgeous Hedy Lamarr as a homewrecker, Frank Morgan as a perennially nervous business partner, and Chill Wills as a crack-shot deputy whose first love is cooking. Funny, touching and at one point thrilling – during a truly terrifying sequence in which McMasters and Sand try to extinguish a wellhead fire – the movie showcases the two stars in top form. It also features a mostly fine script by John Lee Mahin and solid direction by silent-movie veteran Conway, who paints a vivid portrait of the near lawlessness in oil country at the time. The movie's only weakness is its portrayal of women: Colbert as Gable's wife, Lamarr as his lover and veteran character actress Marion Martin as his occasional mistress. Somehow, none of them gets a truly satisfying moment – but boy-oh-boy are the guys terrific! [Trivia notes: 1) During their fistfight, Tracy accidentally landed a haymaker on Gable's jaw that knocked out a couple of his teeth. From then on Tracy never did an intense fight scene, relying instead on stunt doubles. 2) There's a funny inside joke in the movie when at one point Morgan utters, "What do they think I am, the Good Fairy?" It's a reference to his title role the previous year in *The Wizard of Oz*. 3) Lamarr's filmography is decidedly mixed, but her real, lasting and surprising legacy is in, of all things, electronics. During World War II, she and a composer friend invented the process that eventually led to the broadband and WiFi systems we use today] **[B&W]**

15. Unforgettable

Each movie in this category contains an actor delivering a performance that is so vivid, so moving, so frightening, so sexy – so mesmerizing – you will never forget it and you could never imagine anyone else in the role. I can attest to this, because a few of these titles I saw only as a child or adolescent but my memory of them has not dimmed in the intervening decades. There are other examples sprinkled throughout the entire list of movies: Spencer Tracey in *Captains Courageous*, Errol Flynn in *The Adventures of Robin Hood*, Humphrey Bogart and Ingrid Bergman in *Casablanca*, Clark Gable and Vivien Leigh in *Gone with the Wind*, James Stewart in both *Mr. Smith Goes to Washington* and *It's a Wonderful Life*, and Bradley Cooper in *American Sniper*. Here, I offer 25 more examples of what acting immortality is all about.

City Lights
1931 – Charlie Chaplin as the Little Tramp
About midway through the shooting of *City Lights*, Chaplin shut down the production for a period that stretched into an entire year. The reason: He couldn't figure out an effective cinematic way for a blind flower girl (the luminous Virginia Cherrill) to mistake his Little Tramp character for a rich man in a critical scene. So he thought and thought about it, until he finally came up with the answer – which you'll discover to your delight if you decide to watch this exquisite silent classic. It was Chaplin's obsessive nature about perfecting every possible moment of his movies, and every detail of his onscreen character, which has rendered all of them timeless. They are works of art, and all are worthy of your attention. But start with this one if you've never

seen him in action – in front of and behind the camera. **[Silent]**
[B&W]

Mr. Deeds Goes to Town
1936 – Gary Cooper as Longfellow Deeds

There's a scene late in this movie where Cooper, as Deeds – a likable but extremely naïve country bumpkin come to the big city – has discovered that the woman he loves (Jean Arthur, in one of her best roles) has been lying to him. He doesn't say a word. Rather, he conveys the realization entirely with facial expression. It's a shattering moment, and only an actor of Cooper's caliber could express such deep hurt so subtly. The scene solidified his career and established him as a movie star of the first rank, a distinction that would last for over 20 years. The movie also sealed the reputation of director Frank Capra as an unparalleled teller of uplifting tales of Americana. In retrospect, both men made much better movies, but this is the one that revealed the extent of their talents and presaged their many successes to come. **[B&W]**

Ball of Fire (and) The Lady Eve
Both in 1941 – Barbara Stanwyck as, respectively, Sugarpuss O'Shea and Eve

As you can see from this list, it's rare for any actor to create an unforgettable role, and rarer still to do it more than once. But for someone to accomplish the feat twice in the same year ... well, this is the only example I can think of. Maybe it was because Stanwyck was working with two of the most talented directors of the era: the splendid Howard Hawks in *Ball of Fire* and the inimitable Preston Surges in *The Lady Eve*. That's no doubt part of it. But Stanwyck in these two movies performs at the height of her talent and appeal, and whether you see one or both you're not likely to forget her. As devised by screenwriter (and future legendary director) Billy Wilder and his longtime collaborator Charles Brackett, *Ball of Fire*'s plot requires Sugarpuss to hide out from The Law for a few days by staying at a Central Park West mansion housing a group of scholars. Wallflower of a professor

Bertram Potts (Gary Cooper) and seven colleagues are painstakingly compiling an encyclopedia. As dedicated as they are, the men quickly abandon their task in favor of socializing with this gorgeous, mesmerizing creature who has suddenly appeared in their midst. And boy, does Stanwyck mesmerize, especially when she's playing romantic foil to Gary Cooper's stodgy but earnest scholar. She crackles with energy, and when she winks and double-clicks her tongue, you're bound to imitate the gesture for days. I'll say no more, except that it ends happily (How could it not?) and, like Sugarpuss, you'll be well entertained by the hijinks and mayhem. You might recognize some of the scholars, by the way. One is played by Henry Travers, quite unforgettable himself as Clarence, George Bailey's guardian angel in *It's a Wonderful Life*. Two others are S.Z. "Cuddles" Sakall and Leonid Kinskey, both employees of Rick's Café Americain in *Casablanca*. And if you took my recommendation and saw *The Best Years of Our Lives*, you'll also see a younger Dana Andrews playing Sugarpuss's lover and erstwhile husband of convenience.

*   *   *

Then there's *The Lady Eve*, in which Stanwyck plays Jean Harrington (aka Eve), a grifter – a con artist – who along with her father (Charles Coburn, giving a pretty good performance himself) attempts to fleece Charles Pike (Henry Fonda, looking quite young and particularly handsome), heir to a brewery fortune. When the con fails, she vows revenge on him but ends up falling in love. Here, she's every bit as smart and self-assured as Katharine Hepburn was in *Bringing Up Baby* (also directed by Hawks) but as sultry as Kathleen Turner in *Body Heat*. And in the scene where she insists that Fonda put her shoes on her feet … guys, I assure you, that's a most shapely pair of legs! [Trivia notes: 1) Seeing Stanwyck's turn in *Ball of Fire* as nightclub "entertainer" Sugarpuss O'Shea, you might not immediately make a connection with Walt Disney's *Snow White and the Seven Dwarfs* (a classic, but not on this list). Believe it or not, that's the source of the story – or, at least, that's where it evolved. Wilder and Brackett patterned each of Prof. Potts's colleagues after one of the Disney characters – maybe have some fun and try to pair them up. 2) Like *Ball of Fire*, *The Lady Eve* also features some familiar faces: two of the prominent cast members of *The Adventures of Robin Hood*. They are Eugene Pallette, who shined as Friar Tuck, here in his best role of all as Fonda's father; and Melville Cooper, who did the wonderful turn as the cowardly Sheriff of Nottingham, playing an associate con man] [Critic's note: Let me also put in a word for Sturges. During this period, the late 1930s to mid-'40s, no one in Hollywood could write and direct a movie with as much wit and skill. He was so good, in fact, that some of the funniest scenes in *The Lady Eve* occur with people speaking (such as on the telephone) but you can't hear their words – they're pantomiming their performances. And his slapstick setups with Fonda and with William Demarest (one of his repertory players) are priceless] **[B&W]**

Born Yesterday
1950 – Judy Holliday as Billie Dawn

Like James Cagney's character in *White Heat* the previous year, Holliday's Billie Dawn has been imitated many times on the screen. But nobody has been able to match her Oscar-winning rendition, possibly because she had perfected it during more than 1,600 performances on the Broadway stage. In a five-minute scene midway through the movie, Billie and her thug of a "fiancé" (Broderick Crawford) play gin rummy, as they apparently do frequently. There's an interlude where all she does is consider her cards, figure out her next move, and sing (sort of), "I Can't Give You Anything but Love, Baby." Holliday is essentially wordless but brilliant – simply brilliant. This isn't a coming-of-age story, because heaven knows Billie has seen her share of life's seamier side. Rather, it's a coming-into-one's-own story where Billie, with the help of a smitten reporter (the inimitable William Holden), gradually realizes how much she has been taken advantage of and what she can do about it. Her line near the finale, where she has gained full confidence and orders a henchman to "Do what I'm tellin' ya!" while imitating Crawford's overbearing manner, is perfect. [Trivia notes: 1)

Holliday originally played the role on Broadway opposite Paul Douglas and Gary Merrill as, respectively, the characters in the film portrayed by Crawford and Holden. 2) Columbia Pictures paid $1 million to playwright Garson Kanin, the highest ever for screen rights at the time] **[B&W]**

The African Queen
1951 – Humphrey Bogart and Katharine Hepburn as Charley Allnutt and Rose Sayer
What to call this classic? An adventure yarn? A romantic comedy with dramatic interludes? A star vehicle? Actually it's all three, and more. Director John Huston transported Bogart, Hepburn and the crew to several African locations – where most of them promptly contracted terrible cases of dysentery – to shoot this exciting story based on a brilliant script by legendary critic James Agee. It follows the relationship that develops between a grizzled riverboat captain and a prim but courageous missionary, and their efforts to represent England in the early days of World War I. Bogart won his only Oscar as Charlie, and Hepburn was nominated for Rose, whose many memorable lines included, "Nature, Mr. Allnutt, is what we were put on Earth to rise above." And nature is abundant here. The lush locales of what was then the Belgian Congo (today the Democratic Republic of the Congo) in Central Africa just drench the movie with atmosphere. Yes, the effects are crude by today's standards – mostly models carrying dummies and projected backgrounds – but they're secondary to the chemistry between the two actors, who are wonderful to watch, and their charm and appeal are unfailing. These two Hollywood veterans, pushed to physical limits by the harsh location environments, both gave performances that will stick in your memory and draw you back for repeat visits over the years. [Trivia notes: 1) Huston and Bogart were the only cast and crew members to escape intestinal distress during the location shoot, a distinction which they attributed to their constant imbibing of alcoholic beverages. 2) Hepburn said Huston gave her a marvelous directorial hint early in the shoot: He told her to play Rose as Eleanor Roosevelt. She

said from then on she knew exactly what to do with her character. 3) There is a moment in Agee's script that, regrettably, Huston doesn't use in the movie. Early on, as Rose plays the pump organ during the opening church service, a huge centipede suddenly attempts to crawl across the keyboard. Rose notices and flicks the thing away without hesitation. It's supposed to foreshadow her courage, and it would have been great to see Hepburn perform it. 4) Hepburn wrote a fascinating book about making the movie. Its unwieldy title is <u>The Making of The African Queen, or How I Went to Africa with Bogart, Bacall and Huston and Almost Lost My Mind</u>. "Bacall" in the title refers to actress Lauren Bacall, whom Bogart had married in 1945]

The Seven Year Itch
1955 – Marilyn Monroe as 'The Girl'
Early in this movie, Monroe's naked girl in the upstairs apartment – whose modesty is preserved behind a battery of potted plants – leans over the balcony to tell her neighbor (Tom Ewell), who is standing mesmerized on his patio below, that she tries to beat the heat in her un-air-conditioned apartment by keeping her "undies in the ice box." That line literally gave me the shivers when I first heard it as a teenager a number of years after the movie's initial release. Monroe, whose famous pose, holding down her loose-fitting white dress above a subway ventilation grating to keep a blast of air from a passing train from blowing it above her head, almost bought the movie a condemnation by the Catholic Church's Legion of Decency. And it wrecked her marriage to baseball legend Joe DiMaggio. Monroe personified sexuality in the 1950s. She captivated countless young men like me with her uninhibited manner, her striking beauty and her incomparable curves. But as the years passed she endured a steady stream of tragedies in her personal life, dying of an apparent drug overdose in 1962 at age 36. But here Billy Wilder, adapting George Axelrod's play for the screen, flawlessly directs this tale of a publisher married seven years who toys with – and is tormented by – notions of infidelity while

his wife and son vacation in the country during a sweltering Manhattan summer. A blend of real and fantasy sequences, the movie at the time was considered quite risqué. Now, it seems playful and innocent – but as funny as ever. **[W]**

The King and I
1956 – Yul Brynner as the King

Another way of describing the titles in this category might be roles that certain actors were born to play, and nowhere is such a description more fitting than of Brynner as the King of Siam in this gorgeous screen rendition of the Broadway musical by Richard Rodgers and Oscar Hammerstein. The stage play, which opened in 1951, marked Brynner's first starring role, and he was so good in it he became the logical choice to reprise the performance in the movie, which became his second major screen appearance of the year (along with his likewise iconic portrayal of Egyptian Pharaoh Rameses II in *The Ten Commandments*). The "I" in the movie's title refers to Anna Leonowens, played wonderfully by Deborah Kerr, the British governess hired to tutor the King's many children. The pair's interplay and conflict are extremely entertaining, and the movie boasts many great songs, including "Getting to Know You," "Hello, Young Lovers," "We Kiss in the Shadows," "The Entrance of the Siamese Children" and Brynner and Kerr's immortal duet in "Shall We Dance?" Even after nearly two decades of screen acting, the role remained so popular that Brynner returned to it on the stage in 1970 and played it until his death in 1985. In all, he performed it more than 4,500 times, and with good reason – he was, as this category asserts, unforgettable! [Trivia notes: 1) Brynner lived one of the most unusual lives of any movie actor. Born in Vladivostok, Siberia, in 1920, he moved to Paris as a young man where he worked as a photographer's model, a stage actor and a trapeze artist before escaping when the Germans invaded. Then he worked as a French-speaking radio broadcaster for the U.S. Office of War Information. Moving to New York after the war he became involved in, of all things, early television, where he directed live shows, acted in a forgettable sitcom and co-hosted, with his first wife Virginia Gilmore, one of TV's first talk shows. 2) While dying of lung cancer, Brynner appeared in several commercials warning against the dangers of cigarette smoking. 3) Two of the Asian characters were played by veteran Hispanic-American actors early in their careers: Rita Moreno, as the beautiful concubine Tuptim, and Carlos Rivas (whose singing voice was dubbed) as her doomed lover Lun Tha. 4) In what has become well-known Hollywood lore, Marni Nixon dubbed Kerr's singing voice. What isn't well known is that Nixon, age 21 at the time and a soprano, faced a challenge portraying Kerr's deeper voice. But she developed a head cold while recording the songs, and she claimed it actually helped her perform them in the alto range. 5) *The King and I* was – and remains – banned in Thailand because of its factual errors and perceived disrespect to the country's history and its royal dynasties] **[W]**

Cool Hand Luke
1967 – Paul Newman as Luke

Newman's acting career spanned six decades, but among all of his roles this one remains unique. It's the story of a chain gang in the South in the 1950s and of the attempt by one inmate to maintain his individuality, even if it meant inviting hardship or physical harm. In fact, Luke literally becomes a martyr to individuality. It's the movie that generated the clichéd phrase, "What we've got heah is a failure to communicate," uttered by the redneck warden (Strother Martin, a frequent supporting player with Newman). Luke as portrayed by Newman has a singular view of the world. It's part humorous and part "I don't give a damn." In the prison environment, however, such characteristics can be dangerous, but Luke takes that risk over and over. Though you're always rooting for him, you know in your gut he's fighting a system that will not tolerate such behavior. Alas, Newman didn't win Best Actor for this performance. That honor went to Rod Steiger for the next movie on this list. But the academy did give the nod to his co-star George Kennedy, playing a hulking but more conventional inmate. Watch for several well-known TV actors in minor roles: Wayne Rogers, who played Trapper John McIntyre on the M*A*S*H TV series; Harry Dean Stanton, who was Roman Grant in the HBO series Big Love, and Ralph Waite, who went on to play John Walton in The Waltons. Lalo Schifrin, most famous for his Mission: Impossible TV theme, composed the laid-back mandolin score. And Conrad Hall, who shot *Butch Cassidy and the Sundance Kid*, did the crisp cinematography. [Caution: sexuality and violence] **[W]**

In the Heat of the Night
1967 – Sidney Poitier as Detective Virgil Tibbs

Incredible, but not only did the motion picture academy not award Poitier an Oscar for his groundbreaking role as a police detective from Philadelphia who suddenly finds himself caught, literally, in a Mississippi town called Sparta, they didn't even nominate him. Rod Steiger, his co-star, playing Bill Gillespie, a redneck southern sheriff, received that distinction, two years after playing an unscrupulous Russian aristocrat in *Doctor Zhivago*. But make no mistake; this is Poitier's movie, in a role that changed Hollywood. He became the first black actor to star in a mainstream attraction, and his precedent influenced the generation of African Americans that followed. As Tibbs, he is poised, professional and more than a match for everyone in Sparta. [Trivia notes: 1) The most sensational moment in the movie is when Tibbs is slapped by Eric Endicott (Larry Gates), a wealthy town resident he is questioning, and then instantly slaps him back. The script, by Stirling Silliphant, had simply called for Endicott to slap Tibbs. But Poitier insisted that his character would not have tolerated the insult. It became electrifying. 2) Over Steiger's objections, Oscar-winning director Norman Jewison wanted Gillespie to chew gum constantly. Steiger eventually relented, and during the shoot ended up chewing more than 250 packs. 3) The movie was shot in a real town called Sparta – but in Illinois, and in autumn. Substituting for Mississippi in the summer caused some logistical problems for the cast and crew. Example: When shooting the night scenes, the actors had to chew on ice cubes before each scene to keep their breaths from fogging] [Caution: sexuality and violence] **[W]**

The Odd Couple
1968 – Walter Matthau and Jack Lemmon as Oscar Madison and Felix Ungar

Neil Simon's hilarious play about two formerly married men with direct-opposite personalities trying to share a West Side apartment in New York City has become a classic storyline and an immortal comedy; first on the stage, here on the screen and eventually as a long-running TV series starring Jack Klugman and Tony Randall. Matthau's Madison (which he reprised from the play) is a consummate slob who loves only baseball, poker and his regained freedom to chase women. Lemmon as Ungar (replacing Art Carney's Broadway role) is a schnook pining for his wife but so compulsive he can incite the people around him to contemplate murder. His neatness obsession is only one of his annoyances. There's a scene early on where Oscar is sitting with Felix in a restaurant watching him trying to clear his sinuses. Lemmon's portrayal of that process alone is side-splitting, but the look on Matthau's face as he watches is hysterical. Likewise, later when Matthau is reduced to tears while telling Lemmon's character to get out of the apartment before he's driven to desperate measures. It's a perfectly executed comedy, well directed by Gene Saks with a witty score by Neal Hefti, and no one has ever portrayed these characters better. [Trivia note: As perfect as Matthau was for the role, when he originally auditioned for the play he wanted to portray Felix. He said at the time that he could play Oscar in his sleep, but Felix would represent a real acting challenge. When Simon heard about Matthau's proposal, he reportedly told him he could play anyone he wanted – anywhere else but in "The Odd Couple." Fortunately for all of us, Simon won the argument, and the two stars and the playwright got rich on the royalties that rolled in over the decades – including from *The Odd Couple II* (not here), which reunited Simon with Matthau and Lemmon 30 years later] [Caution: just a little bit of adult material] **[W]**

213

Patton [100]
1970 – George C. Scott as General George S. Patton

Russell Crowe, Robert De Niro and Daniel Day-Lewis, eat your hearts out. Scott's performance in this movie is the best ever by an actor. Period. It is towering. Only 43 at the time, he plays the famous World War II general, whose nickname was "Old Blood and Guts," at ages 58 through 61 as a man without fear or even a shadow of doubt, but with an unmistakable human gleam in his eye. Patton was a flamboyant figure, but Scott's portrayal makes you feel as though you don't care what the real man was like – you could follow this guy anywhere. It's no love letter, however. Patton's flaws are clearly visible: his impatience, his penchant for drama, his tendency toward arrogance and his deluded sense that he had been reincarnated many times. Winner of seven Oscars, including Best Picture, with Francis Ford Coppola's terrific script and Franklin Schaffner's brilliant direction, this is one of the landmarks in movie biographies. The battle sequences are enormous, using real planes, tanks and heavy guns – and this was decades before computer animation could supply such scope artificially. Shot in Spain and Morocco with a cast of thousands, *Patton* presents an immense tableau of *men* in war. I mean this literally. As in *Lawrence of Arabia*, women are almost completely absent from the story. The few female characters are marginal, and only two of them even speak. Jerry Goldsmith contributed the glorious music fanfare, one of the greatest works for the movies ever written, a rich thematic orchestration that reaches a thrilling, minor-key crescendo in scenes leading up to the infamous Battle of the Bulge in December 1944 and provides a satisfying coda at the fadeout. *Patton* is another title worth seeing on the biggest screen available – it is overwhelming in that format. [Trivia notes: 1) Scott's Patton roars like a human lion, with a deep, bellowing voice that makes those around him feel cowed and intimidated. But the real general actually spoke with a high-pitched, whiny nasal tone. It was the reason, Patton admitted, that he resorted frequently to profanity. 2) Scott hated doing the signature five-minute prologue, in which Patton addresses off-camera troops from a stage backed with a huge

American flag. Schaffner reportedly assured him that the scene would appear under the movie's end credits – but then the director featured it at the beginning. Good thing, too. It remains one of the most effective movie openings ever] [Caution: wartime violence and profanity] **[W]**

Dog Day Afternoon
1975 – Al Pacino as Sonny Wortzik

The year after he wowed movie audiences with his frightening portrayal of Michael Corleone in *The Godfather Part II*, Pacino plays a big-dreaming loser named Sonny Wortzik, based on a real-life character whose attempted bank robbery in Brooklyn went bad on a hot August weekday. The movie's other stunning role-reversal involves John Cazale, who played Michael's weak-willed brother Fredo in both Godfather movies. Here he portrays Sal, a truly scary Vietnam veteran and Sonny's partner in crime. The story starts rather routinely, but director Sidney Lumet soon pulls your stomach into a knot from the suspense. In the centerpiece scene, the police confront Sonny with hundreds of their weapons trained on him. What he does in response, as portrayed by Pacino, is one of the most rousing sequences ever – it's unmatched as a show of individual courage and foolishness. With Charles Durning as a detective sergeant, James Broderick (Matthew Broderick's father) as an FBI agent, and Chris Sarandon in his acting debut playing a character too unique to reveal. [Trivia note: Cazale, who died three years later at age 42, holds a unique distinction among film actors. He appeared in only five movies – as mentioned the two Godfathers, as well as *The Conversation* (not on this list), *Dog Day Afternoon* and *The Deer Hunter* (also not here) – but all five received Best Picture nominations, and three of them won] [Caution: plentiful profanity and one moment of shocking violence] **[W]**

Body Heat
1981 – Kathleen Turner as Matty Walker

Turner was only 26 – the same age as Jean Harlow in her prime – when she played the femme fatale role of Walker, the frustrated

215

wife of a shady businessman (Richard Crenna) who starts up a feverish romance with a gullible South Florida attorney, Ned Racine (William Hurt). This stylish update of *Double Indemnity* (not on this list) broke new ground in explicit sexuality on the mainstream American screen, and it's all due to Turner's uninhibited displays of herself on camera and her sultry manipulation of Hurt's character. When he thinks he's conquered her, it's exciting to watch, but we eventually learn that he's the one who's been conquered and being led to his doom. You could say that Turner's character is the evil twin of Eve played by Barbara Stanwyck in *The Lady Eve*. Speaking of sultry, John Barry's score surely deserves that description. Watch for Ted Danson (Sam in the beloved Cheers TV series) in an early role as a district attorney who fancies himself a dancer, and Mickey Rourke as a convict who's an expert at arson. [Caution: Need it be said?] **[W]**

Tootsie [100]
1982 – Dustin Hoffman as Michael Dorsey/Dorothy Michaels
This is a wonderfully written and acted comedy, and the amazing thing is that as quirky and neurotic as Hoffman can be sometimes (he's never been one of my favorite actors – he's just too self-affected), here you actually forget it's Hoffman under heavy makeup and women's clothing. He plays Michael Dorsey, a talented but egotistical and perennially unemployed actor who finds fame by secretly impersonating a woman – Dorothy Michaels – on a TV soap opera in New York City. Along the way, or so the plot goes, he discovers some insights about himself and about male–female relationships, and he falls in love for the first time with Julie Nichols (Jessica Lange in an Oscar-winning role), who plays the promiscuous nurse in "Southwest General," a soap opera – "daytime drama," as the cast is required to explain. The fine supporting players include Charles Durning as Julie's father, Teri Garr as Michael's friend and sometime lover, Dabney Coleman as the show's director – who's even more self-absorbed than Michael – and Bill Murray in a terrific turn as Michael's roommate. Sidney Pollack, who

216

directed the movie, also plays Michael's agent, and their hilarious onscreen conflicts apparently mirror the offscreen arguments that frequently transpired between Pollack and Hoffman. Despite the tension and the reported multiple script rewrites, they teamed to deliver a seamless and often hilarious story about gender role reversal. Dave Grusin did the light-and-lively score. [Critic's note: As you've read by now, I frequently disagree, sometimes strenuously, with the members of the motion picture academy about their Oscar choices. And here I go again. I thought Jessica Lange did a fine and appealing job in this movie, but I also thought Teri Garr's performance bested Lange in every way as Michael's neurotic friend Sandy. Her final scene with Hoffman alone should have clinched a Best Supporting Actress win] [Caution: mild profanity and sexuality] **[W]**

Dave
1993 – Kevin Kline as Dave Kovic/President Bill Mitchell
It's difficult enough for an actor to turn in an unforgettable performance; it's also quite remarkable to do it in a movie that's not very good. But Kline not only does it here, he also does it playing a dual role – and making us believe both of his characters are separate individuals. William Harrison Mitchell (read: William Jefferson Clinton) is a U.S. president who's a poor excuse for a human being: outwardly charming but self-centered and a habitual, probably predatory philanderer. Dave Kovic is a decent guy who runs an employment agency in Washington and moonlights as a Bill Mitchell lookalike. At one point a Secret Service agent (a stone-faced Ving Rhames) seeks out Dave to impersonate Mitchell briefly at a public appearance – not because of security concerns but because the president wants an opportunity to engage in a private dalliance in a hotel with one of his secretaries (Laura Linney, whose appeal and talent are wasted here). Dave complies, but a sudden emergency prompts Mitchell's two top aides (Frank Langella, in a fine, menacing turn as an even bigger schmuck than Mitchell, and Kevin Dunn) to persuade him to continue the role, this time in front of the whole country. I'll stop the plot description there. It's hugely

contrived and formulaic, it bashes conservatives in Hollywood's standard way, and for the most part the real-life Washington politicians and media types look wooden and sound silly – come to think of it, that fits them to a tee. What saves the movie and makes it so memorable is watching Kline's metamorphosis from Joe Everyman into a highly admirable if brief tenure as president. He looks like he's having the time of his life, infectiously so, as he warms to the idea that even as an imposter he can help people. As I said, it's contrived, but Kline makes you want Dave to succeed in this most unusual role. It's his finest performance, and he's helped greatly by Sigourney Weaver as the first lady (a totally idealized vision of Hillary Clinton) and Ben Kingsley as the vice president. James Newton Howard's capital score constantly provides just the right mood. [Viewing note: There's a brief scene where Dave, impersonating Mitchell, throws out the first pitch of the Major League Baseball season. It recalls not Clinton, but George W. Bush's electrifying performance at Yankee Stadium shortly after 9/11. Dave's pitch is fun, but Bush's brought you to tears, because the country needed to see something inspiring at that moment] [Trivia note: Kline and Weaver co-starred again four years later in Ang Lee's melancholy drama *The Ice Storm* (not on this list)] [Caution: mild profanity and fleeting (male) nudity] [W]

The Fugitive [100]
1993 – Tommy Lee Jones as Deputy U.S. Marshal Samuel Girard

This remake of the 1960s television series was meant to be a star vehicle for Harrison Ford, and he is appealing in the role of Dr. Richard Kimble, a Chicago surgeon wrongfully convicted of killing his wife (the radiant Sela Ward). But Jones steals the movie right out from under him. The members of the motion picture academy thought so as well, because they awarded him the Best Supporting Actor Oscar. Jones plays Girard with a combination of toughness and humor that's irresistible, and his great moments on the screen are too numerous to mention. He makes you feel, as did George C. Scott's Patton, that you'd follow this guy anywhere. The movie hums along at a fine clip under the assured direction of Andrew Davis, also propelled by the versatile James Newton Howard's thrilling score. Eventually, the story breaks down into a rather dumb indictment of a pharmaceutical firm and ends in a ridiculous climax. But Jones never loses his edge – he's terrific! [Trivia note: Girard's first name was Philip in the TV series. What was wrong with that?] [Caution: violence and language] **[W]**

Geronimo: An American Legend
1993 – Wes Studi as Geronimo
This superior western marked the best work of several people, including director Walter Hill, writer John Milius and actor Jason Patric. But Studi's portrayal of Geronimo, the Apache who fought the U.S. Army in New Mexico in the 1870s and 1880s, trumps everyone else. It's like the other performances in this category. When he's on the screen, even briefly, he is riveting. Studi, a Cherokee who attended Native American schools as a child, has played several striking roles, including a menacing Pawnee in *Dances with Wolves*. But here he delivers a masterful portrayal of Geronimo, giving him a fierce dignity and embodying all of the sadness and fury that must have powered the real man whose family was wiped out by Mexicans and whose trust was betrayed repeatedly by the U.S. government. Hill and Milius present a balanced and full-bodied look at this sad episode in American history when whites and natives alike slaughtered one another for a decade. With majestic Arizona and Utah scenery as backdrops, and solid performances by Gene Hackman as Brigadier General George Crook, who negotiated the treaty with the Apache; Robert Duvall as Al Sieber, a grizzled tracker; and a young Matt Damon (who looks a lot here like the young Ron Howard) as a junior officer and the movie's narrator. Lloyd Ahern did the striking cinematography – though I thought he and Hill used a "tobacco" (brown-hued) lens filter a bit too much. [Trivia notes: 1) Geronimo (Goyahkla in his own language) lived until 1909. Reportedly, on his deathbed he expressed regret at having surrendered and said, "I should have

219

fought until I was the last man alive." 2) (a spoiler) The real Al
Sieber didn't meet his end as portrayed in the movie. He died
much later in a construction accident] [Caution: violence] **[W]**

The Shawshank Redemption
1994 – Morgan Freeman as Ellis Boyd "Red" Redding
Freeman, who has become one of the screen's great actors,
demonstrates the impressive range and appeal of his talent here
by contributing the meat of his performance offscreen as the
movie's narrator. In the story, based on a Stephen King short
novel and skillfully directed by Frank Darabont (who also did
The Green Mile), Freeman plays Red as a soft-spoken, steady,
aging man whose wild youth has been replaced by painful
wisdom. Convicted of murder and sent to prison for life, he
settles into the routine almost comfortably as the years pass,
maintaining a modest living as a procurer of non-dangerous but
contraband goods for inmates and guards alike. When he
befriends newcomer Andy Dufresne (du-FRAYNE – Tim
Robbins), a former banker convicted of killing his wife and her
lover, the two form one of the most unusual relationships ever
portrayed on the screen. Robbins is good as Dufresne, but
Freeman provides the movie's heart, so much so that you begin
to think if you ever found yourself in prison, you'd pray to find
a friend like Red. Thomas Newman wrote the sad and brooding
score. [Caution: violence and rough language] **[W]**

Devil in a Blue Dress
1995 – Don Cheadle as Mouse Alexander
Sometimes an actor will make an entrance relatively late in a
movie and still walk away with it. That's exactly what Don
Cheadle does in this detective thriller based on the Walter
Mosley novel. The versatile Cheadle plays Mouse, who might be
the most nonchalant hit man ever. Though he arrives well into
the plot, he immediately takes over, and the movie is his from
then on. Not that *Devil in a Blue Dress* isn't gripping in its own
right. Skillfully directed by newcomer Carl Franklin, the story
takes place in post-World War II Los Angeles amid political

220

intrigue and scandal involving the race for the city's next mayor. Ezekial "Easy" Rawlins (Denzel Washington) is out of the Army and looking for a job. He finds one, a lucrative one, in the employ of a most shady character named Dewitt Albright (Tom Sizemore). But he soon discovers his assignment is so dangerous he might not live long enough to spend his money. So, he puts in a call for help to his old friend Mouse, who soon thereafter is in charge of Easy's safety – and the movie. In one scene, after Mouse has strangled a hoodlum in his custody, Easy explodes in frustration with him. Mouse seems genuinely puzzled at the reaction and replies, "If you didn't want him killed, why'd you leave him with me?" [Caution: violence and sexuality] **[W]**

Get Shorty [100]
1995 – John Travolta as Chili Palmer
Here's a character who personifies absolute confidence – cool, if you will. You couldn't ruffle his feathers if you hit him with a brick. Or, as he tells someone in so many words, if you put a gun to his head *maybe* he would stand for further discussion. The movie, skillfully directed by Barry Sonnenfeld and written by Scott Frank (based on Elmore Leonard's novel), is done in high style, with quirky camera angles and moves, rapid-fire editing and razor-sharp, dead-pan dialogue. But Travolta anchors it. He plays Chili to perfection. Along with supreme confidence he conveys a sense of fun – he seems to be having a great time here, and it infects the other cast members. Gene Hackman enjoys a wonderful turn as a schlock movie producer; Rene Russo has rough-hewn charm as a B-movie star with higher ambitions; Danny De Vito has a pretty good time as well, playing a bona fide Hollywood star (the "Shorty" in the title); Delroy Lindo holds his own as a drug dealer masquerading as a car-rental operator and Dennis Farina shines as a mobster trying to collect a payoff from Palmer. Farina's repetition of a cab driver's description of recent Los Angeles weather alone is worth the price of admission. Also watch for James Gandolfini (now immortal as Tony Soprano of the HBO series The Sopranos) in an early role as a redneck ex-stuntman-turned bodyguard. And

TV veteran Alex Rocco contributes a funny cameo reprising (approximately) his most memorable scene in *The Godfather*. Consistently witty and clever, and often laugh-out-loud hilarious, the movie presents a savagely sly take on La-La Land culture. John Lurie wrote the hip and unusual score. [Trivia note: Lindo and Gandolfini appeared again together six years later as two military officers in the flawed and overblown *The Last Castle*, and in the same year Lindo co-starred as Hackman's partner, with De Vito as their mutual nemesis, in *Heist*, David Mamet's not-quite-successful … heist drama (neither movie on my list)] [Caution: constant profanity and some graphic violence though in a humorous context] [W]

Amistad
1997 – Djimon Hounsou as Cinque

Steven Spielberg missed twice in the '80s at winning a Best Picture Oscar with his superb screen versions of *The Color Purple* and *Empire of the Sun*. Though he finally won in 1993 with *Schindler's List*, he missed again twice during the '90s, with *Saving Private Ryan* and here, with *Amistad*. This is a beautifully crafted movie depicting a shocking but eventually triumphant episode of American history. The title refers to a slave ship taken over by its African captives in the West Indies in 1839. Intercepted by a U.S. Navy vessel, the ship, La Amistad, and its occupants were interned in Boston while a federal judge tried to rule on their status, and various interest groups attempted to intervene in the case – including the prepubescent Queen Isabella II of Spain, who claimed ownership of the slaves. Eventually they were defended by former President John Quincy Adams, who argued on their behalf before the U.S. Supreme Court. Central to this story is Cinque (SIN-kay), the leader of the slaves. Djimon Hounsou (JI-mon HOON-soo), a former male fashion model and screen newcomer, is outstanding – electrifying even. He is so good that he outshines his formidable co-stars Morgan Freeman, Matthew McConaughey and Anthony Hopkins (who plays Adams). His range of emotions is vast, and he plays them with the subtlety of a screen veteran. His capacity to portray anger is awesome. Spielberg's enduring reputation has come from his crowd-pleasing blockbusters, but over the years he has made some unparalleled movies and has directed some remarkable actors – and *Amistad* and Hounsou are shining examples. Every second Hounsou is on the screen you cannot take your eyes off him. John Williams, who at this point had collaborated with Spielberg for a quarter-century, contributed the sensitive score, which presages his work on *The Patriot* and *Munich*. [Caution: scenes of graphic violence and non-sexual but explicit nudity] **[W]**

L.A. Confidential
1997 – Russell Crowe as Officer Bud White

New Zealand-born actor Crowe appeared in several Australian and minor U.S. features before he won his breakthrough role here in Curtis Hanson's crime thriller set in Los Angeles – and break through he does. From his very first moment on the screen until his last, Crowe dominates the movie with a ferociousness rarely seen. No one else in the cast even approaches his combination of toughness and raw emotional honesty. Here, Crowe does what only a handful of actors have done before: move irrevocably from obscurity to star status with one performance. He's very big, but the movie has other attractions, including fellow Aussie actor and newcomer Guy Pearce as a straight-arrow, second-generation cop; James Cromwell as a corrupt and opportunistic police captain; David Strathairn as a slimy flesh peddler, and Kevin Spacey in a terrific turn as a smooth but cynical detective. There's also a fine if workmanlike score by Jerry Goldsmith – returning to the L.A. detective genre 23 years after *Chinatown* – and some truly distinctive work by character actors both veteran and novice. Oh, the plot? L.A. cops deal with crime and internal corruption, as well as a mob conflict created when the local kingpin Meyer Harris "Mickey" Cohen goes to prison, leaving a vacuum in the city's drug trade. [Critic's note: Kim Basinger won the Best Supporting Actress Oscar for a decent but ordinary performance in this movie, beating out 86-year-old Gloria Stuart in a supporting role for the ages as the centenarian Rose in *Titanic* and marking another of the motion picture academy's worst misjudgments] [<u>Caution</u>: sexuality and graphic violence] [**W**]

The Green Mile
1999 – Michael Clarke Duncan as John Coffey

In this often deeply sad and haunting fantasy, Duncan plays John Coffey, a condemned murderer awaiting his execution in a Louisiana prison in 1935. An enormous man who seems utterly childlike (he's even afraid of the dark), Coffey's guards (Tom Hanks, David Morse and Barry Pepper) come to suspect there's more to this prisoner than meets the eye. And there is – much more – as the big man begins to display some extraordinary abilities and insights. In the process, both his captors and the audience become drawn in ever closer to, and feel more and more protective of, this most unusual character. One of the final scenes, which takes place in a nearly empty prison movie theater, will probably move you to tears with its combination of rapture and tragedy. Though surrounded by fine supporting players, including Patricia Clarkson, James Cromwell, Bonnie Hunt, Gary Sinise and Harry Dean Stanton, Duncan commands the screen anytime he's on camera. His massive face is astoundingly expressive, and as the story unfolds you find yourself hoping for his deliverance as much as he seems accepting and even welcoming of his fate. Like *The Shawshank Redemption*, it's based on a novel by Stephen King and written and directed by Frank Darabont. Unlike its predecessor, however, this movie frequently veers too far into implausibility, and the special effects aren't particularly convincing. Nevertheless, don't miss this one – but keep the kids away. As he did for *The Shawshank Redemption*, Thomas Newman contributed the painfully sad but memorable score. [<u>Trivia notes</u>: At six feet, five inches, veteran actor Duncan was a large man (he died of a heart attack in 2012 at age 54), but he wasn't nearly as large as the movie portrayed him. His size was the result of clever camera tricks] [<u>Caution</u>: scenes of highly disturbing violence and harsh language] [**W**]

Flight

2012 – Denzel Washington as Whip Whitaker

So many of the movies I've seen over the years start out strong and move along well, only to fizzle at or near the denouement. This one, as directed by Robert Zemeckis, is a rare reversal of that pattern – in the extreme. For much of the time, watching *Flight*, I grew impatient and even angry at the way the story was unfolding. I found it frustrating and objectionable, seeing Whitaker, an alcoholic, coke-sniffing, serial liar of an airline pilot, escape liability for endangering his passengers and trashing one relationship after another because of his dangerous habit of getting drunk at night and the following morning, and using cocaine to snap himself back into action. When destiny takes a hand, as it so often does in self-destructive situations, and things go very, very wrong on a short hop from Orlando to Atlanta, it appears as though Whitaker's secret life will be exposed. Even then, Whitaker just might escape his moment of truth – with the help of his longstanding drug dealer (John Goodman, in a sensational but neglected performance). But that's when the story suddenly and wrenchingly heads in a new direction. From that point on, although it's near the end, the movie soars and rewards your patience. The reason? One of the most astounding moments on the screen you'll ever see. Washington, whose Oscar-winning performance in *Glory* was extraordinary, tops himself here as a man whose conscience finally overcomes – smashes, even – a lifetime of deception and denial. His epiphany is palpable, meaning that you will literally feel both his pain and ultimate peace. Yes, he is indeed unforgettable. [Trivia note: *Flight* reunites Washington with Don Cheadle, who stole *Devil in a Blue Dress* from him. But here, it's all Denzel's show] [Caution: sexuality, drug and alcohol abuse, rough language, adult material and two extremely tense scenes in the air] **[W]**

225

16. Incomparable Cagney

Call this an addendum to the Unforgettable category, because it involves an actor whose entire body of work comprises indelible performances. In the annals of great movie stars, no one was more versatile than the man born James Francis Cagney. Consider someone who could play the beloved song-and-dance man George M. Cohan – and do the singing and dancing for real – then portray the criminal psychopath Cody Jarret, and then dramatize the resourcefulness and courage of Admiral "Bull" Halsey during the earliest days of World War II, and you get an idea of his range. Yet unlike some of the chameleon-like actors of more recent times – such as Russell Crowe and Daniel Day-Lewis – Cagney was always Cagney, no matter the role. As he once described his acting, it was about "planting your feet, looking the other guy in the eye and telling the truth." That fits him to a T, and though he often played "sons-of-bitches," as George C. Scott once described Cagney's characters, "they still make you care." Here are four reasons why he will reside forever among favorite movie actors.

Yankee Doodle Dandy
1942 – as George M. Cohan
The premier Hollywood studio for musicals was Metro-Goldwyn-Mayer, but Warner Brothers, best known for war movies and westerns, once in a while turned out its own excellent version of the genre. Perhaps none was more successful than this biography of the great song-and-dance man George M. Cohan. James Cagney is superb in the role, particularly when he performs the tunes that Cohan made famous, including the title number. The movie proceeds as many biographies do, in

flashback. We first meet Cohan, as an elderly man, just after his performance of President Franklin D. Roosevelt (who isn't named) in the play "I'd Rather Be Right" in the early days of World War II. Cohan receives a telegram from the White House requesting his presence there. He complies, ending up in a one-on-one meeting with the president (who's shown with his back to the camera). From there, in the course of the conversation, Cohan recounts his long life on the stage, including his performances as a member of "The Four Cohans," including his father, mother and sister (Walter Huston, Rosemary DeCamp and Cagney's real sister Jeanne). And what a rousing, thoroughly patriotic reminiscence it is, including Cohan's courtship of, marriage to and onstage partnership with his wife Mary (Joan Leslie, who was only 17). Directed by Michael Curtiz just before he did *Casablanca*, this is a delightful and stirring tribute to an American institution and distinctly American music. It won Cagney his only Oscar. [Trivia note: If you watch Cagney's dancing closely, you'll probably conclude that he looks good. But he wasn't a trained dancer; he just rehearsed and rehearsed the numbers until his feet bled] **[B&W]**

White Heat
1949 – as Cody Jarret

"Made it, Ma! Top of the world!" is such a famous last line (though it's often misquoted as "Top o' the world, Ma!") that it has worked its way into the popular culture, and here is the movie where it was first uttered. Cagney's Jarret is one of the great movie psychotics, a man whose character has been imitated and parodied countless times. He's a murderous mama's boy, beset with fits of temper and possibly epilepsy, but he rules his gang – and his moll (Virginia Mayo) – with an iron hand. Along with the famous finale, there are several other great scenes. One of them depicts Jarret's reaction when he's notified in prison that his mother has died, and he sobs and moans in grief while punching out the guards trying to subdue him. There's also a rare moment of black humor where a stooge, whom Jarret has locked in the trunk of his car, complains that he's not getting enough air – so guess what happens? Given his monstrous nature, you can't like Cody Jarret, but as played by James Cagney, and flawlessly directed by Raoul Walsh, you'll never forget him. [Trivia note: Jarret's explosive outburst in the prison cafeteria even shocked the cast, because Cagney wouldn't let anyone else know how he planned to perform the scene. So, the reactions of everyone else were genuine] **[B&W]**

Mister Roberts
1955 – as Captain Morton
The second of two movies director John Ford took from stage plays, this one won Jack Lemmon his first Oscar as the mischievous Ensign Pulver. Henry Fonda, reprising his Tony Award-winning stage role, plays Lieutenant (junior grade) Doug Roberts, a man who longs for a combat assignment in the waning days of the war in the Pacific but instead must endure the boredom of a supply ship well away from the action. Both Roberts and Lemmon are foils to Cagney's Captain Morton, which he plays wonderfully by evoking Ford's personality – though he's onscreen a lot less than the other principals. Morton's a stickler for the rules, driven by an inferiority complex and a royal pain in the butt. As such, he's in constant conflict with Roberts, who channels his frustration by standing up to the captain on behalf of the ship's crew. Shot on Midway Island and off the coast of the Hawai`ian island of Oahu, as well as on a large set representing the cargo ship's deck, most of the story is played for laughs – particularly a recurring incident involving Morton 's treasured potted palm tree – but there is one heartbreaking moment. William Powell, in his last film role, plays the ship's doctor. [Trivia notes: 1) The movie lists two directors, including Mervyn Leroy along with Ford. That's because at one point Ford got into a heated argument with Fonda and ended up punching him, severing their long friendship and resulting in the director's quiet dismissal from the production. But the resulting chaos actually required Joshua Logan, who co-wrote both the play and the screenplay, to help with the directing as well; likewise cast member Ward Bond, a

longtime Ford player and friend – though both contributions were uncredited. 2) The filming on Midway represented a homecoming of sorts for Ford. Stationed there by the War Department in 1942, he had shot 16-millimeter footage of the Japanese attack on the island and compiled it in the short film *The Battle of Midway* (coming in my next compilation). 3) That other Ford movie taken from a stage play? *The Long Voyage Home*, in 1940 (also in the next compilation)] **[W]**

The Gallant Hours
1960 – as Fleet Admiral William F. "Bull" Halsey, Jr.

A most unusual war movie, this is an almost reverential look at Halsey – complete with frequent (and mostly male) choral accompaniment in the background. Commander of U.S. Navy forces in the South Pacific during World War II, and of Colonel James Doolittle's daring raid on Tokyo, Halsey didn't get his nickname, "Bull," for nothing. His stubborn refusal to retreat at the battle of Guadalcanal in the face of far superior Japanese forces became the stuff of legend, as was his daring and successful effort to shoot down an aircraft carrying Isoroku Yamamoto, the Japanese admiral who commanded the attack on Pearl Harbor on December 7, 1941, and who commanded the fleet that Halsey was charged with destroying. Cagney's next-to-last starring role is a fine one, but it's also his most restrained, made all the more admirable by the limitations placed on his character. Except for a few exterior scenes, this could have been done as a stage play. There are no battle sequences, and most of the action, so to speak, takes place at Halsey's headquarters or in the stateroom aboard his flagship. So do the interactions among the Japanese commanders. A narrator provides much of the background detail, and some sequences consist entirely of Cagney alone in a room – such as a long sequence depicting Halsey tensely waiting for word about the outcome of the infamous sea battle to save Guadalcanal – but he's so compelling you can't lose your interest in what's happening, or in him. That, dear reader, is star power. **[B&W] [W]**

17. Big-Name Directors But Did You Know They Also Did...?

One of the traits that makes a fine movie director is the willingness to attempt a variety of subjects. The attempts don't always work, of course, but in the hands of masters of the medium even their relatively minor productions can be valuable. If you're a fan of these three moviemakers, you might want to sample their lesser-known works, including this trio of my favorites.

The Sugarland Express
1974 – Steven Spielberg

Ordinarily I don't like movies featuring pampered Hollywood actors playing bumpkins, but this one got to me because it treats the main characters with affection and pathos. Based on a true story, Goldie Hawn and William Atherton play Lou Jean and Clovis Poplin, a pair of white-trash Texans who scheme to kidnap their own son, a toddler taken from them when Lou Jean was sent to prison. Out on parole but notified she can't regain custody, she schemes to spring Clovis – also a prisoner – and reclaim their baby. Naturally, the plan goes wrong, so the couple compounds the problem by commandeering a police car and ordering the officer (Michael Sacks) to drive them to Sugarland, Texas, and their son's foster home. When word gets out about the hijacking, the chase is on, led by Captain Harlin Tanner of the Highway Patrol (Ben Johnson, in his best role). Eventually, Lou Jean's quest to recover her baby becomes a statewide media sensation, and hundreds of people turn out to watch the train of patrol cars pursuing the fugitives. Spielberg, who was only 26 at the time, handles the action scenes like a veteran and gets strong performances from all four main characters. And John Williams provides the twangy, melancholy score in his first of many collaborations with the director. [Caution: violence] **[W]**

Tucker: The Man and His Dream
1988 – Francis Ford Coppola

The subject of maverick automaker Preston Tucker had fascinated Coppola for a long time before he was able to bring it to the screen, and the writer–director spent years doing basic research on the man. The result doesn't rank anywhere near Coppola's magnificent renditions of *The Godfather* saga, or even his extravagant folly of *Apocalypse Now*. But it's a highly stylized, interesting piece of cinema storytelling, with Coppola often using vivid primary colors to portray the enthusiasm of post-World War II advertising. Jeff Bridges stars as Tucker, a real-life industrialist who dreams of starting his own automobile line and emphasizing safety and innovation instead of the assembly-line mentality of the Big Three automakers at the time: Ford, General Motors and Chrysler. With the help of Abe Karatz (Martin Landau, in an Oscar-nominated performance), his agent and financier, Tucker raises enough capital to build a vehicle with a lightweight helicopter engine placed behind the passenger compartment; a pop-out windshield; an extra headlight in the center of the grill that follows the turn of the wheels; and seatbelts – the first time they're featured in an automobile. After some initial success – though the car's rollout is a nail-biter – Tucker runs afoul of the big carmakers and their man in Washington, Senator Homer Ferguson (Lloyd Bridges, Jeff's father, in a fun cameo role). They conspire to run him out of business, but not before he has his day in court. It's a handsome production and to date the last really good movie Coppola has made. Watch for a weird but witty cameo by Dean Stockwell as eccentric billionaire Howard Hughes. [Trivia note: Joan Allen, who plays Tucker's wife Vera here, would reunite with Jeff Bridges 12 years later as a (platonic) compatriot in the political thriller *The Contender* (coming in a later compilation)] **[W]**

Crimes and Misdemeanors
1989 – Woody Allen

Since the late 1960s, Allen's movies have alternated between the terminally silly and the insufferably self-indulgent – sometimes morbidly so – with just a couple of standouts (*Annie Hall* and *Hannah and Her Sisters*) in between. This title is unique to him. It's silly and superfluous some of the time, but it also contains a solid, wrenching drama at its core. Martin Landau was nominated for Best Supporting Actor for the second consecutive year, here playing a doctor locked in an ill-fated affair with an obsessive woman (Anjelica Huston). Allen can't resist his habitual nebbishness, and he gives Alan Alda a thankless role as a vapid TV producer, but whenever he's directing Landau, and the great Jerry Orbach as Landau's brother, he's dead on. [Trivia note: Landau, whose career spanned five decades and 125 movies, finally won an Oscar as Best Supporting Actor five years later for portraying the legendary vampire persona Bela Lugosi in the otherwise forgettable *Ed Wood* (not here)] [Caution: violence, harsh language and sexuality] **[W]**

18. Fine Westerns, Straight and Offbeat

Even to this day, Hollywood has probably produced more westerns than any other genre; yet many, many of them are forgettable. Here – along with others listed elsewhere – are six that decidedly are not.

Red River [100]
1948 – Howard Hawks

The best movie made in the year of my birth also happens to be THE most rip-snortin', rootin'-tootin' western – ever, depicting the establishment of the Chisholm Trail after the end of the Civil War. On that trail, hard and desperate men drove cattle from pastures in southern Texas to railroad terminals in Kansas and Missouri, a thousand miles away. John Wayne plays one of his most memorable roles as Thomas Dunson, an obsessive cattle baron who is determined to take his 9,000-strong herd – portrayed by a real herd of 6,000 – to market despite the rigors of the trail and the threat of attack by Indians and bandits, as well as growing disgruntlement among his men. Wayne's endearing gruffness and his lanky gait reach the peak of their development here. Montgomery Clift as Dunson's foster son Matt Garth is no slouch, either. Joanne Dru provides more than enough love interest for both men. Walter Brennan is at his flinty-eyed best as Dunson's toothless sidekick and camp cook. And of course the famous Hawksian dialog, which flavored such classics as *Bringing Up Baby* and *His Girl Friday*, is in full display. Russell Harlan's cinematography is sweeping, and composer Dimitri Tiomkin produces his first great score. But the real standout in this movie is the herd. In this day of computer-generated images of everything from fleets of starships to swarms of giant insects, there's an awesome aspect to seeing a cattle drive conducted with such realism, with actors sitting astride horses amid thousands of potentially dangerous animals. There are many classic scenes, but when Wayne tells Clift to begin the drive with the line, "Take 'em to Missouri, Matt," and every cowboy lets out a whoop and a holler, it makes you want to saddle up and sign on for the ride. At one point in the climactic fight between Wayne and Clift, Wayne strides through a herd of cattle and scatters them like chickens – and solidifies his twin titles as king of the westerns and America's most iconic actor. Pauline Kael called it "a magnificent horse opera," and I think you'll agree. [Trivia note: The reason the cattle herd used for the movie actually numbered about 6,000, instead of 9,000, is possibly because each of them rented at $10 per day, and the studio balked at the extra cost] **[B&W]**

Jeremiah Johnson [100]
1972 – Sydney Pollack
In this languid but absorbing and beautiful-looking movie, Robert Redford plays the title role, a mysterious mountain man whose exploits in the 1830s are loosely based on a real character named Johnston, whose nastier habits included cutting out the livers of his enemies and consuming them. Redford's Johnson is decidedly more genteel; he simply forsakes civilization to live out his life in solitude in the wilderness. Along the way, he encounters an assortment of bizarre characters, including Hatchet Jack, a man frozen to death on a mountain; Bear Claw, a bear hunter with a devilish sense of humor (Will Geer, best known as Grandpa on The Waltons TV series); a demented woman (Allyn Ann McLerie, who played a minor role with Redford in *All the President's Men* four years later, and was the neurotic mother in the quirky TV series Days and Nights of Molly Dodd); Swan, an Indian woman whom Johnson must take for a wife (Delle Bolton, in her one and only movie role), and Del Gue (Stefan Gierasch), another mountain man, who shouts to himself deliberately. There are also many, many Indians. This mix makes for some vivid action sequences, but the movie is at

234

its best in the long, quiet scenes set amid the stunning Utah landscapes, where backdrops include high, sheer mountainsides that once lay buried under an ancient ocean. For that reason, *Jeremiah Johnson* is best appreciated in the theater, or on the biggest video screen you can find. The music of Tim McIntire and John Rubenstein provides a perfect mood, and you might hear yourself mimicking McIntire singing the title song in his gravelly voice for days afterward.

> *The way that you wander*
> *is the way that you choose;*
> *the day that you tarry*
> *is the day that you lose.*
> *Sunshine or thunder,*
> *a man will always wonder*
> *where – the fair wind blows.*

[Trivia notes: 1) In the scene where Johnson is catching fish in a mountain stream, Redford appears rather jolly. That's because he had grown so cold after multiple takes in the icy water that the hypothermia actually made him giddy. 2) Redford was so taken by the Utah landscape used in the movie that he settled there permanently] **[W]**

Junior Bonner
1972 – Sam Peckinpah

For those of you too young to know the name Sam Peckinpah, let's just say that from the late '60s through the '70s he pushed the outside of the envelope for movie violence, particularly with such titles as *The Wild Bunch* and *The Getaway* (neither here), and two more repulsive movies from that time period you're not likely to find. This is the one movie he made that bucks the trend. It's a simple tale, well told, about an aging rodeo rider (Steve McQueen) who returns to his hometown of Prescott, Arizona, to ride a notorious bull that had busted his ribs on a previous occasion. While there he pays a visit to his mother (Ida Lupino, a fine actress and a pretty fair director herself), carouses with his father (Robert Preston, in yet another top-grade performance neglected by the motion picture academy),

235

exchanges punches with his brother (Joe Don Baker), and enjoys a fling with a pretty girl (B-movie player Barbara Leigh). Oh yes, he enters several rodeo events and faces a rematch with his nemesis bull. In the process, however, Peckinpah paints a vivid but affectionate portrait of the lives of rodeo riders, and before you know it the movie saunters its way into your good graces. [Trivia notes: 1) The annual Prescott Rodeo, first organized in 1888 and presented here as the action centerpiece, is America's oldest. 2) There's a reason why rodeo animals buck so violently. If you notice, they all have thin straps wrapped around their hind quarters. Those straps cause the animals reflexively to kick their hind legs. They're not, as some might think – and I've been guilty of this myself – squeezing the testicles, something that would cause excruciating pain, rider or no rider] **[W]**

The Shootist
1976 – Don Siegel
John Wayne's 169th and last Hollywood movie provides a fitting closure to the career of one of Hollywood's greatest stars and – as I declared above – an American icon. Wayne is John Bernard Books, an aging gunfighter who, when he learns he is dying of cancer, decides to settle some old scores and go out in a blaze of glory. The movie begins with a delightful montage ostensibly depicting Books in his earlier years. It's actually a series of clips of Wayne in his earlier westerns, so we watch him as he ages onscreen. Shot almost entirely on location in Carson City, Nevada, on the shores of Lake Tahoe, the scenery is gorgeous, and the old part of town is charming. Lauren Bacall plays a widow who runs a boarding house where Books takes up residence temporarily. Even though Wayne at the time was suffering from prostate problems and the aftereffects of pneumonia, he played the role of Books with relish, and as usual he outclassed just about everyone else on the screen. The movie's best parts involve Books, the killer of more than 30 men, simply coming to terms with his own mortality. In a way it makes the climactic gun fight somewhat anticlimactic. With Ron Howard as Bacall's rambunctious son, Harry Morgan as the town

marshal, Scatman Crothers as a feisty livery stable owner, Richard Boone and Hugh O'Brian as two of Books's mortal rivals, and James Stewart – who co-starred with Wayne only once, in *The Man Who Shot Liberty Valence* – in a small role as the doctor who gives him the bad news. **[W]**

Silverado
1985 – Lawrence Kasdan
An all-star cast graces Kasdan's first and most successful foray into westerns, a sometimes overwritten but otherwise entertaining and lively tribute to the genre. Silverado refers to a fictional town (which the production company built from scratch in New Mexico) that draws the four main characters – played by Scott Glenn, Kevin Kline, Danny Glover and Kevin Costner – to join forces to fight Brian Dennehy and the rest of the bad guys. This also marks the major movie debut of Costner, who shines in his role as a flamboyant gunfighter from his very first scene. There also are pretty good minor turns by former Monty Python troupe member John Cleese as a sheriff, and Linda Hunt as Stella, owner of The Midnight Star saloon. James Gammon, one of my favorite character actors, is wonderful in a small role as a bandit leader, and Jeff Fahey is all evil menace as Kline's nemesis. There's the usual fightin' and fussin' and feudin', with some killin' mixed in, but it's a tongue-in-cheek love letter to every western you've ever seen, and everyone seems comfortable on horseback. John Bailey's splendid cinematography gives a pretty luster to the southwestern landscapes, and Bruce Broughton's orchestral score with a western twang is rich and memorable. [Trivia notes: 1) In what has become familiar lore in the wake of Costner's now-stellar career, he was originally cast as Alex, the (now-unseen) character who commits suicide in *The Big Chill*. But when writer–director Kasdan decided to cut the part from that movie, he offered Costner the sensational role of Jake in *Silverado*, joining Kline and Jeff Goldblum (in a lesser role here) from the earlier title. The rest, as they say, is history. It was only five years later that Costner directed and starred in the magnificent *Dances with*

Wolves. 2) Meanwhile, Cleese went on to write and star in *A Fish Called Wanda* (coming in my next compilation) three years later. He invited Kline to co-star, in a role that would win him a Best Supporting Actor Oscar] **[W]**

City Slickers
1991 – Ron Underwood
Maybe they should have called this one "Three Men and Some Cattle." An example of the sensitive-male-bonding genre that emerged in the 1980s and '90s, this one concerns Mitch, Ed and Phil (Billy Crystal, Bruno Kirby and Daniel Stern). Like the trio in *Three Men and a Baby*, they're New Yorkers in their late thirties. But each year, this bunch tries to recapture their receding youth by sharing some sort of adventure. At the opening we find them fleeing the bulls running through the streets of Pamplona, Spain, a foolish feat that results in Mitch being gored. Flash forward one year later when Mitch, stuck in a dull job of selling radio airtime to advertisers, decides to rekindle his excitement for life – and possibly save his foundering marriage – by joining his pals for a two-week cattle drive from New Mexico to Colorado. The thing is, it works, though not without some nervous and cathartic moments for all three would-be cowboys. It's pretty good fun and even occasionally rousing, made particularly so by the movie's real star, veteran actor Jack Palance, who won a Best Supporting Actor Oscar for his portrayal of Curly, the tough trail boss with a gleam in his eye. [Trivia notes: 1) Speaking of eyes, here's a test for yours about movie details. There's a moment in *City Slickers* where the boys are riding toward the camera. It matches a shot – same situation, location and camera angle – you saw in *Silverado*. Can you spot it? 2) Playing Mitch's young son here is Jake Gyllenhaal, who grew up to become a fine and serious actor, portraying a cowboy himself in 2005 in Ang Lee's version of Annie Proux's novel *Brokeback Mountain* (coming in my next compilation), and positively shining in 2012 in the shattering police drama *End of Watch*] [Caution: mild violence, but lots and lots of rough and raunchy man-talk] **[W]**

19. 'John Ford, John Ford and John Ford'

That's how Orson Welles once replied to the question, "Who are your three favorite directors?" If ever there was a consummate American moviemaker, it would be the legendary "Pappy" Ford, a World War II Navy veteran who helmed more than 140 titles – beginning with silent westerns in 1917 and ostensibly ending in 1964 with the widescreen epic *Cheyenne Autumn* (not on this list). Winner of four directing Oscars – more than anyone else – Ford was most responsible for the rise and enduring fame of John Wayne, though their lifelong friendship was a stormy one. He also shepherded Henry Fonda's career to a great extent, as well as a host of other character actors. Ford's genius at dramatizing the human condition, particularly the experience of men in combat, whether in the Old West, in wartime, on the job or even one-on-one in the Irish countryside, was unparalleled. Likewise, his portrayal of the loves and conflicts and struggles within families, as in *The Grapes of Wrath* and *How Green Was My Valley*, both coming in my next compilation and the latter winning a Best Picture Oscar in 1942. That same year he displayed great personal courage in creating his short documentary *The Battle of Midway* (also coming in the next compilation), which he filmed during the Japanese attack on the island. For these and other reasons, John Ford remains – even for many other directors – the best who ever was. Steven Spielberg said Ford will live forever because his movies will live forever, and it's true. Don't ever consider yourself movie savvy unless you have made the effort to become acquainted with at least some of his works, and by all means track down and watch Peter Bogdanovich's fine two-hour documentary *Directed by John Ford*, which he originally produced in 1971 (and which Welles narrated) and then updated for

Turner Classic Movies in 2006. Along with *How the West Was Won* and *Mister Roberts*, both of which he co-directed, here are four of my very favorites.

They Were Expendable [100]
1945

This might be the most understated, straightforward movie ever made about men in combat. Written by former Navy commander-turned-screenwriter Frank W. "Spig" Wead, who became the subject of one of Ford's rare biographies 12 years later in *The Wings of Eagles* (coming in the next compilation), it's the story of a patrol torpedo boat squadron in the South Pacific in the early days of World War II, one of whose missions is to ferry General Douglas MacArthur secretly to Mindanao, in the Philippines, from Bataan in 1942. The PTs, as they were called, were small but high-powered plywood vessels meant to elude enemy guns in order to deliver their ship-killing torpedoes at close range. The boats were so small that many in the Navy did consider them expendable to accomplish a mission – almost like the Japanese Kamikaze pilots later in the war, though not deliberately suicidal. The movie features some harrowing battle scenes, particularly during the climax, but much of the story is devoted to some surprisingly quiet, thoughtful times, such as a prolonged, memorable scene during which one of the boat captains (John Wayne) and fellow officers entertain a nurse (Donna Reed, in her first significant role) at an impromptu dinner. The longing in the men's eyes for the young and beautiful nurse is palpable, but their civilized and restrained kindness is almost heartbreaking. With Robert Montgomery in a fine performance as the squadron's commander, and longtime Wayne and Ford regular Ward Bond as a crew member. It's a deeply moving tribute to American military personnel serving at a time when the outcome of the war and the odds for their survival were in considerable doubt. The climax is quietly shattering, involving decisions about who will remain on Bataan and face almost-certain death, and who will escape to fight another day. Ford's affection for this story is evident in every scene, and I urge you to to see it sometime in your life. [Trivia notes: 1) The scenes in which Montgomery pilots his PT look authentic, which is fitting because during the war he actually did command one of the boats. 2) At the end of the war, the Navy stripped and burned all of the remaining PTs in the Pacific because they weren't considered worth transporting all the way back to the States or even to Pearl Harbor. 3) Ford broke his leg just before the end of production, so Montgomery pitched in to direct the remaining scenes] **[B&W]**

The Quiet Man
1952

Many movie lovers consider *The Searchers* (not on this list – though I will be including it in my next compilation) to be Ford's masterpiece. No doubt it's a classic, quintessential Western, but my choice is *The Quiet Man*. It's a surprisingly subtle and tremendously entertaining story about loss, love and redemption. It concerns Sean Thornton (John Wayne), born in the village of Inishfree and who emigrated to America as a boy, but who has returned for mysterious reasons. There, he meets Mary Kate Danaher (Maureen O'Hara, who never looked more alluring), with whom he falls in love and marries, but not before he runs afoul of her brother and guardian, Will (Victor McLaglen, in his best role). To tell any more would be to spoil the many, many surprises and delights. Let's just say that Wayne and O'Hara make one of the finest screen couples ever filmed, and their tempestuous romance is sophisticated and compelling (Steven Spielberg even excerpted one of their moments for a pivotal scene in his popular sci-fi tale *E.T.* – not on this list). Above all, this is Ford's paean to Ireland, and a more poignant love letter there never was. Shot on location in glorious Technicolor by Winton C. Hoch, it won Ford his fourth and final directing Oscar. [Trivia note: Ford named the character Mary Kate for the two female loves of his life – his wife Mary Smith and his favorite actress and one-time rumored romantic interest Katharine Hepburn – and Ford named Wayne's character Sean because that was his real first name]

241

The Horse Soldiers
1959

I loved *They Were Expendable,* and I deeply admire *The Quiet Man*, but this rousing Civil War-era story might just be the most entertaining of the John Ford/John Wayne movies. It's so lively, and in its own way good-humored, that it's irresistible. Wayne stars as Colonel John Marlowe, a Union commander given secret orders to drive his cavalry regiment through the South to Baton Rouge, Louisiana. William Holden co-stars as Major Hank Kendall, the unit's surgeon, who has no love for his commander, and the feeling is mutual. Together, the two men create more friction and sparks than any other male duo on the screen since Clark Gable and Spencer Tracy, a distinction for which Wayne and Holden were paid handsomely at the time. Their encounters are always sharply and smartly executed – as is Ford's effortless direction – and they're punctuated with wry humor. Relative unknown Constance Towers provides the love interest as Hannah Hunter, a loyal southerner who becomes an unwilling and unwelcome member of the regiment's push toward Baton Rouge. Based on a real incident involving a Union officer named Grierson, I admit it's not a great movie, but as Duke Wayne might have said, it's a helluva good time, Pilgrim! [Viewing notes: 1) There's a movie production cost-saving technique on display here. At first, Marlowe leads his sizable complement of Union troops on horseback until they're ambushed on the way to their first objective. Wanting to fool the enemy into thinking he and his men have retreated, he dispatches two-thirds of the troops back to their starting point and resumes heading south with the bare-bones complement. Later, we see a large column of Confederate cavalry riding past while Marlowe's men hide in the woods – with the rebels now played by the same men (and the same horses) who had been outfitted in Union duds earlier. 2) Despite the fact this is a war movie, there's surprisingly little killing, though Wayne and Holden do start fixin' to get into one terrific fistfight – before they're interrupted by more pressing matters] [Caution: some wartime violence] **[W]**

The Man Who Shot Liberty Valance
1962

This is one of Ford's most unusual movies, because aside from its opening and closing sequences and a couple of quick scenes in the middle, it takes place on a huge sound stage. That's appropriate, however, because the story is a classic morality play. It concerns Ransom Stoddard (James Stewart), a law school graduate from back East who follows legendary newspaper editor Horace Greeley's advice and goes West. He travels to the fictional town of Shinbone in post-Civil War days to practice his profession and help turn the undisclosed territory into a new state. The problem is, en route to Shinbone his stagecoach is held up by a vicious gang led by Liberty Valance (Lee Marvin), who proceeds to welcome Stoddard to his new home by beating him severely. Left to die, he is rescued by Tom Doniphon (John Wayne, in yet another great performance), a fierce individualist who warns Stoddard that the only way to fight Valance is with a gun, not a law book. That admonition places the two men in disagreement for the duration. It's a simple tale but told ever so skillfully, with a terrific twist at the end – and in these days of national doubt about the need to confront evil in all of its forms and sponsors with all of the forces at our disposal, it conveys a powerful lesson about the heroes among us who protect us from that evil, and the price they often must pay for accepting the burden. The movie is rough-hewn greatness. [Trivia notes: 1) The morality play aspect aside, most of the movie was shot on a sound stage for a more mundane reason: Paramount studio executives weren't fond of the script and therefore would not fund a location shoot. 2) Wayne was 54 and Stewart 53 during production, despite their characters being supposedly much younger. 3) In the opposite direction, one of the minor players, a teenager, was portrayed by O.Z. Whitehead, who was 50 at the time. 4) Ford greatly admired Lee Marvin, who had served with distinction in World War II and was badly wounded in battle. 5) The song "The Man Who Shot Liberty Valance," sung by Gene Pitney, became a big hit that same year – but it wasn't used in the movie because it was considered too modern] **[B&W] [W]**

243

20. Three Classics by Hitchcock…

For many years, the name Alfred Hitchcock was synonymous with suspense, and although he did direct one Oscar-winning feature – *Rebecca* in 1940 (not on this list) – his filmography largely consists of titles that fall short of those that have been the most honored or most popular. These three are the exceptions. All were big hits at the box office, all remain highly respected because they are impeccably styled and well-crafted thrillers, and all are favorites of mine.

Rear Window
1954

Like several of Hitchcock's movies, *Rear Window* is based on a gimmick – but it's a clever one. James Stewart plays L.B. Jefferies, a news photographer who's been laid up with a broken leg in a cast, the result of an injury sustained while shooting a Grand Prix auto race. During his convalescence, L.B. amuses himself by observing his neighbors through his … rear window. They include a frustrated composer, a newlywed couple (who quickly disappear behind a drawn window shade), a lonely spinster and a voluptuous and uninhibited dancer. But that's not the gimmick. It's that Hitchcock shot the entire movie on a single large sound stage built to represent the inner courtyard of a block of apartments in the Greenwich Village section of New York City. It's an exceptionally well-plotted mystery, with a host of interesting characters, and it features a young and gorgeous Grace Kelly as L.B.'s love interest, an always sly Thelma Ritter as his housekeeper and a menacing Raymond Burr (Perry Mason in the long-running TV series) as a neighbor who might or might not have murdered his wife. What's so absorbing about the movie is how slowly and methodically – and relentlessly – it builds suspense, courtesy of John Michael Hayes's excellent script. It's so subtle and frequently humorous you might not even realize how much tension it's building, until the denouement. [Trivia notes: 1) All of the action takes place from the vantage point of L.B.'s third-floor apartment, so the production crew built it at street level to facilitate easy entrances and exits by the cast and crew. It seems higher because the set builders excavated the floor of the sound stage to install the lower apartments and the fake street. 2) That same year, Burr also appeared as an American broadcast newsman in the delightfully clunky Japanese horror movie *Godzilla: King of the Monsters!*] [Caution: mild sexuality and violence]

Vertigo
1958

I regard this as Hitchcock's masterpiece; a gripping, atmospheric and complex psychological mystery involving romantic obsession. The movie brings together co-stars James Stewart and Kim Novak for the first of two times in the same year (they also did *Bell, Book and Candle,* another one of my favorites). Stewart plays Scotty Ferguson, a San Francisco police detective forced into retirement after he develops a bad case of the title condition by narrowly escaping a fatal fall from a San Francisco rooftop. During his recovery, Scotty is asked by a friend to tail his wife because he suspects she's having an affair. But that simple request leads to an incredible web of intrigue, woven by the friend and his "wife," Madeline (Novak). Beyond that I won't go, except to say the story is spellbinding, Novak is hypnotic, San Francisco never looked better on film, and Bernard Herrmann's truly haunting score is his most beautiful. Saul Bass contributed the (literally) eye-catching title sequence. [Trivia notes: 1) At one point when Scotty asks Madeline where she's from, she replies "Salina, Kansas." That's the location of *Picnic,* a 1955 movie starring Novak. 2) Hitchcock reportedly took delight in ordering Novak to jump repeatedly into the chilly waters of San Francisco Bay because Novak had challenged his directorial authority. 3) Steven Spielberg once told the story of meeting Herrmann during a scoring session for *Taxi Driver,* Martin

Scorsese's violent drama (not on this list), on Christmas Eve, 1975. He said Herrmann, who had a reputation as an unpleasant person, was sitting smoking a cigar and listening to the Warner Brothers orchestra play his dark and foreboding music for the movie. Spielberg approached him smiling and telling him what an honor it was to meet him and what a genius he was. But Herrmann just scowled back and said, "Then why do you always hire John Williams?" Herrmann died later that day] **[W]**

North by Northwest [100]
1959
Hitchcock's biggest crowd-pleaser is a mystery thriller that becomes less and less plausible the more the story unfolds. But it doesn't matter, because the movie is so entertaining and enjoyable, and its lead characters so appealing, that you easily suspend your sense of disbelief. Cary Grant plays Roger O. Thornhill (his middle initial becomes a plot device), a dapper Manhattan advertising executive with a healthy appetite and capacity for cocktails (another plot device). Through a series of terrible misunderstandings, Thornhill becomes pursued by both a nest of enemy spies and the police. As he struggles to solve the mystery and clear his name, he meets Eve Kendall, an alluring woman (Eva Marie Saint at the peak of her beauty) who figures to be either his undoing or his salvation. Once Thornhill and Kendall meet, the chase really begins, with Ernest Lehman's script providing wonderful dialogue throughout. The scene in the train's dining car where Kendall lures Thornhill into her berth is electric, and the movie's most improbable sequence, involving Grant being chased on the flat Illinois prairie (actually near Bakersfield, California) by a crop-dusting biplane, has become its most famous. With James Mason as Phillip Vandamm, the villain; Martin Landau as his henchman; and Leo C. Carroll as a shadowy government official. Bernard Herrmann's alternately bombastic and romantic score is probably his most popular as well. [Trivia notes: 1) In the scene in the Mount Rushmore cafeteria, watch the small boy in the background. Several seconds before Saint pulls out a gun and

246

shoots Grant, the boy has already covered his ears with his hands. Apparently, he didn't like the loud noise the stage gun made as Saint fired it several times over several takes. She revealed the trivia bit publicly in a documentary retrospective, now included in the DVD and Blu-ray versions. But years earlier in an interview, she told my friend Hap Erstein, former drama/film critic for The Washington Times and the Palm Beach (Florida) Post, that no one spotted the boy's antics on film until after the movie was released. 2) Jessie Royce Landis, who plays Thornhill's mother, was only eight years older than Grant. 3) The entire climactic sequence, from the time Thornhill meets Kendall in the woods to his rescue of Kendall atop Mount Rushmore, was shot indoors on studio sets. 4) Gentleman's Quarterly magazine in 2006 called the dark-gray suit Grant wears, essentially, during the whole movie the greatest movie suit ever. Probably, but I'm still partial to the light-gray suit donned by Sean Connery in *Goldfinger* – and duplicated by Leonardo DiCaprio in *Catch Me If You Can*] **[W]**

A Hitchcock Postscript:

I can't move on from the celebrated director without covering a now-standard movie device closely associated with him – yet one he used only sparingly in his movies: a MacGuffin. Its connection with Hitchcock began in one of his earliest titles, *The 39 Steps* in 1935 (coming in a future compilation). Simply defined, it's the object everyone is pursuing, often in desperation and usually at their peril. In *The 39 Steps*, it was a military secret. Among the titles here, for example in *The Maltese Falcon*, it's the title object. Likewise, in *Raiders of the Lost Ark*, it's the lost Ark. In *Monty Python and the Holy Grail*, it's the … you know. In the original *Star Wars*, it's the plans to the Death Star. In *Road to Rio*, it's the mysterious "papers." And, of course, in *Citizen Kane* it's the meaning of "Rosebud." Confused? Don't be. A MacGuffin is an artificial device that simply keeps the plot moving forward. It can be anything, as long as it serves that purpose. Now that you know, keep an eye out for it. You'll spot it more often than you think.

21. Three by Wilder...

In the history of the movies, there probably has been no wittier or more versatile moviemaker than Billy Wilder. Born Samuel Wilder on June 22, 1906, in Sucha, Poland, he started writing for the German cinema in the 1920s, but his family left for America in 1933 just as the Nazis seized power. It took him a few years, but he rose to become one of Hollywood's brightest and best screenwriters, creating or co-creating such classics as *Ninotchka* and *Ball of Fire*. Eventually, he grew weary of what other directors were doing to his work and decided to take up directing. The rest is history. Over three decades, Wilder created some of the most memorable works of the screen, including two Best Picture winners: *The Lost Weekend* in 1945 (not on this list) and *The Apartment* in 1960. Along with *Some Like It Hot* – which I consider his comedic masterpiece – *Sabrina*, *The Seven Year Itch* and *The Spirit of St. Louis* in other categories, here's a trio of favorites that Billy Wilder co-wrote and directed.

Stalag 17
1953
One of the most popular TV comedy shows of the late 1960s, Hogan's Heroes, dealt with a group of American and British airmen held in a German prison camp. The show had its suspenseful moments, but mostly it was played for laughs. Here, over a decade earlier, Wilder gives the POW scene his own treatment, and though it's quite funny in places it's a much darker story. Based on a stageplay by Donald Bevan and Edmund Trczinski (I have no idea how to pronounce it), *Stalag 17* concerns a spy among the inmates who's been alerting the Germans to their escape plans. As a result two Americans are

shot, and the push is on to find the traitor. The chief suspect is Sergeant J.J. Sefton (William Holden, incredibly in his only Oscar-winning role), an unscrupulous wheeler-dealer and cynic who trades with the Germans and has made few friends among his comrades. Not nearly as exciting or entertaining as *The Great Escape*, it nevertheless has its moments – for example, the Christmas dance. There, a scruffy character the guys call "Animal" (the gravelly voiced Robert Strauss, who received an Oscar nomination), who has grown so lonely he imagines his costumed buddy Harry (Harvey Lembeck) is actually pin-up sensation Betty Grable. It's painfully funny. There's also the scene where the inmates restrain Sefton and exact punishment on him. His defiance is admirable but excruciating to watch. [Trivia note: The dance scene between Strauss and Lembeck is actually Wilder's homage to a similar scene in the great French movie *La Grande Illusion*] **[B&W]**

Witness for the Prosecution
1957

I think Wilder's *Some Like It Hot* is the best comedy ever, but his second superlative offering of '57 (along with *The Spirit of St. Louis*) might qualify as the best courtroom drama, featuring a boffo performance by Charles Laughton as defense attorney Sir Wilfred Robarts. The scene is London a few years after the end of World War II, and the crime is murder. Specifically, an aging spinster (Norma Varden) is found dead in her home, and the primary suspect is Leonard Vole (Tyrone Power), an American with a German wife (Marlene Dietrich, in one of her best roles – including a stunning surprise). The evidence against Vole seems quite incriminating, so he seeks the counsel of Robarts, who is still recovering from a heart attack and has been advised to avoid excitement – no more criminal trials. Good thing for us he ignores the warning, because Laughton turns in one of his best in a long string of fabulous performances. And under Wilder's script and direction – adapted from the stage play by immortal crime novelist Agatha Christie – we're treated to a very, very clever whodunit with a quadruple-cross at the end. With Elsa

Lanchester (Laughton's real-life wife) in a fun role as a fussy nurse, and veteran character actor Torin Thatcher as the prosecutor. It's great fun, and the ending most likely will shock you; it surely did me. [Trivia note: The cast member with the real heart problem was Tyrone Power. This was his last completed movie, and he died within a year at age 42] **[W]**

The Apartment
1960
As you might have read already, I thought *Spartacus* should have taken the Oscar instead of *The Apartment*, but Wilder's second of two Best Picture winners (his first was *The Lost Weekend* – not listed) is an extremely enjoyable and worthwhile comedy-drama. Moreover, I'd place Wilder's quartet of *The Spirit of St. Louis*, *Witness for the Prosecution*, *Some Like It Hot* and this title as the finest four movies ever made by anyone in such a short time period. Sparklingly written by Wilder and his longtime collaborator I.A.L. Diamond, you might say *The Apartment* is a "wise" movie, because that word figures into much of the dialogue – although for unexpected reasons. It's the story of C.C. Baxter (Jack Lemmon), a minor employee working for a very large insurance corporation in a cavernous Manhattan office (actually an enormous Hollywood soundstage), who figures to work his way up the organizational ladder by lending his apartment to executives so they can pursue their extramarital assignations. What he doesn't count on is falling for one of the building's elevator operators, Miss Kubelik (Shirley MacLaine at her most appealing and in her best role), who's having a secret affair with Baxter's boss, Mr. Sheldrake (Fred MacMurray). Complications arise when 1) Miss Kubelik takes an overdose of sleeping pills while in the apartment after a bitter exchange with Sheldrake, and 2) Baxter determines he must protect her, advancement or no advancement, and despite the suspicions and accusations of his neighbor Dr. Dreyfuss (Jack Kruschen, in his best role). Laugh-out-loud funny sometimes but also tender and poignant – and quite racy for its time, in terms of the subject matter – *The Apartment* won the Oscar. But its true value, as

Baxter might say, is that movie-wise it's just about perfect. Adolph Deutsch contributed the score, which is ordinary, but the theme song, titled "Jealous Lover" and composed by an uncredited Charles Williams, became a big hit that year. [Trivia notes: 1) One of the characters in the movie, known in the script only as "The blonde" (Joyce Jameson), looks, acts and talks like Marilyn Monroe, with whom Wilder and Lemmon had worked the previous year in *Some Like It Hot* and who had driven everyone involved to distraction with her tardiness and petulance. 2) In the early scene where Baxter settles into his chair for the evening, TV dinner on his lap, to watch television, and he begins switching channels, there's a shootout in progress on one of the shows, a Western. If the gunfire sounds familiar, you've heard it before if you've seen *Some Like It Hot* or *The Magnificent Seven*. Both movies, along with *The Apartment*, were produced by The Mirisch Company, which owned those specific sound recordings] **[B&W] [W]**

And a Postscript to Wilder: One of the trademark attributes of Billy Wilder's movies are stretches of wise-acre, rapid-fire dialog that seem to emerge, spontaneously and wholecloth, from the characters' own mouths – all of it seeming so real it must have been improvised. Not so. Barbara Diamond, widow of Wilder's longtime writing partner I.A.L. "Izzy" Diamond, once revealed in an interview that both men would talk, out loud, to their typewriters while composing dialog, constantly reciting and repeating the words, and relentlessly striving for just the right pitch and cadence for each scene. As I hope you'll notice if you watch any of these three titles, or the other I've mentioned, so often they succeeded brilliantly.

22. And Two from the Best Director You Never Heard of

He achieved nowhere near the name recognition as John Ford, Alfred Hitchcock or Billy Wilder, but Austrian-born Fred Zinnemann, who made 45 movies over a career that spanned five decades, created dramas that will live as long as there is an American cinema. They include *The Day of the Jackal* and these two Best Picture winners, each of which also earned Zinnemann a director's Oscar. His unique gift was storytelling at such a mature level that he often sent moviegoers home feeling both elated and troubled at the same time. They felt elated at the masterful entertainment they had just enjoyed, but they also were troubled by the complex human emotions the movie had stirred up inside them. With the possible exceptions of *Gone With the Wind* and *The Wizard of Oz* by Victor Fleming, the first two parts of *The Godfather* by Francis Ford Coppola or *The Right Stuff* and *The Unbearable Lightness of Being* by Philip Kaufman, this pair of titles by Zinneman is as good as any individual has ever directed, and for once the members of the academy agreed.

From Here to Eternity
1953
Zinnemann's melancholy but toned-down version of the James Jones novel is nearly perfect, weaving six main characters – two couples and two bitter adversaries – into a seamless tapestry. The story takes place in Honolulu in the last days before the Japanese attack on Pearl Harbor, which began America's entry into World War II. It examines the lives of a maverick soldier (Montgomery Clift) who refuses to box in a military tournament because he had injured a fellow fighter back in the States, and

who falls in love with a B-girl (Donna Reed), a woman who works in a bar keeping company with customers and encouraging them to buy drinks. There's a hard-bitten sergeant (Burt Lancaster) who starts an affair with his superior officer's attractive wife (Deborah Kerr). There's a happy-go-lucky private (Frank Sinatra in an Oscar-winning role) who runs afoul of a sadistic stockade sergeant (Ernest Borgnine, two years before he won the Best Actor Oscar as the loveable schnook in *Marty*). It's a compelling but tragic story of lost souls whose fates and personal tragedies are washed away by the enormity of the war – hence the obviously symbolic and now-classic scene on the beach with Lancaster and Kerr, where the surf wafts over their bodies locked in a reclined embrace. And Burnett Guffey's stark, black-and-white cinematography subdues the great scenic beauty of Hawai`i, as though its azure-blue skies, lush vegetation and tropical sunshine will not return until the war is over. Now, six decades later, its emotional power remains undiminished. [Trivia notes: 1) When you watch the movie's most famous shot – the embrace in the surf – feel a little fortunate, because you're seeing it in its entirety. During the movie's original release, many audiences saw shorter and shorter versions of it, because theater projectionists kept snipping out film frames as keepsakes for themselves and friends and family. 2) The movie's theme song became a classic love ballad that Sinatra himself performed frequently] **[B&W]**

A Man for All Seasons
1966
The definition of martyrdom has been perverted to a great degree in recent years by Islamic extremists bent on destroying themselves and as many bystanders as possible in their demented zealotry. But the story of Sir Thomas More, at least as portrayed here so indelibly by Paul Scofield in Robert Bolt's Oscar-winning screenplay, is the story of a true martyr: Someone who is willing sacrifice everything he holds dear, including his life – and no one else's – in order to stand for a principle of faith. Thomas More was declared Chancellor of England in 1529 by

253

none other than King Henry VIII. Henry (Robert Shaw, in his first major role) wanted to divorce his wife and marry Anne Boleyn (Vanessa Redgrave, in a stunning cameo), but the Roman Church, headed by Pope Clement VII, refused his request. Henry wanted More's support in his effort to father an heir to his throne, but when More refused, the king imprisoned him and eventually had him beheaded. Like Gary Cooper's Will Kane in *High Noon* (also directed by Zinnemann but not on this list – though I'll be profiling it in my second compilation), Scofield gives an unforgettable portrayal of personal courage laced with ironclad stubbornness. He portrays this historical role with great dignity and a surprising amount of wit. Agree or disagree with More's moral position, he's undeniably and non-violently heroic in defense of his religious conviction. At one point, More discovers he has been betrayed by Richard Rich (a young John Hurt), a former protégé who has been appointed Regent of Wales, essentially as a reward for his treachery. "Richard," Moore says soulfully, "it profits a man not if he gains the whole world but loses his immortal soul – but for Wales?" Along with the Best Picture honor, and Bolt's screenplay, the movie won four other Oscars, including one for cinematographer Ted Moore's sumptuous English landscapes and another, richly deserved, for Zinnemann. [Viewing note: Bolt's screenplay contains a now-famous scene that, inadvertently or not, makes the story even more memorable for its cautionary tale about the supreme importance of following the law, no matter who might be considered deserving of vigilante justice. Scofield delivers it with such conviction it's doubtful you'll ever forget it – nor should you] **[W]**

23. Air Power

The landmark documentary series of the same name, which aired on the CBS television network in the late 1950s, traced the history of aviation, particularly the role of aviation in warfare. There's no doubt that, beginning with World War II – the German *Blitzkrieg*, the Battle of Britain, Pearl Harbor, etc. – military aviation played a decisive role. And here are six really good movies that illustrate my point.

Thirty Seconds Over Tokyo
1944 – Mervyn Leroy
This exciting and enthralling story is based on the true account of Lieutenant Colonel James Doolittle's daring and supremely dangerous raid on Tokyo in the early days of World War II, when the United States had suffered a string of crushing defeats by the Japanese in the Pacific theater. For the raid, Doolittle (played in the movie by Spencer Tracy) trained 16 crews to fly their B-25 twin-engine bombers from the deck of the aircraft carrier U.S.S. Hornet, which sailed close enough to Japan that the bombers could reach the enemy's homeland on a one-way mission – hitting Tokyo and several other cities in highly symbolic bombing raids and then flying to secret airstrips in non-occupied China. Some of the real footage of the raid is mixed in with skillful recreations, including a giant set replicating the flight deck of the Hornet – complete with full-size aircraft – as well as some large and obvious models, but the combination provides a gripping portrayal of the events. The story, based on the memoir of Army Air Corps Lieutenant Ted Lawson, centers on the crew of his aircraft the "Ruptured Duck," which successfully bombed Tokyo in the raid but crashed just off

the China coast. Lawson, played by Van Johnson, injured his leg badly in the crash and had to be sheltered and cared for by the Chinese allies who were fighting the Japanese invaders. Some of the scenes between Lawson and his wife (Phyllis Thaxter) might seem hokey by today's standards, but the emotions are heartfelt, and the half-hour sequence depicting the carrier takeoffs and the flight to Tokyo is heart-pounding. [Trivia notes: 1) The real footage of the B-25s taking off from the carrier was shot by none other than director John Ford, whose military duty had assigned him to document the beginning of the raid. 2) Lawson actually appears in the movie, in a brief scene from behind. When you see what happens, you'll understand] [B&W]

God Is My Co-Pilot
1945 – Robert Florey

Another Hollywood depiction of a true story, this one features excitingly staged aerial combat scenes (filmed over California landscapes) cleverly mixed with real war footage, miniatures and full-size models. The movie follows Robert L. Scott, (Dennis Morgan) a native of Macon, Georgia, who joined the U.S. Army Air Forces in the 1930s and headed to China to stage a lightning bombing raid on Tokyo after World War II broke out. When the raid was canceled, in favor of a carrier-launched assault (see *Thirty Seconds Over Tokyo*), he ended up fighting with the famous Flying Tigers under General Claire L. Chennault (Raymond Massey). The title, taken from Scott's autobiography, refers to his crisis of conscience during wartime and his embrace of the Christian faith. Yes, it's a bit corny in that respect, as many movies of the period were, but there's also emotional truth in Morgan's performance. The movie is weakest when it dehumanizes the Japanese, particularly the villain of the story, an ace fighter pilot nicknamed "Tokyo Joe" (played by Chinese–American actor Richard Loo, who thrived during the war portraying snarling Japanese). But it positively soars when depicting the fighting spirit of the men who served in the struggle against an evil and treacherous invader. [Trivia note: Scott died in 2006 at age 97. His one and only aviation-related injury occurred in 1920 at age 12, when he attempted to fly a makeshift glider] **[B&W]**

Command Decision
1948 – Sam Wood

This exceptional war story started out as a stage play by William Wister Haines, and though the screen version offers compelling combat documentary footage, it likewise takes place mostly on sound stages. Clark Gable plays Brigadier General K.C. "Casey" Dennis, commander of a B-17 bomber wing in England during World War II. Despite extremely heavy losses, Gen. Dennis continues to send his planes against heavily defended German targets – and risks losing his command – in an effort to stop the Nazis from deploying the first jet fighter aircraft, a weapon which could turn the tide of the war against the Allies. The one integral action sequence uses models and miniature sets, which diminish its impact, but the movie's real interest stems from the emotional and intellectual conflicts between Gen. Dennis and his commander, Major General Roland Kane (Walter Pidgeon, in one of his best roles). There's a great scene, mid-movie, in which Pidgeon compellingly describes the struggle to build aviation as a viable force in the U.S. military. Then Dennis follows him with an equally forceful monologue, reminding his superior of the need to press on with the attack plan. It's an intelligent and thought-provoking effort, beautifully written by William R. Laidlaw and George Froeschel, with a fine supporting cast that includes Brian Donlevy, Van Johnson and Charles Bickford. Its portrayals of conflicting war priorities and the politics of military funding remain relevant to this day. [Trivia notes: 1) Gable's emotions here were real. In 1942, he had enlisted in the Army Air Forces the Air Force's original name) after his wife, actress Carole Lombard, died in a plane crash. He flew many combat missions, attained the rank of major and was awarded the Distinguished Flying Cross. 2) Gable's wartime service didn't go unnoticed across enemy lines. Adolph Hitler reportedly offered a large cash reward to anyone who could confirm they had shot down Gable's aircraft] **[B&W]**

Twelve O'Clock High
1949 – Henry King

The movie's time frame, setting and plot are all similar to *Command Decision* but with a different cast and much more action. Gregory Peck plays Brigadier General Frank Savage, a man who has been given a critical task. In 1942 in England, early in World War II, Savage must restore the effectiveness and morale of the men of the 918th bomber group while replacing their beloved commander, Colonel Keith Davenport (Gary Merrill). The way he does it is tremendously difficult for both him and his men, but given what's at stake – possibly the outcome of the war in Europe – you can see he has no choice. This movie was cited most often by members of the U.S. 8th Air Force as the most accurate representation of their lives and missions dramatized on film. Written by Beirne Lay, Jr. and Sy Bartlett from their novel, it is an intelligent, highly engaging portrayal of the stresses of command in wartime, and it is a tribute to the quiet but amazing heroism of the men who flew bombing missions against Germany. The 12-minute combat sequence, featuring B-17 bombers against Messerschmitt and Focke-Wulf fighters, is incredibly harrowing and realistic – because it uses real battle footage. Dean Jagger won a Best Supporting Actor Oscar for his portrayal of Peck's top aide, and Peck himself is terrific, as are Millard Mitchell as the Air Force commander in England, and Hugh Marlowe (in possibly his best role) as a trouble-plagued officer. [Trivia note: The movie was turned into a pretty good TV series that lasted three years in the '60s. It starred Robert Lansing in the Gregory Peck role with Frank Overton replacing Dean Jagger] [B&W]

The Big Lift
1950 – George Seaton

A unique cinema treasure, this is the story of American and British courage and persistence in the face of a determined foe, the Union of Soviet Socialist Republics. On April 1, 1948 (two days after I was born), the Soviets blocked all highway and rail access to Berlin, Germany, which had been divided into four quadrants after World War II – American, British, French and Russian – but which lay within the borders of Communist East Germany. The Soviets were trying to provoke a confrontation with the allies, particularly the United States. Their goal was to force the West to give up on Berlin so it could fall under their control. What they didn't count on was the backbone of President Harry S. Truman. He ordered the U.S. Air Force to begin dangerous flights across a narrow air-access route into Berlin's Tempelhof Airport to deliver critical supplies – including 4,000 tons of food per day – to the city's millions of residents. The flights began on June 24, and this movie, shot on location during the actual airlift, dramatizes the incredible effort required to fulfill that mission and save the people of Berlin from starvation and Soviet domination. Montgomery Clift and Paul Douglas (a bit of a screen treasure himself) star as American airmen participating in the lift. They were among the few professional actors in the cast. Everyone else involved in the operation was portrayed by Air Force personnel. It's a fascinating look at how military airmen undertook the enormous task of supplying one of the biggest cities in the world under the most difficult circumstances. The accompanying melodrama also provides a rare view of the wasteland that was still Berlin in the late 1940s, following years of relentless bombing by the Allies during World War II. Seaton's crew must have worked frantically to capture some of the footage, and it shows. There are scenes where real Russian fighters buzz the C-54 military-transport planes ferrying supplies into Berlin, coming so close they nearly bump wings. It's all the more harrowing knowing the Russkies were not playacting. Likewise, you won't believe how scary it was to land a plane at Tempelhof ("Like landing in the Rose Bowl," one pilot quips), with apartment buildings jutting up right around the edges of its runways. It wasn't aerial combat, but the adrenaline level must have run awfully high for these brave men. [Trivia note: American and British aircraft flew a combined 92 million miles during the 11 months of the airlift, delivering over 2.3 million tons of food. At peak times, planes landed at Tempelhof every 30 seconds, night and day, in rain, snow and fog. In all, the operation cost 25 planes and the lives of 101 airmen – an astoundingly small toll given the hazards – but it led to the development of better radar systems to help pilots in conditions of poor visibility] **[B&W]**

The Bridges at Toko-Ri
1954 – Mark Robson
This fictional story about Naval aviators (that's what they called themselves) in action during the Korean War is based on a bestseller by James A. Michener – which is in turn based on a real incident – and features some strong aerial sequences, superior (for its day) miniature effects and a frightening and fierce shootout on the ground. The main mission involves blowing up three railroad bridges over the Yalu River, which the Russians and Chinese have been using to supply the North Koreans. William Holden stars as Lieutenant Harry Brubaker, pilot of a Grumman F9 Panther jet fighter-bomber who's based aboard an aircraft carrier in the Sea of Japan commanded by Rear Admiral George Tarrant (Fredric March). Also serving is a flamboyant rescue helicopter pilot (Mickey Rooney), who always wears a green scarf and matching top hat that becomes a most welcome sight for downed fliers. There's also Grace Kelly as Brubaker's wife, whose presence intensifies the shattering climax and drives home the piercing question, uttered by Admiral Tarrant at the fadeout: "Where do we get such men?" [Trivia notes: That real incident was even more harrowing and suspenseful – and involved more men and aircraft – than portrayed in the movie, though its outcome was considerably more positive. Also, the bombing of the bridges was carried out by propeller-driven Douglas AD Sky Raiders, which actually were considered more capable – and lethal – for carrying out such missions than the Panthers. 2) Michener titled his novel by combining the names of two Korean villages – Toko-san and Poko-ri – located near Samdong-ni, the canyon spanned by the real bridges of the battle] **[W]**

24. Men at War

I've seen hundreds of war movies over the years, and for a long time, I confess, I thought the best of them were made in the 1940s – that modern moviemakers could never match the quality of those classics in terms of dramatic power as well as physical production. But on further consideration I stand corrected. Some of the greatest titles in the genre – including the ones I've listed elsewhere, such as the monumental *American Sniper*, George C. Scott's performance for the ages in *Patton* and Steven Spielberg's overwhelming *Saving Private Ryan* – often surpass the best wartime features of the old days. Here are 10 more of my favorite titles featuring men immersed in the desperate struggles that wars demand.

49th Parallel
1941 – Michael Powell
This is an unusual war movie, but one you might not soon forget. It concerns the fictional exploits of six survivors of a German U-boat that has been sunk in Hudson's Bay as they struggle to sneak their way across Canada to reach the United States – which had not yet entered the war and still was considered a neutral country. Powell made the movie to persuade Americans to become involved in the war, or to at least support the efforts of their northern neighbors, and in doing so he portrays the Germans as either brainwashed or outright evil – but not entirely so. The movie, retitled *The Invaders* for U.S. distribution, became a major hit on both sides of the Atlantic. The fine cast includes Raymond Massey, Leslie Howard and Glynis Johns (as a teenager), plus Finlay Currie and Laurence Olivier as unfortunate Canadians who cross paths with the

fugitives. And the formidable production crew includes the great cinematographer Freddie Young and his most famous collaborator, David Lean, who edited the movie. Most of all, it's a fascinating and loving look at Canada as it appeared so many years ago. [Trivia notes: 1) The transition from peacetime to wartime footings affected the cast and crew in some inconvenient and potentially hazardous ways. For example, British authorities arrested screenwriter Eric Pressberger when he returned to England after the shoot. That's because as a Hungarian expatriate he was considered an enemy alien. Only director Powell's intervention kept him out of jail. And Peter Cushing (the evil Governor Tarkin in the original *Star Wars*), working at the time on the production, was nearly jailed when his landlady discovered some of the Nazi props he had created for the shoot. 2) The movie received several Oscar nominations, but under its U.S. title] **[B&W]**

Guadalcanal Diary
1943 – Lewis Seiler
Based on the bestselling, and raw, World War II memoir by Richard Tregaskis, this episodic and somewhat sanitized production nevertheless provides a reasonably good sense of what it was like for members of U.S. Marines First Division going into the first offensive battle in the Pacific Theater. Guadalcanal is one of the Solomon Islands, east of what was then the Australian Territory of New Guinea. In August 1942, the Marines landed there to destroy a Japanese stronghold that could have threatened the ship convoys supplying New Zealand and Australia. It was the first victory on land in the war against Japan for the United States – but it was a costly one. At first the Marines faced only token resistance, but that turned out to be enemy strategy. Soon, Japanese troops began fighting back fiercely, and over the next four months both sides took heavy casualties and endured unimaginable suffering in the steamy, rotting jungle environment. The movie contains an effective mix of real military footage with staged sequences shot on Catalina Island off the California coast. Though it doesn't rank with the

262

greatest war movies – and it exhibits the racism of the time – it's a gripping story and a heartfelt tribute to the men involved in one of the most horrible battles of the war. An American grave at the cemetery on Guadalcanal contains this iconic poem inscribed on its headstone:

> *And when he gets to heaven,*
> *To Saint Peter he will tell;*
> *One more Marine reporting sir.*
> *I've served my time in Hell.*

The fine cast includes William Bendix, Richard Conte, Preston Foster and Richard Jaeckel (who was only 17 at the time) in the leading roles, and features a young Anthony Quinn. [Trivia notes: 1) The U.S. military decided to invade Guadalcanal because an American scout plane discovered a Japanese airstrip under construction; hence the perceived threat to the convoys from the mainland supplying New Zealand and Australia. 2) The great NBC documentary series Victory at Sea, which first ran from 1952 to 1953, contains a terrific episode covering the battle of Guadalcanal – and includes that aforementioned headstone inscription] [B&W]

Battleground
1949 – William Wellman

Six months after the D-Day invasion at Normandy on June 6, 1944, the German Army launched a surprise counterattack. Tens of thousands of tanks, artillery and men broke through the Allied front lines and pushed far into Belgium in what became known as the Battle of the Bulge. In this powerful, vivid portrayal of a part of that battle, soldiers from the 101st Airborne Division, known as the "Screaming Eagles," become trapped along with thousands of their fellow soldiers in the town of Bastogne. There, the Airborne mounts a desperate defense, spurred on by their commander, General Anthony McAuliffe, who responded to a German demand for surrender with his famous, one-word answer: "Nuts!" The movie, shot in California with soap chips substituting for snow, and intercut with actual battle footage, effectively conveys the hardships those men

263

suffered during that frigid winter battle, which cost more than 20,000 American and British lives, an unknown number of local civilians and equally massive losses on the German side. There's a scene toward the end where the men gather for an impromptu religious service with their company chaplain (Leon Ames). He speaks to them about why they were called to perform a mission to defeat fascism, and his words uncannily parallel the current war against Islamic terrorism. The performances are completely solid, but the standout is James Whitmore as a grungy, tobacco-chewing, bow-legged drill sergeant, who more than anyone else I can think of on the screen, personifies the affectionate nickname applied to the American soldier during the war: "Dogface." [Trivia note: The studio that produced this gritty movie was none other than MGM, which up to then was home almost exclusively to family fare, particularly its lighthearted and splashy musicals. But the new head of production, Dore (DOR-ee) Schary, apparently felt compelled to take the venerable dream factory in a new direction, at least with some of its titles. Though studio head Louis B. Mayer protested, Schary won out] [Caution: intense battle scenes] **[B&W]**

The Longest Day
1962 – Produced by Darryl F. Zanuck
A meticulous and epic-scale re-creation of the events preceding and during the invasion of Europe, which began on the beaches of Normandy, France, on June 6, 1944, by an initial Allied force of 135,000 men carried across the English Channel in 4,000 vessels, making it the largest armada in history. Zanuck was the visionary behind this huge production, which involved four directors (himself included), five writers, 42 international stars – including, among many others, Richard Burton, Sean Connery, Henry Fonda, Robert Mitchum and John Wayne – and thousands of extras and crew members. Because of its faithful attention to documented details, much of the time it isn't very exciting, but it does have its moments, including the first appearance of the fleet as witnessed by German sentries, the initial bombardment, and particularly an aerial shot of the

landing of the invasion force, which was not computer generated and seems to go on and on and on. This was one of the most momentous events of the modern era, when the fate of the civilized world hung in the balance of what happened on D-Day, as it was called. My own father, F.A. Berardelli, participated in the invasion as a truck driver in the Army Corps of Engineers, transporting heavy equipment onto Utah Beach only two hours after it was secured. As one of the characters, a ship commander (played by Rod Steiger) says early on, "We are on the eve of a day that people are gonna talk about long after we are dead and gone." The battle marked the beginning of the end of the occupation of Europe by the armies of Adolph Hitler. For anyone interested in the events of that day – and in this day and age of the renewed and growing global threat of fascism – this is a must-see, in terms of what was required back then to dislodge a tyrant from the throat of Europe. [Trivia notes: 1) Zanuck shot almost the entire movie in France, using authentic locations whenever possible. 2) Three of the actors in the battle scenes actually had served on D-Day and recreated their roles during the invasion] [Caution: intense battle scenes] **[B&W] [W]**

Tora! Tora! Tora!
1970 – Richard Fleisher, Kinji Fukasaky and Toshio Masuda
Eight years after *The Longest Day*, another international cast and crew gathered to produce an enormous re-creation. This time it involved the events that occurred on one of the darkest days in American history – which President Franklin Delano Roosevelt called "a day that will live in infamy" – as they affected the people on both sides of the battle. The movie documents the attack by aircraft from a Japanese carrier task force on Pearl Harbor, the U.S. Pacific Fleet's home base in Honolulu, Hawai`i, shortly after 8 o'clock in the morning on Sunday, December 7, 1941. The production effectively uses three directors: Fleisher for the American sequences and Fukasaky and Masuda for the Japanese segments, as well as six writers – including the great director Akira Kurosawa, who was uncredited. Like *The Longest Day*, it bogs down in places in its attempts to be objective and

265

historically accurate, but it soars otherwise. With only a few clumsy exceptions, it's a totally authentic-looking depiction of the attack. For the 25-minute centerpiece sequence, the moviemakers assembled a dozen vintage Japanese fighters and bombers, launched them from an aircraft carrier deck (constructed on land) and flew them over the real Pearl Harbor and Hickam Field in Honolulu. Through clever coordination and skillful editing, they made the squadron seem like hundreds of aircraft, often engaging in convincing bombing, strafing and torpedo attacks on the fleet, and on military aircraft stuck on the ground. They also used surprisingly little archival footage, a tribute to the daring of the technical people and, especially, the stunt players, many of whom looked very much at risk during some of the scenes. Where the moviemakers differed from *The Longest Day* was in not casting big-name American stars in the key historical roles, using instead solid character actors such as old pros Joseph Cotton, James Whitmore and E.G. Marshall, as well as relative newcomers Martin Balsam and Jason Robards, Jr. (who split Oscars when they worked together in *A Thousand Clowns* in 1965 and *All the President's Men* in 1976). Also memorable is veteran Japanese actor So Yamamura playing Vice Admiral Isoroku Yamamoto, the architect of the attack on Pearl Harbor. Yamamoto had studied in the United States at Harvard University and had learned a great deal about the country's character and enormous industrial capacity. When he was informed that the attack had taken place before Japan delivered its ultimatum to President Franklin Roosevelt, he immediately understood how the event would enrage the American public. His reported response was, "I fear all we have done is to awaken a sleeping giant and fill him with a terrible resolve." The moviemakers use those prophetic words at the fadeout, and they're chilling, given the context of what eventually happened. [Caution: intense battle scenes] **[W]**

Valkyrie

2008 – Bryan Singer

On July 20, 1944, seven weeks after the Allies invaded Normandy, a group of German officers attempted to assassinate Adolph Hitler and end the war. As history notes, they failed. The story isn't well known, but it's something that should be a common part of World War II history, and this movie tells it skillfully. The keystone of the plot was a German aristocrat, Count Claus Philipp Maria Schenk Graf von Stauffenberg (pronounced SCHTAU-fen-berg), played here with surprising conviction and skill by Tom Cruise. A man of basic decency but military loyalty, he had served in combat in North Africa, losing his left eye and hand in one battle. Gradually but inexorably, he becomes convinced that Hitler is evil and must be removed from power if Germany is ever to regain its soul. So he conspires with other conscientious members of the military and the government to carry out the assassination. It's a gripping tale, produced on a grand scale and enhanced by some fine performances, including Kenneth Branagh, Tom Wilkinson and Bill Nighy as co-conspirators. These . well-known actors are overshadowed, however, by a brief but stunning turn by David Bamber as Hitler. Before this role, he was best known as the bumbling and prissy Mr. Collins in the wonderful BBC TV miniseries production of Jane Austen's <u>Pride and Prejudice</u>. He also played a bit part as a jaded theater director in *The King's Speech*, where I commented earlier on his versatility. [<u>Trivia note</u>: The swastika, the symbol of Hitler's Third Reich, remains so reviled in Germany that the movie's producers had to obtain, with some difficulty, special permission to display it during filming at German locations] [<u>Caution</u>: wartime violence] **[W]**

Special Forces

2011 – France – Stéphane Rybojad

In this well-crafted and often heart-pounding tale, a mission to rescue a French journalist (Diane Kruger, who played the legendary Helen in the clunky but watchable movie *Troy* – coming in a future compilation) kidnapped by a murderous

Taliban leader turns into a desperate attempt to flee to freedom when a planned rendezvous goes bad. The rescue team comprises six members of France's elite Forces Spéciales – their equivalent of the U.S. Navy SEALs – veterans all of the war in Afghanistan. They are led by Kovax (Djimon Hounsou, who delivered a stunning debut in Steven Spielberg's *Amistad*), a fierce and fearless commando who is relentless about rescuing the woman. His five other team members are equally determined to save her from Zaief, the warlord (played with true menace by Israeli actor Raz Degan), and bring her home. That's the pretext. The bulk of the story involves their attempted escape after the rescue, and it's unrelentingly tense, punctuated with scenes of sudden, shocking violence. French moviemakers are best known for their complicated adult dramas and witty comedies, but this one ranks up there with the best American military thrillers. [Viewing note: Be sure to watch the coda at the end of the credits] [Caution: rough language in both English and French] **[W]**

Act of Valor
2012 – Mike McCoy and Scott Waugh
Here's another gripping story about a secret military mission, with episodes based on actual events. In 1961, newly elected President John F. Kennedy established a program to develop supremely skilled special-operations teams that could perform the most difficult missions on any terrain in any kind of weather, night or day. That program gave birth to the U.S. Navy SEALs – standing for, in case you didn't know, Sea Air and Land. This movie not only portrays the SEALs in action, but it also features real members (with disguised identities) of the outfit, and what a show they put on! As in *Special Forces*, the plot here concerns a rescue mission, but it expands to include the capture of a dangerous terrorist and the interception of a cache of deadly and undetectable weapons moving into the United States. The scenes depicting those missions are literally stunning, but what distinguishes this title from all of the other war/action movies I've listed here is that a dozen of the cast members are genuine,

active-duty SEALs, and the missions are based on incidents these men probably – they don't talk about their real work – experienced. As such, we moviegoers owe them much more than just appreciation for keeping us glued to our seats for two hours; we owe them undying respect and gratitude because they are the best in the world at what they do. Thank heaven they're on our side! [Trivia note: Some of the weapons fired in the movie used real bullets, and the production used SEAL training sites, all to provide as much realism as possible] [Technical note: A sure sign the digital movie age has arrived: *Act of Valor* was shot with Canon Eos digital *still* cameras with HD video capability. Much more compact and versatile than motion-picture cameras, they've quickly become an industry standard. In fact, as of 2011, all of the major motion-picture camera manufacturers had ceased operations. Though at this writing some directors still choose to shoot much of their movies on film, the day is coming when we'll be saying R.I.P. to Panavision, Arriflex and Aaton; likewise, to Bolex, Beaulieu and Éclair] [Caution: rough language and intense battle scenes] **[W]**

Lone Survivor
2013 – Peter Berg
The third title in this category dealing with covert missions by military special forces – and the fifth on this list if you add *Zero Dark Thirty* and *American Sniper* – *Lone Survivor* is an extremely intense movie based on a true story. Some sequences are so vividly portrayed you could find yourself covering your eyes as they unfold. And the outcome is so heartbreaking it makes you want to scream at the incompetence of our political and military leadership. In June 2005, the military inserted a small team of U.S. Navy SEALs into a rugged and treacherous part of Afghanistan. Their mission: to assassinate a Taliban leader suspected of killing at least 20 of our military. As well trained as the men were, unfortunately their superiors made several critical mistakes in supporting them. As a result, the team spent five days in a deadly firefight and was nearly wiped out. What happens should give you undying respect for the dedication of

269

our fighting forces, deep sadness at their fate and, as I said, outrage at how haphazardly the command structure functioned during this episode. [Trivia notes: 1) Despite being set in the rugged mountains of Afghanistan, the movie was shot entirely in New Mexico. 2) The other emotion the movie should elicit in you is tremendous respect for the Afghan people and their devotion to *Pashtunwali*, the code of ethics to which they are fiercely devoted. In the case of this story, following that code meant literally risking their lives to shelter an American against the dreaded Taliban] [Caution: extreme battle violence] **[W]**

13 Hours: The Secret Soldiers of Benghazi
2016 – Michael Bay

On September 11, 2012, on the 11th anniversary of the worst terror attack in U.S. history, waves of radical Islamists stormed and eventually overran a State Department mission in Benghazi, Libya. Also on that date and into September 12th, they mounted a siege of a secret CIA compound nearby. During those battles, four men were killed: Ambassador J. Christopher Stevens, his aide and protector Sean Smith, and CIA contract security officers Glen Doherty and Tyrone S. Woods. The incident has become one of the most notorious in our diplomatic history, because the assault lasted, literally, 13 hours, during which time no aid or reinforcements were sent by the Pentagon, the CIA, the State Department or the White House. I'll leave my personal feelings out of this, but whatever you might believe, *13 Hours* represents a true telling of those events based on the eyewitness accounts of those who were there, on the ground, that night. By all means draw your own conclusions, but however you react, never forget Doherty and Woods, whose bravery and self-sacrifice allowed dozens of their colleagues to be evacuated. Until this movie, Bay seemed content to rake in hundreds of millions of dollars from CGI fantasies such as *The Transformers* (not on this list) and producing features related to the music industry. But here he has done his country a fine service by allowing the story of Benghazi to be told in meticulous and terrifying detail. [Caution: rough language and intense battle scenes] **[W]**

25. Men at Sea

Each of this trio of little-known features about naval combat offers suspenseful wartime drama, and each is well worth a look.

The Enemy Below
1957 – Dick Powell
A fine but ultimately fanciful tale involving a deadly conflict between a U.S. Navy destroyer and a German U-boat during World War II. Robert Mitchum plays the new and seemingly untested captain of the destroyer on patrol in the South Atlantic, where it encounters the submarine and proceeds to engage it in a game of cat and mouse, as Mitchum matches wits and daring with the U-boat commander (Curt Jurgens). Based on the novel by D.A. Rayner, the story alternates between the two crews until they meet in a final battle. If you've ever seen *Action in the North Atlantic* (coming in the next compilation), then you've seen several of the plot devices employed here by the opposing captains. But despite its derivative nature, the movie remains suspenseful and entertaining, with several unexpected twists. Shot aboard a real destroyer – though in the Pacific, not the Atlantic – the movie builds great tension before it eventually disintegrates into an implausible climax. But it's entirely diverting until then. [Trivia notes: 1) That sign hanging above the control room in the sub that the captain regards so disdainfully; translated it reads, "The Führer leads, we follow!" 2) Jurgens's real first name is Curd – something the Hollywood execs thought wouldn't go over well with American audiences. 3) You can watch this storyline and several of the plot devices repeated in one of the best episodes of the original Star Trek TV series, "A Balance of Terror," which first aired in 1966] **[W]**

Sink the Bismarck!
1960 – England – Lewis Gilbert

Imagine Titanic with four pairs of 16-inch guns (the size of the barrel openings for the one-ton shells, which the guns could hurl over 20 miles) and moving nearly 10 miles-an-hour faster over the water, and you'll have an idea of the fearsome nature of the Bismarck, a huge German battleship that kept the entire British Navy at bay for a brief time during the early days of World War II. Bismarck was designed to raid the convoys crossing the Atlantic that were supplying Britain with staples and war materiel. But with its massive guns it also could hold its own against an assault by a battle group. That it did – and then some. On May 24, 1941, the Bismarck encountered a trio of warships, including the H.M.S. Hood, a heavy cruiser and the largest ship in the British Navy. At a range of about 9 miles, a shell from one of the Bismarck's guns scored a direct hit on the Hood's armory, and the great ship exploded, killing more than 1,400 sailors, most of them instantly. Only three men survived. This occasionally stodgy, but more often thrilling, dramatization portrays the resulting desperate hunt for the Bismarck, including the fateful battle on May 27, when a British force attacked and sank the ship. The producers augmented the movie's documentary style by including a sequence featuring famed U.S. newsman Edward R. Murrow reprising his reports on the incident from London. The stodgy part involves some fictional melodrama about the people at the naval command center who are attempting to coordinate the operation. But the scenes at sea, even though some involve models and miniatures, depict the true story quite closely. [Trivia notes: 1) The wreck of the Bismarck was discovered in 1989 by undersea explorer Robert Ballard, who also discovered the Titanic. 2) The 1960 hit song, "Sink the Bismarck!" by Johnny Horton, wasn't used in the movie. But it seemed to spawn a string of other ballads using the titles of movies in which they weren't used, such as "The Guns of Navarone" as well as "The Man Who Shot Liberty Valance," which I mentioned earlier, among others. 3) If the voice of the Bismarck's Kapitän, Ernst Lindemann (Carl Möhner), sounds

272

familiar, that's because he's being dubbed by veteran Italian actor Robert Rietty, who also dubbed Adolfo Celli's voice as Emilio Largo in *Thunderball*. Rietty, who died in 2015 at age 92, logged nearly 300 credits in his lengthy career] **[B&W] [W]**

The Bedford Incident
1965 – James B. Harris
Based on the novel by Richard Rascovich, this British production is a variation on the story portrayed in *The Enemy Below*. Instead of chasing a German U-boat, however, a U.S. Navy destroyer plays cat and mouse with a Russian nuclear submarine, and although the two nations are not at war, the commanders of both vessels attempt to press each other as closely as possible to that condition. Richard Widmark, in one of his best roles, plays Eric Finlander, the obsessive captain of the Bedford, and he is determined to best his Russian counterpart even at the cost of pushing his crew to the point of nervous exhaustion. Sidney Poitier, playing Ben Munceford, a photojournalist assigned to cover the ship's mission, proves an exasperating foil for the captain. Martin Balsam (the same year in which he won a Best Supporting Actor Oscar for *A Thousand Clowns*) plays a Naval Reserve doctor who's been detailed to the Bedford and finds much more than he had bargained for. Wally Cox plays an exhausted sonarman, and James MacArthur is a young seaman driven to making a disastrous error. It's a well-done story with strong production values, lots of suspense and a shattering climax. [Trivia notes: 1) Though Widmark and Poitier play antagonists here, they were actually longtime close friends from their early days in Hollywood and had starred together twice before, in *No Way Out*, about an attempt to contain a virus outbreak, in 1950; and in the Viking tale *The Long Ships* in 1964 (neither on this list). 2) Watch for a young Donald Sutherland ("Hawkeye" Pierce in *MASH*) in a small debut role] **[B&W] [W]**

26. The 'Silent Service'

That's what the U.S. Navy calls the cadre of sailors who inhabit its submarine fleet. Hollywood has a rich tradition of movies about submarines, and these five (four from Hollywood and one from Germany) are the best of the bunch.

Destination Tokyo
1943 – Delmer Daves
This is often called the granddaddy of submarine movies, and it's still one of the most famous. Made in the middle of World War II, with the outcome still in doubt, it conveys the fears and determination of the entire country as its citizens faced a powerful and equally determined enemy in Japan. Cary Grant is superb in a dramatic role as captain of the U.S.S. Copperfin, assigned to a penetrate Tokyo Bay to gather intelligence in advance of an aerial bombardment, an approximation of the raid by Lt. Col. James Doolittle and his squadron of carrier-launched, B-25 aircraft, which had taken place the previous year (see *Thirty Seconds Over Tokyo*). Along the way, the sub stops in the Aleutians to pick up a naval commando being sent on the top-secret mission. It's definitely a product of its time, and the studio effects seem dated, but get set for a riveting wartime drama. [Trivia notes: 1) The movie so successfully depicted submarine operations – without divulging any wartime secrets – that the Navy used it for a time for the recruiting and morale-building of sailors. 2) As I mentioned earlier, this movie served as the inspiration for Tony Curtis to join the Navy during the war, and it gave him the idea to ask Grant to co-star with him in *Operation Petticoat* in 1959] **[B&W]**

Operation Pacific

1951 – George Waggner

John Wayne tries his hand at commanding a submarine during World War II, and though the movie was made six years after the war's end and contains perhaps a bit too much melodrama, it still packs a punch now and then and conveys a good sense of the emotions of the time – the movie even pays homage to *Destination Tokyo*. The submarine U.S.S. Thunderfish returns to Pearl Harbor in mid-mission because its torpedoes have begun misfiring. The episode mimics a real event during the war, in which many sub crews were experiencing the same problem. It required a desperate effort to find the source of the misfires, because without their torpedoes subs were virtually defenseless. Wayne's perennial sidekick Ward Bond and co-star Patricia Neal contribute strong supporting roles. Martin Milner, best-known for his role as Todd Stiles in the popular 1960s TV series Route 66, appears as a young sailor. **[B&W]**

Run Silent, Run Deep

1958 – Robert Wise

Another solid World War II submarine drama, though made over a decade after the war ended, this one features Clark Gable as "Rich" Richardson, captain of the U.S.S. Nerkel with Burt Lancaster as Jim Bledsoe, his first officer. Richardson is haunted by the loss of many of his crew on a previous command. His submarine was destroyed, apparently, by the Akikaze, a fast Japanese warship the Nerkel encountered in a narrow passage called the Bungo Strait, which sits at the entrance to Japan's inland sea off the main island of Honshu. Now he's intent on avenging his dead men by taking on the Akikaze anew – except that Bledsoe decides Richardson has become so obsessed with vengeance that he must assume command, which he does when the captain is injured after an unsuccessful attack on the enemy vessel. The incident precipitates a test of wills between the two men but one with an outcome that surprises them both. It's a bit contrived but effective, an action movie from versatile director Wise. It also turned out to be one of Gable's last and best roles.

[Trivia notes: 1) The real Akikaze was actually an aging Japanese ship whose captain sacrificed it by steering into the path of an oncoming American torpedo meant for another vessel. The torpedo sank the Akikaze and cost the lives of the captain and 147 of his crew. 2) Gable and Lancaster show a testy relationship onscreen, because offscreen Gable's daily antics – he was a stickler for quitting at 5 p.m. on the dot, regardless of whether a scene was in progress – frequently annoyed Lancaster, who also co-produced the movie and therefore owned a direct financial stake in its success. 3) Character actor William Campbell played a crewman both in this movie and *Operation Pacific*. 4) Don Rickles, who eventually became famous for his outrageous but hysterically funny standup-comedy routines, plays a straight role here as a crewmember. 5) Lancaster's longtime friend and frequent co-star Nick Cravatt (who played the mute Ojo in *The Crimson Pirate*) also plays a seaman] **[B&W] [W]**

Das Boot
1981 – Germany – Wolfgang Petersen
Of all submarine movies, this is the most realistic – and the most harrowing. Originally a six-hour television miniseries, it's a superb German production about the young (and growing younger) men recruited to serve in the U-boat fleet in the waning days of World War II, of whom some 300,000 never returned home. Petersen, who went on to a successful career in Hollywood, practically reimagined the submarine movie genre, using the latest technology to portray the lives of underwater warriors more vividly – and frighteningly – than ever before. The crew built three large models for the ocean and underwater shots, and filmed them in slow motion to make them appear more real. The actors were kept indoors during the entire shoot to simulate the pale faces of real submariners. And though the interiors were built on sound stages, Petersen insisted that they be complete replicas, instead of the standard practice of removing the left or right half of a sub's interior to make shooting easier. The result is palpable for claustrophobics (like me). There's a sequence that's nearly unbearable to watch where

a machinist must crawl into a narrow space beneath the floor plates to make a repair. Yikes! [Trivia note: The full-scale submarine model also appeared briefly that same year in *Raiders of the Lost Ark*, along with a remaining German sub base on the French coast used in an early scene] [Caution: sexuality, language and intense suspense] **[W]**

The Hunt for Red October
1990 – John McTiernan
A taut Cold War thriller based on the Tom Clancy bestseller that's contrived as can be but benefits from the performances of its cast – another case where fine actors trump mediocre material. Sean Connery plays Marko Ramius, captain of the super-secret Russian sub of the title. He has turned renegade, but is he planning to attack the U.S. mainland, or does he intend to defect? CIA analyst Jack Ryan (Alec Baldwin) thinks it's the latter, but he's got plenty of opposition within the government, including Bart Mancuso (Scott Glenn), captain of the attack submarine U.S.S. Dallas, along with many in Washington's senior officialdom. Therefore, Ryan must somehow contact Ramius and learn his intentions – an extremely difficult task given that the whole Russian Navy is attempting to stop Ramius before he reaches American shores. Some of the story is utterly implausible, but it's more than offset by McTiernan's sure-handed direction and by that strong cast, including Sam Neill as Ramius's second in command, Fred Thompson as a wily fleet admiral, James Earl Jones as the CIA director, Courtney Vance as a hotshot sonar officer and Richard Jordan as a national security adviser who's as shrewd as they come. [Trivia note: Connery became Ramius when Klaus Maria Brandauer, a fine German actor who probably would have done an even better job, injured himself before production began. Brandauer recommended Connery, with whom he had become friends while shooting 1983's *Never Say Never Again* (coming in my second compilation). They then worked together that same year in *The Russia House* (coming in my third compilation), a romantic spy thriller adapted from the John le Carré novel] **[W]**

27. Men at Play

The list of good movies portraying the lives of professional athletes or sports personalities is surprisingly small. Along with *Pride of the Yankees* and *Jim Thorpe: All American*, I like these five best – four fictional and one based on a true story.

Slap Shot
1977 – George Roy Hill
A profane comedy about smalltown professional hockey, it's the third pairing between Paul Newman and director Hill, following *Butch Cassidy and the Sundance Kid* and *The Sting*. Newman plays Reggie Dunlop, player–coach of the fictional Charlestown Chiefs (the movie was shot in Johnstown, Pa.). As the story begins, both team and town are about to suffer hard times; the team is losing money and the steelmill that is the biggest local employer is closing. Dunlop's desperation leads him to concoct a phony story that a Florida syndicate is buying the team – if they can perform well enough during the remainder of the season. By "perform," Dunlop means play dirty, so he uses every ploy he can think of to fire up the players before the games. He also recruits the Hanson brothers, a trio of hulking but immature and most unsportsmanlike skaters. As you can guess, the plan doesn't go as expected, but in any event it's only pretext for hijinks on ice. I'm fond of the movie, but it's definitely not for everyone. One problem, admittedly not so big these days, is the obscenity-loaded dialogue. Pauline Kael wrote that the dirty words seemed sprinkled into script like manure. "But they're 'plastic turds,'" she added. "You're conscious of every dirty word." Maybe so, but Hill insisted on the language because he wanted the movie to reflect accurately the world of smalltime pro hockey. With Strother Martin (Newman's sadistic warden in

Cool Hand Luke) as the team's general manager; Jennifer Warren, Melinda Dillon and Lindsay Crouse as, respectively, Dunlop's ex-wife, occasional lover and potential new love interest; and former hockey player Michael Ontkean as the Chiefs' only star, who brings the final game to a most unexpected close. [Trivia note: 1) Many members of the cast (including Newman) said they had so much fun making the movie they considered it their favorite production. 2) Ned Dowd, the notorious "Ogie" Oglethorpe, was a minor league hockey player. His experiences inspired his sister Nancy to write the screenplay. 3) The Hanson "brothers" were actually two brothers named Carlson, plus a third actor/hockey player named Hanson. Three Carlsons had been cast to play the Hansons, but one of the brothers was called up to the National Hockey League before shooting started. So Hanson replaced Carlson to become the third "Hanson." Confused? How about this: Jeffrey Hauser's character in the movie was named "Killer" Carlson. Must've been fun to keep track of everybody on the set] [Caution: sexuality, on-the-ice violence and, as mentioned, plentiful profanity] **[W]**

Bull Durham
1988 – Ron Shelton
A sassy, whimsical, funny and profane but basically sweet-tempered comedy about minor-league baseball. Written and directed by former minor-leaguer Shelton, it stars Kevin Costner as Crash Davis, an aging catcher who's hired by the Durham (North Carolina) Bulls to spend a season helping prepare Ebbie Calvin LaLoosh (Tim Robbins), a promising rookie pitcher, for the "Show," as minor-leaguers call the majors. In the words of the assistant manager (Robert Wuhl), "He's got a million-dollar arm but a five-cent head." Resisting at first but unable to withdraw from the world he loves, Crash begins to enjoy tormenting his young charge, and eventually the two men develop a tentative bond – though it's complicated somewhat by their mutual love interest, Annie Savoy (Susan Sarandon, in one of her best roles), a philosophical baseball groupie who acts as the movie's narrator, as well as their natural competitive

279

instincts. Don't expect it to lead up to The Big Game, because it doesn't. But that's one of the reasons the movie is so special. [Trivia notes: 1) The veteran-rookie interplay between Crash and "Nuke," as LaLoosh is eventually nicknamed, works well even though Costner is only three years older than Robbins. 2) The romance between Nuke and Annie also worked well, both onscreen and off. Robbins and Sarandon remained partners for the next two decades and had two sons together] [Caution: sexuality and rough language] **[W]**

Major League
1989 – David S. Ward
Sometimes, a movie succeeds in spite of itself, and here's a perfect example. Ward, who penned the Oscar-winning script for *The Sting*, wrote and directed this crude and predictable comedy about the Cleveland Indians, a perennially sagging baseball franchise whose late owner's widow (Margaret Whitton), a former Las Vegas showgirl, wants the team to do even worse so she can exercise an option to move it to Miami. Her strategy is to populate the ball club with such poor players that they'll drive away the crowds. The pathetic losers she hires include Tom Berenger as a has-been catcher; Charlie Sheen as a pitcher with poor control, a punk hairdo and a prison record; Dennis Haysbert as a Cuban exile and Voodoo practitioner; Wesley Snipes (in his first significant role) as a training camp crasher; and James Gammon as a minor league manager who sells tires on the side. There's also Rene Russo as Berenger's former fiancée and Corbin Bernsen (from TV's L.A. Law) as a preening, overpaid holdover. Somehow, despite the stock ingredients, it all works, and you find yourself not only watching the thing but also enjoying it as well – more than a few times laughing out loud and actually rooting for the team. The lively, catchy score is by ever-versatile James Newton Howard, Randy Newman sings the sweetly laconic title tune. By the way, Whitton's (obscene) last line is the funniest in the movie. [Trivia notes: 1) Five years later, most of the main players and crew reunited for *Major League II*, a perfectly dreadful sequel but

outdone by an even worse third outing that featured an entirely new cast. 2) Berenger and Sheen end up close friends here, but three years earlier, in Best Picture winner *Platoon* (coming in the next compilation), they played mortal enemies] [Caution: rough language and sexuality] **[W]**

61*

2001 – Billy Crystal

The asterisk is no mistake; nor does it connect to a footnote here. Rather, it's part of Crystal's affectionate telling of a standout year in the history of the New York Yankees and the remarkable achievement of one of their players. The year, coincidentally, was 1961 and the achievement was breaking Babe Ruth's one-season homerun record by 27-year-old Roger Maris, a promising second-year player picked up by the Yankees to bolster their outfield and take up some of the hitting slack for their fading star, Mickey Mantle. For much of that season, Mantle and Maris both looked to threaten Ruth's 34-year-old record. But eventually Mantle's health and rambunctious lifestyle caught up with him, and the quest for the record rested solely with Maris. That became a problem for many fans because Ruth and Mantle were beloved, while Maris's shyness and seeming sullenness turned off a lot of fans. A further problem arose because Maris eventually broke Ruth's record, but in 162 games instead of Ruth's 154. This caused Ford Frick, the Commissioner of Baseball, to add the asterisk to Maris's record, diminishing the achievement. Crystal, a lifelong Yankees fan, cast two fine young actors to play the baseball stars: Barry Pepper as the lanky Maris, and Thomas Jane, who is a dead ringer for Mantle in his prime. An affectionate portrait, but it doesn't gloss over the demons afflicting both sports heroes. [Trivia notes: 1) Crystal used the same trick with Pepper that moviemakers employed 59 years earlier in *Pride of the Yankees*: He shot the right-handed Pepper in mirror image so he could appear to be left-handed on film. 2) Recent history has tainted part of this movie. Mark McGwire, of the St. Louis Cardinals, who finally broke Maris's record in 1998 later admitted taking steroids to maintain his strength as he

281

aged, even though Major League Baseball prohibited their use. Likewise Barry Bonds of the San Francisco Giants, who eclipsed McGwire's single-season record with 73 homers in 2001 and exceeded Hank Aaron's home-run total, which Aaron had held for 33 years, by reaching 756 in 2007] [Caution: rough language and hints of sexuality] **[W]**

Draft Day
2014 – Ivan Reitman
Once each year, 224 talented, ambitious young athletes wait as 32 older men and their staffs negotiate, manipulate and horsetrade their way into would-be genius status attempting to put together a winning season – or squander millions of dollars on bad decisions. In other words, the general managers of the teams of the National Football League pick their newest players. The NFL draft at this writing comprises seven rounds – hence the number of draftees – but the most intense activity and biggest stakes involve the first round and particularly the first few picks, called the franchise players. The movie depicts the lead-up to that event – beginning 12 hours before and occasionally posting a clock graphic showing how much time remains – all the while following one of the general managers, the fictional Sonny Weaver, Jr. (Kevin Costner), as he agonizes over his strategy to exploit the team's coveted number-one pick. This is Sonny's first draft as GM for the Cleveland Browns, following the recent death of his father, the beloved coach who had guided the team for years. It's now Sonny's team to build or destroy, and we watch him plot what he must do – and what he must risk – to attain his goal. No more details, except to say the script by Scott Rothman and Rajiv Joseph is razor-sharp, Reitman's direction is surprisingly crisp for someone known for comedies, the production values are first-rate, and Costner's performance is among his best. Likewise Jennifer Garner's as the Browns' finance manager and Sonny's secret lover. The outcome will be hard to guess but satisfying, and it's a terrific look into this arcane world. [Caution: language and a tiny bit of sexuality] **[W]**

28. Workin' on the Railroad

For some unexplained reason, very few movies have been made about trains, and even fewer good ones. Along with the famous dining-car/Pullman-car scenes in *The Palm Beach Story, White Christmas, Some Like It Hot, From Russia with Love* and *North by Northwest*, these three top my list for romance and/or thrills on the rails.

Union Pacific
1939 – Cecil B. DeMille

If you've seen the *Star Wars* saga you remember the dazzling opening title sequences, where the words of the written prologue for each episode lie flat and slide off horizontally into space. But if you've seen this sprawling epic western you know it used precisely the same device nearly four decades earlier – and that's only the beginning. No one but DeMille would be so audacious as to stage not one but two spectacular train wrecks in a single movie or build a miniaturized set so large that it looks amazingly real. This is his version of the story – albeit highly fanciful and full of 1930s-style stereotyping of Native Americans – of the building of the first transcontinental railroad in the 1860s. It begins after the Civil War, when Congress voted to span the United States with tracks in an attempt to fulfill the wish, posthumously, of President Abraham Lincoln to unify the country, both symbolically and literally. Legislators commissioned two private corporations – the Central Pacific Railroad and the Union Pacific Railroad – to undertake the daunting task. The Central Pacific headed east from Sacramento, California, and the Union Pacific worked its way west from Omaha, Nebraska. Together they laid nearly 1,800 miles of track (700 by the Central Pacific and 1,100 by the Union Pacific),

283

meeting at Promontory Point, Utah, on May 10, 1869 – only 70 years before the movie was released. DeMille, who already had been directing epics for two decades, constructed several sprawling sets to represent the huge work camps that were repeatedly established and then dismantled and moved as the Union Pacific pushed onward at a rate of about 3 miles per day. He also depicts in some detail the brutal work required to accomplish what became at the time the greatest engineering feat in history. Then there's the movie's melodrama: a love triangle involving a gambler (Robert Preston at his most dashing), a man hired to protect the interests of the railroad (Joel McCrea, pretty dashing himself) and a *bona fide* railroad brat (Barbara Stanwyck). Their interplay is always sassy and engaging. Russian-born Akim Tamiroff (playing a Mexican named Fiesta) and Lynne Overman are irresistible as a pair of mangy bodyguards. They alone are worth, as I say occasionally, the price of admission. DeMille directed with his usual flair and unabashed patriotism, and as always the movie became a big deal. In fact, its world premiere in Omaha was the biggest in history – much bigger, even, than for *Gone with the Wind* that same year. It drew more than 200,000 people and required the Nebraska governor to dispatch the National Guard to keep order. Nearly forgotten now because of its dated aspects, *Union Pacific* remains a terrific ride. [Trivia notes: 1) DeMille so exhausted himself working on the movie that he had to be hospitalized and even spent a couple of weeks directing from a stretcher. 2) The golden spike used in the scene joining the eastern and western halves of the railroad (which actually was shot on the Paramount back lot in Hollywood) was the real artifact from the ceremony in 1869. The studio managed to borrow it for the movie. 3) Paramount needed so many engines and trains for the production that the Interstate Commerce Commission required the studio to obtain a railroad operating license] **[B&W]**

The Train
1964 – John Frankenheimer

Based loosely on a true story, this thrilling movie follows an attempt by the French Underground to prevent the Nazis from plundering the country's artistic masterpieces as they flee the advancing Allies in August 1944. Burt Lancaster – the only American in the cast – stars as Paul Labiche, a switchyard foreman and undercover resistance fighter. Reluctant at first, he eventually leads the effort to save the artworks from the clutches of the German colonel, von Waldheim (Paul Scofield, two years before his Oscar-winning performance in *A Man for All Seasons*), conducting the operation. He's motivated to do so when von Waldheim allows the execution of the gruff old engineer "Papa" Boule (venerable Swiss actor Michele Simon), whom the Germans catch trying to sabotage the train. Helping the Underground notwithstanding, Labiche also finds time for a little romance with a war-weary but sympathetic innkeeper (French star Jeanne Moreau). No computer graphics here and very few models. All of the train sequences – and the train wrecks – are real and spectacular, and with one understandable exception Lancaster performs all of his own stunts. At its best, it's thrilling under Frankenheimer's skillful direction and a moving tribute to the sacrifices of the men and women who pulled off the real operation. Maurice Jarre contributed the energetic score, using instrumentation and arrangements presaging his work in *Doctor Zhivago* two years later. [Trivia notes: 1) About that exception to Lancaster performing his own stunts: He injured his knee playing golf during the shoot, so Frankenheimer worked the injury into the script, having a stuntman playing Labiche appear to get shot in the leg while running to escape German soldiers, thereby allowing Lancaster to limp during the rest of the movie. 2) The scene of the bombing raid on the rail yard, shot at Gargenville about 30 miles northwest of Paris, provided a service to the French National Railway. The explosions – which took six weeks of preparation – demolished an old part of the yard that railway officials had

been planning to modernize but lacked the funds to proceed]
[B&W] [W]

Runaway Train
1985 – Andrei Konchalovsky
A superlative but hard-edged and often profane thriller with a
script based on a story by legendary Japanese director Akira
Kurosawa. The story is an allegory about humans attempting to
control their lives aboard runaway fate. Jon Voight, in an over-
the-top performance, stars as "Manny" Manheim, an escaped
criminal accompanied by fellow prisoner Buck (Eric Roberts)
and a stowaway railway employee (the implausibly cast Rebecca
De Mornay), the three of whom find themselves trapped aboard
a runaway train in Alaska. As in John Frankenheimer's *The
Train*, Russian director Konchalovsky eschewed models and
matte effects for real trains and stunts – and the results are often
heart-stopping, particularly the climax, when the prison warden
(John P. Ryan) attempts to capture Manheim by dropping onto
the train from a helicopter. Not for children or the faint of heart,
but in terms of sheer thrills, this is the most intense of the three.
Trevor Jones did the throbbing electronic score. [Trivia note:
Nearly all of the train scenes and many of the stunts are real, but
as a concession to the safety of Voight, Konchalovsky shot one
particularly dangerous sequence in a studio, using stationary
train cars with the tracks and frozen ground represented by a
moving conveyor belt] [Caution: rough language, violence and
graphic depictions of prison life] [W]

29. 'To Boldly Go' ... But Only So Far

Beginning in 1966 and persisting to this day, over five decades later, Star Trek has been a perennial presence in movies and TV. The original series ran only three seasons and racked up 80 episodes, but it began an uninterrupted run in syndication rivaled only by I Love Lucy and M*A*S*H. As you read this, somewhere, someone is probably still rerunning Star Trek – it's on Netflix, for example – and that grammatically incorrect prologue phrase "to boldly go where no man has gone before" has become a cultural icon. The problem, with a few notable exceptions, is that all of the spin-offs have proven fairly lame and often insufferable, including the 1979 movie version I mentioned earlier; so, in retrospect, was much of the original. The exceptions include the second TV series, called Star Trek: The Next Generation – which boasted a fine cast, decent effects and, after the first two wobbly seasons, some really good stories – and *parts* of three of these five movies.

Star Trek II: The Wrath of Khan
1982 – Nicholas Meyer

After the original movie in the series registered such a crashing thud, this first sequel managed to re-insert some excitement – at least for a while. Just as in *Star Trek: The Motion Picture*, creator Gene Roddenberry borrowed heavily from the plot of one of the TV episodes, and he brought back that particular show's lead guest character, Khan Noonien Singh, and the actor who played him, Ricardo Montalban. The deal is that Khan still holds a grudge against James T. Kirk (William Shatner), captain of the federation starship Enterprise, for marooning him on a barren planet, and he vows to destroy him. Most of the main plot (the secondary stuff is forgettable) involves the battle of wits between the two men and the damage they inflict on each other, which makes for two reasonably good 20-minute battle sequences. Unfortunately, the story eventually breaks down into either over-the-top rants by Shatner and Montalban or sentimental nonsense. James Horner did a good job supplying the updated series music in his first major movie score. [W]

Star Trek IV: The Voyage Home
1986 – Leonard Nimoy
This is one instance where arriving well after the opening credits and expository scenes becomes an advantage. Those parts and maybe the last 10 minutes are, as is much of the whole movie series, entirely dispensable – but the middle is lots of fun. Once again, a powerful alien probe – which looks like a giant Peter Paul Mounds candy bar – threatens to (what else?) destroy Earth, unless Captain Kirk and his crew can travel back to the 20th century and retrieve two humpback whales in order to repopulate the species, which has been hunted to extinction. They end up in San Francisco – coincidentally the headquarters of the United Federation of Planets – where they meet a feisty cetacean specialist (Katherine Hicks), who naturally needs to be persuaded they're telling the truth about their mission. When she is finally convinced she proves most helpful and even heroic, but in the meantime there's quite a bit of hilarity from the collision of cultures that are centuries apart. It's really pretty good, as *Star Trek* movies go, and Nimoy proves a skilled director – who decided, to his credit, to go against the annoying trend of the series and allow the humor to bubble to the surface in the scenes – as well as the best actor of the bunch. [W]

Galaxy Quest
1999 – Dean Parisot
Technically speaking, this isn't a Star Trek movie, but it's an often dead-on sendup of the series. So, rather than place it among the comedies elsewhere, I've dropped it in here. Tim Allen (of the Home Improvement television series) plays Jason

Nesmith, the aging and jaded star of a TV show that has grown legions of fans in its years of reruns (sound familiar?). One day he's paid a visit by a bunch of strange-looking folk who request his help to perform an important task. They seem to be dressed in sci-fi costumes, so Nesmith complies, figuring his participation will earn him some sort of payday or at least some fun. But to his shock and temporary horror, the strange folk turn out to be a race of real aliens who promptly transport him into space and explain that they are desperately in need of someone with his supposed skills. They have picked him because they have been monitoring his TV adventures, not knowing those adventures were fictional. The premise might seem hokey, but it's good for lots of laughs and even some genuine excitement. Alan Rickman, Tony Shalhoub and Sigourney Weaver are all in fine form as Nesmith's former fellow officers, as is Enrico Colantoni as the head alien and Robin Sachs as a particularly nasty enemy. I'm a lifelong fan of the real series, but it's a pity more of it wasn't this entertaining. [Trivia note: Seeded among the cast in a minor role is the only eventual Oscar-winner in the bunch: Sam Rockwell, who plays Guy, the nerdy crewmember. He won Best Supporting Actor for the unpleasant *Three Billboards Outside Ebbing, Missouri* (not on this list) in 2017] **[W]**

Star Trek
2009 – J.J. Abrams
In 2006, *Casino Royale* – albeit temporarily – revitalized the James Bond saga by re-introducing Agent 007 at the beginning of his career with a talented new star, Daniel Craig, and a consistently terrific production. Likewise, this *Star Trek* installment re-introduces the original characters fresh out of Starfleet Academy. We meet Kirk, Spock, McCoy, Scott, Uhura, Chekov and Sulu personified by a stellar new cast under Abrams's energetic directorial hand. And for much of the time, it's eye-popping, boffo entertainment. Nevertheless, like most of the movies in the series, this one doesn't always know when to quit. Its excesses are excessive. The plot concerns a revenge-bent Romulan named Nero (Eric Bana), who talks like a street tough and looks like,

along with his crew, one of the Dark Lords of the Sith in the *Star Wars* saga. Nero chases Spock back through time to punish him for failing to prevent the destruction of Nero's home planet in the future. Naturally, it falls upon the young and untested crew of the starship Enterprise to stop him. The key plot point is that when Nero disrupts the spacetime continuum, he sets Kirk & Co. in new directions in terms of destinies and relationships (e.g., the original Kirk and Spock were close and longtime friends; here they begin as disdainful rivals). Go with the premise or not, but you can't say cast and crew haven't gone all-out to show you a good time. Michael Giacchino did the knockout score, Chris Pine deserves raves as the new Kirk and Zachary Quinto gives a fine portrayal of Spock (he's a dead-ringer for Leonard Nimoy). Trekkies will find inside jokes aplenty, and there's yet another dignified appearance – after 43 years – by the venerable Nimoy, who sorely deserved an honorary Oscar before his death in 2015. [Trivia note: This movie enjoys the distinction of being one of the very last shot on film with Panavision cameras and anamorphic (widescreen) lenses, which director Abrams wanted because of the format's abilities to display grain, lens flaring and richness of color] [Viewing note: Speaking of Giacchino's score, you might want to watch through the end-credit sequence because his composition for that part of the movie is marvelous] [Caution: sci-fi violence and some brief – though alien – sexuality] **[W]**

Star Trek: Into Darkness
2013 – J.J. Abrams

As in my chapter elsewhere, another superior sequel. Like its predecessor, this episode portrays the crew of the Enterprise at younger ages than when the original TV series began. Both movies also use the contrivance that a spacetime distortion has placed everyone in essentially a new reality, allowing for different setups and outcomes. A few times, however, *Into Darkness* goes a bit overboard with effects and suspenseful situations, causing viewers to retract their suspension of disbelief once in a while. But that's a quibble. For nearly all of its 132 minutes, the movie does very, very well. It's a solid piece of

290

science fiction and a grand, lavish-looking even, production, though it's somewhat of a retread. A mysterious figure with seeming superhuman powers mounts a singlehanded attack on Star Fleet headquarters in San Francisco, prompting Kirk & company to hunt him down. The man turns out to be none other than Khan Noonien Singh, the villain of *Star Trek II* – except here instead of Ricardo Montalban, Khan is played by the dashing and talented Benedict Cumberbatch of the Sherlock series from British TV and the excellent movie *The Imitation Game*. After several twists, turns and, as I mentioned, overblown action sequences, the plot ends up putting Kirk in the same predicament as Spock in the earlier movie, with the result drawing laughs from anyone who's seen *STII*. It's a clever way of redoing the original plot, and it's a rollicking good time. With Bruce Greenwood reprising his role as Captain Christopher Pike; Peter Weller as Marcus, a rogue Starfleet admiral; and Alice Eve as Marcus's daughter, Carol, who was also a character in *II*. The regulars, including Chis Pine as Kirk, Zachary Quinto as the young Spock, Karl Urban as McCoy, John Cho as Sulu, Anton Yelchin as Chekov, Zoë Saldana as Uhura and especially Simon Pegg as Scotty, are uniformly skilled, witty and appealing, with Pegg proving himself the best comic presence. Michael Giacchino updates his superb themes, and of course, Leonard Nimoy contributes a sly cameo in his last big-screen appearance. [Viewing notes: 1) The movie repeats a nifty technique used in its predecessor: a simulated quick zoom from a distant perspective to a close-up – except the effect isn't real, because the object or objects the camera is tracking are computer-generated. 2) Along with shooting on film, Abrams also insisted on creating very large sets or using real buildings and facilities where possible – instead of computer simulations – to help his actors play their scenes more realistically. He also resorted to clever tricks such as shaking the camera and employing mirrors as effects shortcuts. The devices all pay off handsomely. Many of both movies' images are dazzling yet deceptively simple] [Caution: language, action violence and a shot of Alice Eve in her skivvies; likewise a couple of rather feline alien females] **[W]**

291

30. International Classics

In the interest of your cinematic education, at some point in your adult life you should become acquainted with these five foreign masterpieces. They represent some of the greatest examples of movies as an art form, produced by individuals whose talent has justifiably earned them acclaim by movielovers the world over. If you are unfamiliar with foreign classics, you should know that they require a lot more effort than Hollywood fare. You really have to pay attention to the dialogue, to the symbolism, to the unspoken communications between characters. But don't be put off by this. Spend a part of your moviegoing life with some of the world's best. If nothing else, when you return to the commercial hits, you might be amazed at how much you recognize what's been derived or outright stolen from these titles. **A heartfelt request**: Please, please resist the temptation to see any of these masterpieces – and any of the titles in the next category as well – dubbed into English. Instead, unless there's no alternative, go to the trouble to view subtitled versions – or opt for subtitles on the DVD – because then you will also hear the movies the way they were meant to be heard. Too often, dubbed versions are more distracting than convenient, because you can sense their artificiality. Listen to the movies in their original language and read the subtitles, and I guarantee you will enjoy a much richer experience for the effort.

La Grande Illusion
1937 – France – Jean Renoir
An exquisitely constructed drama by the renowned director, and many movie lovers consider it the greatest anti-war movie ever made. At the least, it's a gripping portrayal of the futility of

warfare as practiced by the Europeans during World War I: ferocious on the battlefield, but civilized – gentlemanly, even – in captivity. Starring Jean Gabin ("Gah-BAHN" – called by some the French Humphrey Bogart) as a French aviator, and director Erich von Stroheim as his German captor. [Trivia note: There's a poignant scene in this movie involving one of the prisoners dressing up as a woman. The scene worked so well that I'm sure Billy Wilder stole it to use in *Stalag 17*] **[B&W]**

Bicycle Thieves
1948 – Italy – Vittorio De Sica

Considered the most famous example of the Italian neorealist style of moviemaking, for decades critics have chosen this Foreign Language Oscar-winning movie, known in Italy as *Ladri di Biciclette*, as one of the greatest ever made. It is an extremely simple story that packs a powerful emotional punch. Antonio Ricci (Lamberto Maggiorani), an unemployed family man in post-war Rome, is given a job as a poster-hanger that requires him to ride a bicycle so he can cover many locations in a day. To get the job, he must retrieve his bicycle from a pawn shop – which his wife enables by pawning her heirloom bed linens. But a thief steals the bicycle on Ricci's first day, requiring him to search desperately for it. His young son, Bruno (Enzo Staiola), accompanies him, and in desperation Ricci contemplates stealing someone else's bicycle, with nearly disastrous results. Essentially, that's everything that happens. But De Sica paints this character study with such simple eloquence that its shattering conclusion can leave you breathless. Orson Welles once said he considered himself a master of the movie camera, but he thought De Sica could accomplish something even more amazing: He could "make the camera disappear." In other words, he could make you forget you're only watching a movie and draw you so deeply inside the slice of life portrayed that you could imagine it's really unfolding before you. [Trivia note: In a striking example of art imitating life, Maggiorani actually was an unemployed family man in post-war Rome, and playing Antonio in this classic was the only work he could find] **[B&W]**

293

Seven Samurai
1954 – Japan – Akira Kurosawa

You might think watching a three hours-plus Japanese martial-arts epic from the early 1950s – in black and white, yet – would be boring and outdated. But it is neither. In fact, if this isn't one of the greatest movies ever made, it's certainly within striking distance of the top. Kurosawa's masterpiece just gets better and better as the years go by. It received a real boost in 2004 when a new print was struck for international distribution to mark the 50th anniversary. That update included a terrific new version of the subtitles, which deepened the story and magnified its already potent emotional punch. The basic tale has been told many times: A humble village is besieged by a gang of bandits who arrive regularly to rape and plunder. Exhausted and on the verge of starvation and despair, the villagers gather their valuables together to hire samurai warriors as protectors. This arrangement proves much more difficult than expected. The bandits don't give up so easily, requiring the villagers to decide whether or not to continue the struggle, which offers them the chance for freedom but also the risk of violent death. And for the samurai, the question is whether to continue to defend peasants who seem less and less grateful for their sacrifices. Skeptical? I hope not. Give this one the patience it deserves, and you just might be amply rewarded. It's one of the finest productions in the history of the medium, not because it is so vast in scale or scope but because it so relentlessly digs at the heart of human nature and can expose feelings within you that you might have not even known existed. [Viewing note: Among those cast as samurai was Kurosawa's most reliable actor and, eventually, Japan's most popular movie star, the great Toshiro Mifune (Miff-OON-ay), who gives one of the most amazing performances in movie history – a performance that Steven Spielberg once said seemed to emerge from seismic activity. You might call his character an offbeat samurai – and Mifune called the role his favorite, the one that most closely reflected his real personality. He plays an illiterate character named Kikuchiyo, which means a

294

thousand-year-old chrysanthemum – and it's actually a girl's name] [Trivia notes: 1) Samurai films previously had been a staple of Japanese cinema for over 40 years, but following Japan's surrender at the end of World War II, the occupying American Army banned all depictions of sword-fighting until 1952. 2) As I hope you already know, Hollywood appropriated this story in 1960, creating one of the best American westerns ever made, *The Magnificent Seven*] [Caution: violence and sexuality] **[B&W]**

The 400 Blows
1959 – France – François Truffaut
In the late 1950s and early '60s, cinema fans packed the world's art houses to savor the works of a group of moviemakers called the French New Wave. These young and brash auteurs energized the medium and created legions of followers and successors worldwide. Truffaut, who started out as a critic and author, provided one of the earliest examples with this crisp, raw, semi-autobiographical story of a young boy's unhappy life. It's the story of Antoine Doinel, a 13 year-old whose (justifiable) disinterest in his studies and tendencies toward dishonesty land him in reform school. But the movie consists of much more, including a fascinating glimpse of Paris in the late '50s and an affinity for young people that Truffaut would use and perfect in several more of his works later on. [Trivia notes: 1) The movie's Anglicized title is actually a bad translation. A better version would be "Live the Wild Life." 2) Jean-Pierre Léaud, also 13 at the time, who plays Antoine, repeated the role in five other Truffaut films as he grew to manhood, concluding with *Love on the Run* (*L'amour en Fruite*) in 1979 (not on this list). 3) Truffaut created the end sequence, in which Antoine responds to questions from an unseen psychiatrist, from the footage of Léaud's unscripted audition before he was cast in the movie] [Caution: language and sexuality] **[B&W] [W]**

The Road Home
1999 – China – Yimou Zhang

This hauntingly beautiful, achingly sad story by the famed director was banned in his home country. Why? Because it dealt with a forbidden subject: a schoolteacher writing his own textbook – not a political textbook, merely an unauthorized one. The schoolteacher is loosely based on Zhang's father, and here he relates how his father courted his mother (played by the beautiful Ziyi Zhang – no relation to the director). The movie actually follows two parallel plots, one in the present day and one in the past – and in a bit of originality Zhang shot the contemporary scenes in black and white, while the past appears in brilliant color. Zhang is one of the most masterful directors ever, and he can take the simplest of devices and elicit strong emotions from them. Consider that in this movie he makes you gasp at a broken teacup and brings you nearly to tears with a lost hairclip. Though a more recent addition, *The Road Home* rightfully belongs among the masterworks of world cinema – and it will always be one of my favorites. **[B&W – with some sequences in color] [W]**

31. International Favorites

From the 1950s through the '70s, many American cities harbored what were called art houses; movie theaters that featured the best of cinema from abroad, bringing titles from many of the directors – also called *auteurs* because they often wrote as well as directed – noted below and greatly enriching the cultural lives of audiences willing to read subtitles. Most of the art houses are gone now, but many of the movies they once presented to grateful, enthusiastic fans remain available through cable and DVD, though not nearly often enough (A Turner International Classics movie channel, anyone?). Watch for them, because you might find they will broaden your horizons and open up a marvelous world of entertainment you didn't realize existed. I greatly enjoyed each of these 23 titles – which include nine foreign-language Oscar winners – many of them in theaters. I hope you will, too, regardless of venue.

Yojimbo
1961 – Japan – Akira Kurosawa

There's a scene in the original *Star Wars* (now known as *Episode IV: A New Hope*) where Obi Wan Kenobi slices off the arm of an aggressive alien with one lightning-fast, graceful move. *Yojimbo* provided the inspiration for that scene as well as others in the *Star Wars* saga, as George Lucas has acknowledged. It's the story of an itinerant samurai named Sanjuro (the immortal Toshiro Mifune) who wanders into a small town beset by two feuding factions and desperately in need of some law and order. We quickly deduce that need when Yojimbo encounters a dog walking along with the severed human hand in its mouth. So, the invincible Yojimbo hires himself out – to both sides! Like or dislike this movie, but there's one thing I'll guarantee: You'll rarely see an actor who can dominate the screen like Mifune. He personifies the term "electrifying." [Trivia note: This scenario has been remade a number of times in a number of guises, but probably the best of the bunch (though still not very good) is the Clint Eastwood drama *A Fistful of Dollars* (not on this list) three years later] [Caution: violence] **[B&W] [W]**

Yesterday, Today and Tomorrow
1963 – Italy – Vittorio De Sica
De Sica eventually moved from his neorealist dramas of the 1940s and '50s (see *Bicycle Thieves*, above) to comedies in the '60s, and this delightful, Oscar-winning trilogy of domestic life, such as it is, in Italy features perhaps the most romantic couple ever to grace the screen: Marcello Mastroianni and Sophia Loren. In "Yesterday," the two play a struggling Neapolitan husband and wife who must take some rather unusual steps to stay ahead of their creditors. In "Today," the scene shifts to Milan where Mastroianni and Loren play upper-class paramours in a love-hate relationship. And in "Tomorrow," she's a prostitute, he's her wealthy client and Loren – arguably the sexiest woman who ever lived – performs a striptease (emphasis on "tease") that's positively knee-wobbling, which is why it's become a classic scene. Uproarious, all in good fun and oh, so Italiano! [Trivia note: Loren's physical beauty was imposing, but don't underestimate her acting ability. She won an Oscar in 1960, at age 26, for her performance in *Two Women* (coming in the next compilation), which De Sica also directed – and that was her 48th film role!] [Caution: Even though it's 1963 there's plenty of ... um, adult material] **[W]**

A Man and a Woman
1966 – France – Claude Lelouche
This Oscar winner was the first foreign-language movie to break through to mainstream American audiences, and though it is beginning to age in some respects it remains a popular cinematic love story. It's also an ultra-stylish movie, made so by auteur

Lelouche, who produced, co-wrote, shot and edited as well as directed. He's also well supported by Francis Lai's now-famous romantic score and by the hugely photogenic leads, Jean-Louis Trintignant and especially Anouk Aimée, playing a widower and widow who meet because their children attend the same school. Though the movie is in color, Lelouche shot it with such subdued tones that it almost seems black and white. He also used overcast days, heavy rain and nighttime to maintain the romantic mood. Manipulative and ultimately shallow, yes, but after over 50 years it's still a great date movie, particularly for guys who want to demonstrate they can harbor a sophisticated side but who lack the patience to sit through *Jules et Jim* (a classic, but not on this list) [Caution: sexuality, albeit brief and oh so tasteful] **[W]**

Day for Night
1973 – France – François Truffaut
This is Truffaut's Oscar-winning love letter to the movies, with the letter wrapped up inside itself, and a more ardent fan of the medium there never was. Truffaut plays a director trying to make a movie with the uninspiring title, "Meet Pamela," and he narrates the challenges and frustrations involved in the process as we watch the scenes unfold one by one. It's enjoyable on two levels. First, the story of making the movie is fairly standard but engaging. Second, watching how the crew engages in the process is fascinating. [Trivia notes: 1) Here's an indication how devoted Truffaut was to the movies. Melinda Dillon once told an interviewer how nervous she felt at the prospect of meeting Truffaut, who co-starred with her in *Close Encounters of the Third Kind*. After all, he was the famous French director and she was a little-known actress. To her surprise and delight, he instantly recognized her and complimented her about a role she had played in an obscure, low-budget movie he had seen years earlier. 2) Watch for Nathalie Baye in a small early role as a script girl. She became much better known nearly 30 years later playing Leonardo DiCaprio's mother in Steven Spielberg's *Catch Me If You Can*] [Caution: sexuality – after all, it's French!] **[W]**

Dona Flor and Her Two Husbands
1976 – Brazil – Bruno Barreto
Based on the hugely popular novel by Jorge Amado, you could call this erotic fantasy a comedy of the outrageous, because Barreto is a moviemaker willing to push the envelope of good taste for laughs. Sonia Braga plays the title character with a sexuality so smoldering she personifies the term "hot." Her husband, Vadinho (Vah-DEEN-yo), played by Jose Wilker, dies at a young age essentially from overdoing *everything*! Example: Vadinho grabs another woman's backside, in public, literally behind Dona's back and proceeds to simulate having sex with her. After Vadinho's demise, Dona eventually remarries Teodoro, a gentle but uninteresting doctor (Mauro Mendonca) whose lovemaking leaves much to be desired. But Dona's dissatisfaction and grief are soon alleviated when Vadinho returns as a ghost – who has miraculously maintained his sexual prowess. That should be enough to intrigue you or turn you away. [Caution: intense eroticism – frequently connected with food and eating – and graphic sexuality] [W]

Fanny and Alexander
1982 – Sweden – Ingmar Bergman
You can divide Bergman's Oscar-winning movie – and his last theatrical feature – into two distinct parts. That's good, because at just over three hours it can use an intermission. Part one takes place at a lavish Christmas party, and its scenes are as gorgeously shot (by the great Sven Nykvist) as any interiors ever appearing in the movies. It is candlelit-warm and glowing and sometimes even funny – particularly a hilarious interlude where a male relative entertains the partygoing children with his … ahem, exceptional ability. But then comes the second half, and it's so jarringly different that it seems to shove you out into the Scandinavian winter. It's cold and stark and shocking, and you might not want to go there. [Viewing note: Just as he did with *Scenes from a Marriage* (coming in the next compilation), Bergman also produced a six-hour version for Swedish television] [Caution: sexuality and a crude but very funny sequence] [W]

My Life as a Dog
1985 – Sweden – Lasse Hallström

Hallström's quirky but heartfelt and Oscar-nominated tale, set in 1959, follows the plight of Ingemar, an imaginative young boy (Anton Glanzelius) who is forced to stay with relatives in another town while his mother fights an ultimately losing battle with tuberculosis. There he meets an exceptionally odd assortment of relatives and residents, many of whom have become preoccupied with the upcoming heavyweight boxing championship fight between their country's Ingemar Johansson (Ingemar's last name is also, coincidentally, Johansson) and the American champion, Floyd Patterson. Others seem intent on pursuing their dreams, no matter how loony. All of it makes for offbeat and appealing entertainment. [Caution: sexuality, including quite a bit of sexual curiosity involving Ingomar, a local girl and some of the town's other children] **[W]**

Tampopo
1985 – Japan – Jûzô Itami

One critic described this movie as a "noodle western," but even that's too restrictive to do it justice. It's a comedy and character study that's above all about cooking perfection – about the desire and determination to prepare and present foods well – especially noodles. The title character (Nobuko Miyamoto – director Itami's real-life wife) inherits her husband's noodle shop after he dies, but she lacks the skills necessary to attract a good clientele because in Japan all of the best noodle experts are men. So she strikes a deal with a mysterious truck driver who rides into town one day (hence the "western" reference) and ends up being her mentor and protector. Along the way, the movie digresses to visit other characters that seemingly have no relation to the main plot – including a white-suited gangster and his girlfriend who engage in some of the strangest "romantic" behavior ever filmed. Confused? Don't be. It's entertaining and remains one of the biggest foreign hits at the U.S. box office. [Translation note: Tampopo means "dandelion" in Japanese] [Caution: sexuality, including one *weirdly* erotic episode] **[W]**

301

The Decline of the American Empire
1986 – Quebec – Denys Arcand

Known as *Le Déclin de l'Empire Américain* in Quebec, this frank and unflinching but irresistible look at the lives and delusions of a group of French–Canadian intellectuals represents veteran Canadian TV director Arcand's smashing debut for U.S. audiences. Two couples and three single friends grapple with themes ranging from love to infidelity, and from democracy to decadence, all while pursuing their academic careers, domestic home lives and extracurricular coupling. It's a fine ensemble piece with a host of distinctive and appealing characters, shot in scenically splendid Magog, Quebec. [<u>Strong caution</u>: explicit sexuality, including one disturbing reference, albeit humorously, to pedophilia, and a graphic and erotic but hilarious scene] **[W]**

Babette's Feast
1987 – Denmark – Gabriel Axel

The year's Foreign Language Oscar-winner is a simple, delicate, bittersweet story, taken from the novel by Karen Blixen (aka Isak Dinesin of *Out of Africa*), and so well told. Babette (Stephane Audran) is a Frenchwoman and former master chef who has fallen on hard times and is forced to work as a servant for two elderly sisters and their even-more-elderly father in a seaside village in Denmark in the late 19th century. When the father dies, and Babette wins a significant sum of money in the national lottery, she decides to commemorate the 100th anniversary of the father's birth with a feast fit for a king. As the makings of the meal arrive, however, the sisters seem horrified at some of the entrees, such as a live (at the time) snapping turtle and some game hens. The naïve women decide that Babette, a Catholic, might somehow be trying to corrupt their Protestant religious purity with the meal, so they resolve not to enjoy or comment on anything she prepares, lest they be damned for their wantonness. But one of the dinner guests they invite, a Swedish general, remembers Babette from her earlier days, and he eventually leads everyone at the table to enjoy the meal of their lives. There's a bit more to the story, but I'll leave that for you to discover and ponder. Just know that the movie carries at its heart the timeless message that all artists wish: to be able to pursue their craft at its finest. **[W]**

Cinema Paradiso [100]
1988 – Italy – Giuseppe Tornatore

Where François Truffaut wrote and directed *Day for Night* as a love letter to the craft of moviemaking, Tornatore's *Cinema Paradiso* creates an enchanting memoir about the *experience* of moviegoing. This widely beloved, Oscar-winning story is actually told in flashback, as a successful moviemaker named Salvatore (French actor Jacques Perrin) returns to his Italian hometown to attend the funeral of an old friend, Alfredo (French actor Philippe Noiret), the projectionist at the local movie house. Salvatore, known as Toto when he was a boy (and played wonderfully by 9-year-old Salvatore Cascio), idolized Alfredo and spent his time at the theater enraptured, as though he had entered Heaven on Earth, just as so many of the town's residents did – and just as legions of us have done all over the world. Like many great movies, this is a deceptively simple tale, but it's an engrossing one, and it had me bawling my eyes out at the ending, which is graced and enhanced by Ennio Morricone's score, one of the most beautiful of all time. [Explanatory note: There are two versions of this movie: the original theatrical release, and the "director's cut," which adds several scenes to the story and shifts its emphasis at the end. Both are satisfying, but the longer release, on DVD, diffuses things, particularly the emotional punch of the fadeout scene in the theatrical version] [Caution: sexuality, mostly in the movies within the movie] **[W]**

Bread and Tulips
2000 – Italy – Silvio Soldini

Rosalba Barletta, a housewife approaching middle age, reluctantly but dutifully accompanies her husband and two teenage sons on a guided tour of Greek archaeological sites in the Italian countryside. When she accidentally drops an earring into a toilet at a rest stop, and the tour bus inadvertently leaves her behind, Rosalba (the bewitching Licia Maglietta) makes what will become a life-changing decision. She abandons the tour and her family and tries to hitchhike home on her own. Sound sinister? Not at all, for what transpires in *Pane e Tulipani* is a charming and delightful – if improbable – tale of renewal, friendship and romance. Instead of going home, Rosalba ends up in Venice, quickly finding: 1) a room courtesy of a polite but brooding and potentially suicidal waiter (the great Bruno Ganz), 2) a job in a flower shop run by a lifelong anarchist and 3) friendship with a ditsy masseuse living in the same building. There's also a plumber-turned-detective hired by her husband to find her and an abandoned accordion, and … well, enough detail. See it. *Buon divertimento*! [Caution: mild sexuality] **[W]**

Crouching Tiger, Hidden Dragon
2000 – Ang Lee

Lee might prove to be one of the most versatile directors ever. This Oscar-winning, fanciful tale of swordsmen – and swordswomen – is continually thrilling and sometimes so electrifying that if the motion picture academy members had any sense they would have refrained from awarding this title the Best Foreign Language Film and instead acclaimed it as Best Picture over the dull, predictable and overblown *Gladiator*. As in so many Asian martial arts stories, the plot is mostly pretext for the action – but the plot is nevertheless engaging, and the action is eye-popping. There is one sensational swordfight between two women (Ziyi Zhang and Michelle Yeoh) that is as fierce and lightning-fast as any hand-to-hand combat ever portrayed. There's also a sword duel executed on the swaying branches of a willow tree that will amaze you. The pint-sized heroine (Zhang) is tiny, yes, but invincible. It does not matter how many opponents she faces or how much larger they are, they simply cannot defeat her – and she makes you believe it's true! Even if you're not a fan of the genre, don't hesitate to sample this one. If you're patient and attentive as the plot unfolds, *Crouching Tiger…* just might astound you. [Trivia note: Zhang, a trained dancer, said her background actually helped more in the sword duels than the martial-arts instruction she received for the movie] [Caution: mild sexuality] **[W]**

Monsoon Wedding
2001 – India – Mira Nair
A middle-class Delhi couple is planning a wedding, as the monsoon season approaches, of their grown daughter to the son of a family of similar background but living in America. By tradition, the marriage was arranged long ago, and the young man and woman have never met as adults. Also the tradition among India's Punjabi people, the bride's parents seek every extravagance for the wedding, even if it means plunging themselves into massive debt. Unbeknownst to them, however, their daughter has been involved for some time with a married man, and she is struggling to decide whether to break off the affair or call off the wedding. Those are the plot essentials, but there's much, much more, creating one of the most lively, captivating screen stories you're likely to encounter. Part of it is the Indian culture, which mixes centuries-old customs and rituals with modern life. Part of it is getting to know the large cast of appealing characters and following their attempts to resolve their respective dilemmas. And part of it involves engrossing yourself in the event itself, as lively a wedding as ever portrayed. I regard Nair as one of the world's finest directors of mature stories, and *Monsoon Wedding* is no exception. From the personal dramas to the throbbing, sexy traditional music, it's a masterpiece of moments. [Viewing note: The dialogue's rapid switching from Hindi to English and back – sometimes in mid-sentence – might prove difficult at first. But stick with it. The excellent cast will convey what you need to know] [Caution: sexuality and adult situations] **[W]**

Mostly Martha
2001 – Germany – Sandra Nettlebeck
If you start watching this import, at first you might not know where it's going. Is it a comedy, a character study, an edgy romance? But sit tight and stay with it. Also known as *Bella*

Martha, the woman of the title (Martina Gedeck) is a temperamental top chef in a pricy restaurant in Hamburg. She whips up gourmet dishes for patrons but can also treat them with massive eruptions of rudeness. Possibly she's starved for love. It might be why she spends part of her time spilling her emotional guts to her analyst. Then Martha's unhappy existence takes a further downturn when her sister is killed in an automobile accident, leaving Martha responsible for her niece, a sullen 8 year-old named Lina (Maxime Foerste). Worse, her employer hires a flamboyant Italian chef (Sergio Castellitto – who resembles Tom Conti in his face, mannerisms and deadpan humor), who quickly becomes her rival. I won't tell you any more except to say that the movie contains equal parts drama, comedy and romance, all of them quite satisfying – and it will probably make you feel ravenously hungry for vino, fresh bread and pasta with sautéed veggies! [Viewing note: This movie would make a dandy, rainy-day double feature with *Bread and Tulips*] [Trivia note: Hollywood, as it does so often, unwisely attempted a remake of this movie called *No Reservations* (not on this list) starring Catherine Zeta-Jones substituting for Martha (but named Kate) and, improbably, the otherwise appealing Aaron Eckhart in Castellitto's role – though mercifully without the Italian accent] [Caution: sexuality and mild profanity] **[W]**

The Barbarian Invasions
2003 – Quebec – Denys Arcand
This sequel to *Le Déclin de l'Empire Américain* takes place some 17 years later, focusing on the imminent death of one of the characters and his family's struggle to provide him with a dignified demise, despite the oppressive, labyrinthine rules and bureaucracy of the Canadian healthcare system – which carries no official name, and which Arcand displays in vivid and disturbing detail in the movie's opening sequence. *Les Invasions Barbares* is a much more serious story than the original movie, but it offers many compelling and touching moments, and Arcand continues to write and direct with a skillful hand – in

this case his talent won him a foreign-language Oscar. [<u>Caution</u>: language and sexuality] **[W]**

House of Flying Daggers
2004 – China – Yimou Zhang

The year is AD 859, and China's Tang Dynasty is mired in intrigue, as several rebel groups compete to overthrow the corrupt empire. One such group, cloaked in secrecy, is the House of Flying Daggers, whose members seem to be able to infiltrate imperial strongholds with impunity. To counter the rebels, the emperor orders two policemen and friends, Jin and Leo (Takeshi Kaneshiro and Andy Lau) to track down the leaders and kill them. What Jin finds, however, to his complete surprise, is that the fiercest rebel of all is a beautiful, slightly built and blind dancer named Xiao Mei (Ziyi Zhang – who was even more invincible in *Crouching Tiger, Hidden Dragon*), who immediately captivates him – and places him in conflict with Leo. But forget the plot. Instead, feast your eyes on a movie of indescribable beauty and thrills, a spectacle once again demonstrating Zhang as one of the most masterful directors on the planet. [<u>Caution</u>: violence and brief sexuality] **[W]**

The Diving Bell and the Butterfly
2007 – France – Julian Schnabel

A unique – and technically true – story. In 1995, Jean-Dominique Bauby, the celebrated editor of Elle magazine, suffered a sudden and rare type of stroke at age 43. The event paralyzed him from head to toe except for his left eye – a condition called locked-in syndrome. Using his tenuous ability to blink (once for "yes" and twice for "no") he managed to dictate his memoir, as friends and caregivers patiently spelled out the alphabet over and over for him and recorded his responses. Mathieu Amalric plays "Jean-Do," as he was known, though for much of the story, Amalric remains the unseen narrator, or he is presented in flashback in his normal appearance. But in several wrenching scenes, we see him as Bauby was seen: paralyzed, with one eye sewn shut, the other eye gaping and his mouth repulsively contorted and

307

drooling. Despite those limitations, Amalric gives a stunning performance, strongly supported by the rest of the cast. *Le Scaphandre et le Papillon* presents a painfully moving portrait of a formerly privileged man now imprisoned in his body, while his mind continues to roam free. Facing mortality, and no doubt with great courage, he manages to leave the world with a remarkable account of that process. [Biographical note: As with so many movie portrayals of real people and events, the story takes liberties with the facts. If you'd like to know more about Bauby's ordeal, read the book of the same name] [Trivia note: Though this is a French production, the original script by Ronald Harwood was in English, and director Schnabel was born in New York City, in Brooklyn] [Caution: sexuality and some rough language] **[W]**

The Secret in Their Eyes
2009 – Argentina – Juan Jose Campanella

You know a director is talented when he can re-imagine a standard action sequence so well that it makes you gasp. That's what Campanella did for me in an absolutely stunning chase scene, which takes place on foot in the middle of a filled-to-capacity soccer stadium – at night, no less. But that's only one brief sequence in a movie that continually moves and amazes. Another Foreign-Language Oscar winner (the ninth and last in this category), *The Secret in Their Eyes* is essentially a murder mystery but with some brand-new twists. Retiring prosecutor Benjamin Esposito (Ricardo Darin) decides to write a novel about an unresolved case that has been haunting him for years. In the process, he is reunited with Irene Menendez Hastings (Soledad Villamil), his former superior and longtime object of desire. From there the story bounces back and forth in time and between Esposito's real life and his literary fantasy, and each is equally fascinating – for the movie's portrayal of life under the Peron regime, for its glimpse of life in present-day Argentina and for its intense assortment of characters. I don't want to give away too much, because this movie is better discovered cold. But you're likely to be as swept away, as I was. [Caution: sexuality and shocking violence] **[W]**

Romantics Anonymous
2010 – France – Jean-Pierre Améris

A lovely trifle of a romantic comedy, this charming story follows a pair of neurotics who fear relationships so much that it drives one of them to faint at the drop of a hat and the other to … well, you'll see. When we first meet Angélique (the lovely Isabelle Carré), she's ambling down a street while singing a variation of "I Have Confidence in Me" from *The Sound of Music*. Turns out she's on her way to a group session with fellow neurotics, followed by a job interview at a chocolatiery owned by Jean-René Van Den Hugde (the wonderfully loopy Benoît Poelvoorde). Naturally, they fall in love, and my guess is you'll love watching it unfold. Three important details: 1) How could you miss what's probably the slowest car chase ever filmed? 2) Wouldn't you want to discover that the lyrics of the old song "Ochi Tchorniye" ("Dark Eyes") are beautiful? 3) If you love chocolate, well then… [Caution: sexuality] **[W]**

The Intouchables
2011 – France – Olivier Nakache and Eric Toledano

For the past decade, Jessie and I have been engaging in what has become an enjoyable and rewarding practice. We browse through Netflix's selections and pick a title we haven't heard of. After 10 minutes, we either agree to keep watching or stop and find something else. Most times, we bail out and move on, but occasionally we'll discover a new treasure. I added *The Secret in Their Eyes* to International Favorites, and quite a few to other categories, based on this activity. Ditto *The Intouchables*, and what a find! Based on the true story of a wealthy quadriplegic who hires a cynical ex-con as his caregiver, the unlikely match irrevocably changes both lives. Featuring knockout performances by Omar Sy in the role of Driss, the caregiver, and François Cluzet (who resembles Dustin Hoffman) as his charge, the movie challenges characterization. It's funny, touching, surprising and altogether wonderful. [Trivia note: You can see photos of the real Driss and Philippe in the closing credits] [Caution: sexuality and rough language] **[W]**

Haute Cuisine
2012 – France – Christian Vincent

Three other titles in this category, and six on the entire list, deal with the subject of cooking. That is, they deal with the *skillful and passionate* preparation of food. I loved watching all of them, including this one. Based on the true story of the first woman chosen to be personal chef to the president of France (at the time, François Mitterand), the movie follows Hortense Laborie (Catherine Frot), a country chef and farm owner who suddenly finds herself summoned to prepare meals at the Palais de l'Elysée, France's equivalent of the White House. You might think Hortense would be overwhelmed by the experience, particularly because she's held in low regard by the chef of the palace's main kitchen. *Mais bein au contraire*! She gives as good as she gets, endearing herself to her small staff – and to the president – in all matters culinary. Yet another simple story, well told. [Caution: just a taste of rough language] **[W]**

Populaire
2012 – France – Régis Roinsard

Want an unusual milieu for a breezy romantic comedy? How about a speed-typing contest? It's the 1950s, and in France every ambitious young woman wants to improve her life and her social standing by becoming a secretary. That's for certain what young Rose (the delightful Déborah François) desires. But she has a problem: She can type rapidly but only with two fingers. Still, when she interviews to be a secretary for M. Louis Échard (Romain Duris), he's immediately impressed by her speed – and her bare shoulder. Thereby begins a lovely but subtle romantic dance between them, propelled by a series of typing competitions but underlain by their characters' appealing natures and flaws. *C'est si bon!* [Caution: sexuality] **[W]**

32. One Singular Sensation

In the entire history of the movies, one attraction remains the most towering achievement of all. Other people have produced longer and grander epics, or more technically proficient ones – and definitely more expensive ones – but no one has ever achieved so much so soon in the evolution of motion pictures and did it with so much passion and vision.

Napoléon
1927 – France – Abel Gance

If you've never heard of this magnificent movie, then your knowledge of the cinema might not run as deep as you think, because this is one of the greatest products of the medium, and it has affected the style of moviemakers ever since. Even though *Napoléon* is four hours long and silent, Gance's epic is never, ever dull, and few movies of any length are as continually lively. He draws you along relentlessly but willingly into a mythic, poetic vision of one of the most familiar and controversial names in history.

*   *   *

The story begins in winter with the young Bonaparte as a child at a boarding school. Then it follows him through the French Revolution in 1789 and ends with his rise to power and dominance of Europe in the early 19th century. For the title role, Gance chose two actors with striking faces and resemblances to the real Bonaparte. Eighteen-year-old Vladimir Roudenko plays him as a schoolboy, and he's marvelous. Then Albert Dieudonne enters as the adult Napoléon. He's a 37-year-old veteran actor whose resemblance is as uncanny as his performance is mesmerizing. But the real power of *Napoléon* comes from its

311

creator. Gance used techniques never attempted before. He mounted his camera on horseback and swung it on cables over a crowd. He sometimes split the screen into 16 squares or edited his sequences so tightly that some shots consist of a single frame of film. Because of this, the snowball-fight and pillow-fight scenes in the early part of the movie have become legendary among film buffs, and they're still dazzling. But Gance saved the most impressive achievement for last. During the final few minutes of *Napoléon,* he added two flanking screens that contain either synchronized or complementary images – a technique not tried again for 25 years, in *This Is Cinerama* (not on this list) in 1952. The movie stunned crowds at its premiere at the Paris Opera House. Sitting in the audience was none other than Charles de Gaulle, the future wartime leader and French president, who reportedly stood up and cheered at the end along with everyone else. He later said he never forgot the experience.

*   *   *

All of this is only part of the story. Like other exceptional movies of the period, *Napoléon* became a casualty of the advent of sound – but a particularly tragic one. After its sensational opening, it soon faded from public consciousness, because by 1930 theaters worldwide had retooled to present "talkies," and audiences had grown uninterested in silent features, even ones as monumental as *Napoléon.* So, like Howard Hughes did with *Hell's Angels,* Gance attempted to remake his masterpiece. In 1934, he produced a new version. Called "Bonaparte and Revolution," it featured a soundtrack that contained recordings of his actors matching their dialogue to what they originally had mouthed on the screen. It failed. Part of the problem was its length – at more than five hours, many people considered it overwhelming and even burdensome. So, as time passed, Gance and *Napoléon* slipped into obscurity. He directed his last theatrical feature in 1938 – a sound version remake of *J'accuse!* (not on this list) his legendary anti-war movie of 20 years earlier.

*   *   *

Then, in 1951, a British schoolboy named Kevin Brownlow ordered a two-reel film from his local library called "Napoléon

Bonaparte and the French Revolution." Brownlow later wrote, "When the parcel arrived, I set up my projector, summoned my parents, and ran the picture on the living room wall. Those two reels changed my life." Even a fragment of the original movie, shown in the tiny 9.5-millimeter format (the British equivalent of Super-8 in the United States), astounded Brownlow, and as a result he spent most of the next three decades tracking down pieces of the long-lost epic. Eventually, he forged a friendship with Gance. Finally, Francis Ford Coppola's Zoetrope Studios sponsored a four-hour restoration of *Napoléon* and commissioned a fine new score by Carmine Coppola, the director's father, who had composed the fine original music for *The Black Stallion* in 1979.

*   *   *

The restored *Napoléon* premiered the weekend of January 23, 1981, at Radio City Music Hall in New York City. Gary Arnold and I traveled there to see the restoration. He attended the first night, and I saw the second screening on the evening of the 24th. The 6,500-seat theater sold out both nights, and the movie was projected on Radio City's giant screen. It was magnificent, thrilling and totally captivating. The elder Coppola was there, and at age 71 (soon to be my current age) he conducted his live orchestral accompaniment with vigor and with only a couple of stretches of relief by a substitute. Despite *Napoléon's* length and detail, it seemed as though Gance had meticulously hand-composed each individual frame of film. Every shot, every composition, every face of every character, seemed perfect. The final, three-screen sequence *was* overwhelming, particularly the very last shot, in which he tinted the two flanking screens red and blue to match the tricolors of the French flag. When it ended, the audience erupted in prolonged applause and cheers.

But there was more…

*   *   *

At the time, I edited American Widescreener, the newsletter of an association of amateur moviemaking enthusiasts. Here's what I wrote about that night in an issue we devoted to the movie:

313

In the advertising that preceded the screenings for that weekend, it was announced that Gance would appear in person. Unfortunately, at the last minute, the filmmaker had decided that his age and health would not permit him to make the trip from Paris to New York. So, following the January 24 show, at about midnight (6 a.m. Paris time) a telephone call was put through to Gance, so he could hear what the audience thought of his newly reconstructed film.

A telephone was brought out on stage, and when the audience was told that Gance was listening on the other end, it exploded into tumultuous applause and cheering that lasted almost ten minutes.

It was an enormously exhilarating and dramatic moment, irresistibly bringing tears to the eyes. And it was a fitting climax to the life story of perhaps the greatest film romanticist of all time: *Napoléon*, forgotten and almost irretrievably lost for over 50 years, now finally recognized for the great cinematic creation that it was. And Gance, equally as ignored, suffering through years of frustration, finally received the fitting tribute – in the last year of his life.

Gance died 10 months later, on November 10, 1981. He was 92. [Viewing note: In 2012, Kevin Brownlow unveiled the fruit of three additional decades of his restoration work: the full, five-hour version of *Napoléon*, complete with a new soundtrack by composer Carl Davis. The re-release dazzled audiences at the San Francisco Silent Film Festival that year. But here's the bad news: The film has not been screened since. Furthermore, though it is available on Blu-ray and DVD, the discs are British productions and are incompatible with players in the United States. So, for the time being, *Napoléon* has once again become a lost treasure] **[B&W with a brief color sequence, part of the widescreen finale]**

33. Let Silliness Reign

"Dying is easy; comedy is hard." That phrase has been attributed to several sources, all of them British and all of them reported to be on their death beds, including the great dramatist Noel Coward, stage actor Edmund Kean and actor/stage director Donald Wolfit. Whatever its true source, the quip is – excuse the pun – dead-on about acting and the difficulty of being truly funny. Small wonder. In all of cinema, relatively few attractions could either sustain laughs all the way through or at least hit some highs of comedy. Not that it's impossible, as the selections below demonstrate, but out of tens of thousands of titles, a list this small does seem to validate the comment; doing comedy *really* is hard. Here are two-dozen-plus-one times when it has succeeded, sometimes sublimely but in all cases at least fitfully.

The Music Box
1932 – Produced by Hal Roach
In this hilarious, Oscar-winning short, Stan Laurel and Oliver Hardy play moving men. Their job: transport a piano by hand to the top of a very long outdoor stairway – whether it should be moved that particular way or not. If you know them, that's all you need. If you've never seen them, you're in for a most silly treat. [B&W]

Duck Soup
1933 – Leo McCarey
I'll say it at the outset: Your knowledge and understanding of movie slapstick comedy will remain incomplete and fatally flawed unless you've seen *Duck Soup* – and I'd even argue you must see it more than once to fully appreciate its genius. Sure,

there had been plenty of hilarious one- and two-reelers produced for years before by the likes of Mack Sennett and Hal Roach, and starring the slapstick luminaries of the period such as the Keystone Cops, Buster Keaton, Charlie Chaplin, Harold Lloyd and even Laurel and Hardy in their silent days. And they were all great attractions that kept audiences in stitches. But this was the movie that perfected using spoken words above all to convey slapstick on film, and few have surpassed it to this day. The words here are delivered by Groucho Marx, the absolute master of the genre. Groucho plays Rufus T. Firefly, who for vague and irrelevant reasons becomes the head of the fictional European state of Freedonia, a country on the verge of war. He announces his new policies to his constituents with a song, "Whatever it is, I'm against it!" and declares, "If you think this country's bad off now, just wait 'til I get through with it!" Two other Marx brothers, Chico and Harpo, provide heavy-duty comedy support, and the durable Margaret Dumont endures Groucho's constant barrage of insults and double entendres. None of it makes any sense, but I doubt you'll care one bit. There is one scene where Groucho pretends to be Harpo's mirror image, and it's considered a classic as well. There's also the required piano concerto by Chico and harp solo by, well, Harpo. But Groucho carries the day. [Trivia note: Nearly three decades later, Harpo recreated the mirror scene brilliantly with Lucille Ball in an episode of her TV series I Love Lucy] **[B&W]**

A Night at the Opera (and) A Day at the Races
1935 and 1937 – Sam Wood
These two Marx Brothers attractions make a perfect double bill, or see just one of them. It doesn't matter, because they're interchangeable and just excuses for the boys to demonstrate their ability to cause mayhem and their signature bits: Groucho's naughty remarks at the expense of Margaret Dumont, Chico's Italian routines and clever piano solos, and Harpo's silent slapstick and beautiful harp performances. There's also the periodic interplay between Groucho and Chico, such as the "sanity clause" discussion in *Night at the Opera*, with its

316

inevitable punchline, and an even funnier bit at an ice cream stand in *A Day at the Races*. Everything else is secondary to the fact that these two movies are rousing good times. Oh, and don't miss the stateroom scene in *Night at the Opera*. **[B&W]**

Way Out West (and) Block-Heads
1937 and 1938 – James W. Horne
Another comedy double-bill for your consideration: For 20 years, Stan Laurel and Oliver Hardy churned out dozens of shorts and a few features for the Hal Roach Studios, and these two represent some of their best. In *Way Out West* the title says it all, but watch for one particularly hysterical scene where the boys are trying to climb up to a second-story window. Just don't be drinking liquids or eating during it – actually that's good advice anytime you're watching these two beloved souls. In *Block-Heads*, Ollie reunites with Stan, who's just returned after 20 years fighting World War I, because he never learned the war had ended. Don't ask, just watch – and don't miss the closing scene! **[B&W]**

The Bank Dick
1940 – Edward F. Cline
The man born William Claude Duncanfield in 1880 in Philadelphia became one of the most distinctive screen presences ever. W.C. Fields was surely the most obnoxious of movie characters, a reputation that loosely paralleled his real life. Here he plays Egbert Sousè (Soo-SAY). a hapless bank guard who becomes involved in one of the screen's funniest car chases – and one that's been imitated many times since. **[B&W]**

The Palm Beach Story
1942 – Preston Sturges
This lively and often hysterically funny Sturges title begins differently from any other movie I can think of: with a prologue ostensibly replaying the climax of another movie that Sturges *never* made! That's right, it delivers an opening montage from a

nonexistent prequel – but it's so good I wish he *had* made the thing. The story concerns a couple dangling on the edge of financial ruin. The husband (Joel McCrea) is an inventor who's always falling short of that one big break, so his wife (Claudette Colbert), tired of being chased by bill-collectors, decides to flee and seek her fortune elsewhere. This she does, first on an overnight train from Manhattan to Palm Beach, where she encounters maybe the most obnoxious social group ever – The Ale and Quail Club, a bunch of besotted twits armed with hunting dogs, shotguns and lots of liquor. She's rescued from the mayhem by a seeming nerd (Rudy Vallee) named John D. Hackensacker (a play on tycoon John D. Rockefeller). And that's where I'll leave you. Just know it's a typically intricate Sturges plot that serves only as pretext for the hilarity, and there's tons of it – and the nonexistent prequel eventually comes in handy. For that matter, Vallee's character's wealth comes in handy as well, such as when he arranges a good-night serenade that's to die for. **[B&W]**

Road to Morocco [100]
1942 – David Butler
In this third installment of the *Road to…* series – which began with *Road to Singapore* in 1940 and *Road to Zanzibar* in '41 (neither on this list) – Bing Crosby and Bob Hope settle into the formulaic but comfortable routines they would repeat over the next decade as they delighted audiences with, respectively, their crooning and manic bumbling. Here, the boys are shipwrecked on the coast of (where else?) Morocco and proceed to run afoul of a local sheik (a young and rather dashing-looking Anthony Quinn, back for the second time as a *Road to…* villain). They also meet a beautiful princess (Dorothy Lamour, a constant romantic presence in the series) who declares she wants to marry Hope but seems to prefer Crosby. Hilarity ensues, as they say, including a scene where Hope pretends to be a statue despite a persistent fly crawling all over his face. This is also the movie that introduced what became Lamour's theme song, "Moonlight Becomes You," performed of course by Der Bingle. **[B&W]**

The Miracle of Morgan's Creek
1944 – Preston Sturges

How's this for a comedy plot? A young woman goes out one night, gets drunk, sleeps with a soldier whose name she can't remember and becomes pregnant. If this sounds like a melodrama, maybe it would be in less capable hands. But with Sturges at the helm, it's one of the funniest – and sweetest – movies ever made. Betty Hutton plays Trudy Kockenlocker, the unfortunate mother-to-be, and the ever-spunky Diana Lynn plays her sister Emily. William Demarest plays their father, and Eddie Bracken plays Trudy's milquetoast suitor, who comes through like a champ when she needs him. It's unique, and some of the sequences are side-splitting funny. As for the plot, don't worry about the kids seeing this one – it plays out so innocuously I doubt they'll grasp the implications. **[B&W]**

Road to Utopia
1945 – Hal Walker

The liveliest, most uninhibited installment of the Hope–Crosby road pictures takes place in Alaska during the Gold Rush (though, as usual, they shot it in California). But it's just an excuse for every single sight gag and pun the moviemakers and the stars could cram into the 90-minute running time, and just about every one of them pays off. The movie also features humorist Robert Benchley making occasional appearances, and silly commentary, as the narrator. **[B&W]**

Road to Rio
1947 – Norman Z. McLeod

Of all the Hope–Crosby road movies, this one has my favorite ending, where Crosby and Hope finally track down "the papers" they've been chasing, while mustachioed, bug-eyed, big-mouthed Jerry Colonna leads a cavalry charge saying ... well, "Ch-a-a-a-a-a-a-a-a-a-a-a-a-a-a-a-a-a-a-a-a-a-a-a-r-r-r-r-r-r-r-r-r-r-g-e! The biggest box-office hit of that year, it also features a lively number, "You Don't Have to Know the Language," sung

319

by Crosby and the fabulous Andrews sisters. [Trivia note: Patty Andrews, the trio's lead singer, lived to be 94 and died in 2013] [B&W]

Bud Abbott and Lou Costello Meet Frankenstein
1948 – Charles Barton
No survey of movie comedies would be complete without at least one title featuring the beloved duo. The plot? I'm not sure I could describe it. Just know it's pure silliness, good-natured fun, plenty of laughs, and it even features appearances by Bela Lugosi (the original Dracula) and Lon Chaney, Jr. (the Wolf Man) – though they couldn't swing getting the inimitable Boris Karloff to reprise his role as Mary Shelley's monster. Instead, they cast 6-foot-5 actor Glenn Strange, who bore a reasonable resemblance to Karloff. [B&W]

A Southern Yankee
1948 – Edward Sedgwick
Another required inclusion in movie comedies: Richard Bernard "Red" Skelton. The loveable, bumbling star of assorted movies became one of the most popular personalities on television for two decades as the star of The Red Skelton Show. Here, he's (what else?) a bumbling hotel bellhop who gets involved in a Civil War spy ring. Endearing nonsense, all. [B&W]

What's Up, Tiger Lily?
1966 – Woody Allen
Unique in all of cinema; simply put, Allen took a low-budget Japanese spy movie called "Key of Keys," removed the dialogue and then dubbed in his own take on what was going on. It's extremely uneven and often stupefying, with way too much filler, but sometimes it's hilarious. Whatever the original plot was, Allen made it about a desperate struggle to acquire – no kidding – the recipe for the world's best egg salad. Maybe the most amazing thing is trying to figure out what the heck those people were doing in the original movie, because it couldn't

320

have made any more sense than what Allen re-conceived for the action, which includes the memorable last line of dialogue, "He thinks he's an airplane." [Trivia note: Two of the co-stars in the Japanese movie are Mie Hama and Akiko Wakabayashi, both of whom appeared the following year as Bond girls in *You Only Live Twice*] [Caution: nudity, lewd references to sexuality and mild profanity] [W]

Take the Money and Run
1969 – Woody Allen

Allen's first original feature is a real gigglefest. It's a pseudo-documentary about a hardened criminal named Virgil Starkwell and the saga of his career, personal life and eventual downfall – but all done for nearly constant laughs. Allen showed in this movie an enormous gift for verbal and slapstick comedy, both in his directing and his acting, but as with his Oscar-winning *Annie Hall* 16 years later, he benefits here from the skills of the great film editor Ralph Rosenblum. Also, composer Marvin Hamlisch contributed a sweet score. Janet Margolin plays his beautiful but long-suffering wife. [Caution: adult humor and mild sexuality] [W]

And Now for Something Completely Different
1971 – Terry Gilliam

In the late 1960s, a troupe of five young British comedians – and one American – began a series on British television. At first, they couldn't think of a name. Then, somehow, they came up with Monty Python's Flying Circus. Each show contained a half-dozen or so sketches that varied in quality from deadly dull to brilliantly funny. Eventually, the troupe decided to assemble some of their best material into a movie, stitched together with one of the cast announcing, in between the bits, "And now, for something completely different." Some of the material has become dated and arcane, but there are still plenty of laugh-out-loud moments, including the now-legendary "dead-parrot" sketch, which transforms into the "I'm a Lumberjack" song. Don't get it? Don't worry. With John Cleese, Graham Chapman,

321

Eric Idle, Terry Jones, Michael Palin and director Terry Gilliam (the American). [Caution: sexuality and adult humor]

Bananas
1971 – Woody Allen
Allen's second movie immortalizes his character as the world's biggest schnook, in this guise a New York products tester named Fielding Mellish. Jilted by his girlfriend (Louise Lasser, to whom Allen was married at the time), he departs for Central America where he fights for the rebels in the fictional country of San Marcos and, after the rebel leader suffers a bit of a breakdown, ends up becoming the leader of the country – albeit in tacky fake beard. Whatever. It's all complete nonsense and done entirely for laughs, including some scenes that basically have nothing to do with the story.[Trivia note: One scene involves Mellish being accosted by a couple of toughs on a subway, one of whom is played by a young and then-unknown Sylvester Stallone] [Caution: humorous sexual references] **[W]**

Sleeper
1973 – Woody Allen
Probably Allen's best pure comedy – though like the rest of them it's uneven. In this futuristic fantasy, he plays Miles Monroe, a health-food fanatic of the 1970s who is frozen and then revived nearly 200 years later. He awakens to a world where the government is run by a dictator named Our Beloved Leader, people smoke and consume decidedly unhealthy foods, nothing much works, and old fashioned sexuality has been replaced by a device called the Orgasmatron, which resembles a bullet-shaped, chrome-plated phone booth, and which apparently delivers the goods within a few seconds. Diane Keaton, in her second co-starring role with Allen (the first was the previous year in *Play It Again, Sam*), plays a spacey socialite – quite a different character from Kay (Mrs. Michael) Corleone, whom she portrayed in the two *Godfather* movies, respectively, the year before and year after *Sleeper*. But maybe that experience paid off, because she does a humorous impersonation of Marlon Brando here that isn't bad.

322

Once again, Marvin Hamlisch contributed a hip, jazzy score. [Trivia note: The movie's climax takes place at a futuristic complex, supposedly the government's headquarters. In reality, it's the main building of the National Center for Atmospheric Research in Boulder, Colorado, which I used to visit periodically back in my days as a science writer] [Caution (naturally): humorous sexual references] **[W]**

Young Frankenstein
1974 – Mel Brooks
Brooks and his perennial players Gene Wilder and Madeline Kahn join Teri Garr, Cloris Leachman, Peter Boyle and British comedian Marty Feldman in this spotty but sometimes screamingly funny send-up of the 1930s James Whale classics *Frankenstein* and *Bride of Frankenstein*, with Wilder as Dr. Frankenstein's grandson, a medical professor who is so embarrassed about his past that he pronounces his name "FRONK-en-steen." Boyle is absolutely terrific as the monster, and he brings a surprising amount of expression and appeal to his character despite the heavy makeup. Kahn is likewise wonderful as Wilder's prissy fiancée, who discovers her womanhood, and then some, at the hands – and other parts – of the monster. Gene Hackman shows up in a hilarious parody of the scene in which the monster encounters a blind monk. Cloris Leachman plays well against type as the dour Frau Blücher, the mere utterance of whose name causes unseen, off-camera horses to whinny in fright. And for those of you who have never had the pleasure of seeing Feldman, here playing Frankenstein's henchman Igor (which he pronounces "EYE-gor"), this is a fine chance. It's all good fun, and the final bedroom scenes are perfect twin denouements. [Caution: humorous sexual references] **[B&W] [W]**

Monty Python and the Holy Grail
1975 – Terry Gilliam
Considered *the* classic Monty Python for aficionados and novices alike, this is unabashed silliness from beginning to end –

interrupted by the usual dull stretches and occasional strokes of brilliance that characterized the troupe (Graham Chapman, John Cleese, Eric Idle, Terry Jones, Michael Palin and director Gilliam) from the start of their TV days. It's the telling of the tale of Arthur, "King of the Britons," and his Knights of the Round Table at Camelot, although there's scant resemblance to the legend. The boys here began employing a device they would use in their three subsequent movies: each playing many different roles. Some of the bits have become immortal, including the discussion about coconuts, the trial of a witch (played by Connie Booth, Cleese's wife at the time), the "bring out your dead" scene, the battle with the Black Knight, the killer rabbit, and an attempted assault on a castle occupied by some obnoxious Frenchmen – which includes a hysterical take on the Trojan Horse. It's the best of all Python on the big screen – and even the trailer, if you can find it, is hilarious. [Trivia notes: 1) Budget and cultural restrictions dictated that cast and crew employ their creativity to make the Medieval Doune Castle stand in for multiple locations. As a result, today the privately owned and operated Doune, about 30 miles northeast of Glasgow, Scotland, has become a haven for *Grail* fans. 2) Budget was also the reason why Arthur and the Knights are on foot accompanied by faithful servants making clopping sounds with coconuts – they couldn't afford horses!] [Caution: fake gore and humorous sexual references] [W]

The Return of the Pink Panther
1975 – Blake Edwards

The third installment in the series exceeds *A Shot in the Dark* (coming in the next compilation) as the funniest and most enjoyable of the bunch. It features the antics of two actors at the height of their appeal: Christopher Plummer (Captain Von Trapp in *The Sound of Music*) and Catherine Schell, playing Sir Charles and Lady Claudine Litton, two suave and sophisticated aristocrats who might be moonlighting as jewel thieves. Peter Sellers reprises his role as Inspector Clouseau of the Sûreté, and he's as bumbling and hilarious as ever on their trail; likewise

Herbert Lom as his neurotic superior and Bert Kwouk as Clouseau's long-suffering-but-loyal manservant, Cato. After seeing this movie, you might be tempted never to pronounce the word "phone" correctly again. The venerable Henry Mancini also returned to contribute a snazzy update of his original score, and animator Ken Harris created the knockout title sequence. [W]

Dead Men Don't Wear Plaid
1982 – Carl Reiner

Here's another unique plot idea along the lines of *What's Up, Tiger Lily?* Reiner fabricated a 1940s-style detective plot and then intercut it with real detective movies from the '40s, some classic and some mediocre, often with hilarious results. Steve Martin plays the protagonist and narrator, a detective named Rigby Reardon. Aside from co-starring with his contemporary, Rachel Ward, the gimmick allows Martin – via clever editing – to interact with some of the biggest stars of the era, including Humphrey Bogart, Cary Grant, Alan Ladd, James Cagney, Barbara Stanwyck, Ava Gardner and Ingrid Bergman. The moviemakers kind of run out of ideas toward the end (coincidentally, when Reiner makes his appearance onscreen), but for an hour or so, it's a rollicking good time. Miklós Rózsa's score adds a flair for the genre and the time period. [Caution: sexuality and some violence] [B&W] [W]

The Naked Gun: From the Files of Police Squad!
1988 – David Zucker

This utterly sophomoric police caper stars drama veteran Leslie Nielsen, playing Lt. Frank Drebin of the LAPD, hot on the trail of … well, we're never sure, but it's got something to do with smuggling and a plot to assassinate Queen Elizabeth of England. But never mind, that isn't important now. What is important are the jokes, which are well-timed and plentiful, and Drebin's trip to the men's room after a speech could be the funniest scene ever filmed. With George Kennedy and O.J. Simpson (back when he was just a popular ex-jock/actor/commercial pitchman and not a suspected double-murderer) as his sidekicks and the pert and pretty Priscilla Presley (forgive the alliteration) as his love interest. [Caution: lewd and crude but entirely funny sexual and men's-room references] **[W]**

Analyze This
1999 – Harold Ramis
Here, Robert De Niro, one of the finest dramatic actors of his generation, demonstrates he can do deadpan comedy as well. He plays Paul Vitti, a gangster who desperately needs psychiatric help to overcome a rash of panic attacks before rival mobsters discover his weakness and assassinate him. So, he seeks the help of family therapist Dr. Ben Sobel (Billy Crystal), an ordinary guy who's otherwise comfortably ensconced in his practice and is soon to be married for the second time to a lovely TV journalist (Lisa Kudrow). But Vitti will not be denied (as Sobel discovers to his horror), and the resulting interaction between the two men makes for a surprisingly appealing and funny story. Also surprising, and delightfully so, is how well Crystal holds his own in his scenes with De Niro. He even proves the dominant character a few times. Perennial screen tough guy Joe Viterelli is terrific as Vitti's affable but no-nonsense henchman, as is Chazz Palminteri as Vitti's rival for mob dominance. By the way, who would have thought the recommendation, "just hit a pillow," could endanger your health? [Trivia notes: 1) Coincidentally, Vitti's affliction mirrors that of America's favorite TV mobster, Anthony Soprano (the great James Gandolfini), who debuted that same year and likewise desperately needed a psychiatrist (in his case, Lorraine Bracco). 2) As mentioned elsewhere, De Niro was originally cast as Elliot Garfield in Neil Simon's *The Goodbye Girl*, but early in the production Simon wisely decided that he wasn't right for the role. De Niro's very good here, but he's playing one of his natural characters] [Caution: sexuality, language and, of course, violence] **[W]**

34. Guilty Pleasures

Go ahead, call them tasteless, stupid or even downright offensive. You'll get no argument from me. I'll even guess you'll cast some disapproving looks at them (and whether you do or not, please keep the kids far away). But I defy you to watch the first two of these four selections all the way through with a straight face. The second two aren't comedies, but each possesses its own brand of guilty fun.

Ruthless People
1986 – Jim Abrahams, David Zucker and Jerry Zucker

The writing-directing trio who gave us *Airplane!* (coming in the next compilation) and *The Naked Gun* set aside their genre send-ups temporarily and instead updated the O. Henry short story "The Ransom of Red Chief." (see *O. Henry's Full House*) And, guess what? They produced a consistently hilarious feature starring Danny DeVito, Judge Reinhold and Helen Slater, with Bette Midler playing the Red Chief role to comedic perfection. DeVito is clothing magnate Sam Stone. He despises his heiress wife, Barbara (Midler), with a passion. "I hate the way she licks stamps," he growls. To be blunt, Sam wants Barbara's money, and he wants her dead. So when an otherwise decent and honest but wronged former employee (Slater) and her husband (Reinhold) kidnap Barbara and demand ransom, Sam refuses, figuring they'll murder her and he'll collect her inheritance. After that, all bets are off about the plot, which produces a steady stream of crude laughs. Watch for Anita Morris as a sexy Jezebel and Bill Pullman in his debut as her lover, a man about whom one police officer says, "This could very well be the stupidest person on the face of the Earth." [Viewing note: You might want to skip the grating opening credits] [Caution: rough language and sexuality] **[W]**

Wedding Crashers
2005 – David Dobkin

Here's another offering that's frequently crude and senseless but also hilarious a good deal of the time, entirely because of the terrific performances of Vince Vaughn as a shameless hound who finally receives his comeuppance, and Isla Fisher as the One-Night Stand from Hell who dishes it. Vaughn and co-star Owen Wilson play a pair of divorce lawyers who crash weddings to pick up single women for the aforementioned one-night stands. And they're really successful at it, as the long and increasingly funny early montage depicts. But when love enters into the picture – Fisher for Vaughn and Rachel McAdams for Wilson – it complicates things, big time. Though the whole concept is offensive, not only do Vaughn and Wilson carry it off, but they also actually make you want to root for their success. Fisher is the mother of all monkey wrenches along the way, however. She's assisted in that capacity, inadvertently, by the great Bradley Cooper (immortal now as Chris Kyle in *American Sniper*) in an early role as McAdams's obnoxious boyfriend – though he receives a comeuppance of his own. Two wrong notes involve former Bond girl (as in James Bond) Jane Seymour in a thankless turn as a mother-of-the-bride on the make, and Will Ferrell as a hideously obnoxious mentor. [Trivia note: The movie features a loose, coincidental association and two repairings. Seymour's husband and father of the bride is played by Christopher Walken. Both had co-starred with Roger Moore as 007; Seymour in 1973's *Live and Let Die*, as Bond's love interest in her debut, and Walken in a rare villainous role in *A View to a Kill* in 1985 (both coming in a later compilation). In 2011, Wilson and McAdams again co-starred as a couple, albeit unhappily, in Woody Allen's shockingly flat romantic fantasy *Midnight in Paris* (not on my lists). And Vaughn and Wilson teamed up two years later in the lame comedy *The Internship* (likewise not here)] [Caution: rough language and sexuality] **[W]**

The Expendables
2010 – Sylvester Stallone

I never really liked Sylvester Stallone's movies, with the possible exceptions of *parts* of the original *Rocky* and the original Rambo installment, *First Blood* – though not enough to include them on my list. But then this irresistible clunker showed up. Plus, in 2015, "Sly," as he's known to his friends, finally won me over with his marvelous, unforgettable performance as Rocky Balboa in *Creed*. No question, this one, made as an updated combination of *The Magnificent Seven* and *The Dirty Dozen* (the latter likewise not on my list), is formulaic, ultra-violent, excessive, derivative and highly dependent on computer effects (and much younger stuntmen) to portray explosions, ultra-heroic deeds and the rending of human flesh. But it's also a roaring good time, offering tons of thrills and deadpan humor. Stallone, here nearly in his mid-sixties, looks fit and relaxed – though a l-i-t-t-l-e paunchy – as the leader of a ragtag band of mercenaries sent on an impossible mission that inevitably goes wrong. He's joined by several action stars of the 1970s, '80s and '90s, plus cameos by Bruce Willis and The Terminator himself, Arnold Schwarzenegger, late of his duties as governor of California (or as he pronounces it, CALL-ee-FOR-nee-ah). Mickey Rourke also appears, though he seems to have morphed into Charles Bronson in his old age, playing a wizened ex-mercenary who now operates a tattoo parlor and drags pensively on his pipe. During all of the accommodations, empty negotiations and apologies that passed for our national foreign policy while this movie enjoyed its theatrical runs, it was genuinely refreshing to watch men who dispatch bad guys without hesitation or remorse. But if your sensibilities would be offended, or if you have to ask more, then you probably should stick with PC material (that's Politically Correct, not Parental Guidance). [Viewing note: My affection for the series mildly improved with the sequel in 2012, which included a few more action stars, and my resistance dissolved with the third installment in 2014, which became so preposterous I gave up my critical objections entirely. I'll have more to say about *Expendables* 2 and 3 in a future compilation] [Caution: needless to say, rough language and *extreme* blood and gore] **[W]**

RED
2010 – Richard Schwentke
My favorite of the bunch. Picture yourself lying awake in your bed in the middle of the night, basically minding your own business, when a full-scale assault team sneaks in, prepared to shred your flesh with automatic weapons. Now, picture that you're so well trained and professional you can escape your would-be assassins and return to wreak havoc on them. That's basically how *RED* gets started, after which Frank Moses (Bruce Willis), a former CIA operative who's "Retired, Extremely Dangerous" (Get it?), recruits some of his old allies to foil a serious plot to kill the President of the United States and take over the government. Those allies include Helen Mirren as a sharpshooter who's a Martha Stewart lookalike, Morgan Freeman as a quietly deadly former agent, Brian Cox as an ex-Russian spy who's kept the lovelight burning for Mirren, and John Malkovich in a wonderfully wild-eyed, over-the-top portrayal of a likewise retired agency guy whose paranoid delusions often turn out to be true. For the bad guys, there's Richard Dreyfuss playing a slithery arms dealer, and Karl Urban (the second iteration of Dr. Leonard McCoy, aka "Bones," in the new *Star Trek* movies) showing considerable menace as a lethal upstart of a CIA operative. Mary Louise Parker plays Willis's at-first-involuntary love interest, and veteran Ernest Borgnine, at age 93, turns in a witty cameo as the keeper of the CIA's deepest secrets. It's a popcorn thriller, frequently improbable but always entertaining. [Viewing note: The gang reunited in 2013 for *RED 2*, but the sequel was predictable and far less entertaining, so coincidentally I didn't include it here] [Trivia note: Borgnine went on to make six more movies (raising his total to an amazing 206) before passing away two years later] [Caution: Like *The Expendables*, the plot is tongue-in-cheek, but the violence, gore and mayhem are intense and unsuitable for kids] **[W]**

35. Tense, Thrilling or Downright Terrifying

Alfred Hitchcock once said the best way to scare audiences is first to bore them to death then spring something unexpected. Maybe so, but my favorite device, also described by Hitchcock, is as follows: If the characters know a bomb is about to go off, it can be reasonably suspenseful. But if a bomb is about to go off, and the audience knows but the characters don't, the tension can be excruciating. There are plenty of ways to thrill or scare moviegoers, and if you spend a couple of hours or so with any of these 22 titles, you might find yourself on the edge of your seat learning more of them.

The Wages of Fear
1953 – France – Henri-Georges Clouzot

Consider this plot outline: Four desperate men, trapped in a godforsaken town somewhere in Venezuela, take jobs transporting two truckloads of unstable nitroglycerin explosives 300 miles to extinguish an oil-well fire and earn enough money to get out of the country. That might be all you need to know, except to say Clouzot was a master of suspense, and some of the sequences are almost unbearable to watch. After nearly 70 years, this remains a knockout adventure yarn, offering hair-raising tension and vivid if unpleasant realism – it's like spending a couple of hours in Hell. It's also international star Yves Montand's first significant role. I thought about including this in the International Classics category, but it more properly belongs here. My only problem with the movie is its ending; I really think it unravels in the last few minutes. [Trivia notes: 1) Linda, the rather seductive bar slut in the movie (particularly for the 1950s), is played by Clouzot's wife, Vera, who co-starred in his other thriller, *Les Diaboliques* (not on this list), which he made the following year. 2) The character M. Jo, Montand's pal and co-driver, is played by Charles Vanel, one of the few actors in the world to appear in more than 200 movies and whose career spanned an astounding 80 years, beginning in 1908 when he was 16] [Caution: sexuality and rough language] **[B&W]**

The High and the Mighty [100]
1954 – William Wellman

For half a century, this movie occupied the Exceedingly Rare category (coming up), because it simply was not available. Then, in 2005, John Wayne's family settled some legal issues surrounding the property and allowed the release of this early CinemaScope gem, a classic aircraft-in-trouble movie with a white-knuckle ending. Wayne plays Dan Roman, a co-pilot with a haunted past flying an 11-hour commercial run (the early airliners only did about 200 miles an hour) from Honolulu to San Francisco when the plane develops severe engine trouble over the ocean. The question becomes whether Roman and pilot John Sullivan (Robert Stack) can keep the ship in the air long enough to land safely, or whether they must ditch in rough seas and hope to survive and be rescued. The uncertainty surrounding their fate compels crewmembers and passengers alike to reflect on their lives – and it gives the moviemakers lots of opportunities to follow increasingly dopey but endearing plot lines involving the characters. The Zucker brothers based *Airplane!* (coming in the next compilation) on the story, and they lifted liberally from it – even casting Stack as an aging, ornery pilot. Nevertheless, it's a highly entertaining and exciting tale of disaster in the air, featuring some of the earliest widescreen footage (shot in glorious Technicolor) of the experience of flight. Its content is suitable for the kids, but it could have you all gripping your seats and clinging to one another as you wait to see if the crippled plane can stay in the air, awaiting one of the all-time great cinematic climaxes, a sequence that will leave you spent and in tears. And for days afterward you'll probably find yourself whistling those memorable notes from Dimitri

Tiomkin's heavenly, Oscar-winning score – just as Dan Roman does during and at the end of the movie. [Trivia note: In one of the strangest and most tragic bits of trivia about the movies on this list, the real DC-4 aircraft used in *The High and the Mighty* crashed 10 years later, when an engine fire forced it down in the Pacific, on a run from Honolulu to San Francisco! No one survived, and the plane was never found] **[W]**

The Guns of Navarone
1961 – J. Lee Thompson
This was a tremendous hit when first released, and it remains a rousing tale, though it's also consistently overacted, excessively melodramatic and damned predictable. As such, I toyed with including it in the Deliciously Bad category along with *Where Eagles Dare* and *Ice Station Zebra*, two other titles based on Alistair MacLean bestsellers. But it contains enough fine moments to earn a slot here. Likewise, I didn't include it in the Men at War category, despite it's World War II battle setting, because it's too much of a star vehicle and suspense yarn – though it is loosely based on a real episode that pitted a team of highly skilled commandos against the German army, in this case in an attempt to disable two enormous artillery guns installed on the fictional Greek island of Navarone. The guns guard a narrow channel, through which a British naval squadron is due to pass to rescue thousands of troops stranded on Kyros, another fictional island. Gregory Peck plays Keith Mallory, the team leader, chosen because he speaks "Greek like a Greek and German like a German" and was reputed to be "the greatest mountain-climber in the world before the war." That last skill proves mighty handy because an early part of the mission involves scaling a massive sheer cliff, which occurs just after the team survives a nasty storm at sea and a perilous – and realistic-looking – landing on a rocky coast. The other specialists include a cynical demolitions expert (David Niven), a guerrilla fighter nursing a grudge against Mallory (Anthony Quinn), a burned-out but expert killer (Stanley Baker), a young but skilled assassin (teen idol James Darren – who even gets to sing), and a pair of

333

female Greek freedom fighters (Irene Papas and Gia Scala). "With every one of us a genius, how can we fail?" Mallory asks. "You can't," his superior replies, and therein begins the tale, punctuated by titles such as "The third day 09.30 Hours." The device is heavy-handed, as are many other moments, but it's best to ignore such indulgences and instead enjoy this as a popcorn thriller, 1960s style, with its Oscar-winning special effects, Greek locales, and another adventure-themed, *basso-profundo* score by Dimitri Tiomkin. **[W]**

Grand Prix
1966 – John Frankenheimer
Half of the movie's three-hour running time contains some standard melodrama with undistinguished performances all around, but the other half more than makes up for it. Frankenheimer installed dozens of cameras along and above race courses in France, Italy, England and California. He also mounted other cameras on the vehicles and shot many of the scenes with the actors actually driving lower-powered versions of real Formula 1 racers. He also insisted on shooting in real time – not slowing down the camera to make the speeds look higher. The results are often electrifying. There are long, long shots from the drivers' points of view screaming along the race courses, and even on video they're realistic enough to make you want to clutch the arms of your chair. In the perfunctory plot, James Garner stars as Pete Aron, an American racer who gets fired from an Italian team for carelessly injuring a teammate, but he's eventually hired by a Japanese team owner (Toshiro Mifune) who's bent on winning the world championship. Aron's chief rival is Jean-Pierre Sarti (Yves Montand), the reigning but aging champion, who has grown tired of the circuit. Much of the melodrama consists of the obligatory entanglements of the competitors with wives, sweethearts and mistresses, but these scenes mostly detract from the superior work by Frankenheimer, his crew and more than two dozen of the world's top racing drivers in capturing the races and the racing environment. Saul Bass contributed the dazzling title sequence, and Maurice Jarre

composed a lively but (for him) ordinary score. [An unusual problem: Like *How the West Was Won*, this move was shot in Cinerama, so its 2.65:1 aspect ratio is so wide that the full images look literally like a letterbox on video. To compound the problem, Frankenheimer sometimes resorted to split-screen shots to tell the story, unfortunately requiring one side or the other to be cropped on the DVD, giving the image a weird look. The solution: If you're lucky enough to live near a vintage Cinerama theater that offers widescreen revivals, wait for it, and bring your earplugs – this is a loud one!] [Caution: intensity and some sexuality] **[W]**

Blue Water, White Death
1971 – Peter Gimbel
This mostly fascinating documentary about finding a great white shark in the wild explores the elusive nature of these fearsome but beautiful predators. Expert diver Gimbel shot the movie off the Great Barrier Reef in Australia with Ron and Valerie Taylor, the two underwater moviemakers who provided the real shark footage for *Jaws*. Actually, the "stars" don't appear until nearly the end of the movie, but there are a couple of interesting sequences in the interim, particularly a frightening, frenzied attack by blue sharks on a whale carcass. Mostly, the early content involves setting up the quest for the great white and a little too much bickering among the documentary crew, but the final sequence is well worth waiting for. [Caution: language and intense shark scenes] **[W]**

Duel
1971 – Steven Spielberg
Spielberg's gripping first feature, a television movie he made at age 23 – and which was eventually released theatrically in Europe – is based on a short story by Richard Matheson that had appeared in Playboy magazine a few years before. A man (Dennis Weaver) traveling alone in his car on a desert highway encounters a tanker truck whose driver suddenly seems determined to kill him. That simple plot device results in quite a

few genuinely frightening scenes, and the beginnings of Spielberg's superior talent at telling stories visually are well evident here. It's also a testament to the young director's abilities that he managed to shoot the whole movie – fully on location – in only 13 days. Even on a TV screen, you might find yourself dropping your jaw and cringing in terror as you wait to see what happens next. [Trivia notes: 1) Spielberg became well-known for storyboarding his movies. That's a technique where each action scene is mapped out in detail as though it were a comic-book story. He started using storyboards with *Duel*, but with a twist: Instead of storyboarding the action, Spielberg actually mapped out the action sequences on the California road where the shooting took place – a certain scene on this curve, another one on that straightaway, and so on. 2) The European release created some technical problems, because the aspect ratio of the film image had to be wider for theatrical projection and therefore caused certain formerly hidden elements to appear. Example: Some of the shots of Weaver in the car, in full frame, also revealed Spielberg directing him from the back seat] **[W]**

The Day of the Jackal
1973 – Fred Zinnemann
The most literate of the bunch. Based on Frederick Forsyth's bestselling novel, it's a finely wrought, meticulously detailed but fictional tale about a plot to kill French President Charles de Gaulle by a professional assassin (Edward Fox), and the desperate search by the French government and law enforcement to locate him before he does the deed. Leading the investigation is Deputy Police Commissioner Claude Lebel (veteran Michel Lonsdale – who played the shadowy patriarch in *Munich*). Lebel's subtle but relentless effort easily matches the assassin's preparations in terms of cleverness, particularly in Lonsdale's wry witticisms. Not related to the real "Jackal," the international terrorist whom the French cornered in Sudan with the help of the U.S. Central Intelligence Agency, this masterful portrayal of the plotting and counter-plotting truly is a nail-biting exercise. [Caution: violence and sexuality] **[W]**

Juggernaut
1974 – England – Richard Lester
Produced on a vastly smaller scale than James Cameron's *Titanic*, the movie nevertheless delivers a surprising amount of intensity. A clever bomber has placed seven sophisticated explosive devices aboard the liner Britannic, which is crossing the Atlantic in a fierce storm – meaning the ship cannot lower its lifeboats. So Scotland Yard dispatches a special bomb-disposal team to disarm the devices before they detonate. Richard Harris is excellent as Jack Fallon, the team's leader, but the otherwise fine supporting cast – including Omar Sharif, Ian Holm, Shirley Knight and Anthony Hopkins – is not up to his level. Lester shot the movie aboard a real ocean liner in a real storm, which helps to sustain the mood of fear. It's a competent, suspenseful, engaging bit of moviemaking, including a terrific sequence in which the disposal team must parachute out the back of a cargo aircraft into the raging sea and then climb up rope ladders onto the liner – and stuntmen did it for real! During the attempt to disable the bombs, Fallon tries to ease the fear of one of his team members. "Haven't I told you about death?" he asks. "It's nature's way of saying you're in the wrong job." [Trivia notes: 1) The story was based on a real incident that turned out to be a hoax. 2) The production team recruited extras by advertising a free ocean cruise for anyone willing to accept – except they had to endure a storm] [Caution: rough language and brief sexuality] [W]

The Taking of Pelham One Two Three
1974 – Joseph Sargent
Based on John Godey's bestselling thriller, this gritty story is about, of all things, the hijacking of a subway train. Robert Shaw, the year after he played the heavy in *The Sting* and the year before *Jaws* made him a star, leads a gang aboard a New York City transit train, where they proceed to hold the passengers hostage for a million-dollar ransom. All the while, the city's government and the cops can't figure out the hijackers' next move – because, after all, as one of them says, "you *know* where a

337

train is going." That doesn't stop the suspense, however, and Walter Matthau gives a strong performance as Zachary Garber, an earthy transit police detective. It's got a few dopey moments, but all in all it's a gripping tale. Jerry Stiller (now immortal as Frank Costanza in the Seinfeld TV series) appears in a rare dramatic role, and Martin Balsam plays one of Shaw's accomplices. David Shire supplied the thumping bass-note theme. [Caution: lots of rough language and some violence] **[W]**

Carrie
1976 – Brian De Palma

When the movie opened in November of that year, Gary Arnold wrote that it would be "guaranteed to leave your nerve ends vibrating far into the night." He was right, because *Carrie*'s ending contains a shocker that had moviegoers at the time screaming and literally jumping out of their seats – and I can attest to the fact, because that's what it did to me. The shock might be less intense now, because so many moviemakers since have copied it (including De Palma), but if you're not expecting it, it's still potent. Based on an early novel by Stephen King, it's the story of Carrie White (Sissy Spacek), a shy and awkward high school girl who possesses telekinetic powers, meaning she can move objects – in some cases, large objects – and accomplish other feats just by willing them to happen. If being shy and awkward and telekinetic weren't problems enough, Carrie's mother (Piper Laurie in a bravura performance that was nominated for and should have won her an Oscar) is completely deranged, thrown far off-balance by a former lover's abandonment of her and her child. Then there are Carrie's tormentors, Chris (Nancy Allen, who eventually married De Palma) and Billy (John Travolta), who plan to humiliate her at the high school prom. All of these elements combine to drive the story – which is not without its witty moments – to a tragic, shattering and extremely creepy conclusion. But just when you think it's over, De Palma saves one more shock for you, and although he plants subtle hints, most viewers don't suspect what's coming; hence all the screaming and jumping. The solid

338

cast also includes Amy Irving and William Katt as sympathetic classmates and Betty Buckley as a supportive teacher. Priscilla Pointer, Amy Irving's real mother, plays her character's mother here. [Trivia note: As happens so often in movies portraying teenagers, several of the key actors in *Carrie* – including Sissy Spacek – were actually in their mid-twenties. In fact Spacek, 26 at the time, was married to the movie's art director Jack Fisk, who had recommended her for the title role] [Strong caution: plentiful nudity, violence and an extremely frightening scene that is likely to give even adults some trouble sleeping afterward – so keep the kids far away] **[W]**

Alien
1979 – Ridley Scott
You could call this story Seven Little Indians in Outer Space. Scott's version of Dan O'Bannon's screenplay creates several moments of utter visceral fear. It was meant to do so. O'Bannon once told me that he had intended his story to be a direct assault on the audience, systematically stripping down their defenses and exposing them to the sensation of sheer terror—and *Alien* comes close to achieving his goal. The crewmembers of the space freighter Nostromo (Veronica Cartwright, Ian Holm, John Hurt, Yaphet Koto, Tom Skerritt, Harry Dean Stanton and Sigourney Weaver), sleeping in hibernation during the long voyage home to Earth, are awakened by the ship's computer to investigate a distress signal coming from an uncharted planet. They should have stayed asleep. Aboard a creepy alien spacecraft that lies derelict on the planet, one of the crew members is attacked by some sort of creature that attaches itself to him. Therein begins a terrifying ordeal in which those seven souls face oblivion one by one in shocking and unexpected ways. Jerry Goldsmith supplied the shiver-inducing score. [Author's note: I once spent a rather unpleasant evening at a small gathering listening to O' Bannon expound on the symbolic meanings of his screenplay and on how director Scott and the producers ruined it. Maybe so, but he was such an insufferable personality that my sympathies

naturally gravitated toward the moviemakers] [Caution: rough language, gross violence and visceral suspense] **[W]**

The Terminator
1984 – James Cameron
No one who sits through this relentless thriller, Cameron's major debut attraction, could doubt that he had arrived fully formed as a top-flight action director. He also wrote this tale about a murderous cyborg from the future, a "Terminator," whose mission is to hunt down the mother of a charismatic rebel leader before she can give birth to him. And who else to play the humanoid machine but "Ahnold" – Arnold Schwarzenegger, that is – about whose performance one wry critic said was the role he was "born to play." Also sent from the future to stop the Terminator and save the mother, Sarah Connor (Linda Hamilton), is a fearless rebel named Kyle Reese (Michael Biehn). As soon as he arrives, the chase is on, and what a chase it is, with a tremendous amount of violent thrills and black, black humor. Example: A landlord bangs on the door of a room the Terminator has rented during his search for Sarah after an intense gun battle with Reese. He's in the process of binding up his wounds, which are beginning to reek of dead flesh. As the landlord yells through the door, we see the room from the Terminator's point of view – a video screen that displays what he sees but also provides alternative vocal responses based on previous encounters with humans. He selects the most appropriate: F**k you a**hole! Despite its often gruesome nature, the movie hits very few wrong notes. Watch for Bill Paxton, who co-starred in two other Cameron movies, *Aliens* and *Titanic*, in an early scene as a young and doomed punk. [Trivia note: In a great bit of irony, one of the early choices for the role of the Terminator was O.J. Simpson (who was widely suspected but acquitted of brutally murdering his wife in 1994), but the producers rejected the former football star and TV personality because they thought he was too "nice" and therefore couldn't project the proper sense of menace] [Caution: prolific violence, rough language and sexuality] **[W]**

Die Hard
1988 – John McTiernan

Sometimes you can tell from the very first shot that a director is due to make a big splash, and that's what happens here with McTiernan's electrifying blockbuster thriller. The same for Bruce Willis, who took a big leap from the TV series Moonlighting with his crowd-pleasing portrayal of John McClane, a gritty, world-weary New York City cop visiting Los Angeles at Christmastime to see his wife and children, from whom he's been separated. McClane arrives at the office of his wife, Holly (the ever-solid Bonnie Bedelia), in time for a holiday party, soon to find that the high-rise building owned by her employer, the Nakatomi Corporation of Japan, has been taken over by a group of heavily armed men. They succeed in killing or capturing everyone except McClane, and it falls upon him to fight and harass them – keeping in touch via radio with Sgt. Al Powell (Reginald Veljohnson, who becomes the movie's heart) until rest of the police arrive. As it turns out, even the cops, the SWAT team and the FBI are no match for this band, led by the crafty and murderous Hans Gruber (classically trained British stage actor Alan Rickman in a terrific American debut). Only McClane, an ordinary cop away from his hometown, seems able to outwit them, and his repeated hairbreadth escapes should keep you glued to the screen for two nonstop hours, with each new thrill improving on the last. The only false note is the ending, which seems gratuitous. That's a minor quibble, however – Die Hard is one wild ride! [Trivia notes: 1) The fictional Nakatomi Building in the movie was actually the brand new and unfinished headquarters of 20th Century Fox in L.A.'s Century City. 2) Willis went on to make four sequels to this movie, none of which was remotely as entertaining. 3) The source novel that eventually became Die Hard was called Nothing Lasts Forever. Written by Roderick Thorp in the late 1970s, it involved terrorists taking over a skyscraper. It contained a distinct downer of an ending and was envisioned as a star vehicle for ... Frank Sinatra! 4) Believe it or not, some misguided souls continue to promote Die Hard as a cult Christmas movie. It's a first-rate actioner, but let's leave it at that] [Caution: sexuality and plentiful violence and rough language] **[W]**

Terminator 2 – Judgment Day
1991 – James Cameron

Cameron took seven years to mount a sequel to his breakthrough hit, and despite some loopy bits of narration he manages to exceed the level of suspense he achieved in the original. The premise begins much the same way: Two individuals from the future, in this case *both* of them cyborgs, return to present-day Los Angeles on a desperate mission. The first (Arnold Schwarzenegger, reprising his Terminator persona) once again plops down from time transport in the altogether and must quickly find clothes that fit him. This he does in a local biker bar, in a scene that's played for laughs as much as shock. The second, instead of a member of the human rebels, is an updated Terminator, called a T-1000, whose structure is made of "liquid metal," meaning it can really take a licking and keep on ticking. If you've seen the first movie, you should get into the second one quickly, so no need for more plot details. Just know this one's got the Mother of All Motorcycle Chases, involving Schwarzenegger on the bike and his nemesis driving an extreme heavy-duty tow truck. Lots of computer-generated effects, but that chase sequence must have been a bear to shoot. Linda Hamilton reprises her role as Sarah Connor, and 13-year-old Edward Furlong gives an impressive debut performance as her fearless son, John (fans of the original will know who he is), particularly when he interacts with "Ahnold." [Caution: lots of violence and rough language] **[W]**

The Horseman on the Roof
1995 – France – Jean-Paul Rappeneau

Talk about being caught between the devil and the deep blue sea! The year is 1832, and much of Europe is in turmoil. (Yes, I know, so what else is new?) The Austrians have taken over northern Italy, and Emperor Francis I's assassins are tracking down and killing anyone supporting the growing rebellion. The killers are even pursuing the rebels into France, which is where this story takes place. One night, they nearly catch Angelo Pardi (Olivier Martinez), one such rebel and a former colonel in the Lombardy cavalry – hence the movie's original title, *Le Hussard* (cavalryman) *sur le Toit*. Pardi manages a hairbreadth escape only to become trapped by an enraged, insane mob intent on killing all outsiders, whom they suspect are carrying cholera, the deadly disease ravaging the country and the continent. These twin threats dog Pardi for much of the time, and director Rappeneau manages some of the most intricately choreographed escapes imaginable – including one where Pardi ends up, literally, on a rooftop. Soon, he is joined in the ordeal by Pauline de Théus (Juliette Binoche), a beautiful and mysterious noblewoman who seems as fearless as he is. In one positively thrilling sequence, the two of them (not stuntpeople) flee their pursuers on horseback at full gallop across breathtaking Alpine countryside – while carrying on a casual conversation! Despite their courage, the close calls continue, and through it all Martinez, as Pardi, creates one of the most dashing movie characters I have ever seen. I almost included him in the Unforgettable category. He's obviously falling for Pauline, but his chivalry runs so deep that he won't allow his feelings to overcome him, even when he must fight to save her life in a most intimate way. Binoche is captivating as ever, and Rappeneau, who directed only eight features (but whose career spanned four decades), proves himself a master of this genre. [Caution: violence and a vivid scene of non-sexual nudity] **[W]**

Open Water
2003 – Chris Kentis

This might be one of the most terrifying movies ever made, which is all the more astounding because it contains no mechanical or computer-generated sharks and, almost the entire time, only two cast members. Loosely based on a true story, a vacationing husband and wife are inadvertently abandoned by their diving boat and left adrift in open ocean for two days. Even the story of the making of the movie is astounding. Director

Kentis and his producer/co-writer/co-cinematographer (and wife) Laura Lau self-financed the project and shot it on long holiday weekends and vacations. They took two young but professional actors and essentially dumped them in the ocean among real sharks – albeit under the supervision of an experienced shark wrangler. Though they borrowed a few pages from Steven Spielberg's book and portrayed some of the more gruesome action offscreen, there are shots of the actors and the sharks in very close proximity. As with *Jaws*, exercise great caution with children and with adults who have low tolerances for fright. A suggestion: Before watching or showing the movie, watch the feature on the DVD about how it was made. It will help the fainthearted acclimate a little better to what happens in the story. [Trivia note: 1) Kentis and Lau shot *Open Water* with a souped-up Sony Digital Handicam video camera – much like the one stored in my own closet. They later transferred the footage to 35-millimeter film after the movie found a distributor at the Sundance Film Festival. 2) The spouses engaged in a bit of real heroism the following year while vacationing in Thailand. The resort town where they were staying was hit by the December 26 tsunami that killed hundreds of thousands of people in the Indian Ocean Basin (see *The Impossible*), but Chris and Laura helped a bunch of people to safety as the waters rose around them] [Strong caution: nudity and, I repeat, this is one of the scariest movies ever made, so keep the kids away] **[W]**

Casino Royale
2006 – Martin Campbell
James Bond is brought back spectacularly alive and well – albeit briefly – in this 21st installment of the series based on Ian Fleming's spy novels, which first hit the big screen starring Sean Connery in *Dr. No* in 1962. Here, Daniel Craig takes on the role of British Secret Agent 007, and with him the series seems freshly imagined, exquisitely produced and highly entertaining anew. That's quite a compliment, considering Connery's dashing, witty and irresistible Bond remains a piece of cinematic immortality, with his every move underscored by the sexy, thrilling music of

344

John Barry – which continues here as the "007" theme. But Craig stakes out his own vision for the character. He's a marvelously versatile actor, and he's riveting. The elegant score by David Arnold – whose only previously notable work was his brassy, military-style suite for *Independence Day* – builds and in some cases even improves on Barry's original orchestrations. It's a beautiful reworking, providing three electrifying action sequences, particularly the opening chase, on foot, between Bond and a terrorist named Mollaka, played by acrobatic dancer Sebastien Foucan, who performed many of the gravity-defying stunts for real. Another surprise is 26-year-old Eva Green as Bond's love interest Vesper Lynd. Only her fourth movie, she nevertheless handles it like a veteran, matching Craig quip for quip. Other members of the cast contribute superlative performances for the genre as well, particularly Danish actor Mads Mikkelsen as the villain Le Chiffre, and Dame Judi Dench assuming the role of Bond's boss, "M." It's all superbly directed by Martin Campbell, a New Zealander with *Goldeneye*, a previous and mostly unremarkable Bond series entry, to his credit – every single moment seems crisp and efficient. The scenery seems fresh and exotic, as the story moves effortlessly from the enormous Atlantis resort in the Bahamas to a posh hotel in Montenegro (portrayed by a stand-in location in the Czech Republic), and then to the canals of Venice and the breathtaking Lake Como in Italy. This is not a movie for young children, but for adults it offers excitement galore. It's just about a perfect rendering of Ian Fleming's immortal spy chronicles. [Viewing note: I had originally ended this capsule with the declaration, "Welcome back, 007!" But my enthusiasm for Craig's Bond has remained dimmed after suffering through the unwatchable *Quantum of Solace,* the depressing *Skyfall* and the ridiculous *SPECTRE* (needless to say...)] [Trivia note: *Casino Royale* marks the reappearance, nearly four decades later, of a cast member from *You Only Live Twice.* Twai Chin, who played Bond's brief consort in the prologue of that movie, appears here in a cameo as Madam Wu, one of the poker players] [Caution: violence, including a scene of torture, and sexuality] **[W]**

North Face
2008 – Germany – Philipp Stölzl
In my Deliciously Bad category I had originally included a Clint Eastwood thriller called *The Eiger Sanction*, which Clint directed and starred in back in 1975. It had its moments, but after seeing this one, which is so superior in every way, I couldn't possibly list the other title – I'll be including it in my next compilation. Meanwhile, this is a wrenching, gut-churning tale based on a true story. Four men – two Germans and two Austrians – mount an attempt in 1936 to tackle one of the most difficult climbs in all mountaineering: the north face of the monolithic Swiss peak called the Eiger. Ostensibly, they want to do it for the greater glory of Hitler's Third Reich in the year of the Berlin Olympics. Quickly, however, as so often happens in such endeavors, their quest for glory becomes a terrifying ordeal of survival. The plot includes a rivalry between the two pairs and a budding, compelling romance involving a young photojournalist and one of the climbers. But you'll likely never forget the gasp-inducing shots of the men making their ill-fated attempt on the vertical side of that mountain. And when it's over, you might need sufficient quantities of hot liquid, several warm blankets and some time to calm your nerves. The snow, wind and vertiginousness gave me a heavy dose of the chills. I acknowledge supreme kudos to Stölzl and his crew for their literal cliff-hanging feats in filming the action. **[W]**

Headhunters
2011 – Norway – Morten Tyldum
The phrase "Norwegian thriller" normally would bring the term "oxymoron" to mind – but not here. Titled *Hodejegerne* in Norway, the country's biggest-grossing international hit is one of the slickest and least predictable movies you're ever likely to see. Based on Jo Nesbø's bestselling novel, the story concerns Roger Brown (Aksel Hennie – and yes, that's his character's name, even though he's Norwegian). Roger is an employment consultant – a headhunter – during business hours as well as an extremely clever art thief (usually) when off-duty. He is driven

346

to his extracurricular activity by his desire to shower his beautiful – and taller – wife Diana (Synnøve Macody Lund) with earthly goods far beyond the limits of his salary. It helps that Diana is an art dealer and therefore an inadvertent source of targets for Roger's thefts, the latest being her potential client who owns a Rubens worth perhaps $100 million. That sets off new plotting by Roger and Ove (Eivind Sander), his loose cannon of an associate in crime, to steal the painting and replace it with a skillful forgery. All goes well until ... well, there's too much to reveal, and doing so would spoil a literally amazing turn of events. Let me just say that among other surprises *Headhunters* offers the most unusual occupant-crash-protection scenario ever seen, and the relentless plot eventually gives new meaning to the phrase "in deep doo-doo." [Caution: sexuality and some gruesome violence] **[W]**

End of Watch
2012 – David Ayer
From 1981 through 1987, millions of TV viewers – myself included – faithfully followed Hill Street Blues, the landmark weekly saga about a fictional police station in an unnamed rust-belt city, where an exceptionally appealing cast of characters constantly fought to retain their sanity in an insane and often violent urban precinct environment. I will always love Hill Street Blues – it remains my favorite TV series – but I wholeheartedly nominate *End of Watch* is its cinematic successor. This is a dramatically and technologically updated take on the same environment, except in the intervening three decades that environment has become even more insane and violent. Instead of presenting a panorama of characters, as Hill Street did unforgettably, this movie focuses on two street patrolmen, Brian Taylor and Mike Zavala (terrifically played by Jake Gyllenhaal and Michael Peña), and their encounters with the worst of the worst of south-central Los Angeles. I said technologically updated because nearly the entire movie was shot using HD video cameras placed in Taylor and Zavala's patrol car, worn by the two men or employed by various other characters. The

method works extremely well, making *End of Watch* a gripping and sometimes terrifying ride from beginning to end. Along with *The Impossible*, it represents a shameful oversight by the motion picture academy in selecting Best Picture nominees for 2012. [Trivia note: To prepare for their roles, Gyllenhaal and Peña spent months riding along with real L.A. cops in the same area of the city portrayed in the movie – Gyllenhaal even witnessed a murder on his first day out – and they improvised most of their dialog based on that experience, and some of it has turned out to be prophetic. At one point Taylor, hearing from an informant that he and Zavala are being hunted by a contract killer, replies, "We're cops. Everybody wants to kill us."] [Caution: constant – and I mean constant – profanity, some sexuality and graphic violence] **[W]**

The Impossible
2012 – Spain – J.A. Bayona
On December 26, 2004, the third-biggest earthquake ever recorded struck the Indian Ocean bottom off the Indonesian island of Sumatra. Some 500 miles to the north, at the Orchid Beach resort in Khao Lak, Thailand, the Belón family was enjoying their second day of vacation. Soon, however, they and millions of other unfortunate individuals would experience one of the most terrifying events of their lives from one of the most destructive tsunamis in history. A tsunami is a great ocean wave generated by an earthquake. In this case, several waves struck the entire coastline of the Indian Ocean, leveling everything in their path and killing more than 200,000 people. The movie, in a 10-minute sequence of astounding, horrifying detail, depicts what happened to the Belóns when the tsunami overwhelmed the beachside resort. Their ordeal is portrayed by the fictional Bennett family – Henry the husband, Maria the wife and their three sons, Lukas, Thomas and Simon – as we watch their impossible story unfold. Director Bayona and his crew created what might be the most realistic depiction of a waterborne disaster ever brought to the screen. In the process, we get to see two great acting performances – one by Naomi Watts as Maria

and the other by 16-year-old Tom Holland as Lukas. Together, they're as compelling as any two actors I've ever seen, portraying people literally swept away from their quiet, normal lives by the immense power of nature. You might never be able to forget them as well. [Trivia note: For some unknown reason, despite the fact that the Belón family is Spanish, the production crew is Spanish and the movie was shot mostly in Spain, the actors playing the family are English and are portrayed as English] [Caution: The tsunami sequence can be particularly terrifying to children, and there is fleeting, though non-sexual, nudity] [W]

Everest
2015 – Baltasar Kormákur
Consider what's required to climb the highest peak in the world. First, you need to set aside tens of thousands of dollars for gear, transportation and lodging. Then you need to endure weeks and weeks of training and acclimation to the harsh environment. Last, assuming you can avoid altitude sickness or plunging into a deep crevice to make the grueling climb to the final camp – which is located at an altitude of 26,000 feet, a mile higher than what's known as the Death Zone, where just being there causes your body to begin to die – you start from there at midnight on a 3,000-foot ascent to the summit (that's nearly three times higher than the Empire State Building, folks). For the next 12 hours, you strain for every yard while your body slowly shuts down, and the hormones governing your emotions throw you into disorientation, depression and possibly delusion. Then, if you manage to make it to the top of the world, you've got another six hours or more to descend, all the while hoping that the jet-stream-force winds of Sagarmāthā – the Nepalese name for Everest – won't suddenly arise and either freeze-dry you or blow you off a ridge to your doom miles below. Yet every year now, hundreds of brave (or foolish) souls make the attempt, many of them fail and a certain number of them die. On the 10th and 11th of May 1996, eight such climbers perished on those slopes through a combination of bad judgment and bad luck. This

349

movie tells what happened in vivid, terrifying and heartbreaking detail. Outdoor journalist Jon Krakauer originally chronicled the event, based on his personal experience on that climb. In his 1997 bestseller Into Thin Air, Krakauer described how the tragedy returned stark reality to the conceit that Everest could be climbed routinely because of improved technology and the systematized procedures developed by expert guides such as Rob Hall and Scott Fischer (well-played here by Jason Clarke and Jake Gyllenhaal). There is no doubt such a perception contributed to the 1996 disaster, because the lanes to the summit on May 10th were nearly choked with climbers, each of whom had paid up to $50,000 for the privilege. For many reasons – some of them understandable – Hall and Fischer chose to ignore their own ironclad rules about the ascent. It cost them, and six others, dearly. [Trivia notes: 1) Given the extreme danger of actually filming on the slopes of Everest, Kormákur and his crew opted to shoot the summit ascent in the relative safety of locations in the Italian Alps – and at much lower elevations. 2) Avalanches on Everest killed 16 and 18 climbers and guides in 2014 and 2015, respectively. 3) At this writing, 152 climbers have died trying to reach the summit since May 11, 1996 – including six more that same year] [W]

36. Six Christmas Classics

Give me a comfortable chair to lounge in, some freshly baked Christmas cookies, a cup of hot chocolate and these favorites, and I'll happily bliss out during several afternoons of the holiday season. What makes them even more enjoyable is, of course, being able to share them with friends and family, particularly the kids and grandkids.

A Christmas Carol [100]
1938 – Edwin L. Marin

The Metro-Goldwyn-Mayer studio built its reputation in the 1930s with lively musicals and lavish productions of literary works, and this version of the Charles Dickens classic is no exception. It's a handsomely mounted telling of the immortal tale of Ebenezer Scrooge, a bitter man whose lifetime of selfishness is challenged by late-night visits from the ghost of his former partner, Jacob Marley, and from three Christmas spirits – representing Scrooge's past, present and future. The role has been played many times, but my favorite remains Reginald Owen, who looks positively Dickensian and receives his redemption with such a sense of joy that it made me positively giddy along with him. I found his brief shaving scene on Christmas morning positively sublime. Gene Lockhart is nearly as good as Bob Cratchit, Scrooge's hapless but goodhearted employee, and everyone else in the cast is just right. [Trivia note: Lionel Barrymore was originally slated to play Scrooge but had to bow out because of the cumulative effects of two hip fractures, one due to a fall and the other from an injury he had received during a previous production – and both ended up confining him to a wheelchair for the rest of his life. So Barrymore recommended his friend and MGM colleague Owen for the role. As much as I admire Barrymore, Owen embodied Scrooge, particularly his redeemed persona, as no one else ever has] [B&W]

Holiday Inn
1942 – Mark Sandrich

This isn't nearly at the level of the previous or next item, and technically it isn't a Christmas movie, but it's still highly entertaining and lots of fun, largely because of Fred Astaire's superb dancing and effortless comedy. As Ted Hanover, he teams with Bing Crosby's singer Jim Hardy as a pair of entertainers who have a falling out over their onstage partner, Lila Dixon (Virginia Dale). Hardy, the loser in the dispute, decides to retire from show business to a farm, where he can be "lazy." As anyone who's lived on a farm knows, that word in no way applies. So, after an exasperating time that lands him temporarily in a rest home, Hardy comes up with an alternative idea that might fulfill his need for downtime: an inn that's open only on holidays – 15 a year. The story follows the outcome of that strategy, with stage numbers created for the occasions and featuring fine songs by the beloved Irving Berlin, including the debut of the biggest-selling ballad of all time, "White Christmas." Marjorie Reynolds joins Cosby as his love interest, Linda Mason, and she proves a fine dancing partner for Astaire as well, though her singing voice is dubbed by Martha Mears. The always-entertaining Irving Bacon plays Gus, the inn's jack-of-all-trades. [Viewing notes: 1) This one is worth having on DVD because it offers two really good pieces of bonus material. First there's "A Couple of Song & Dance Men," a charming 45-minute documentary hosted by Ava Astaire McKenzie, Fred's daughter, and film historian Ken Barnes, which traces Crosby's and Astaire's careers. There's also a 10-minute featurette, "All Singing, All Dancing," which shows how complex it can be to shoot a musical number for the screen. 2) Here's a trivia question: Which American actor appeared in the most movies? Answer: Irving Bacon, who plays Gus, the yokel chauffeur. From

1923 through 1958 he racked up almost 500 cast credits, far more than anyone else. 3) The movie is a product of its time, meaning the moviemakers and the cast had no problem appearing in what was called blackface – very dark makeup applied to the skin – and mimicking African Americans in stereotypical fashion. The stereotype also extended to the character of Mamie (Louise Beavers), Crosby's housekeeper, and her two young children. Take all of that with a grain of salt and consign it to movie and cultural history] **[B&W]**

It's a Wonderful Life [100]
1946 – Frank Capra

It's a toss-up between this one and *Singin' in the Rain* as my all-time favorite. It's so good it could fit into many of the categories on this list, including Should Have Been Best Pictures; Unforgettable, because of James Stewart's performance; Hollywood's Best (still to come), and so on. But its most appropriate classification is as one of the great Christmas movies, because it's one of the best holiday stories ever told. Not that you could ever forget Stewart or this movie regardless of the season. For that matter, just about every other actor's performance in this cinematic treasure is indelible, from the superb supporting cast to the bit players. If you haven't seen it (and if that's the case, by all means drop what you're doing and go find it), it's the story of George Bailey, a selfless and compassionate young man who yearns for travel and adventure but never escapes the small town where he has grown up. Stewart plays that young man, and I can't think of a better performance by him. His George Bailey is Everyman embodied – basically good and decent but also humanly flawed. He finds love with Mary Hatch (Donna Reed, near the beginning of her career but at her very best), a younger woman who proves his perfect match. Nevertheless, George's fundamental unhappiness seethes beneath the surface for most of his life, and when a crisis interjects itself, his unhappiness boils over to the point where George considers suicide. That's when Providence intervenes, literally, by sending Clarence Oddbody (Henry Travers, in a

353

perfect performance), an "Angel, 2nd Class," to present George with a most unusual gift: the opportunity to see what the world would have been like if he had never been born.

As with so many classics listed here, I choose to reveal no more. You will have to discover the rest for yourself. Know, however, that this is as good as moviemaking gets. It's Frank Capra directing at the zenith of his powers, digging profoundly into the human psyche with a vision as affectionate and positive as anything ever portrayed on the screen. And if you don't find yourself weeping unashamedly at the finale, possibly the most rapturous eight minutes in all of cinema – because, as someone once said, no tears are more intense than those of longing fulfilled – then we're living on different planets.

*   *   *

About that exceptional supporting cast, there's Samuel S. Hinds as Bailey's salt-of-the-earth father, Thomas Mitchell as his eccentric uncle Billy, Beulah Bondi as his mother, Ward Bond as Bert the cop, Frank Faylen as Ernie the taxi driver, Gloria Grahame as the town flirt, H.B. Warner as Mr. Gower the druggist, Lillian Randolph as the Bailey family housekeeper, and a young Sheldon Leonard (who became a major TV producer in the 1950s and '60s) as Nick the bartender. Last but not least, Lionel Barrymore plays Mr. Potter, "the meanest man in town" and George's frequent foe and tormentor. As for the bit players, you'll understand how vivid Capra has painted them during the movie's last scene, where he pans the camera across a grouping, and you recognize and appreciate everyone. [Trivia notes: 1) This treasure of a movie might have sunk into oblivion if not for a quirk of fate. Sometime after its initial release, It's a Wonderful Life fell into legal limbo, allowing its copyright to slip into the public domain. This meant TV stations could show the movie at any time without having to pay for it. Somehow the word spread, and stations around the country began broadcasting it during the holidays each year. As a result, it won legions of new fans and eventually achieved its richly deserved classic status. 2) The fictional town of Bedford Falls was built as a huge outdoor set on a ranch in Encino, California, owned by the RKO studio. The snow was a mix of soap, water and a firefighting chemical – something that proved problematic when George rescues Clarence in the river because the stuff stuck to both actors like wet flour dough. 3) Hinds worked often with Barrymore in the Dr. Kildare movie series in the 1940s and with Stewart in three other movies, including the Oscar-winning *You Can't Take It With You* in 1938 (not on this list), in which Barrymore also appeared as the benevolent family patriarch. 4) Believe it or not, Ward Bond's duet serenade for Donna Reed marked the second time in two years he performed that task. He also did it as part of a quintet, singing to Reed's character, in John Ford's magnificent but heartbreaking *They Were Expendable* in 1945] [Viewing note: This timeless classic suffered from an affectation of the 1980s, in which some video production houses thought audiences would enjoy old black-and-white movies better if they were re-released in color. They called the process "colorization," and each time it's been used it detracts from the movie instead of enhancing it. Avoid it like the plague. Try to see movies the way their producers originally meant for them to be seen – particularly immortal titles like this one and *Miracle on 34th Street*] **[B&W]**

The Bishop's Wife [100]
1947 – Henry Koster

Enchanting and affecting, this Christmas fantasy utterly captivates me every time I see it – and I usually screen it every holiday season. A forlorn and increasingly discouraged bishop named Henry Brougham (David Niven), who is seeking to raise money to build a new cathedral, prays for divine guidance and, as such things are realized in dramatic terms, is visited by an angel named Dudley (Cary Grant, in one of his most appealing roles), who proceeds to turn Henry's life upside down. Immediately, Dudley begins to rekindle happiness and purpose in the title character (Loretta Young at her most lovely), as well as in three supporting characters – a shopworn professor (Monty Woolley), a listless cab driver (the always-dependable James

355

Gleason) and an embittered heiress (Gladys Cooper). In doing so, Dudley arouses feelings of resentment in Henry, who wonders whether Dudley's intervention will cost him his family. As seemingly slight as this movie is, it contains some deeply memorable moments, particularly a beautiful performance of the hymn "On This Happy Day" by the Robert Mitchell Boychoir; a thoroughly delightful ice skating sequence – expert skaters doubling for the actors notwithstanding – and a cathartic moment as the heiress confesses her deepest secret to Dudley. What makes *The Bishop's Wife* so special is it portrays life as we might wish it to be and Dudley as the person we might wish *we* could be. It creates such feelings of hopefulness and well-being we start to feel as though we really have been visited by an angel. [Trivia notes: 1) The movie went through two directors (the first was George Seiter) and several screenwriters, including the legendary Billy Wilder and one of his best collaborators, Charles Brackett. 2) Originally, Niven was supposed to play Dudley and Grant was set to play Henry, but after producer Samuel Goldwyn fired Seiter, Henry Koster decided Grant should play the angel – a wise choice. 3) The previous year, Karolyn Grimes, who plays the Bishop's daughter, appeared as the character Zuzu in *It's a Wonderful Life*. Bobby Anderson, who played George Bailey as a boy in the same movie, likewise has a small role in this one. 4) Grant and Woolley shared a previous connection. Six years earlier, Grant was set to play the title role in the movie version of *The Man Who Came to Dinner* (not on this list), but Warner Brothers eventually chose Woolley, who had performed it on Broadway for two years, and the studio heads cast Grant as Mortimer Brewster in *Arsenic and Old Lace*] **[B&W]**

Miracle on 34th Street [100]
1947 – George Seaton

The year 1947 produced two Christmas tales for the ages: *The Bishop's Wife* and this one. Though they differ in tone, both reach deeply into human emotions and create experiences that really do border on the miraculous. The story concerns the sudden appearance at Macy's department store in New York City of a man who goes by the name Kris Kringle and claims to be the real Santa Claus. There is conflicting evidence, but Kris (Edmund Gwenn, in a well-deserved, Oscar-winning role) does seem to have special knowledge about Christmas. And whether he's real or delusional, Mr. Macy (Harry Antrim) wants him on the job because he's getting everyone into the holiday spirit – and significantly improving the store's bottom line. So it falls upon Doris Walker (Maureen O'Hara) the store's employee responsible for its annual Thanksgiving Day Parade – whose belief in miracles has been sorely tested by a bad marriage – to host Mr. Kringle for the holiday season. That arrangement brings him into contact with Doris's young daughter Susan (an amazingly good Natalie Wood at 9 years old) and her sympathetic neighbor Fred Gailey (John Payne). Things seem to be going fine when … well, that's far enough. Just know that the story proceeds to the most delightful courtroom scene ever, and that by the time the movie is over, you just might recover your belief in both Santa and miracles. [Viewing note: This one's available in a colorized version, too, but please try to avoid the temptation] [Trivia notes: 1) Though this is a Christmas classic, 20th Century-Fox for unfathomable reasons released it in June 1947, promoting it with trailers that failed to mention its seasonal focus – even titling it, nondescriptly, "The Big Heart" for its run in England. The ploy worked, however, and the movie remained a big hit all the way through to the holidays. 2) The brief role of the inebriated Santa near the movie's beginning was played by Percy Helton, one of Hollywood's most durable character actors. He appeared in more than 220 movies and TV episodes. 3) This was the second of three onscreen romantic pairings of Payne and O'Hara. Five years before, they had co-starred in the decent World War II drama *To The Shores of Tripoli*. Then, in 1950, they reunited for the pitifully inept historical adventure *Tripoli* (neither on this list), which depicted the famous battle memorialized in that line from the "Marine's Hymn." Stick to this one, because they're great together here]

[B&W]

White Christmas
1954 – Michael Curtiz

Like *Holiday Inn*, which premiered the title song, this is not really a Christmas story, either. But I've always had a soft spot for it as a holiday favorite. Released under the full title *Irving Berlin's White Christmas*, it's a carefree musical starring Bing Crosby and Danny Kaye as two army buddies who team up in show business after World War II. The meandering plot ties them to a pair of singing sisters, played by dancer Vera-Ellen and soloist Rosemary Clooney (George Clooney's aunt), and their former commanding officer, General Waverly (Dean Jagger). That's as much background as you need, because it's all just pretext for Berlin's musical numbers, including the immortal title song, which remains to this day the all-time best seller. Berlin composed hundreds of popular melodies before he died in 1989 at age 101. Fellow composer Jerome Kern was once asked where he would place Berlin in American music. Kern replied, "Berlin *is* American music." Still, I admit, it's a trifle, and there might be one or two too many dance numbers, but they're all terrific, including an intricately choreographed one called … "Choreography." It's pleasant holiday fun, Kaye was never better and Rosie Clooney never looked lovelier, especially singing her show-stopping number, "Love, You Didn't Do Right by Me," and wearing what has become known by the movie's fans as "that dress!" [Trivia notes: 1) Early in the movie, Judy Haynes, Vera-Ellen's character, produces a snapshot supposedly of her ugly brother, Benny. It's actually Irving Berlin as a younger man. 2) If the Pine Tree Inn looks familiar, it should. It's the same set used in *Holiday Inn* 12 years earlier. 3) Among Rosie Clooney's three dancing partners for her "Love, You Didn't…" number is George Chakiris, who became a veteran TV actor but is best known – and an Oscar winner – for playing Bernardo in the movie version of *West Side Story* in 1961 (not on this list). 4) Percy Helton, whom I just mentioned in *Miracle on 34th Street*, enjoys another small bit here as a train conductor] **[W]**

37. Great Movies for the Youngest Kids and Grandkids

So many contemporary movies made for the littlest viewers are either formulaic, cloying or just sequels or remakes of past hits. That isn't to say some of them aren't pretty good, but few can match the charm and excitement of these six classics or near-classics that have withstood the test of time and passed with flying colors.

Dumbo [100]
1941 – Produced by Walt Disney
Let's not mince words. Hands down, this is the most joyful, touching and all-around satisfying animated feature ever made. *Pinocchio* might be Disney's masterpiece, but this one has stayed locked in my heart and touched me in ways I wouldn't have thought possible. It's the story of a baby elephant delivered by a stork to a circus-performing mother in Florida, just as the troupe is getting underway on a tour of the country by train. And his momma and the other elephants are delighted – until they discover the baby's most unusual feature: his enormous, ears, which to his little body are almost the proportion of butterfly wings. It's a simple but exquisitely told tale of motherly love, friendship and finding value in one's own uniqueness, and a sweeter story there never was. Grow old and wise as you might, but don't ever let your age or sophistication interfere with enjoying this eternal classic, produced by Disney's animators at the peak of their powers and preserved in glorious Technicolor.

The Shaggy Dog
1959 – Charles Barton
Not to be confused with the 2006 version starring Tim Allen, this is a completely silly but also thoroughly engaging fantasy from Disney – which is commendable because it was the studio's first try at a live-action comedy feature. Tommy Kirk, a Disney regular on TV in the 1950s, plays Wilby Daniels, teenage son of an otherwise normal middle-class family, whose parents are played by Fred MacMurray and Jean Hagen. Let's not worry about how Wilby manages to turn into a sheepdog – he does, and at the most inconvenient times, but the transformation does come in handy in helping Wilby to uncover a spy plot. **[B&W]**

The Absent-Minded Professor
1961 – Robert Stevenson
Another delightful and hilarious live-action entry from Disney, this time with Fred MacMurray playing the eponymous Professor Ned Brainard, a man so preoccupied with his research that three times he forgets to attend his own wedding, causing his fiancée Betsy (Nancy Olson) to consider dumping him. The preoccupation turns out to be well worth it, however, because Brainard has discovered something amazing: flying rubber, which he immediately names "flubber." Upset that Betsy's affections might be redirected toward an obnoxious colleague (Elliott Reid), Ned decides to demonstrate his invention at a basketball game. The result is one of the funniest sequences ever conceived. His school's team, which had gotten creamed during the first half by much taller rivals, dominates the floor by being able to jump higher – make that *much* higher – than the opposing team. The process is likely to keep you and your kids and grandkids in stitches. The rest of the plot deals with Brainard's attempt to recover the other demonstration vehicle – a vintage Model T Ford – from an unscrupulous businessman (Keenan Wynn) and prove its value to the U.S. government. Whatever. The point is the whole family can have a fine time watching the hijinks. **[B&W]**

Hatari!
1962 – Howard Hawks

The trick to showing this exciting wildlife adventure yarn to the youngest viewers (and I haven't met one yet who didn't love it) is to skip the intervening episodes involving the adults in the cast – something you can do easily on DVD – and stick to the outdoor scenes, which are thrillingly shot and staged mostly for real. Then, if you want, watch the movie all the way through later, because the adult interactions are witty and diverting if a bit dated. John Wayne stars as the chief of a crew that captures wild African animals for zoos. This requires them to get up close and personal with some of the most dangerous creatures on the continent, including water buffalo, leopards, full-size giraffes and, most of all, a couple of very angry rhinoceroses. The movie was shot entirely in the wildlife preserves and parks of Tanganyika (now Tanzania), and often you get to watch Wayne and crew actually chasing down and capturing the animals. It's a little frightening, but it should not be beyond the emotional limits of even the youngest children. Along with the corralled critters, the movie features a trio of adorable baby elephants, which at the time inspired a popular Henry Mancini song called "Baby Elephant Walk." Mancini did the rest of the score as well, and it's pretty good. The title, by the way, means "Danger!" in Swahili. **[W]**

Mary Poppins
1964 – Robert Stevenson

No matter your age, this Disney fantasy about a nanny who appears suddenly one day to take charge of two incorrigible youngsters in 19th-century London ought to amuse, please, delight and even touch you. Over half a century later it's still sublime. If it weren't such a children's classic – based on the popular novels by P.L. Travers – I would have listed it in the Should Have Been Best Pictures category for 1964, because it's far better than the frequently stodgy *My Fair Lady* (not on this list), and it became Disney's biggest hit and most critically acclaimed feature up to then. Julie Andrews won the Best

Actress Oscar for the title role, her screen debut, and she's fine as the prim and proper – and magical – nanny who literally blows in with a change in the wind. But Dick Van Dyke steals the movie with his inimitable turn as Bert the chimney sweep. It's by far the best thing he's ever done (and I say this as a lifelong fan of his TV series The Dick Van Dyke Show). The effects might seem dated by today's standards but not enough to detract from the feelings of blissful satisfaction the movie accumulates, or from the dazzling musical numbers, particularly the rousing "Step in Time," which took 6 weeks to rehearse and lasts over 8 minutes; the Oscar-winning "Chim Chim Cher-ee"; the exuberant "Let's Go Fly a Kite" and the lilting "Feed the Birds," which Walt Disney said was his all-time favorite. Watch for Reginald Owen, who remains the best Ebenezer Scrooge of all, as a rather blustery neighbor, the appropriately named Admiral Boom. [Viewing note: By all means, enjoy this movie with your kids and/or grandkids. But also take the time, by yourself or with fellow adults, to watch and enjoy the marvelous *Saving Mr. Banks*, about Travers and Disney and the making of *Mary Poppins*] [Trivia notes: 1) After he did this movie, Dick Van Dyke enjoyed a reputation as a song-and-dance man. In fact, before *Mary Poppins*, though he had studied mime, he had received no dance training – his talent was, as the expression goes, God-given. 2) On Sunday March 19, 1961, Julie Andrews and Richard Burton appeared on The Ed Sullivan Show, singing "What Do the Simple Folk Do?" from their Broadway hit, "Camelot." I had never seen Andrews before, but even as a 12-year-old kid I recognized her special talent. Well, apparently so did Robert and Richard Sherman, who were composing the songs for *Mary Poppins*. Likewise, she impressed Don DaGradi, the movie's screenwriter. The next day, the three men approached Walt Disney and enthusiastically recommended her for the title role. Disney, in turn, flew to New York to see her performance in person. Afterward, he went backstage and implored her to do the role] **[W]**

Winnie-the-Pooh and the Blustery Day
1968 – <u>Produced</u> by Walt Disney

This Oscar-winning, animated short might be the gentlest movie the Disney studio has ever made. It's utterly devoid of conflict – the only bit of excitement at all is the appearance of the irrepressible Tigger. Nevertheless, it's captivating and delightful. The chemise-thin plot involves a windstorm – the story takes place on "Windsday" – that strikes the Hundred Acre Wood, where Pooh and his friends –including the little boy Christopher Robin – live. [<u>Viewing note</u>: If you enjoy this one, then you might want to try the others in the series, including *Winnie the Pooh and the Honey Tree*, *Winnie the Pooh and Tigger Too*, and *The Many Adventures of Winnie the Pooh*, All are included in the video, originally produced in 1997, *The Many Adventures of Winnie the Pooh*, but *Blustery Day* is my favorite] [<u>Trivia note</u>: As gentle and sweet as the Pooh stories are, they're underpinned by the sad personal saga of Adam "A.A." Milne, the author. A World War I combat veteran who returned home to England with what we now call PTS, or post-traumatic stress, Milne originally created the Pooh narrative to entertain his six-year-old son, Christopher Robin Milne. First published in 1926, the book became an instant sensation in England, and its popularity quickly spread to America and elsewhere. But that intense spotlight focused on Christopher Robin, who later described the experience as having destroyed his childhood, to the point where it estranged the younger Milne from his parents for the rest of his life. Adults can find an absorbing and mostly factual account of this facet of English cultural history in the fine 2017 movie, *Goodbye Christopher Robin* (coming in my second compilation)]

38. For the Kids and Grandkids – a Little Later

In Bruno Bettelheim's groundbreaking book, <u>The Uses of Enchantment</u>, he argues that fairy tales can help children grapple with their fears in ways not necessarily available to them in real life. In other words, experiencing powerful emotions symbolically, such as by reading, or in this case watching movies, can help them grow emotionally. When you decide they're old enough to bear some suspense or fear in their viewing, along with *The Wizard of Oz* elsewhere, here are eight fine titles to introduce to your not-so-little ones – and for you to enjoy all over again.

Pinocchio
1940 – <u>Produced</u> by Walt Disney
Now approaching eight decades old, this classic animated feature – each one of its 125,000+ frames was hand-drawn by a team of 95 artists – remains Disney's towering achievement, a masterpiece of storytelling and an immortal moviegoing experience. The story of a wooden puppet who longs to become human has been told countless times, but never this well. And Cliff Edwards's performance of the signature number "When You Wish Upon a Star," which was composed by Leigh Harline with lyrics by Ned Washington, is probably the most heartfelt song ever brought to the screen. [<u>Caution</u>: Some of the scenes involving Pinocchio's encounter with Monstro the whale could frighten the youngest viewers]

Lassie Come Home
1943 – Fred M. Wilcox

The moviemakers at MGM really knew how to tug on the heartstrings, and here they do it irresistibly and in Technicolor. The first of what would become a long stretch of movies featuring the smart-as-a-whip female collie (who often was played by males) also features outstanding performances by Roddy McDowall and Elizabeth Taylor in the early and most appealing years of their careers. And I don't care who you are, like me you're probably going to shed joyful tears at the ending.

National Velvet
1944 – Clarence Brown

MGM in its most glorious period produced this handsomely mounted, Technicolor telling of the Enid Bagnold novel, and the movie stars one of the most popular names in the studio's stable at the time – Mickey Rooney – with Elizabeth Taylor only a year older than in *Lassie Come Home* but already sprouting into young womanhood. She plays Velvet Brown, the 12-year-old, horse-loving daughter of a family of modest means living along the seacoast in prewar England. Rooney plays Mi (pronounced "MY") Taylor, the orphaned, vagabond horserider and trainer who wanders into town in search of work but with an eye out for a quick, ill-gotten gain. The Browns take him in as a worker, and when he discovers their secret stash of money, he considers running off with it. But that doesn't happen. What does transpire becomes a marvelous tale of a girl's quest for an impossible dream, riding in – and winning – the greatest horserace in the world at the time: England's Grand National Sweepstakes. This is a wonderful tale for kids to learn the value of striving, even when the odds seem out of reach. And though the ending is bittersweet, the lesson is no less effective for it. Taylor is captivating as Velvet, and her riding skills are impressive at such a young age, but Rooney is great as Mi, and this is the first of two times he should have won the Best Supporting Actor Oscar. The other was, ironically, when he played a much older version of a similar character: Henry Dailey in *The Black Stallion*.

Trivia notes: 1) There's a photo of Rooney in *The Black Stallion*, supposedly showing Henry in his younger years, which was actually taken from his performance in this movie. 2) During filming of the race sequence, Taylor fell and badly injured her spine. 3) Taylor loved doing *National Velvet* so much that MGM gave her the horse that played The Pie after the filming wrapped]

A Connecticut Yankee in King Arthur's Court
1949 – Tay Garnett

Two good reasons for showing young kids this somewhat dated Bing Crosby time-travel musical: 1) It's based on a novel by none other than Mark Twain, so it might interest literate youngsters in reading the perfectly delightful source book, and 2) They'll probably delight in watching Hank Martin (Crosby's character) frighten and amaze the crowds in Arthur's time with objects and references we take for granted today. Besides, it's harmless fun, with just a little bit of menace and the suffering of medieval times thrown in. William Bendix plays the bumbling but lovable Sir Sagamore; the ravishing Rhonda Fleming is Hank's love interest, Alisande, in both the 6th and early 20th centuries; and the great Cedric Hardwicke plays Arthur as well as his distant descendant. The songs might be forgettable, but Crosby and Bendix are endearing, and the Technicolor is, as always, glorious.

The Sound of Music [100]
1965 – Robert Wise

For his second Best Picture winner (he also won with *West Side Story* in 1961 – not on this list), Wise brought the Rodgers and Hammerstein stage musical to the screen with a sweeping grandeur marked by stunning Austrian locales and an energy that's absolutely contagious. It's based – loosely – on the true story of the Trapp family, who escaped from their home outside Salzburg in 1939 as the Nazis were taking over the country in an action called the Anschluss, or "Annexation." Julie Andrews, in one of her best movie roles, plays Maria, an impetuous novice

366

who can't quite conform to convent life. So, when her mother superior (Peggy Wood) orders her to serve as a governess for the seven children of a widower naval commander (Christopher Plummer, in a fine early role), the association quickly and dramatically changes the lives of all concerned. The story, beautifully written by Ernest Lehman, is full of humor and joyfulness but also great pathos, particularly for the terrible losses wrought on the Austrian people by the Nazis – to which the movie alludes but does not portray directly. Many screen musicals are lucky to produce one or maybe two unforgettable songs, but this one boasts 11, including "My Favorite Things," "Climb Every Mountain," "Edelweiss," "Sixteen Going on Seventeen" and "The Lonely Goatherd" (performed by the wonderful Baird Marionettes); not to mention the show-stopping "Do-Re-Mi" and the spectacular title number, which introduces Maria at the end of a breathtaking aerial shot as she stands in the middle of a high mountain meadow. More than any other title in this category, this is an essential. Suitable for all, it's the one of the most glorious musicals ever made, and if you haven't seen it you owe it to yourself and your family to include it in your moviegoing experience. [Trivia note: Eleven years after they escaped from Hitler's *Anschluss*, the family established the Trapp Family Lodge in Stowe, Vermont, which welcomes guests to this day] **[W]**

Born Free
1966 – James Hill
This popular feature of the time tells the story of Elsa, one of a trio of orphaned lion cubs and the most beloved, adopted by Joy Adamson (Virginia McKenna) and her husband George (Bill Travers), both naturalists living in Kenya in the 1950s. As the cubs grew too large to be fully trusted around humans, the Adamsons arranged to ship them off to zoos. But Joy just couldn't part with Elsa, so she and George resolved to train the lioness to survive back in the wild. The saga of that experience constitutes the bulk of the movie, and most youngsters are captivating by it as well as the gorgeous Kenya locations and

John Barry's score, which presaged his work on *Out of Africa*, and the main theme of which became a hit song by Matt Monro. [Trivia note: Much has been written in the intervening years about the raucous lives of the Adamsons. If you'd like to learn more, you can see the more mature version in *To Walk With Lions* from 1999, which I'll be covering in my second list] [Caution: a couple of intense scenes involving fierce wild lions] **[W]**

Charlotte's Web
1973 – Produced by William Hanna and Joseph Barbera
The studio responsible for the most popular animated TV shows of the 1960s – including The Flintstones, The Jetsons, and Yogi Bear, among others – created this utterly captivating rendition of E.B. White's classic children's story about a friendship between a pig and a spider, and made it a charming musical to boot. Wilbur the pig (voiced by Henry Gibson), the runt of a litter born on Mr. Arable's farm, is rescued by Fern, the farmer's young daughter, from a premature death. Pig and child quickly become bonded, but they are separated when Arable sells Wilbur to a neighboring farmer named Zuckerman, who plans to slaughter him when he is fully grown. Wilbur is saved again by the extraordinary actions of Charlotte, a clever barn spider (voiced by Debbie Reynolds). Though there are several references to the killing of farm animals and death, the movie's gentle and sweet tone conveys those episodes as parts of the natural cycle of life, so they should not disturb the littlest viewers. In fact, it might be a good way to introduce such themes to them. The movie also contains plenty of subtle humor and observations, and sophisticated song lyrics to entertain adults. Speaking of which, the songs – by brothers Richard and Robert Sherman (the talents behind many of the most popular songs from the Walt Disney movies) – are delightful, as are the supporting voice performances by Agnes Moorehead as a mother goose; Paul Lynde as Templeton, a crafty and self-centered rat; the great Martha Scott in a small role as Mrs. Arable and Lex Barker as the narrator. The movie also features one of the cleverest fadeout

lines ever, though it's probably appreciated most by individuals – me included – of a certain professional persuasion.

Babe
1995 – Australia – <u>Produced</u> by George Miller

This is the live-action equivalent of *Charlotte's Web*, in terms of its theme of camaraderie among barnyard animals, but it's a far funnier and less sentimental tale – though it doesn't lack wondrous moments. It's likewise the story of the runt pig of a litter who seems destined for an early demise, until he's taken in by a kindly farmer named Hoggett (James Cromwell) and his happily plump wife (Magda Szubanski). Just like Wilbur in the E.B. White classic, Babe is quickly befriended by the other critters, including Ferdinand the Duck (who fancies himself a rooster), and particularly Fly, the maternal border collie. Because life and death are part of farm existence, those themes appear here, and in slightly more explicit terms than in *Charlotte's Web*. But they're still subdued enough not to traumatize the little ones. And besides, the movie's humor is its strong suit. You might find yourself laughing hysterically at some of the scenes, particularly when Babe and Ferdinand attempt to steal an alarm clock from the Hoggetts' home without waking the dreaded cat, Duchess. Then there's that Greek-chorus trio of mice... [<u>Trivia notes</u>: 1) Technically, Chris Noonan is listed as the director of Babe, but the artistic vision belongs to Miller. Famous for his brutal action tales featuring the character of Mad Max (none on this list), Miller had nursed this project for a decade before he thought moviemaking technology had advanced enough to bring Babe the talking pig to life. 2) Even though the technical wizards could manipulate the real pig playing Babe to make him seem to talk, they faced an unforeseen problem: baby pigs grow rapidly. So, the crew ended up using 48 different piglets during the production, sometimes applying makeup and other cosmetics to maintain Babe's appearance] **[W]**

39. For the Kids and Grandkids – Later Still

When Gary Arnold and I recommended movies on our TV show, The Moviegoing Family, we always took a tolerant view of attractions for children, particularly where intensity was involved. One of the biggest problems to evolve with the Motion Picture Association of America's ratings system was the penchant by the board of people evaluating movies to impose strict criteria for a title to receive a "G" rating, meaning it was considered suitable for all audiences. At the slightest bit of intensity, the board would opt for a "PG," advising parental guidance. The problem, as we saw it, was that the ratings often judged material too harshly that could be beneficial to young viewers. So we based our recommendations on how a movie presented some of the basic themes of life: good versus evil, courage, self-sacrifice, friendship and family, striving for a just cause and doing what you know to be the right thing even when others attempt to discourage you. Along with *The Black Stallion* and *Never Cry Wolf* elsewhere, here are a dozen titles (plus one reprise) to nourish young and growing movie-loving minds.

Captains Courageous
1937 – Victor Fleming
Two years before he directed two of the best-loved movies of all time, *Gone with the Wind* and *The Wizard of Oz*, Fleming made this magnificent version of the Rudyard Kipling classic. It's the story of Harvey Cheyne (Freddie Bartholomew), a spoiled brat of a rich kid who eats too much ice cream on a trans-Atlantic voyage with his father (Melvyn Douglas) and falls overboard in an indigestive faint. He is rescued from the drink by a Portuguese fisherman named Manuel (Spencer Tracy), who takes the boy

under his wing aboard a fishing schooner named the We're Here, working the Grand Banks, east of Gloucester, Massachusetts – and thereby transforms the lad from brat to budding decent young man. Tracy is so good in the role of Manuel that you quickly forget who he is and accept him as a simple fisherman, and you grow to love him as much as Harvey does. Speaking of Harvey's character, Bartholomew, who was only 10 at the time, delivers a knockout performance, including allowing himself to be put in physical danger in some scenes. Tracy credited the success of the movie, and even of his own Oscar-winning performance, to the quality of his young co-star's acting. This is a terrific tale, and it offers priceless lessons for kids in humility, courage, honesty and the meaning of friendship. It is graced by the presence of some of the best character actors of the 1930s – all from the MGM stable – including the great Lionel Barrymore (best known as the evil Mr. Potter in *It's a Wonderful Life*) as Disko Troop, the boat's captain; and John Carradine (patriarch of a fine acting family) as Manuel's rival and Harvey's nemesis, Long Jack. There's a scene where Troop deals with Harvey's sassiness that tends to draw silent cheers from exasperated parents. Mickey Rooney, in an early role, appears as Troop's son, Dan. [Trivia notes: 1) The movie's opening credits are among the most unusual, and beautiful, I've ever seen – and darned if I can tell you how the production people created them. 2) About those opening credits: they're presented in reverse – highly unusual for Hollywood at the time – with director Fleming's name at the beginning and the cast of characters at the end. 3) Tracy reportedly fussed incessantly about having to have his hair dyed black and curled for the role – and frankly it did make him look a bit like Chico Marx, particularly when he wore his cap] [Caution: The movie's climax is emotionally intense and shattering, so be careful with the youngest children. 4) Though the movie contains some thrilling sequences at sea, including a race back to Gloucester when the boats' holds are full of fish, all of the scenes involving the actors were shot using a nearly full-scale model of the We're Here constructed in a huge indoor studio tank] **[B&W]**

The Adventures of Robin Hood [100]
1938 – Michael Curtiz and William Keighley

Like *Captains Courageous*, I originally placed this movie in the Unforgettable category, because Errol Flynn's performance in the title role has thrilled audiences, young and old, for over three-quarters of a century. His uninvited appearance at a dinner at Nottingham Castle honoring Prince John (Claude Rains) alone stands as one of the greatest entrance scenes of all time. As the outlaw Robin of Loxley, Flynn is brash, brave and loaded with charm, and despite his rather dainty costumes he's a man's man. But I think *The Adventures of Robin Hood* more appropriately belongs here, among classics for children, because it conveys important themes for them within the context of a fictional story. Yes, there was a King Richard the Lionhearted, and there was a Prince John, but there was no Robin Hood, and the lives of the real Richard and John turned out quite differently than portrayed here. This is not history; it's wish-fulfillment, pure and simple, produced with all of the skills Hollywood's movie factory (in this case the Warner Brothers studio) possessed. It's the way you'd like things to turn out, which is why the story packs so much emotional punch, such as when Richard finally returns to England from the Crusades in the Holy Land and reveals himself to Robin and his band of men. It's also a fine morality tale. There's heroism, humor, honor, courage and loyalty. There's also cruelty, deceit, cowardice and treachery. It's all presented without subtlety, how good people must contend with evil in this world. Set in England in the 10th century, the movie was shot entirely in California in glorious Technicolor, with a strenuously complex but rousing and Oscar-winning score by Erich Wolfgang Korngold. Its look and energy remain undimmed, and Flynn's Robin Hood is the best ever. He's joined by his onscreen regulars Olivia de Havilland as Lady Marian, Basil Rathbone as the evil Sir Guy of Gisborne, and Alan Hale as Little John. And stalwarts Eugene Pallette and Melville Cooper turn in witty performances as, respectively, the jovial but dangerous Friar Tuck and the pompous but cowardly Sheriff of Nottingham. [Trivia notes: 1) The horse ridden by Lady Marian

372

was none other than Trigger, the famous golden palomino that came to be owned by western star Roy Rogers. 2) The real expert archer in the movie was Howard Hill, who played Robin's opponent in the contest. Hill handled all of the scenes where arrows hit human targets, and he executed the movie's most famous shot. 3) Warner Brothers brought in Curtiz to replace Keighley as director – even though Flynn and Curtiz had developed a dislike for each other, and Flynn considered Keighley his friend – because the studio's executives thought the action scenes as first staged needed more energy. 4) Speaking of disliking, Flynn and Rathbone weren't friends, and Rathbone injured Flynn several times over the years during their swordfights]

Captain Horatio Hornblower
1951 – Raoul Walsh

This handsome rendering of the C.S. Forester novel, about the exploits of a British naval officer during the Napoleonic wars in the early 19th century, is a little dated and formulaic for adults, but it's just right for kids who haven't been overwhelmed by the computer-effects-laden *Pirates of the Caribbean* series. It's also much less graphic than 2004's *Master and Commander*, which is a terrific movie but too intense for kids. Gregory Peck is in fine fettle in the title role as the brave and clever but sometimes stodgy captain of the H.M.S. Lydia, on a secret mission for His Majesty King George III. He gets what he needs to loosen his stern jaw a bit from the attention of a beautiful woman, in the person of Lady Barbara Wellesley (Virginia Mayo), sister of the Duke of Wellington, whom Hornblower is compelled to rescue and conduct back to England from Central America. Soon afterward he and his crew are captured by the French Navy and held prisoner – until they plot a daring escape, and he can return to England and the arms of Lady Barbara. It's not as consistently thrilling as *The Adventures of Robin Hood*, and though Peck is a solid actor he's no Errol Flynn, but the Technicolor photography is excellent, and there are enough exciting moments to rivet young attention. [Trivia notes: 1) Actually, this movie has some direct connections to *The Adventures of Robin Hood*. Both were produced by Warner Brothers, and Flynn was originally set to play Hornblower, but "problems" with the actor caused the studio to seek an alternative star. 2) That enormous docked ship, seen near the end of the movie in Plymouth, is no prop. It's the H.M.S. Victory, which was Lord Nelson's flagship and after 200 years is still a commissioned vessel in the British Navy]

The Crimson Pirate [100]
1952 – Robert Siodmak

One of the most entertaining swashbucklers ever, this is a dear, dear favorite of mine, as it was for many men whose boyhoods spanned the 1950s, and it's always a thrill to introduce it to young viewers. Burt Lancaster, who never looked more dashing, plays Captain Vallo, leader of a fleetingly loyal pirate crew on a caper to rob both the English crown and the rebels on a fictional Caribbean island. But Vallo doesn't count on losing his heart to the daughter of the rebel leader (Eva Bartok), or on being betrayed by his men – one of whom (Torin Thatcher) reminds him that any pirate worth his salt would be willing to sell out his best friend or even his own mother. Robust, rousing and often laugh-out-loud funny, Lancaster and his boyhood pal and circus-acrobat sidekick Nick Cravat perform their own stunts, providing many surprises and delights. The violence is mostly of the comic book variety, so there's no problem for young kids. So, "Gather 'round, lads and lasses, gather 'round" for a rollicking good time, all in gorgeous Technicolor!

It Came from Outer Space
1953 – Jack Arnold

Now, I've come full circle. If you've read my Introduction, you know this was the first movie I ever saw, at a drive-in theater in the year it was released. Clunky by today's production standards, the story holds up surprisingly well, and the lead characters are appealing. Richard Carlson stars as John Putnam, a scientist (what else?) living in the desert and courting his love interest, Ellen Fields (Barbara Rush). One night he asks her to join him outside by romantically asking, "Let's see what the stars have to say." Well, any moviegoer worth his or her salt would know that such a remark must lead to something bad or amazing. Here it seems decidedly bad at first, because a fireball streaks through the sky and crashes through the desert. Naturally Putnam investigates, and what he sees stuns him – though just as naturally, no one believes him. But then strange and disturbing events occur in and around the nearby town, and eventually Putnam learns the truth. A benign (though physically repulsive) race of aliens has crashed in their spaceship. As soon as they can make repairs – and provided Putnam can keep the fearful townspeople, and law enforcement, from attacking them – they will leave our planet in peace. For young audiences it's a suspenseful and engaging tale – one that's likely to give them a (healthy) scare or two. **[3D in some versions]**

20,000 Leagues under the Sea
1954 – Produced by Walt Disney
A grand telling of the classic Jules Verne story about a supposed sea monster terrorizing shipping in the late 19th century that turns out to be an electric-powered submarine called the Nautilus. The movie started a tradition of excellence in live-action titles by Disney, whereas before *20,000 Leagues* the studio had produced only animated features. The story begins with reports trickling in from around the world about the monster's rampage and a scientific party departing from San Francisco to seek and encounter the creature, only to be lost as another of its casualties. Three members of the party manage to survive: Professor Arronax (Paul Lukas), a scientist; Conseil (the always wonderful Peter Lorre), his assistant; and Ned Land (Kirk Douglas having a grand time in a movie-stealing role), a scalawag sailor and harpooner. Soon they are taken aboard the Nautilus, where they experience some of the wonders of the deep, meet the brooding and mysterious Captain Nemo (the great James Mason), and must fight a giant squid to the death in a raging storm. Over 60 years of progress in moviemaking technology notwithstanding, this one still looks terrific. It's high

adventure on the high seas. [Trivia notes: 1) The Disney team achieved such a realistic look for the Nautilus by building a smaller mock-up and attaching it to a real submarine, so it held steady in the water and made enough of a disturbance when it moved to look powerful and menacing. 2) That raging storm, in which the Naultilus crew fights the giant squid, was actually a necessity. The beast was such a complex mechanical contraption of cables and gears that the moviemakers couldn't conceal them. Hence, they created high wind and heavy seas to mask the slimy critter's workings – which made the scene thrilling and terrifying. 3) See if you can spot some of the messages painted on the foreheads of the actors playing the cannibals. One reads "Eat at Joe's" and another is "I ate Joe"] **[W]**

Moby Dick
1956 – John Huston
In this gripping version of the immortal Herman Melville story, Richard Basehart (who was 40 years old at the time) plays Ishmael, the narrator, a young New England man determined to set sail on a whaling ship in the early 19th century. He gets his wish, and much more, as a crew member on the Pequod, which is captained by the notorious Captain Ahab (Gregory Peck in a surprisingly effective role, though he was only 38), a man consumed by hatred for the eponymous white whale and a burning desire for vengeance. Years earlier, Ahab's encounter with the whale had resulted in the loss of one of his legs, and like Captain Hook's bout with Peter Pan (who cut off Hook's left hand and fed it to a crocodile as a prank), Ahab can't forget the incident or forgive the creature that wounded him. The script, by Huston and famed science-fiction writer Ray Bradbury, has become a little dated. But the great casting of British character actors, the on-location filming in the Irish Sea with a full-sized version of the ship, and some very large whale props give the movie an authentic feel. And the suspense building to the fateful encounter between man and beast is palpable. There's also a wonderful cameo by Orson Welles, who wrote his own dialogue, as the preacher at the whalers' church in New Bedford,

376

Massachusetts, where he delivers sermons from a pulpit built like a ship's bow. It's a dark but rousing adventure tale for kids, the only downside being the shots of real whale hunts showing actual deaths of the intelligent giants. [Trivia notes: 1) Over 30 years before Melville published his novel in 1851, a real whaling ship sank after being attacked, reportedly, by an albino sperm whale in an incident that took place off the coast of Chile. Ron Howard attempted to tell that tale in 2015 in the beautiful-looking but overblown and effects-laden *In the Heart of the Sea* (not on this list), but the movie failed to capture audiences and sank at the box office. 2) The Starbuck's chain of coffee shops was named for the first mate of the Pequod] **[W]**

Journey to the Center of the Earth
1959 – Henry Levin

A forgotten delight from my childhood, this '50s-style, CinemaScope telling of the Jules Verne tale remains a silly treasure, and just as youngsters should like *A Connecticut Yankee* my guess is they'll thoroughly enjoy *Journey to the Center of the Earth*. James Mason – in the same year as his wry performance as the villainous Phillip Vandamm in *North by Northwest* – puts in an appealing turn here as obsessive scientist Sir Oliver Lindenbrook. And speaking of appealing, there's the pert Diane Baker as the professor's daughter, Jenny, and the emerald-eyed Arlene Dahl as Carla Göteborg, Lindenbrook's foil and eventual love interest. There's also Bernard Herrmann's dark and moody but rapturous score and some eye-catching set pieces and American desert locations. But the real fun of the movie comes from Pat Boone's multiple songs and, believe it or not, a whip-smart duck named Gertrude. [Trivia note: Whatever was supposed to happen between their characters, Dahl got along better on the set with Gertrude the duck than with Mason] [Caution (an unusual one): In case your children are sensitive to such things, you should know that this movie breaks a longstanding taboo about harming animals playing significant characters. In other words, the unfortunate Gertrude doesn't make it to the closing credits] [Another caution – but a mild one:

Jules Verne imagined the center of the Earth to be the lair of monsters, but here they're obviously iguanas shot in extreme close-up or in split-screen] **[W]**

Young Einstein
1988 – Yahoo Serious

As offbeat as a movie can get, this inoffensive musical easily could have degenerated into a vanity production, because it was written, produced and directed by Australian writer, producer and director Yahoo Serious (born Gregory Pead – yes, I'm serious), who also stars as the title character. But as they say Down Under, "No worries." It's a genuinely charming debut – breezy, funny and fundamentally sweet, portraying the young Albert Einstein as a Tasmanian apple farmer with a curious mind, a constant taste for the fruit and flowing red hair that recalls folk singer Arlo Guthrie more than the great physicist. You have to pay attention, because the clever visual gags and verbal puns appear quickly and often. The humor bits and the plot are both pretext for the musical numbers, of course, which are lively, catchy and often rousing, particularly Yahoo's lip-syncing of "Rock and Roll Music" at the end, and the hit song, "Great Southern Land," by the Aussie band, Icehouse, overlaying Albert's humorous (but unnecessarily arduous) quest to leave home and seek his fortune. The charming French actress Odile Le Clezio plays Albert's love interest, Marie Curie – another fictional take on a historical figure. [Slight caution: some mild and oblique sexuality, mostly in the form of double entendres, plus some views of bare male derrieres] **[W]**

Fly Away Home
1996 – Carroll Ballard

I've mentioned two movies by the great Carroll Ballard, the director of *The Black Stallion* and *Never Cry Wolf*, at the beginning of this category. You'll hear more about those titles later, but this one and *Duma* likewise demonstrate Ballard's unparalleled ability to work with animals – though he uses some computer-generated effects here. The story concerns a lonely young girl

(Anna Paquin), survivor of an automobile crash that took the life of her mother, who learns to pilot an ultralight aircraft with the help of her father (Jeff Daniels). She then flies the ultralight on a long trip south to lead a flock of Canadian geese to their wintering grounds. Based on a true story and featuring the actual aircraft used in that story, it's surprisingly compelling; you'll find yourself rooting for the girl – and the geese! **[W]**

Duma
2005 – Carroll Ballard
Here, Ballard again portrays the healing of a child via interaction with an animal. Duma, an orphaned baby cheetah, is adopted by a South African farmer (Campbell Scott) and his young son, Xan (Alexander Michaletos). As Duma grows full-sized under the watchful eyes of the father and son (including a terrific sequence in which they clock the young cheetah's speed by racing it with a motorcycle), they come to realize that eventually they will have to return him to the wild. But the father dies of cancer, and the mother (Hope Davis) is forced to sell the farm and move to the city. She decides Xan (pronounced "Zann") must send his beloved animal to a zoo. The family, including Duma, must stay temporarily with the mother's sister, but Duma escapes. Xan rescues him, steals his father's cycle and heads north to the wilderness to find the cheetah's birthplace. This precipitates an engrossing adventure involving scrapes with crocodiles, lions, a warthog and swarms of biting insects – and an encounter with a vagabond named Ripkuna (Eamonn Walker), who at first seems a nemesis but turns into a trusted friend. Not at the sublime level of Ballard's *The Black Stallion* or *Never Cry Wolf*, it's nevertheless highly diverting. [Caution: some staged scenes of animal intensity] **[W]**

Buck
2011 – Cindy Meehl
From the title, you might surmise this is some cowboy story. Actually, it is, but not anything you'd expect. It's a surprisingly engrossing and touching documentary about a man called the

379

real Horse Whisperer – the inspiration for the so-so movie of the same name starring Robert Redford (not on this list). They call him the Horse Whisperer because Buck Brannaman communicates with horses as few humans can. His instinctive mastery of the skill is something to admire, particularly because his childhood was riddled with physical abuse from a cruel father. You wouldn't think someone with his background could grow up to exhibit such a rare ability, but Buck does, and with great insight. As he says, "A lot of times, when I'm helping people with horse problems, I'm [actually] helping horses with people problems." It's a must-see for all kids who have an interest in horses or in raising animals. [Caution: some adult material] **[W]**

Hugo (*reprise*)
2011 – Martin Scorsese
This is one of only two movies on the list I've encapsuled twice, in this case first in They Should Have Been Best Pictures, and now here. It's appropriate in both places. Scorsese, a champion of film preservation, directed this love letter to the early cinema that's wrapped within an utterly charming tale of redemption. Hugo Cabret, played by 14-year-old Asa Butterfield, is a gifted orphan who secretly inhabits the attic of a Paris train station in the early 1930s (impersonated by the Peterborough Station in England). He survives there by engaging in petty theft from the vendors below, and he serves a useful purpose – one of the movie's themes – by keeping the station's clocks running. One day he attempts to steal a mechanical mouse from a toy vendor (Ben Kingsley, in a great role), and therein a marvelous story begins to unfold, one of searching and learning and remembering and, finally, tearful reconciliation. This is a wonderful feature for children ages 10 and older. Based on the illustrated novel The Invention of Hugo Cabret by Brian Selznick, it presents two children – Hugo and his newfound friend Isabelle (15-year-old Chloë Grace Moretz) – as both curious and courageous. Comedian Sacha Baron Cohen

contributes a witty and surprisingly touching performance as the stationmaster, a wounded World War I veteran. **[3D] [W]**

The Book Thief
2013 – Brian Percival

Here's a tricky one. I considered adding it to the Flawed But Not Fatally category because it suffers from a clumsy device inherited from Marcus Zusak's bestselling novel, as well as one other problem. On further consideration, I decided it properly belongs here, intense and frightening as it is sometimes. But as youngsters emerge from childhood and begin to ponder the world they live in, and the history they've inherited, *The Book Thief* gives them a vivid and often moving glimpse of what other children in another era in another part of the world had to endure. The title character is named Liesel (Sophie Nélisse, who delivered a terrific debut performance two years earlier in *Monsieur Lazhar* – coming in my second compilation). She's a young girl abandoned by her mother, for unexplained reasons, in Germany in 1938 during Adolph Hitler's rise to power. She is adopted by Hans and Rosa (Geoffrey Rush and Emily Watson), who seem to be harboring secrets of their own. Shy at first but spirited, Liesel is befriended by Rudi (Nico Liersch), a neighbor and classmate. From there the story proceeds in a parallel way to another favorite, *Hope and Glory*, except that movie is about a young boy growing up in London during the Blitz, and it's basically a comedy. Though *The Book Thief* contains humor, it's definitely not a comedy. In fact, much of it is heavy-going, with a heartrending conclusion. And yes, the title reflects the theft of a book. But this is more a story about the blessed persistence of the human spirit despite the attempts of tyrants and others like them to extinguish it. For that reason, I highly recommend it for young teens. It takes a while to congeal, so it requires some patience, but it packs a powerful emotional punch. I'll leave the clumsy device for you to discover and judge, but the other problem, again in my view, is the movie's abrupt ending and epilogue. [Caution: as mentioned, some intense scenes and violence] **[W]**

40. Movie Magic

I have often heard people assert they don't like movies with special effects. That's like saying they don't like movies at all, because in a sense every movie is a special effect. Take the term, "movie" (or "motion picture"), itself. In every one that you've ever seen, during every moment, whether in a theater or on a video screen, you've *never* really seen anything move. Instead, the physical process that produces movies and video projects a rapid series of *still* images to create the *illusion* of motion. On film, 24 separate images, called frames, are flashed by the projector per second; while video or digital projection uses at least 30 frames per second. In both cases, it's the property of your optical system called persistence of vision that tricks your brain into believing you're seeing motion. The method has been used since the beginning of movies, back in the late 19th century. Even before that, enterprising individuals shot bunches of photographs, or they created drawings, and bound the images into flip books, which when thumbed rapidly produce the illusion of motion. Then, others capitalized on the process by opening establishments called nickelodeons, in which patrons watched simple movies by sliding nickels into the slots of hand-cranked machines. The phenomenon expanded further in the 1890s, when Thomas Edison and others developed the first practical projectors, which allowed groups of people to watch movies together. Then, artists such as George Méliès and Edwin S. Porter introduced audiences to movies as storytelling devices with arresting short features such as *A Trip to the Moon* and *The Great Train Robbery* (neither on this list). During those early years, the process was so crude that the light from the projection machines flickered. That's how the term "flicks" originated to describe movies. From that basic process, two equally important offshoots emerged: 1) If one image follows another, then a different image can be inserted at any time – and so began editing; and 2) each individual image can be constructed from multiple elements, meaning two or more objects can be combined onto a frame of film even though those objects were never together in real life. Getting confused? Don't worry. All you need to remember is that special effects have been integral and essential to movies all along. Moviemakers constantly employ them to push the limits of illusion, trying to top everyone else by showing something new that will cause audiences to gasp and utter a collective "Wow!" You'll find examples of effects-laden movies elsewhere on my list, but I chose these eight titles because each, with one exception, represents the pinnacle of the techniques of its day. When you watch, consider the effort required to produce them, which in most cases employed moviemaking methods that had never been tried or even conceived of before. That was the genius of these wizards of movie magic.

Mighty Joe Young
1949 – Ernest B. Schoedsack

This is *King Kong*'s lesser-known cousin, a story that parallels the tale of the great ape in all respects. But here the star primate is essentially tame, taught to get along with humans by the young girl who buys him as a baby and raises him as her lifelong companion. The movie also parallels the 1933 version of *King Kong* because it's the product of the same creative team – including director Schoedsack, producer Merian C. Cooper, expert animator Willis O'Brien and even Robert Armstrong (who played Carl Denham in the original) – plus two conspicuous additions. The great director John Ford helped to bankroll the production as executive producer, and Ray Harryhausen, the famed master of stop-motion animation from the 1950s through the 1970s, debuted here as supervisor of nearly all the effects shots.

The key to understanding how *King Kong* and *Mighty Joe Young* – as well as similar features – were made is a technique called stop-motion animation. It's simple in principle, and it's based again on that property of your brain called persistence of vision. You take a single photo of an object, move the object slightly – or in the case of animation draw or paint a new image that implies a slight amount of motion – and then take another photo. If you repeat this process over and over then project 24 new images per second, the object will appear to move on its own. In practice, it's an excruciatingly slow and complex process that can take days or even weeks to produce just a minute or two on film. But as in *King Kong*, O'Brien's team did it well. The action flows so seamlessly – and sometimes spectacularly – that you quickly forget you're watching a small mechanical ape doll whose position has been shifted minutely and painstakingly by the technicians. In addition, it's a well-told tale, and though it doesn't rise to the level of its predecessor, it does offer some dazzling and heroic moments. With Lora Lee Michel and Terry Moore playing, respectively, Joe's benefactor as a child and young woman, and Ben Johnson as her friend and eventual love interest. This is a good movie to show to children before they are old enough to see *King Kong* without becoming terrified. [Trivia notes: 1) O'Brien refined the animation technique used in *King Kong* by developing a rubberized surface for the miniature ape, whereas in the original they covered the miniature with dyed rabbit fur. The problem was that each time the animators moved the model, they disturbed the fur. If you watch *King Kong* closely, you'll see the "fur chatter," as the effects team called it. 2) I know personally how painstaking stop-motion can be. I once made two short movies with my daughters when they were young. In the first, called "The Big Race," I had them sit down on the local high school's running track and pretend to race each other. I'd click off a single frame of movie film, have them scoot forward about a foot, and then take the next frame. The movie lasts about two minutes but took nearly four hours to shoot. The girls complained a lot but they hung in like troopers, and we finished what became a family treasure. In the other, a cut-paper

384

animated cartoon called "Mouse in the Rain," the first shot called for a mouse to walk across the frame in a downpour. We had to move each "raindrop" individually between frames, so an eight-second shot took eight hours to film. 3) There's a scene where Mighty Joe engages in a tug of war with a group of the world's strongest men at the time, including former heavyweight boxing champion Primo Carnera. In this fantasy, he bests them all, but even a normal-sized gorilla is powerful enough to have matched his feat] [B&W]

The War of the Worlds
1953 – Produced by George Pal

Yes, Steven Spielberg mounted a big-budget remake of the H.G. Wells classic novel in 2005 (see below), but this version, with its still-convincing – and scary – effects, remains the better movie, and at a cost of over $2 million it boasted its own big budget for the time. The story involves an attack by Martians on the people of Earth. They descend from the sky in what appear to be hollow, giant, flaming meteors, each of which opens after it cools to unleash a trio of seemingly invincible, manta-ray-like war machines that feature death rays delivered by long, swan-necked arms crowned with brilliant, jeweled eyes. The machines easily resist everything the humans attempt to throw against them, including an atomic bomb. Gene Barry (who starred in two TV series in the 1950s and '60s: the western, Bat Masterson, and the detective drama, Burke's Law) plays Clayton Forrester, a scientist whose attempt to understand and fight the Martians becomes an exercise in futility. Ann Robinson, another TV veteran from the same period, plays Forrester's love interest, Sylvia Van Buren. Together they must brave some too-close-for-comfort encounters with the Martian invaders and their hardware. George Pal, who is considered the godfather of sci-fi movies, and his team made a bunch of effects-laden features from the late 1940s through the early '60s, but they pioneered or perfected their best techniques with this one, skillfully combining elaborate and expansive models with optical, physical and even previously unheard sound effects, to give everything associated with the Martians an otherworldly feel. Example: They suspended, moved and controlled each of the war machine models with nearly two-dozen thin wires. They used composite and reverse audio recordings to create new sounds – paving the way for many of the techniques used in the best sound-effects movies of all: the *Star Wars* sagas. Yes, *The War of the Worlds* has aged quite a bit after over half a century, but it still packs a remarkable amount of entertainment value and even thrills. [Trivia notes: 1) One of Pal's closest friends was Walter Lanz, the creator of the cartoon character, Woody Woodpecker. So, Pal concealed a doll of the mop-headed bird in this and in every other one of his movies. 2) Robinson continued her role as Van Buren in a short-lived TV series of the same name, again as a grandmother in Spielberg's update, and even in a forgettable B-movie called *The Naked Monster* (obviously not here), also in 2005]

Godzilla, King of the Monsters!
1954 – Japan – Ishiro Honda and Terry O. Morse

Here's the exception I mentioned. The effects are bargain-basement, even for their day: obviously miniature buildings, model planes and tanks, and of course a guy in a big rubber monster suit. But I included *Godzilla* here because it's a feature that entertains *despite* the bad effects. I can state this confidently; the movie engendered a long line of ridiculous but endearing Japanese monster movies, not to mention several big-budget, computer-generated remakes by Hollywood. In this one – the original version – atomic testing has unleashed a giant creature that had been slumbering for untold thousands or millions of years. So now, as they say, he's back, and he's ticked off! At over 300 feet tall and breathing fire, Godzilla makes mincemeat of any defenses humans can deploy as he runs roughshod over the Japanese countryside. At least, that's what's supposed to be happening. Actually – as I mentioned and as we can plainly see – it's a guy in a big rubber suit (the actor's name is Haruo Nakajima) who romps around a sound stage and exhales animated flames. But don't knock it; it's so awful you can't help but love it. [Trivia notes: 1) Japan's Toho studio created a version of *Godzilla* especially for American audiences. Dubbed into English, it featured Raymond Burr (Perry Mason in the long-running TV series of the same name) as an American reporter witnessing the monster's ravaging of Tokyo. For his role, Burr never left the United States, shooting all of his scenes in one long day on a Los Angeles sound stage and studio backlot, and pretending to view the mayhem and carnage somewhere offscreen – hence the T.O. Morse director's credit (he handled that chore for Burr's scenes). 2) Toho's talent scouts picked Nakajima for the title role in this movie because he had performed effectively as one of the bandits in the great *Seven Samurai*, also produced in 1954] **[B&W]**

Forbidden Planet
1956 – Fred M. Wilcox

This title would fit well into the Deliciously Bad category, but some of its special effects remain flashy even after all these years, and it will always hold the twin titles of the first big-budget sci-fi movie (from Metro-Goldwyn-Mayer, no less) and the first movie to use an entirely electronic score. Essentially, the story is Shakespeare's "The Tempest" set among the stars but with the clunky sensibilities of the 1950s. A spacecraft from Earth travels to the planet Altair 4, where a previous Earth mission had landed and been presumed lost. When the crew arrives – commanded by Leslie Nielsen, who became popular in the 1990s in the *Airplane!* (coming in the next compilation) and the *Naked Gun* comedies – they find the planet populated only by a rather crabby scientist named Dr. Morbius (Walter Pidgeon), his nubile and restless daughter, Altaira (Anne Francis), and a robot named Robby (more about him shortly). Morbius refuses to be rescued, however, because he has discovered a secret so important he does not want to share it. Actually, the storyline is hokey, but the movie looks splendid, almost like a comic book come to life. The effect is achieved by a technique called matte painting, in which live action is mated in the film-printing process with artwork meant to depict, in this case, alien landscapes and structures. It's campy fun. Married composers Louis and Bebe Barron took nearly a year to develop that aforementioned otherworldly score. [Trivia notes: 1) If the garden on the planet looks vaguely familiar, that's because it's the same set – reconfigured a bit – used for the Munchkin village sequence in *The Wizard of Oz*. 2) Among its other distinctions, *Forbidden Planet* marked the first appearance of Robby the Robot, a mechanical contraption that became possibly the longest-lasting movie and television character of all time. Robby is best remembered as a regular in the 1970s TV series Lost in Space, but he's appeared in dozens of other venues. Designed by Japanese-American engineer Robert Kinoshita and built by MGM prop technicians (voiced by actor/announcer Marvin Miller and performed by actor/stuntman Frankie Darro), the robot was rumored to have cost $125,000, more than many movie budgets at the time. Robby would remain the most famous movie robot until a rather foppish android and a vacuum-cleaner-sized critter overtook him more than two decades later: C-3PO and R2-D2 in *Star Wars*] **[W]**

Superman
1978 – Richard Donner
Forget about the fancy remakes of 2006 and 2013. This version is far more entertaining and appealing. Christopher Reeve – whose life was cut short by a tragic horseback-riding accident – plays the Man of Steel from the late planet Krypton with tremendous warmth and charm. He's surrounded by a strong supporting cast, including Margot Kidder as Lois Lane; Glenn Ford and Phyllis Thaxter as Jonathan and Martha Clark Kent, his adoptive Earth parents; Gene Hackman as archvillain Lex Luthor; and Marlon Brando and Susannah York as Superman's real parents. It also reunites Brando with screenwriter Mario Puzo six years after *The Godfather*. The tag line in the newspaper ads that ran before the movie's release exclaimed: "You'll believe that a man can fly!" Well, yes, you do, because the special-effects artists who made the movie possible tried things never attempted before, employing complicated cable-and-harness rigs and

groundbreaking background photography. Most of the time it works very well, but that's not what makes this movie so good. It belongs to Reeve, who was 26 at the time. An unknown before the release of *Superman*, the movie propelled him to instant stardom with his terrific looks and tremendous screen charm. He appeared in nearly 20 other movies and did a lot of television and theater, but nothing ever surpassed this performance – as both Superman and his alter ego, Clark Kent, the mild-mannered reporter for the fictional Daily Planet newspaper. The same can be said for Margot Kidder as Kent's newspaper colleague Lane, who serves as both the object of Kent's affections and Superman's would-be consort. The chemistry between them just sparkles – though reports of the production have mentioned sparks flying between the two on the set. Hackman, Ned Beatty and Valerie Perrine are just fine as the villainous trio of criminal-mastermind Luthor, his henchman Otis and his voluptuous secretary Miss Tessmacher. And Jackie Cooper contributes some fun as the gruff newspaper editor Perry White. John Williams created another famous score, including the great title theme. [Author's note: My family and I attended the world premiere of *Superman* on December 10, 1978, at the Uptown Theater in Washington, D.C., at Gary Arnold's invitation. Several of the cast members attended the premiere as well, and they watched the first full screening along with the enthusiastic, standing-room-only crowd. But one person who attended did not watch the screening: director Richard Donner. He spent the whole two hours and 23 minutes in the lobby, pacing back and forth, most of the time with a worried look on his face. Such was the pressure he apparently felt about whether the movie would be a hit. He needn't have worried, however. The audience loved it!] [W]

2010
1984 – Peter Hyams
Many people of my age consider Stanley Kubrick's *2001: A Space Odyssey* to be the finest science-fiction movie ever made. It's positively majestic and, as I'll describe later, should *only* be

watched on a theater-sized screen. One of the unique qualities of that movie is how quiet it is most of the time. In fact, its first line of dialogue isn't uttered until nearly 26 minutes after the fade-in. Not so with this sequel, released 16 years later and written, directed, produced, photographed and edited by Hyams. Its first words are spoken within a minute of the fade-in, following a texted prologue meant to acquaint you with the original movie, as well as the title sequence. From there on, it does a *lot* of talking, and most of it is either pedestrian or New Age. *2010* is based on 2010: Odyssey Two, the second story in the series by Sir Arthur C. Clarke about a tremendously advanced alien civilization keeping tabs on both earthlings and our solar system for unfathomable reasons. In this case, three Americans hitch a ride aboard a Russian spacecraft headed for Jupiter, looking to find out what happened to the Discovery, the 900-foot-long spaceship that appeared in *2001*. This time out, Roy Scheider plays Dr. Haywood Floyd, the role which previously went to William Sylvester. Scheider does a credible job, and Helen Mirren is very good as the plucky Kirbuk (which is "Kubrick" backwards phonetically), the often-stubborn commander of the Russian craft. The actors playing the rest of the Russian crew are pretty good as well; likewise John Lithgow and Bob Balaban on the American side. But some of the cast, including Dana Elcar and especially Mary Jo Deschanel, are laughably bad, largely due to their scripted lines or Hyams' lackluster direction. The same for David Shire's overblown and hollow score. Despite its shortcomings, the movie's space sequences are for the most part terrific, and Keir Dullea does a nice turn reprising his role of David Bowman, as does Douglas Rain, the voice of the HAL 9000 computer. [Trivia notes: 1) Arthur C. Clarke appears twice in the movie in cameos, once as a man feeding pigeons from a park bench in front of the White House, and the other pictured on the cover of TIME magazine as the U.S. president – with Kubrick's image representing the Russian premier. 2) MGM arranged for an email connection between Hyams in Hollywood and Clarke at his home on the island of Sri Lanka so they could confer easily and quickly while Hyams wrote and directed the

390

movie – the first such connection in the industry. Too bad it didn't help much] [W]

The Abyss
1989 – James Cameron
Every single one of Cameron's major movies has featured groundbreaking effects, and *The Abyss* is no exception. But this one also required a grueling and dangerous shoot, sometimes lasting 16 hours at a time, to bring this story to the screen. The star, Ed Harris, nearly drowned at one point, and for a long time he rarely spoke about the production, which has been called the toughest shoot in film history. Co-written and co-produced by Cameron and Gale Ann Hurd, his wife at the time, it's a science-fiction story about contact between humans and a superior alien race that lives or has created a colony in the depths of the Cayman Trench in the Gulf of Mexico. The story begins with an American nuclear missile submarine tangling with an unknown craft and sinking on a ledge above the trench – but still nearly half a mile down. A team of Navy specialists has been assigned to visit the sub's wreck, search for survivors and remove its deadly warheads. Ordered to help is the crew of the deep-sea submersible oil rig, Deep Core, operated under the supervision of Virgil "Bud" Brigman (Harris). For the live-action underwater scenes of the rig and the submarine, Cameron's production team employed two of the biggest water tanks in the world, both former nuclear reactor vessels in Gaffney, South Carolina. For some of the scenes of the submersibles moving about, the team shot them using stop-motion, including tiny projection screens displaying one frame at a time of the actors supposedly inside the vehicles reacting to what was happening. Some of the other underwater scenes were shot using a technique called dry-for-wet, in which optical effects supplied the illusion of water. For still others, they used underwater or topside miniatures. For the aliens they used underwater illuminated puppets. And for the scenes in which Bud must dive deep supposedly using a liquid-breathing system, Cameron placed him underwater and allowed his suit to fill up – and Harris simply held his breath during the

takes and took breaths from an oxygen hose in between. If it sounds scary and claustrophobic for the actors, it was! But the results are astounding. Alan Silvestri supplied a pretty good score. [Viewing note: Two versions of this movie are available: the original theatrical release and the "special edition," which is considerably longer. Take my advice and stick with the original, which is available on both the DVD and Blu-ray versions. It's tighter and more sharply focused, and the plot is much less sappy] [Caution: language and brief, non-sexual nudity] [W]

War of the Worlds
2005 – Steven Spielberg

When all was said and done, I didn't particularly like this movie. But for one brief sequence, it's amazing. Spielberg's version of the H.G. Wells novel stars Tom Cruise as a single dad whose weekend hosting his two kids turns out to be anything but ordinary. First, there's a nasty looking thunderstorm with lightning that keeps striking in the same place, causing a widespread power outage. Then there are the strange disturbances under the pavement on a street corner. That's when *they* emerge! The five-or-so minutes when an alien machine rises from the ground and begins vaporizing humans are among the most stunning effects sequence ever shown – and the *only* reason to watch the movie. Though almost entirely computer generated, the action is totally believable and frightening. After that, the story becomes less and less logical and more and more depressing, so it's up to you how long you want to stay with it. As you've seen in these capsules, Spielberg has directed many of my favorites (including the next one on the list), but he's capable of misses, too, and this is one of them. He's the Babe Ruth of modern moviemakers, almost always swinging for the bleachers, and succeeding lots of times, but striking out a lot as well. I couldn't include this in the Flawed But Not Fatally category because it just doesn't hold up well enough and, unlike Spielberg's *1941*, I couldn't include it in the Deliciously Bad list, either, because it's no fun to watch. But as I said, for a short time early on it's extraordinary. [Caution: language and violence] [W]

41. Once Lost, At Last Regained

It might seem strange to classify a movie as lost when you could have seen it anytime on commercial or pay TV over the years, or easily purchased it on video or DVD, or rented it via Amazon or similar services. But trust me, there was a time when viewing this one on any of those venues meant you never really saw it. Fortunately, the 30th anniversary re-release in 2007 allowed audiences to rediscover the original theatrical version of a science-fiction classic.

Close Encounters of the Third Kind [100]
1977 – Steven Spielberg

Between autumn 1975, after *Jaws* had become such a, excuse the pun, monster hit the previous summer, and November 1977 when *Close Encounters* finally opened, it held the distinction of being the most eagerly awaited movie since *Gone with the Wind*. Alas, it didn't turn out to be the attraction for the ages that so many people, myself included, had hoped – in his review in The Washington Post, Gary Arnold called me and other members of this group his "movie-demented friends" – but it does deliver a terrific amount of entertainment value. The title refers to a phrase invented by science author J. Allan Hynek (who shows up in a cameo role) to describe three potential interactions between humans and alien beings. The first involves a sighting, the second produces physical evidence, and the third results in some sort of contact. In the story, Roy Neary (Richard Dreyfuss), an Indiana electric-utility worker and family man, experiences a close encounter of the first kind one night while investigating a power outage. He sees something extraordinary that scares the wits out of him and also leaves him with an encounter of the second kind (a partial sunburn). The experience obsesses him so severely that it eventually estranges him from his wife Ronnie (Teri Garr) and his children. But the episode also endears him to Jillian Guiler (Melinda Dillon), a similarly tormented, single mother whose son (played amazingly well by four-year-old Cary Guffey) has been kidnapped, presumably by the aliens. While Neary tries desperately to figure out what is going on, in another part of the country a secret team led by French scientist Claude Lacombe (director François Truffaut) is investigating the recent strange occurrences, and the efforts eventually draw everyone involved to a climactic meeting at a most distinctive geographic landmark. Spielberg orchestrated that climax with so much visceral power that I once saw a fellow moviegoer weeping uncontrollably after the house lights came back up. The movie's emotional punch even caused Stanley Kaufman, august movie critic of The New Republic magazine, to call Close Encounters not so much a movie as "an event in the history of faith." In more proper perspective, Gary concluded his review in the Post by saying that if real aliens ever landed and they didn't resemble Spielberg's vision, "they obviously aren't movie lovers, have no romance in their souls, and to hell with 'em." However you end up reacting, you'll probably agree that Close Encounters demonstrated how Spielberg was destined to become a giant of American cinema. In an interview with Film Comment magazine, Spielberg once summed up his abilities by saying, "I sort of know what works." It's true. What's also true is Close Encounters works powerfully on an emotional level despite making very little sense – if you start asking obvious questions the whole story begins to fall apart. No matter. Spielberg communicates subliminally to moviegoers so effectively that they willingly buy in, whatever the logical shortcomings. Perhaps more than any other movie on this list, Close Encounters illustrates the point I made in the Introduction. We love movies because the best of them do more than just entertain us. They crawl inside our souls and, as the lyrics of "When You Wish Upon a Star" (played quietly during one scene) tell us,

Fate is kind.
It brings to those who love
The sweet fulfillment of
Their secret longing.

Along with Spielberg's considerable skills at cinematic storytelling, the movie boasts dazzling and groundbreaking visual effects by Douglas Trumbull; gorgeous, Oscar-winning cinematography by Vilmos Zsigmond, and possibly the best work that composer John Williams has ever done. It's an absolute crowd-pleaser.

*   *   *

For 27 years, however, this was the problem: Spielberg re-edited the movie and shot expensive new sequences for a re-release in 1980, but that version was inferior to the original and relatively unsuccessful at the box office. Yet, ever since "The Special Edition," as it was called, was released, each time the movie appeared it seemed to contain a different configuration. Usually it retained some of the scenes from 1980, lost several scenes from the first version and mixed up the chronology of the original edit. It might not mean much to anyone who didn't see *Close Encounters* as it was first presented, but for those of us who experienced the well-edited and coherent original, seeing any of these mishmashes became highly frustrating. Worse, for a while it appeared that the original version was not available at all, because the prints had been recalled and feared shelved or even destroyed. Also, very few theaters have ever shown the movie properly, because it was meant to be heard as well as seen.

*   *   *

My first encounter with *CE3K*, as it's also known, occurred in December 1977 at the huge Ziegfeld Theater in New York City, which at the time boasted one of the best sound systems in the country. Audiences there could *feel* the sound as well as hear it, particularly the final chord of the title sequence, which might be the most exciting single moment I've experienced in my moviegoing life. It surprised and delighted everyone there so much it literally lifted them out of their seats. So it came as welcome news that Spielberg had restored the original *Close*

Encounters in the new DVD release, and it meant fans equipped with superior sound systems capable of reproducing the soundtrack's low-frequency components with sufficient power could enjoy the rare treat of seeing – and hearing – the movie the way Spielberg first meant it to be presented. Now, the original version presumably will remain available for the ages. [Viewing note: If you're going to watch the DVD of the 30th Anniversary Edition, make sure you turn up the sound – it's really meant to be loud!] [Trivia notes: A lot of trivia has been written about this movie, but here are four items you might not have known. 1) Roy Neary's name in Spielberg's original script was Norman Greenhouse. 2) The timeframe of the movie was at one point set in October, approaching Halloween. A vestige of that script element remains in the form of the three small, brightly illuminated alien spacecraft that appear during the climax at Devil's Tower, Wyoming, and present themselves to the humans gathered at the secret base there. The orb-like craft are meant to resemble jack o'lanterns. 3) Instead of Devil's Tower, the climactic scene was at first intended to take place at a fictional location called Wamsutter Canyon. 4) Another vestige of an earlier story iteration: that dark shadow that gradually blankets the people on the ground at the secret base as the Mothership prepares to land. It does so because Spielberg had formerly conceived the massive spacecraft as a dark and potentially menacing object. How do I know these things? Because a long time ago, even before the movie was released, a friend slipped me a purloined copy of Spielberg's draft] **[W]**

42. Exceedingly Rare

You'll almost never find these three titles in any DVD catalog, let alone on Netflix, Amazon or any of the movie channels. Even YouTube often lacks clips for them. That's a shame, because each is well-made and distinctive, which is why I included them. Just in case they resurface someday – on TCM, for example – please keep them in mind.

The Lady Wants Mink
1953 – William A. Seiter

At first, this seems like a completely lightweight and badly outdated comedy, with Ruth Hussey playing Nora Connors, wife of Jim Connors (Dennis O'Keefe), whose best friend and next-door neighbor (Eve Arden) has received a mink coat from her husband (William Demarest), stirring pangs of envy in Nora. Stopping there would do the movie a disservice, however, because it turns out to be deeper and more subtle than that. It's a surprisingly touching and affecting story of a woman who's driven to take bold and risky action because she realizes it's the only way to save her family. This was another one of my very first movies, seen as a little kid at the drive-in with my parents in the year it was made. I was even younger than the two boys in the story, yet it has stuck with me all this time because there is something so compelling about the way Nora and Jim, through a somewhat emotionally painful process, come to realize they must take a different path than the one they've been following. What makes the story memorable is you don't quite realize what's going on for a while, but when you do, you know it's the right thing to do. A little movie almost no one knows, but one that will stick with you, if you're able to find it and are willing to give it a try. [Viewing note: Used VHS and DVD copies occasionally turn up for sale on the usual venues]

Gizmo! [100]
1977 – Produced by Howard Smith
I have never laughed so hard or so long as when I first watched this brilliant compilation of humanity's misguided attempts at fame and fortune – and I laugh just as much every time I see it. A combination of documentary footage and original songs depicting the limits to which people will go to realize their dreams, *Gizmo!* is unique and in some ways indescribable. Well, no, it's just that this little movie is too precious to describe. It's better to search high and wide for it and, at least once in your life, try to see it and be witness to these wacky dreamers. Narrated with just the right blend of enthusiasm and tongue-in-cheek by Milt Moss, it's perfectly innocuous, except that in the case of kids you need to make sure they won't be tempted to copy some of the insane behavior they're sure to enjoy. The phrase, "Don't try this at home!" applies throughout. [Trivia note: One of the most amusing aspects of *Gizmo!* is the witty dialogue – much of it unintentionally witty – that accompanies many of the segments as you hear people describing their pet projects or their intended achievements. The thing is, however, almost all of the footage collected by Howard Smith and his production team is silent – there was no audio recording at the time. That missing material required an ingenious solution: The moviemakers employed skilled lip-readers to determine what the people on camera were saying, and then they used voice-over actors to perform the transcripted dialogue with appropriate emotion. The effort paid off. The on-camera commentary rendered *Gizmo!* even more of a cinema treasure]
[B&W – with a brief color sequence at the end]

Hot Tomorrows
1977 – Martin Brest
Here's another one that might no longer be possible to see in its entirety, but I mention it because it remains, arguably, the most

sensational student film ever made. Brest, who later would direct *Midnight Run* and *Beverly Hills Cop*, was a fellow at the American Film Institute's Center for Advanced Film Study, and for his graduation effort he made this 75-minute comedy on the subject of death. I've sat through many student films over the years, and most are clumsy, deadly dull, pretentious and interminable. Not *Hot Tomorrows*. Seeing it, you could tell immediately that a major moviemaking talent was emerging, someone with a strong visual sense coupled with a wry view on the human condition. And it contains a musical number finale that rivals the best of Busby Berkeley. As Washington Post critic Tom Shales put it at the time, the movie treats death as "the great pie waiting for all our faces." [Trivia note: Despite Brest's enormous potential and talent shown here, he only directed six features before inexplicably quitting Hollywood in 2003. They included the hit Eddie Murphy actioner *Beverly Hills Cop*, the terrific Robert De Niro crime caper *Midnight Run* and the drama *Scent of a Woman* (not on this list), which won Al Pacino his only Oscar. I intend to cover more of Brest's titles in a future compilation] **[B&W]**

43. Hollywood's Best

People were making motion pictures in several countries by the turn of the 20th century, but the movie industry as a global phenomenon arose in Hollywood, California. Lots of cheap land and plenty of sunshine made the area in northwestern Los Angeles ideal for year-round production. After just a few decades, eight major studios – Columbia, Metro-Goldwyn-Mayer (MGM), Paramount, Republic, Radio-Keith-Orpheum (RKO), 20th Century Fox, Universal and Warner Brothers – plus a couple of significant independent companies, routinely produced movies that would entertain up to 90 million Americans every week and hundreds of millions more people around the world. Let's start this section off with 10 of the best movies ever to come out of the place that came to be known as The Dream Factory – and because I'm paying tribute to the studio system, I'll list the studios along with the directors.

Frankenstein (and) Bride of Frankenstein
1931 and 1935 – James Whale (Universal)
This classic story, written – at age 21, no less – by Mary Shelley, wife of 19th-century poet Percy Bysshe Shelley, has been made into a movie many times in many lands – and has even been the subject of a classic parody, Mel Brooks's *Young Frankenstein*. But few versions compare with this one or its sequel. Boris Karloff stars as The Monster, a human being constructed from parts of deceased people and then re-animated by electricity and the skills of his master, the eponymous doctor. And Elsa Lanchester shines as the bride (as Mary Shelley in the movie's prologue as well). Seeing them both for the first time, you'll probably be amazed at the melding of technical and directorial skills

exhibited so many decades ago. [Trivia notes: 1) If you've seen *Young Frankenstein* as well as these two titles, you might have been thinking that Brooks was able to approximate the laboratory set from the originals very well. He did more than that – he tracked down Ken Strickfaden, builder of the mechanical and electrical lab components, and discovered that Strickfaden had kept that equipment in his garage. 2) If you view the credits for these movies, you won't see Stickfaden's name – but you will see it in the Brooks parody] **[B&W]**

Tarzan the Ape Man (and) Tarzan and His Mate
1932 and 1934 – W.S. Van Dyke and Cedric Gibbons (MGM)

For over a century now, readers and movie audiences have remained fascinated with the Edgar Rice Burroughs tale of a child of an English lord who becomes lost in a remote African location and is raised by apes. Though the story has been brought to the screen many times, these first two sound versions remain the best – though they require some tolerance and forgiveness from today's moviegoers. MGM cast Johnny Weissmuller, son of a Pennsylvania coal miner but an Olympic gold-medal-winning swimmer, in the title role; and the beautiful young actress Maureen O'Sullivan as Jane Parker. Despite the age of these productions, they remain enthralling entertainment. Their use of special effects is still skillful enough to keep even the most tech-savvy audiences on edge, and the initial sexual sparks between Weissmuller and O'Sullivan are intense. In *Tarzan and His Mate*, a former suitor of Jane's arrives in Africa to search for her and bring her back to England. As Tarzan fights to keep her, he is wounded and must be nursed back to health by the apes. There's an incredible battle between elephants and lions, and quite a racy underwater sequence that, as in *King Kong*, was removed by censors and remained inaccessible for years. It isn't O'Sullivan in the underwater sequence, however. Instead, it's Olympic swimmer Josephine McKim doubling for her, and the nudity – innocent though it may be – is much more visible on the video screen than in the theater. [Trivia note: In an interview, Weissmuller once admitted that Louis B. Mayer decided to cast him as Tarzan – a role he would immortalize – because when he showed up for his screen test Mayer said Weissmuller had the dumbest look on his face he had ever seen] [Caution: The one drawback of this early version of the series is its patronizing and offensive portrayal of Africans] **[B&W]**

Gold Diggers of 1933
1933 – Mervyn LeRoy (Warner Brothers)

You might not be familiar with the Hays Code, which set the rules Hollywood used beginning in 1934 to govern moral conduct on the screen, but this movie – as innocuous as it seems by today's standards – represents an example of the type of entertainment the code was meant to restrict. Known as a backstage musical, it involves the plight of four showgirls, including Ginger Rogers in the same year as when she first teamed up with Fred Astaire in *Flying Down to Rio* (not on this list, but another movie that helped to provoke the Hays crackdown). Rogers sings and stars in the movie's crackerjack opening number, "We're in the Money," involving a chorus of girls in flesh-toned body suits, strategically shielded by giant coins. The suits stay, but the coins get pulled off by the sheriff and his men suddenly raiding a dress rehearsal. This is the Depression, and the show's producer hasn't been paying his bills. The sudden closure means four of the girls – Joan Blondell, Aline MacMahon and Ruby Keeler, as well as Rogers – find themselves out of work. From there they use every trick and feminine wile to stay afloat, including an elaborate deception perpetrated on two wealthy men. But it's mostly in fun, and eventually we're treated to one of the most unusual musical numbers ever performed, "Pettin' in the Park," staged by the legendary Busby Berkeley and featuring, among other things, a voyeuristic child (actually Billy Barty, one of the Munchkins in *The Wizard of Oz*), and a long sequence where women (who have been doin' some of that there pettin') get drenched in the rain, retire to change their clothes in full view of the audience (though they're doing it behind a translucent drop screen), and emerge – I'm not kidding – in sheet-metal outfits. And wait until you see where that leads! If it all sounds confusing and contrived, don't worry, it's harmless and well worth watching for the Berkeley numbers and the vintage gender interplay. **[B&W]**

King Kong
1933 – Merian C. Cooper and Ernest B. Schoedsack (RKO)

Twice in later years – in 1976 (see Deliciously Bad) and 2005 (not here) – Hollywood tried big-budget remakes of this all-time classic, but neither matched the appeal of the original, a movie whose centerpiece was an 18-inch puppet. As I explained in the Movie Magic introduction, the moviemakers used a technique called stop-motion animation – which even back then had been employed for over a decade – and in which chief animator Willis O'Brien and his team painstakingly photographed puppets a frame of film at a time and moved their parts slightly each time in between. Then, when projected at 24 frames per second, and combined with other, extremely inventive and groundbreaking movie tricks, the puppets magically came to life. The two remakes boasted superior special effects – particularly in 2005, where Kong became a computer-animated creature – but somehow the closest emotional attachment remains with the 1933 version, as crude and creaky as it appears today (watching with my grandsons one afternoon, even the youngest could easily detect its moviemaking trickery). But it's a better-told tale, with Robert Armstrong as showman Carl Denham, who captures Kong to bring him to New York and infamy; and Fay Wray, probably the best screamer of all time, who looks incomparably lovely and vulnerable here. Yes, the movie displays the repulsive racist and sexist attitudes of the time, but it still packs plenty of entertainment value for everyone. Kong of '33 is still King! [Trivia notes: 1) The version of the movie now available contains three scenes originally deleted by the Hays Code censors. In the first, Kong explores Fay Wray's body with his fingers and then sniffs them, giving a strong sexual suggestion. In the second, Wray plunges into the ocean after a fall, and when she resurfaces there is a glimpse of her bare breast. And in the third, Kong displays his disgusting penchant for trampling and snacking on humans – and murderously discarding other women if he picks them up by mistake. All were regarded as too objectionable to be included in the movie's original theatrical release. 2) In the scene above the Empire State Building, the pilot and gunner shown in one of the airplanes are Cooper and Schoedsack] **[B&W]**

Tarzan Escapes (and) Tarzan Finds a Son!
1936 and 1939 – both by Richard Thorpe (MGM)
The third and fourth installments in the MGM series feature a wide assortment of action and situations, such as Tarzan being captured by opportunistic men intending to put him on display. Johnny Weissmuller and Maureen O'Sullivan return in the lead roles, and their affection for and playfulness with each other seem entirely authentic. The plot of *Tarzan Escapes* is pretty much self-explanatory, while *Tarzan Finds a Son!* introduces the character of "Boy" (Johnny Sheffield), who becomes like a son to the Ape Man when Tarzan rescues him after his parents die in a plane crash. Like the first two movies, these sequels feature plenty of African animal action – with on-location shots interspersed with scenes involving the principal actors produced on the MGM lot or in Southern California locales. And the portrayals of African natives are, alas, no more enlightened than in installments one and two. [Trivia notes: 1) Though all of the movies in the series suffered from problems and turmoil, *Tarzan Escapes* turned out to be a particularly troubled production. In all, five directors and four producers attempted to complete it. Along with Thorpe, who ended up as the director of record, John Farrow, James McKay, Andrew Seitz and even William Wellman (who did *Wings* and *The High and the Mighty*) had eventually taken their turns, unsuccessfully. And though Sam Zimbalist was credited as producer, studio regulars Jack Cummings, Phil Goldstone and Bernard Hyman also had given the movie a try. Quite a few other changes occurred during filming among cast and crew as well. 2) Speaking of John Farrow, he and O'Sullivan met on this production and quickly married] **[B&W]**

Top Hat [100] (and) Swing Time
1935 and 1936 – Mark Sandrich and George Stevens (RKO)

Both titles feature Fred Astaire and Ginger Rogers at the top of their game. In all, the duo danced, sang and romanced in 10 movies together, but these are by far their best and my favorites. It's kind of pointless to discuss the plots, because in both cases the stories mostly fill in between the song-and-dance numbers. But what numbers! From the ultra-smooth title song in *Top Hat* to the deceptively simple "Pick Yourself Up" in *Swing Time*, Fred and Ginger demonstrate why they are considered the greatest dance team ever. It's been said about Rogers that she did everything Astaire did, but backwards and in high heels. True enough. Still, there's a moment in "Pick Yourself Up" where Astaire lifts her effortlessly over a railing and then glides over it himself as though it wasn't even there. It's a tiny bit, but if you notice it will tend to leave you breathless, and you'll see why Astaire's dancing reigns supreme and why his contributions to the movie musical will last forever. Just don't shortchange Rogers. No other woman in the movies ever combined acting, dancing and singing as well as she did. <u>Example</u>: In the duo's climactic number, "Never Gonna Dance" in *Swing Time*, which Astaire wanted filmed in one take, the dance included a breathtaking finale atop a spiral staircase. That part reportedly took 47 tries. By the end, Rogers was bleeding through her shoes, requiring stagehands to sponge and towel her feet. But she never complained and nailed that last attempt, an incredibly complex series of spins and moves. She drew cheers from the crew and created a moment of cinema immortality. [<u>Technical note</u>: These two titles vividly illustrate the technique that Astaire developed – and on which he insisted for the rest of his career – for filming his dance numbers. He wanted the numbers to be shot as completely as possible, with few if any edits, allowing audiences to view the dancing uninterrupted. The approach created major problems, because even the slightest error required reshooting an entire number. But the results speak for themselves. The dance scenes remain most brilliant and unforgettable] **[B&W]**

44. Hollywood's Best Year

Many lifelong movie lovers and critics consider Hollywood's output of 1939 to be the best the industry ever produced, with more classics and near-classics released than in any year before or since. Along with *Union Pacific* elsewhere, here are four examples of the excellence of that year. They include what confidently can be called, respectively, one of the greatest movies ever made, an American political classic, an absolute gem of a romantic comedy, and perhaps the most beloved movie of all time – with all four nominated for Best Picture. Continuing from the last category, I've included the studios that produced them.

Gone with the Wind
1939 – Victor Fleming (Selznick International Pictures)

I get really annoyed when I read or hear news reports that the box-office grosses of the latest movies are breaking records, because such figures are misleading. As ticket prices go up, any mediocre or lame attraction can suddenly out-produce the revenues of a genuine blockbuster in a previous decade. The only true standard of a movie's popularity and power is the number of tickets sold – which is something the studios don't usually release. But by that measure, *Gone with the Wind* – which premiered at a time when tickets averaged 25 cents apiece and were sold for this movie at the outrageous price of $1.50 – remains the all-time box-office champion. There's no doubt that *GWTW*, as it's sometimes known in movie shorthand, also sits atop the list of Hollywood's 1939 offerings. The screen version of Margaret Mitchell's bestselling novel about the waning days of the Old South was the biggest production of its day, and it made legends out of its two co-stars, Clark Gable as Rhett Butler, the scalawag and opportunist; and Vivien Leigh as the equally opportunistic but courageous Scarlett O'Hara. The movie contains so many superlatives it belongs in at least three other categories as well: It's among the best of the Best Picture winners, for example, and the performances of Gable and Leigh both qualify as Unforgettable. That distinction also goes to Hattie McDaniel, the first African American to win an Oscar, playing Mammy, the feisty O'Hara family servant. She gave one of the most gracious acceptance speeches in academy history. *GWTW* also fits well in the Movie Magic category, because so many of its most famous scenes involve clever, groundbreaking effects. But most of all, this movie, produced in glorious Technicolor, with Max Steiner's soaring score, typifies Hollywood at its very best and in its best year – even approaching 80 years old it's the melodrama for all time. [Trivia notes: 1) I know it's probably grown tiresome for me to assert this, but *GWTW* represents yet another example of how wrongheaded the members of the motion picture academy could be. It won five of the biggest awards, including Best Picture, Best Director for Fleming, Best Actress for Leigh, Best Supporting Actor for Thomas Mitchell as Scarlett's father and, as already mentioned, Best Supporting Actress for McDaniel. But instead of awarding the Best Actor Oscar to Gable by acclamation – because few actors have ever dominated a movie the way he did – the members chose to give it to Robert Donat in the syrupy *Goodbye, Mr. Chips* (not on this list). They also chose the now-obscure drama *The Rains Came* (likewise not here) for best effects. Well, award or no award, Gable became known as "The King" for his performance, and deservedly so. With *It Happened One Night* and *Mutiny on the Bounty*, this made a still-unmatched third time in six years that Gable dominated an Oscar-winning picture. 2) Margaret Mitchell wasn't above being wrong-headed about the movie version of her story as well. Her original choice to play Rhett Butler – a choice she reportedly made while still writing the novel – was veteran screen villain Basil Rathbone. 3) In the famous scene where Rhett spirits Scarlett in a horse-drawn wagon past a burning and collapsing structure in Atlanta, that structure is actually the great wall featured in the original *King Kong* a few years earlier. The huge outdoor set had been scheduled for demolition anyway, so Selznick took advantage by torching it as well as several other edifices built for previous movies. Leigh wasn't in the wagon (neither was Gable), because the dangerous scene was handled by stuntpeople. But she was on hand as a visitor to the set and watched the fiery destruction as she stood next to producer David O. Selznick – who had not yet cast the role of Scarlett. 4) Speaking of Leigh, she holds a singular distinction with this movie: She was chosen as Scarlett after the moviemakers considered 1400 other actresses for the role – at least, that was the official version from Selznick's studio] **[B&W]**

Mr. Smith Goes to Washington [100]
1939 – Frank Capra (Columbia)
This is James Stewart's second-best role and Capra's second-best movie, a timeless, cautionary tale about the American political system losing its way (or, as a 19th-century French commentator famous wrote, *"plus ça change, plus c'est la même chose"*). It's the story of Jefferson Smith, a young and idealistic leader of a group called the Boys Nation who is appointed by the governor of his unnamed state to fill a vacancy after the death of one of its senators. Arriving in Washington, he's at first wildly enthusiastic about his new position and living in the nation's capital, but he quickly encounters the cynicism of just about everyone, including a hard-bitten staff aide (Jean Arthur, who had played his love interest the year before in *You Can't Take It With You* – the Best Picture winner but not on this list), as well as his fellow senator and boyhood idol, Joseph Harrison Paine (Claude Rains), who it turns out sits in the pocket of back-home political boss Jim Taylor (Edward Arnold, who had played Stewart's father in *YCTIWY*). Smith's innate goodness and moral courage eventually put him on a collision course with Taylor, and his trial by fire involves scurrilous accusations planted by Taylor's machine that he proposed legislation to create a reserve for the

Boys Nation so he could gain from it financially. Reviled by machine-controlled newspapers back home, and faced with expulsion from the Senate, Smith tries a last-ditch, desperate act to persuade the public he is not corrupt. He begins an electrifying one-man filibuster that lasts for 24 hours, until … well, it's worth not giving away anything else. Just know that you're likely to feel breathless with a patriotic lump in your throat when it's all over. The cast includes three actors destined to work with Stewart seven years later in his and Capra's masterpiece, *It's a Wonderful Life*: Thomas Mitchell as a hard-drinking, sharp-tongued reporter; Beulah Bondi as Smith's mother (a role she would reprise in *IaWL*); and H.B. Warner as a hostile Senate colleague. There's also a wonderful performance by Harry Carey, Sr. – a star of silent screen westerns, 16 of them for director John Ford – as President Pro Tempore. In the quality-packed field of 1939, *Mr. Smith Goes to Washington* won only one Oscar, for best original story (and not for its superior screenplay), out of 11 nominations, but it stands among the best American dramas ever produced. [Author's note: *Mr. Smith…* was considered such an insult to reporters, characterizing them as a swarm of vultures and the newspapers of Smith's state as under the thumb of the Taylor machine, that it was banned from showings at the National Press Club, which was portrayed in one scene as harboring nothing but a bunch of disrespectful cynics. That ban persisted until December 1987, when the club finally invited Stewart to introduce the movie at a screening as it neared its 50th anniversary, which Stewart graciously accepted. I was a Press Club member back then (and still am), and I attended the screening. There, Stewart confided that he had achieved the raspy voice he needed for the climax of Jeff Smith's long filibuster by having a doctor administer a solution of dichloride of mercury to his tongue, which irritated it so badly he could barely speak for days] [Trivia note: This would be the first of two times that Stewart played a politician representing an unnamed state. He did the same with his character Ransom Stoddard in *The Man Who Shot Liberty Vallence*, 33 years later] **[B&W]**

Ninotchka
1939 – Ernst Lubitsch (MGM)

The trailer for this witty, elegant, sophisticated and altogether delightful love story began by declaring, "Garbo laughs!" Yes, Greta Garbo does laugh, playing a straightlaced, sourpuss official of the Soviet Union who melts against the backdrop of Paris in the late 1930s – as well as the advances of a decadent, pleasure-loving French nobleman (Melvyn Douglas). But calling *Ninotchka* merely a comedy would be a disservice. As screenwriters Billy Wilder and Charles Brackett crafted the story, war clouds were gathering in Europe; the days in Paris of wine, women and song were rapidly waning; and the Russian people had already been through decades of hell. So the moviemakers wisely inserted moments of genuine poignancy to deepen the story. The result is perfection. Douglas is wonderful in his best role, and the dark humor is priceless. Example: At one point, a trio of Soviet emissaries in Paris (Lubitsch regulars Sig Ruman, Felix Bressart and Alexander Granach) ask Ninotchka how things are going in Moscow. She replies that because the latest round of political trials was successful, "there will be fewer but better Russians." [Trivia note: You might be wondering why MGM used the "Garbo laughs!" line in promoting the movie. It was a play on an earlier tagline, "Garbo talks!" for the 1930 movie *Annie Christie* (not on this list), which represented Garbo's first foray into the movie sound medium] **[B&W]**

The Wizard of Oz [100]
1939 – Victor Fleming (MGM)

To place this title among Hollywood's best is almost an understatement, because it probably is the most beloved movie of all time, a tale for the ages known and cherished by young and old for over three-quarters of a century. Kansas farm girl Dorothy (Judy Garland) attempts to rescue her little dog Toto from the clutches of the mean old Mrs. Gulch (the wonderful Margaret Hamilton). While attempting to run away, she becomes trapped inside her house during a tornado (one of the scariest movie effects of all time) and is transported to the magical Land of Oz. There, in her effort to return home, she meets her three comrades, the Scarecrow (the limber Ray Bolger), the Tin Man (the sympathetic Jack Haley) and the Cowardly Lion (the hilarious Bert Lahr), not to mention the Wicked Witch of the West (also Margaret Hamilton, in her most famous role) and the title character himself (the avuncular Frank Morgan). *The Wizard of Oz* needs no introduction, and if you have not seen it, go out and find it immediately, surround yourself with the youngest members of your family, and enrich your moviegoing background, because few attractions are as essential – and as perfect – as this one. "Oh, Auntie Em, there's no place like home!" [Trivia notes: 1) When they learned the movie would run over 2 hours, which they considered commercially unacceptable, MGM's executives ordered it trimmed by 20 minutes. One target for the cutting room floor, particularly by studio head Louis B. Mayer, was the song "Over the Rainbow," which he thought too melancholy and undignified (Garland sang it in a barnyard, after all). Fortunately, associate producer Arthur Freed prevailed on the issue, arguing that the song was "essential" to the story, and Judy Garland's immortal rendition remains. 2) Speaking of that song, lyricist E.Y. "Yip" Harburg once related how he and composer Harold Arlen had agonized over the process of writing it. For days, all they could come up with for the first line was "Somewhere, on the other side of the rainbow…" which they hated. Finally, they found the word "over," and today we can't imagine the lyric any other way. It's a lesson about how sometimes the smallest change can mean the difference between something ordinary and something timeless. 3) In the black-and-white scene set inside Dorothy's house after the tornado has deposited it back on the ground, and she opens the front door and enters Munchkin Land, a double for Judy Garland wearing a gray-and-white costume, goes to the front door then retreats out of the frame and hands the basket and Toto the dog to Garland, who then steps into the frame and out the doorway, wearing her famous blue dress and white blouse] **[B&W in Kansas – and glorious Technicolor in Oz]**

411

45. More of Hollywood's Best

Accept this challenge from me. Watch these 17 titles plus the previous four – and the 10 before that – all in sequence (you can stream them for a few dollars each on Amazon or YouTube, for example), and within as short a timeframe as you can manage, and I'll bet you two things: 1) you'll spend the rest of your life remembering the experience most fondly, and 2) you'll never look at current movies the same way again. I think you'll agree that these three groups represent, collectively, the pinnacle of pure entertainment in American cinema.

The Shop Around the Corner [100]
1940 – Ernst Lubitsch (MGM)

This exquisite romantic comedy by Lubitsch, the acknowledged master of the genre, represents one of the shiniest gems in the bunch. James Stewart and Margaret Sullavan are Alfred Kralik and Klara Novak, co-workers and antagonists at a small gift shop in Vienna, Austria, that is owned by Mr. Matuschek (Frank Morgan). Despite their conflicts, and unknown to each other, Alfred and Klara have become affectionate but anonymous pen pals. The story concerns how they eventually discover their respective identities and what that discovery means for their relationship. There really isn't much more than that – other than a subplot involving Matuschek's attempts to determine whether his wife has been having an affair with one of his employees. But that's what can make great moviemaking; taking the simplest of premises and exploiting it to perfection, to the point where, by the end, it resides lightly but forever in your memory. [Trivia notes: 1) The fertile source story for *The Shop Around the Corner* was a 1937 Hungarian play by Miklós László called

"Parfumerie," and it has been remade multiple times, both onscreen and back on the stage, under at least three more titles. In 1949, for example, it became the movie musical *In the Good Old Summertime* (not on this list) with Van Johnson and Judy Garland. In 1963, it emerged as the stage musical "She Loves Me," and again as a movie in 1993's *You've Got Mail* (coming in the next compilation), starring Tom Hanks and Meg Ryan. The stage revivals continue as I write, and as far as I know there might be yet another movie in the works. But none has ever been done as exquisitely as here. 2) Lubitsch had wanted to make the movie for over a year, but scheduling problems kept his two stars unavailable. So, while he waited, he directed *Ninotchka*. How's that for exhibiting genius in your spare time?] **[B&W]**

The Maltese Falcon
1941 – John Huston (Warner Brothers)
In my humble opinion, this classic detective story based on a bestselling novel isn't really a detective story at all. For one thing, the mystery at the movie's center is never resolved. For another, the plot is so elusive that it would be difficult to describe, except to say that a collection of shady characters are all chasing the eponymous bird, a rare statuette said to be worth a fortune. But trust me; none of that matters, because *The Maltese Falcon* is just a great tongue-in-cheek yarn. Written by master plotter Dashiell Hammett, and faithfully followed by Huston, it's as intense a character study as you could find on the screen in the 1940s. It's the tale of Sam Spade (Humphrey Bogart, in his breakthrough role), a hard-bitten, San Francisco-based detective who's (what else?) drawn into a dangerous situation by, as Spade calls her, "a dame" (Mary Astor). Before he knows it, he's being stalked by a murderous young thug (Elisha Cook, Jr.), threatened by an inept but creepy character named Joel Cairo (Peter Lorre at his most witty), and lured by a conniving ne'er-do-well (British theater veteran Sydney Greenstreet in his screen debut). There's also the mysterious character Floyd Thursby, who's never seen, but that's another story. Sometimes shocking in its nastiness, Huston's directorial debut is still a whopping

413

good time. My guess is you won't have the slightest idea what has transpired over the past hour and 41 minutes, but you will have enjoyed it just the same. [Trivia notes: 1) Huston shot the climactic seven-minute scene, in which all of the principal characters are waiting for the falcon to be delivered, in one take. Despite the lack of individual shots, the scene took two days to complete. 2) Spade's last line, "The stuff that dreams are made of," which is a crib from Shakespeare's "The Tempest," is one of the few that differs from the novel. 3) The falcon was supposed to be priceless, but Warner Bros. prop men manufactured three of them for the movie for under $700 – one of which Bogart dropped and damaged irreparably. 4) On the other hand, each of the two surviving falcons have been valued at over $1-million, making them the most expensive movie props, ever. 5) Mary Astor's offscreen amorous exploits had become legendary in Hollywood by the time she made *The Maltese Falcon*. For example, during the production she was carrying on an affair with Huston] **[B&W]**

Sullivan's Travels [100]
1941 – Preston Sturges (Paramount)
This funny but poignant tale about a successful Hollywood director who decides to quit making popular comedies and attempt socially conscious dramas is arguably the best movie Sturges ever did. The title character is John L. Sullivan (Joel McCrae), a man who continually confounds his entourage by attempting to contact the country's troubled, struggling masses still suffering from the effects of the Great Depression of the 1930s in a quest to gather material for his upcoming epic, "Oh Brother, Where Art Thou?" The problem, from his point of view, is his team of aides – played by several distinctive actors who appeared in most of the Sturges titles – who always lurk close by and eventually discover and rescue him, voluntarily or not. During one such escapade, he meets a beautiful young woman (Veronica Lake) who gradually becomes his soulmate. But when "Sully" decides to embark on just one more mission to contact the downtrodden, a brutal twist of fate threatens to ruin his life.

The acting is standard, but the storytelling is superb, including the undeniably moving centerpiece sequence, which takes place in a humble country church, and which you are likely never to forget. It's one of the greatest scenes in all of cinema. **[B&W]**

Tarzan's New York Adventure
1942 – Richard Thorpe (MGM)
Talk about a fish out of water. In this, the fifth installment of the *Tarzan* series, "Boy" (Johnny Scheffield) is kidnapped by agents from a circus and whisked off to New York City. So, Tarzan, Jane and Cheetah (Johnny Wiessmuller, Maureen O'Sullivan and … Cheetah) must travel there to try and rescue him. Okay, it's a ridiculous premise, but it's also frequently amusing and suspenseful, and the kids will love it. There's a particularly funny scene where two tailors are trying to fit Tarzan for street clothes and a thrilling scene where he must jump from the Brooklyn Bridge to escape his pursuers (though it's done with a stunt dummy). **[B&W]**

Casablanca [100]
1943 – Michael Curtiz (Warner Brothers)
A noted film critic once called *Casablanca* "the best bad movie ever made." But I can't agree. It's a first-class movie, one that has captivated audiences, stuck in their memories and roused their spirits ever since its release. It's a classic wartime melodrama, an unforgettable love story and a suspense thriller rolled into one, with a great and underrated score by Max Steiner, some truly funny and memorable lines, and arguably the greatest scene in movie history thrown in for good measure – all reasons why the motion picture academy, in its occasional wisdom, voted it Best Picture.

American expatriate Rick Blaine (Humphrey Bogart, in the role of a lifetime) owns a café bearing his first name in Casablanca, Morocco, at the beginning of World War II. A former mercenary, he tries to play both sides in an increasingly desperate struggle between individuals attempting to leave Casablanca – which is falling under German control – and the

Nazis and their Vichy collaborators who are attempting to stop them. Chief collaborator is police captain Louis Renault (Claude Rains, in his best role), a suave, slick and thoroughly corrupt character. In all this, Rick is managing pretty well … until she walks back into his life. "She" is Ilsa Lund (Ingrid Bergman, playing one of the great romantic characters of all time), wife of Victor Lazlo (Paul Henreid), a Czechoslovakian freedom fighter being hunted by the Nazis. Unbeknownst to Victor, Rick and Ilsa had engaged in a love affair in Paris before the city fell to Hitler's army in 1940, and now they have some explaining and reconciling to do. That explaining and reconciling constitute Hollywood moviemaking at its finest, with the all-time classic love song "As Time Goes By" as its centerpiece; along with a rendition of "La Marseillaise," the French national anthem, that might leave you in tears; and maybe the best ending and fade-out line ever. If no one has ever told you this before, believe it now: In your moviegoing lifetime, *Casablanca* is essential.

[Trivia notes: 1) Probably the least-appreciated actor in the cast was Conrad Veidt, who played Major Strasser, the snarling Nazi commander. Veidt was a German, but he escaped from his home country just ahead of a squad of storm troopers ordered to kill him and his Jewish wife. Moving to Hollywood, Veidt insisted on playing only Nazi villains to help the war effort. Discussing the character, he once told an interviewer, "I know this man well. He is the reason I gave up Germany." Tragically, Veidt died of a heart attack soon after filming ended, leaving his portrayal of Strasser as his immortal legacy. 2) About that greatest scene in movie history? It's the singing of "La Marseillaise." It deserves that distinction because, aside from the principal cast members, almost everyone else in that scene had escaped the Nazis advance across Europe. The tears you see on their faces were real. 3) Let's be thankful Warner Brothers decided not to use the title of the source material, a play called "Everybody Comes to Rick's," though it's a line spoken in the movie. 4) Released in 1943, and winning the Oscar for that year, *Casablanca* actually premiered in New York in November 1942, which is why it's listed in some movie databases as a 1942 production] **[B&W]**

Meet Me in St. Louis [100]
1944 – Vincente Minnelli (MGM)

Trivia question: After *Gone with the Wind*, which movie was the biggest box-office hit of the 1930s and '40s? Only five years after *The Wizard of Oz*, Judy Garland appeared all grown up in this lovely musical, which takes place from 1903 to 1904, the year the city hosted the World's Fair. Judy plays Esther Smith, one of five children in the Smith family, whose lawyer father Alonzo (Leon Ames) has been offered a job with a firm in New York. The announcement throws everyone into a tizzy because of the changes the move will impose on their lives. That's the libretto underlying some wonderful songs and one sublime sequence, much of which was based on Sally Benson's autobiographical novel. The songs include "The Boy Next Door," "The Trolly Song" (which is much more fun than it sounds) and the beautiful and heartrending "Have Yourself a Merry Little Christmas" – all sung by Judy, of course, at the height of her talent. The sublime sequence takes place on Halloween night, and it stars the youngest Smith child, Tootie (Margaret O'Brien). It's far too precious to give away. Shot in Technicolor by George Folsey, it remains one of the great MGM musicals and one of the greatest movies about family life ever brought to the screen. Audiences seemed to agree, because they made *Meet Me in St. Louis* such a smash at the time and a classic ever since. [Trivia notes: 1) The reason Garland could appear so grown up in this movie, only five years after she played the young Dorothy in *The Wizard of Oz*, was that she was already 17 back then. MGM's people had created the illusion of her youth in the previous movie by strongly binding her bosom and, essentially, starving her during the production. 2) The Benson family, about whom the original story is based, actually did move to New York and never returned to St. Louis. 3) A real romance associated with the movie happened for Garland, who met Minnelli during the production and married him the next year]

An American in Paris
1951 – Vincente Minnelli (MGM)

This Best Picture winner followed a longstanding MGM tradition of shooting (with the exception of stock footage for exteriors) stories ostensibly taking place in foreign lands entirely on studio sets and backlots in Hollywood. It's a gorgeous musical, based on George and Ira Gershwin's immortal compositions, starring Gene Kelly as Jerry Mulligan, an American ex-serviceman who remains in Paris after World War II to pursue a career as painter. As he ekes out a marginal living, supplemented by driving a taxi, he makes two lasting friendships; one with a French entertainer (Georges Guetary), and another with an American expatriate pianist (Oscar Levant). He also attracts a sponsor and would-be lover (Nina Foch) but falls in love with Lise Bouvier, a beautiful French girl (20-year-old Leslie Caron in her first movie role), whose pre-existing commitment complicates things. But all is pretext for the great songs, including "I Got Rhythm," "Embraceable You" and the title number, which Kelly directed and runs nearly 20 minutes – and which took a month to shoot. The scene is widely regarded as the greatest piece of choreography ever filmed. Shot in Technicolor, the movie, as one of the songs declares, "S'wonderful!" [Trivia notes: 1) Caron, whose family had endured the Nazi occupation of Paris, still suffered from malnutrition six years later and could work on the production only about every other day. 2) The centerpiece love ballad of the movie, "Our Love Is Here to Stay," was the last song George Gershwin wrote before his death of a brain tumor at age 38. Ira wrote the lyrics after George died, and singer Michael Feinstein has said he thinks the lyrics represent Ira's love letter to his brother]

Singin' in the Rain [100]
1952 – Stanley Donen and Gene Kelly (MGM)

They don't call this everybody's favorite musical for nothin'. It's as good as the genre gets and as perfect as a movie can be. And it was a crime it did not win Best Picture and an even bigger crime

– imagine this – it wasn't even nominated! It's the fanciful story of how Hollywood adapted to the advent of sound in movies, but that's only pretext for some of the most wonderful song-and-dance numbers you will see, particularly the immortal title song, probably the most sublimely happy sequence ever filmed, one that composer Leonard Bernstein once described as "a reaffirmation of life." In one of the most memorable moments of *my* life, I attended a screening of the movie at the American Film Institute at the Kennedy Center in Washington, D.C., with Gene Kelly in the audience. When the title song began, half of the audience started to clap and cheer, while the other half began shushing them so they could enjoy the number – the shushers won. Then, when the number ended, the entire audience erupted in a prolonged standing ovation for Kelly – who walked out on stage after the screening and promptly praised his co-star Donald O'Connor, whose performance of "Make 'em Laugh" is equally classic. Likewise, his two amazing duets with Kelly, "Fit As a Fiddle and Ready for Love" and "Moses Supposes." The two female leads – the young Debbie Reynolds and the versatile Jean Hagen – are sensational, as is Cyd Charisse, who dances a duet with Kelly that's as sexy as musical interludes get on the screen. This is a joy from beginning to end, and like *The Wizard of Oz* and *It's a Wonderful Life*, something to be savored again and again. Don't ever consider your moviegoing life complete without seeing it. [Trivia notes: 1) *Singin' in the Rain* contains maybe the best inside joke in movie history – but there's more to it than has been commonly reported. In one scene, Reynolds, as Kathy Selden, supposedly dubs the speaking voice of Hagen's ditzy blonde star Lina Lamont. Actually, it's Hagen's real voice dubbing for Reynolds. Meanwhile, though you can hear Reynolds's voice in some of the numbers, such as "Good Morning," and in others, such as "You Are My Lucky Star," she's also being dubbed by veteran singer Betty Noyes. In some cases Noyes's voice is used only for certain passages within songs. It makes sense. Reynolds was only 19, and her vocal ability was still developing. 2) O'Connor once told of how he often worked himself into exhaustion or even injury, trying to please the perfectionist Kelly. The same day they completed the "Moses Supposes" number, Kelly decided they could also try to do "Fit As a Fiddle..." As the takes progressed, O'Connor realized he was on the verge of collapse. But then Kelly suddenly threw a fit of anger on the set, supposedly because the bow on his violin was too short. He stormed off to his dressing room in a huff and shocked O'Connor and the rest of the crew. A few minutes later, O'Connor tentatively knocked on Kelly's door. Kelly answered and told him to enter. When he saw Kelly sitting comfortably with his feet up, he asked him what was wrong. "Nothing," Kelly answered congenially and confessed to O'Connor that he was tired, too, but didn't want to admit it. The two men became lifelong friends after that. 3) Reynolds, in a 2004 interview with Turner Classic Movies host Robert Osborne, described the grueling ordeal of rehearsals for the dance numbers, which went on for days and days under Kelly's tutorage. "But he must have taught me well," she said, "because here I am, 52 years later and still in the movie business, and it was because of Gene Kelly's teaching"]

A Star Is Born
1954 – George Cukor (Warner Brothers)
This is the ultimate movie about Hollywood and the best version of the story, which was made twice before – first as *What Price Hollywood?* in 1932 (also directed by Cukor – but not on this list) and again as *A Star is Born* in 1937 (likewise not here) with Janet Gaynor and Frederic March. This time, it's a CinemaScope extravaganza and one of the first movies to use stereophonic sound. It stars Judy Garland and James Mason, who was never better than in this fine if slightly flawed effort by Cukor. It's the story of Vicki Lester (née Esther Blodgett) and Norman Maine. She's an obscure nightclub singer with a fantastic voice, and he's the most popular male actor in Hollywood. The plot might be obvious – her star is ascending while his is crashing and burning – but don't let that discourage you. This well-worn tale is exceptionally well-told, and the songs by Harold Arlen, with lyrics by Ira Gershwin, are wonderful, particularly Judy's show-

stopper, "The Man That Got Away" along with the centerpiece "Born in a Trunk," which runs 15 minutes, and the brilliantly clever "Somewhere There's a Someone." My one complaint – and Cukor's flaw – is he allows Judy to blubber and over-emote when the going gets tough. It's Mason's greatest role but Garland's least appealing – though her singing is as fine as ever. [Triva notes: 1) A problem with the movie now is that Warner Brothers cut nearly 30 minutes from the original three-hour length, and some of the missing footage has never been found. But in 1983, film historian Ron Haver managed to restore all but five minutes. He also recovered the full soundtrack, however, so in some sequences the movie must substitute still photos from the shoot or promotional materials so the dialogue or music can continue. 2) Cukor died on January 24, 1983, the day before the restored version premiered. 3) The Esther Blodgett/Vickie Lester transformation isn't too far-fetched in Garland's case, given that her real name was Frances Esther Gumm] **[W]**

Gigi
1958 – Vincente Minnelli (MGM)

Minnelli's second Best Picture winner in seven years (the movie also took eight other Oscars) features an impressive list of superlatives. For example, Leslie Caron, likewise in her second Best Picture winner – again under Minnelli's direction – gives her finest performance in the title role. Louis Jourdan was never better, including his show-stopping rendition of the beautiful title song. And there probably has never been a more gorgeously mounted screen production – with each scene composed and colored to resemble paintings by Renoir or Toulouse-Lautrec – or such lovely songs, courtesy of the supremely talented Alan Jay Lerner and Frederick Lowe. Plus, Maurice Chevalier capped a distinctive, four-decade-long career with his role here. In all, *Gigi* represents the pinnacle of productions by MGM, the studio that had reigned for 30 years as the leader in the genre. It's a breezy but masterfully told tale about high-class French society around the turn of the 20th century, where rich playboys enjoyed sequential relationships with women known as courtesans – the European equivalent of geishas. In reality, it speaks about the eternal conflict between men and women. Gigi, a young girl who's a courtesan in training, enjoys the friendship of Gaston (Jourdan), nephew of Honoré (Chevalier), who once courted Gigi's grandmother (Hermione Gingold). Naturally, a romance builds, as Gigi stands "trembling on the brink" of womanhood, as the title number tells us, but not without conflict along the way. What a lovely, lovely movie, with great tunes you are sure to remember always, including one of my personal favorites, "I'm Glad I'm Not Young Anymore." **[W]**

Some Like It Hot [100]
1959 – Billy Wilder (The Mirisch Corporation)
Just as *Singin' in the Rain* is everybody's favorite musical, many people consider this their favorite comedy, an absolute gem by Wilder and his longtime writing partner, I.A.L. Diamond, who lifted wholesale from an obscure 1951 German comedy titled *Fanfaren der Liebe* ("Fanfare of Love" – not on this list). The plot, for anyone who hasn't yet had the pleasure, involves two down-and-out musicians (Tony Curtis and Jack Lemmon) who witness the infamous St. Valentine's Day massacre in Chicago in 1929 and are forced to hide from the mob – "go on the lam," as was said at the time – by disguising themselves as female musicians Geraldine (Curtis) and Daphne (Lemmon) playing in an all-girl band. The lead singer is none other than Marilyn Monroe, who creates arguably the sexiest female character of all time, "Sugar Kane" Kowalczyk (Ko-WALL-chek). The dialogue is extremely clever, the jokes are legendary, the situations hilarious and the laughs constant. Movie comedies don't get any better, and going on 60 years later there still has not been a funnier fade-out line. [Trivia notes: 1) The story required Curtis at one point to impersonate a rich, sophisticated man. But growing up in the Bronx, New York, he had never met anyone who fit the bill. So he winged it, imitating his movie idol Cary Grant's distinctive speaking voice to give the character some class and a hint of snobbery. 2) In answer to a question from me, at an American Film Institute screening of the movie I attended decades ago,

422

Lemmon said Monroe had become pregnant during the shoot (she eventually lost the baby), and the extra weight she put on made her look even more voluptuous. 3) Curtis once told a story about getting fitted for the women's outfits he had to wear for the movie. He said the tailor who took his measurements commented that Curtis had a better-looking derriere than Monroe did. When he told Monroe about the remark, her response involved another part of her anatomy, and the quote isn't fit for a family movie list. 4) *Some Like It Hot* was the first big hit for Mirisch but not the last. Though smaller than the other Hollywood studios, they went on to produce nine more of my favorites – including the next two] [Caution: mild sexuality and violence] **[B&W] [W]**

The Magnificent Seven [100]
1960 – John Sturges (The Mirisch Corporation)
Many times, Hollywood has attempted to make its own version of a fine foreign movie, usually with disastrous results. Not here. This great western – arguably the most entertaining ever made – is based on Akira Kurosawa's classic samurai movie and represents a flawless transition from one genre to the other. Instead of seven samurai warriors, here we have seven itinerant gunmen, each of whom, for his own reasons, takes a low-paying job guarding a tiny Mexican farming village against 40 bandits. If you've seen *Seven Samurai*, you will appreciate how well screenwriter William Roberts integrated the original story. If you haven't seen it, you'll still be treated to a first-rate action movie. Yul Brynner and Steve McQueen head the cast, supported by Charles Bronson and James Coburn, all of whom are terrific in their roles as gunslingers. Robert Vaughn (from TV's The Man from U.N.C.L.E. series), Brad Dexter and German-born Horst Buchholz (whose character mirrors the one created by Toshiro Mifune in the antecedent) play the other three guns for hire. But the movie belongs to Eli Wallach, a Brooklyn-born, Actors Studio-trained stage performer playing Calvera, the chief bandito, with such relish that he influenced at least a generation of movie villains. Topping it all is Elmer Bernstein's immortal

score, which could be the most heroic and exciting movie music ever produced. More than anything else, the score endows what would still have been a fine movie with greatness. [Trivia note: 1) Wallach said in an interview he was reluctant to play the part of Calvera until he fixated on the idea of wearing a sombrero that was bigger than everyone else's. 2) Speaking of hats, McQueen, still early in his career, tried to attract attention to himself onscreen by frequently repositioning his hat. The habit annoyed Brynner so much he told director Sturges at one point if McQueen didn't stop it he was going to smack him. 3) Brynner and Dexter teamed up again two years later in the stiff and silly *Taras Bulba* (*definitely* not on this list) 4) You might recall earlier in this text that I mentioned my late friend Sheldon Tromberg, who worked in the movie business. Shelly hired McQueen for his first starring role, in 1958 in a turkey of a sci-fi thriller called *The Blob* (nope, not here). 5) For those with keen ears, there's an unusual connection between this movie and the previous title, *Some Like It Hot*: Both produced by Mirisch, the former features the same sound effects used for gunshots in the latter's opening scene] **[W]**

The Great Escape [100]
1963 – John Sturges (The Mirisch Corporation)

This is the ideal double-bill with *The Magnificent Seven*, because it reunites director Sturges with composer Elmer Bernstein and co-stars Charles Bronson, James Coburn and Steve McQueen. It's also a richer and more complex story. Based on the book by Paul Brickhill, it is the dramatization of a real event: the biggest prison break of World War II. In 1942, the Germans had moved several thousand Allied prisoners of war deemed incorrigible to a special high-security camp near Sagan, Poland, where they were supposed to be contained. But the German high command badly underestimated the determination and resourcefulness of those prisoners, who planned, literally, the Great Escape: springing 250 of the prisoners simultaneously. Sturges and his production team turned that true story into a sprawling, thrilling, engrossing movie, with a centerpiece motorcycle chase

424

involving McQueen that remains unsurpassed to this day, because he did nearly the whole thing himself and for real – though the incident itself is fictional. His expression at the end of the chase remains a classic example of the glorious wiseacre nature of American soldiers, sailors, marines and airmen of the war. Shot entirely on location in Germany – though the real prison camp was in Poland – the movie represents nearly a decade of effort by Sturges to find a studio that would back the project. With Richard Attenborough as "Big X," the escape's mastermind; James Garner as Hendley, "The Scrounger;" Donald Pleasance as Blythe, "The Forger;" and Angus Lennie as Ives, "The Mole," who at 5-feet, 4-inches provides much of the story's heart and tragic soul. Yes, it is definitely a Hollywood production, and as such it takes certain liberties with history, but *The Great Escape* stands as a fitting tribute to the courage and daring of the men it portrays, and Bernstein's thrilling, at times pulse-pounding score ties everything together. [Trivia notes: 1) Brickhill, a British fighter pilot during the war, was shot down and spent time at the German prison camp where the event took place. He had helped in the planning but did not participate in the escape. 2) Several of the men in the cast, including Pleasance, actually were prisoners of war and suffered brutal treatment by the Germans. 3) During the motorcycle chase, McQueen also doubled in several scenes as a German biker in pursuit of his character. 4) The real commandant of the camp, called Stalag Luft III, shocked and remorseful that the Nazis had murdered 50 of the escapees who were captured, permitted the POWs to build a memorial to their fallen comrades – outside the boundaries of the camp. The memorial remains to this day. 5) Over the years, several fine documentaries have been produced, both about making the movie and about the real Great Escape. You can find them on YouTube] **[W]**

The Godfather [100]
1972 – Francis Ford Coppola (Paramount)
Along with *Gone with the Wind* and *Casablanca*, this is a quintessential American movie, and one of the greatest.

Coppola's version of Mario Puzo's historical novel about a New York gangster family's rise and fall is a landmark, and it has become so famous it probably needs no introduction or description. But briefly, it's the saga of the fictional Corleones, the most dominant of five New York crime families in the 1940s. All of the major male characters engage in criminal activities, including murder, but they adhere to a mutually acknowledged code of behavior, the most basic of which is founded on the law of the animal world: Show weakness or carelessness and you risk annihilation. That message is brought home time after time by spectacularly violent means. Yet for all of the monstrous behavior, you can't resist caring about – and even admiring – these characters. That's a triumph of storytelling. With Marlon Brando in his notorious Oscar-winning turn in the title role, and relative newcomers Al Pacino, James Caan, Robert Duvall and Diane Keaton on their way to stardom. Nino Rota's score and "The Godfather" love theme are now iconic, as are so many pieces of dialogue, including, "I'm gonna make him an offer he can't refuse," and "Leave the gun; take the cannoli." Maybe the most amazing aspect, however, is although *The Godfather* won the Best Picture Oscar, the motion picture academy gave it only two others: best actor to Brando (more about that below) and best adapted screenplay to Puzo, based on his novel. That means this classic is among the least-honored Oscar winners, despite its exceptional status in the culture. [Trivia notes: 1) Marlon Brando was only 48 when he played Don Vito Corleone. At first, the executives at Paramount didn't want him. But Coppola persuaded him to do a screen test, in which he transformed himself into the Don in front of the camera by stuffing cotton balls under his cheeks and approximating the facial expression, posture and gestures he eventually used in the movie. 2) Related to Brando's young age, the four actors who played his sons (Pacino, Caan, Duvall and John Cazale) were all within 16 years of him. 3) Coppola not only infused *The Godfather* with anecdotes drawn from his own life but also used several of his family members in the cast. Most prominent was his father Carmine, a musician who can be seen playing one of his original

426

compositions on an out-of-tune piano during the montage in aftermath of a particularly shocking and dramatic scene. 4) I called Brando's Oscar-winning performance "notorious" above because at the awards ceremony in 1973 he not only refused to accept the honor, he also failed to attend. Instead, he sent a young woman named Shacheen Littlefeather, an activist who proceeded to lecture the audience about Hollywood's mistreatment of Native Americans – and then capitalized on her five minutes of fame by posing nude for Playboy magazine] [Caution: graphic violence, sexuality and rough, sometimes racially charged language] **[W]**

The Sting
1973 – George Roy Hill (Universal)
Hill and his *Butch Cassidy and the Sundance Kid* co-stars Paul Newman and Robert Redford reunited four years later to make this audience-pleasing, period caper comedy. Instead of outlaws, the two play Henry Gondorf and Johnny Hooker, a con-man duo attempting to fleece gangster Doyle Lonnegan (Robert Shaw) out of a fortune and exact a little revenge on him in the process. This is fine fun, with colorful characters and plenty of plot twists to keep you guessing. Marvin Hamlisch adapted the ragtime music of Scott Joplin for the lively but sometimes melancholy score – and he performed the piano solos. With screen and TV veterans Harold Gould, Ray Walston, Jack Kehoe, Dana Elcar, Eileen Brennan and Sally Kirkland among the supporting players, and with Robert Earl Jones (father of James Earl Jones) as Redford's character's early partner in the con. The movie won seven Oscars, including Best Picture. [Trivia note: If the diner in the scene where Hooker meets Lonnegan looks familiar, congratulations. You've recognized the diner set on the Universal backlot used in *Back to the Future*] [Caution: violence and sexuality] **[W]**

That's Entertainment!
1974 – <u>Produced</u> and directed by Jack Haley, Jr. (MGM)
This is a special case because I'm actually recommending four movies here that are bound together thematically and by their creative teams. In their entirety, they offer a unique and often enchanting compilation of the best scenes from the best musicals and other movies made by Hollywood's best studio of the 1930s, '40s and '50s, Metro-Goldwyn-Mayer. Each segment presents some of the history of this great and distinctly American cinematic genre. Each begins by showing some of the earliest efforts at movie musicals, most of which were laughable at best. For example, the original starts off with a clip from *The Broadway Review of 1929* (not on this list), a little-known and dreadful musical, in which Cliff Edwards (the voice of the Disney animated character Jiminy Cricket in the beloved *Dumbo*) strums his ukulele and croons a song that all genuine movielovers will recognize in an instant. Then we jump to a clip of Judy Garland singing the same song in 1940 in the long-forgotten *Little Nellie Kelly* (likewise not here). And then we're treated to the opening of what's been popularly known for years as everybody's favorite musical – which in case you've forgotten I listed eight titles ago. After that, it's two hours-plus of brief clips mixed with nearly complete musical numbers, interspersed with commentary and voice-over narration (some of it pretty good, some not so) from 11 of the biggest stars of that era, including Fred Astaire, Bing Crosby, Gene Kelly, Debbie Reynolds, Donald O'Connor and Frank Sinatra. The collective excerpts represent some of the most sublimely entertaining moments in the genre. You'll see a young Judy Garland singing a knockout version of "You Made Me Love You" accompanied by a montage of Clark Gable movies. There's part of the rapturous fantasy ballet sequence from *An American in Paris*; the splashy finale of *The Great Ziegfeld* (a Best Picture; capsule coming later), staged by the inimitable Busby Berkley; Gene Kelly trading steps with Jerry the Mouse in *Anchors Aweigh* (nope); powerhouse dancer Eleanor Powell matching Fred Astaire tap for tap in "Begin the Beguine" from *Broadway Melody of 1940* (not here); Donald

428

O'Connor performing his wonderfully comic rendition of "Make 'em Laugh" from *Singin' in the Rain*; a lovely montage of Judy Garland's best numbers, beginning with "C'mon, Get Happy" from *Summer Stock* (coming later); and Astaire's sublime dance with a coat rack (Yes, a coat rack, part of a number he does in a gymnasium, and it's all amazing.) from *Royal Wedding* (later). Uneven as it might be, *That's Entertainment!* leaves you in a happy mood and wanting more.

*   *   *

In *That's Entertainment, Part II*, released in 1976, Gene Kelly took over as director and wisely confined hosting duties to himself and Fred Astaire, with each man introducing and paying tribute to the other's eight best clips. It turns out that *Part II*, which packs nearly 100 musical numbers and other clips into its two-hour-and-10-minute running time, also features lots of MGM's classic comedy, drama and star-power moments. There's a nice montage of some of the best-known screen comedians, the full-length and classic "stateroom" scene from the Marx Brothers' *A Night at the Opera*, a witty if too-long stretch about songwriting, a compilation of scenes from the movies of Spencer Tracy and Katharine Hepburn, and so on. But *Part II* doesn't neglect the MGM musicals, presenting some of the most beloved in the studio's repertoire, such as "Good Mornin'" from *Singin' in the Rain* and Judy Garland's immortal rendition of "Have Yourself a Merry Little Christmas" from *Meet Me in St. Louis*. There's also Bobby Van's two-and-a-half-minute "Take Me to Broadway" dance in *Small Town Girl* (regrettably, not here), probably the most astounding example of sheer physicality and precise stage direction ever seen. And Kelly and Astaire are just great when they appear together throughout the movie to introduce new sequences. Even at ages 63 and 76, respectively, they demonstrate why they'll always be remembered as the two greatest movie dancers – and one reason why this is my favorite of the bunch.

*   *   *

That's Entertainment! III, released in 1994 – coincidentally, MGM's 70th anniversary – and co-directed by Bud Friedgen and

429

Michael J. Sheridan, reverts to using nine famous stars from the musicals to frame the segments – which include appearances by 79 stars from MGM and elsewhere. But instead of those individuals engaging in standard patter and introduce selected numbers, this third installment focuses on songs and performances not seen in the finished movies (none of them on this list). As a result, *That's Entertainment! III* turns out to be the most fascinating of the trio. For example, there's the amazing dancing of Eleanor Power in *Lady Be Good* (not here) shot with a second camera and showing how the crew and primary cameras were scrambling to capture her performance. There are several lively numbers by Judy Garland, all cut from her movies for various reasons but fascinating nevertheless. We see Ava Gardner singing in her lovely real voice in *Show Boat* (not here), before the producers decided she should be dubbed. There's the dance by Fred Astaire and Ginger Rogers at the end of *The Barkleys of Broadway* (coming later). There's also Astaire performing "I Wanna Be a Dancin' Man" in *The Belle of New York* (not here) but uncharacteristically in casual clothes and shown, side-by-side, with the dance in the finished movie.

*   *   *

Then, going back in time a bit, the companion compilation, 1985's *That's Dancing*, directed once again by Jack Haley, Jr., focuses entirely on – no surprise – the best dance numbers from the MGM musicals. Among its many delights, you'll be treated to the breathtaking acrobatics of the Nicholas Brothers, plus an endearing sequence performed by Ray Bolger as the Scarecrow that was inexplicably pared down from his "If I Only Had a Brain" number in *The Wizard of Oz*. If Bolger's complete rendition had been left in, I think you'd agree it would have transformed the entire feel of the movie. The collective benefit of these four attractions is they relieve you of the trouble of having to watch many of the musicals all of the way through – including the substandard numbers – to get to the most worthwhile songs or dance routines. It's a great advantage, and if you doubt me, try watching the entire *Ziegfeld Follies* sometime (as if I have to mention – not here). When Sinatra introduces the Astaire and

Powell number in Part 1, he says, "You know, you can wait around and hope, but I tell ya, you'll never see the likes of this again." It's true, and because of these compilations the treasured moments of our greatest musical performers will not be lost. **[W]**

Titanic [100]
1997 – James Cameron (20th Century Fox and Paramount)
Among all American movies, only three can be called magnificent productions – in their epic sweep, their exceptional attention to detail, their storytelling and emotional power, and their indelible impression on the memory. The first two are *Gone with the Wind* and *The Godfather* – parts I and II taken as a whole (*Lawrence of Arabia* and *Doctor Zhivago* are likewise magnificent, but they're British productions). *Titanic* is the third and likely to stand as Cameron's masterpiece (particularly after his overblown dud *Avatar* in 2009 – not on this list). In fact, *Titanic* is probably the most immense spectacle ever brought to the screen. Other great movies, such as *Lawrence* and *Zhivago*, involve huge battle sequences or vast sets. But no one has ever attempted to portray a disaster at sea using, essentially, a full-size ship going down with more than 2,000 visible souls aboard. The premise is unsurpassed. Yes, *Titanic* is a colossal spectacle, but it's also an enduring, universal love story of two fictional characters who convey emotional truth during the most famous oceangoing tragedy in history. Titanic sank after midnight on April 15, 1912, about 160 minutes after colliding with an iceberg in the North Atlantic. At the time, it was the largest and most luxurious ship afloat – and foolishly considered unsinkable by Britain's White Star Line. The two young actors in the historical part of the movie, Leonardo DiCaprio and Kate Winslet – playing, respectively, Jack Dawson and Rose De Witt Bukater (byoo-KAY-ter) – are terrific and tremendously appealing. But the heart of the movie belongs to Gloria Stuart, who was 86 at the time, playing Rose as a centenarian in the contemporary sequences. The motion picture academy's denial of the Best Supporting Actress award to Stuart represents maybe the greatest of the many Oscar injustices – matched only by their

failure to award Best Actor to Clark Gable for *Gone with the Wind*). As meticulous as *Titanic's* production values and special effects are – and Cameron went to extraordinary lengths to reproduce the ship's interior down to the smallest detail, as well as the collision and sinking – it would not be nearly as good without her performance. That's not to minimize Cameron's visionary storytelling, however, including his flawless, sometimes breathtaking transitions between the present and the past. James Horner supplied the fine dramatic score, and Celine Dion's melancholy song, "My Heart Will Go On," is unforgettable. Savor and enjoy the story, and go ahead and sob at its heartrending conclusion, but don't leave it too soon. Be sure to watch all the way through the extensive closing credits – which run almost 10 minutes – so you can appreciate the legion of dedicated professionals who contributed to this unparalleled epic under Cameron's guiding hand. In particular, notice the small army of stunt performers, perhaps the biggest such group ever assembled for a movie. [Trivia notes: 1) Gloria Stuart died in her sleep on September 27, 2010, two months and 23 days after her 100th birthday on the Fourth of July. She lived nearly as long as the fictional Rose. 2) The charcoal portrait of the young Rose in the nude, which Jack produces and is the story's romantic centerpiece, actually was done by Cameron, as were all of Jack's drawings. 3) The production crew built a nearly full-size reproduction of Titanic for the movie, but the enormous prop was complete only on its starboard side. So, for the entire opening flashback sequence, which shows Titanic docked on its port side, Cameron shot it and then reversed the images – meaning all the visible signs, lettering and even most of the clothing had to be painted and tailored in reverse to appear correctly. 4) Two ships associated with Titanic likewise met tragic fates. Its sister liner Britannic, launched in 1914, struck a mine and sunk two years later in the Aegean Sea during World War I. Carpathia, which rescued Titanic's survivors the next morning, was sunk by a German U-boat off the Irish coast in 1918] [Caution: sexuality and intense scenes of the sinking] **[W]**

46. Canicular Cinephilia

I invented this term for America's summer movie craze in an unpublished essay I had written about one of the titles below for The Washington Post in 1993. These eight, blockbusters all, combine thrills, laughs and some of the best-loved movie music ever, and audiences embraced them with great enthusiasm, starting with the attraction that ignited the phenomenon in 1975, when it took the country by storm, to the tune of more than 65 million tickets sold – among a population of 210 million or so.

Jaws [100]
1975 – Steven Spielberg
As I was walking out of the theater after introducing a friend to this movie, I noticed he was white as a sheet and looking distressed. When I asked him what was wrong, he said, "I grew up in Daytona Beach, Florida, and we used to go swimming in the ocean at night all the time. I had no idea there were things like *that* in the water!" Another friend heard the following remark as he left a theater after a screening, "Man, I've seen scary movies before, but goddamn!" Those were typical reactions among moviegoers during the summer of *Jaws*. It genuinely terrified people. They didn't know it at the time, but they were witnessing the beginning of a phenomenon: the summer blockbuster craze. *Jaws* launched a trend that has continued uninterrupted for nearly half a century, as people flock to the movies during the summer to be scared, thrilled, amused or tickled to death by the best effects, pop spectacle and silly comedy Hollywood can deploy. Everyone should know this particular story by now: A great white shark stakes out territory in the waters off the fictional New England island of Amity (it

433

was shot on Martha's Vineyard) and starts munching on swimmers. The local chief of police (Roy Scheider), a marine biologist (Richard Dreyfuss) and an obsessive shark hunter (Robert Shaw) set out to catch and kill the beast. They do find it but in the process get much more than they bargained for – hence, Scheider's character's famous quip, "You're gonna need a bigger boat." Spielberg and screenwriter Carl Gottlieb took Peter Benchley's rather pedestrian though bestselling novel and, with the help of veteran film editor Verna Fields, the brilliantly unnerving but thrilling music of John Williams, and the tremendously appealing performances of the three lead actors and the entire supporting cast, streamlined it into an express-train of a thriller. It grabs you from the first deep bass note of the score that made Williams a legendary composer – and about whom Spielberg wrote, "He has made our movie more adventurous, gripping and phobic than I ever thought possible." Some of the mechanical shark scenes seem dated in this age of CGI, but there's still no denying its power and sense of adventure – and its surprising amount of humor. Even now, over four decades later, it remains one of the very best of the summer blockbusters. [Viewing note: No question, *Jaws* sparked the summer movie blockbuster tradition, but the precise distinction should go to one riveting moment. The scene begins ordinarily enough, with two Amity Island locals rowing toward shore amid an early morning fog. Their plan is to catch the shark by attaching a large piece of raw meat to a steel hook connected by a length of heavy chain to a thick wooden column holding up a dock. The plan works. The shark takes the bait and begins swimming out to sea – but apparently is large and strong enough to rip away both the column and part of the dock and carrying one of the locals with it. Eventually, the man falls into the water and starts swimming back to shore. As soon as he does, the floating dock fragment swings around with a groan and pursues him. John Williams augments the action with the shark theme: three sets of four strong strokes by cellos. The first time I watched that scene, I and everyone else in the audience cringed or screamed at what we imagined was now chasing that vulnerable would-be shark hunter. For the rest of the movie, the tension and excitement kept on growing. Those twelve ominous notes changed cinema history] [Trivia notes: 1) Severe and prolonged problems with the array of mechanical sharks constructed for the movie pushed the shooting schedule to an unprecedented 159 days, wreaking havoc with morale among cast and crew alike, and at one point erupting in a cathartic food fight at a party. During much of that time, Spielberg was forced to film many of the scenes without the shark – which resulted in their being much more frightening to audiences because they preyed, so to speak, on the imagination. Hence, the scene with the two locals and the dock. 2) *Jaws* actually approximates a true story that had taken place nearly 60 years earlier when a (much smaller) great white shark staked out territory along the New Jersey shore and claimed five victims – including two children – before being caught and killed. 3) In the aftermath of *Jaws*, a worldwide frenzy of shark hunting began. Millions of the animals were killed. The phenomenon eventually prompted Benchley to initiate a personal campaign to help protect them. 4) The movie's role in sparking the summer movie craze wasn't entirely accidental. Universal Studios spent nearly a million dollars on TV ads for *Jaws*, a huge sum at the time. Also, the studio expanded the movie's bookings to nearly 500 theaters simultaneously – an unprecedented strategy – to create excitement nationwide. It worked. *Jaws* became a, excuse the pun, monster hit, quickly achieving the highest box-office gross in movie history, a distinction it held for two years before being superseded by *Star Wars*. 5) Spielberg once told how, when he first approached Williams about scoring the movie, he had in mind something like Williams's moody, creepy music for *Images* (not on this list), a Robert Altman mystery released three years earlier. When he suggested as much, Williams reportedly replied, "No, no, no, dear boy, this is a pirate movie!" He meant that the score should express high adventure and thrills as well as fear – which it does, in spades! 6) A second story about the movie's score: When Williams invited Spielberg to listen to what he had composed for *Jaws*, he began by playing the shark's theme with two fingers on the piano – including the long pauses at the beginning. Spielberg said his first reaction was to laugh, as if Williams was joking. But Williams assured him that the simple – "mechanical," as he put it – theme would work. Indeed, it did. 7) The movie's three sequels grew progressively more stupid and should be avoided at all costs] [Strong caution: As I described, this movie can frighten adults, so be *extremely* careful where children are concerned. My advice is to refrain from showing it to anyone under high school age] [Another viewing note: This might seem an odd thing to mention, but in the movie's DVD and Blu-ray releases, the Oscar-winning audio mix is often missing, including nearly all of the most distinctive, original sound effects. It's a subtle change. The missing or altered items include the sound of a tin can bouncing along a floor, a license plate being tossed onto the same floor, and the sounds of gunfire and mayhem from the shark. You might not care, unless you've heard and remember the originals, in which case the differences are obvious and grating. The good thing is you can still hear those sounds – but you have to select the monaural option on the disc's audio menu. Then you'll be able to listen to as well as see *Jaws* as it was originally presented] **[W]**

Star Wars [100]
1977 – George Lucas

Everyone thought *Jaws* would remain unchallenged at the box office for decades to come, but George Lucas surpassed it just two summers later and began what would become a multibillion-dollar franchise in the process. This remains one of the most fun-filled experiences ever to hit the big screen. I saw it the first day it opened, on May 25, 1977, and went back over and over again that summer, many of those times with my daughters Angela and Melissa, ages 7 and 6 at the time. During one screening, as it ended and we were listening to that spectacular John Williams theme over the credits, Melissa said to me, "Dad, the music makes me want to see it again!" Indeed, it did, to legions of fans. Now billed as *Episode IV: A New Hope* (because Lucas decided to start the story in middle, do two sequels, then return to the beginning), it is the saga of Luke Skywalker (Mark Hamill), Han Solo (Harrison Ford) and Princess Leia Organa (Carrie Fisher, the daughter of *Singin' in the Rain* star Debbie Reynolds). Along with a wise old Jedi Knight (Sir Alec Guinness), two comic robots named R2-D2 and C-3PO (performed, respectively, by Kenny Baker and Anthony Daniels), and an 8-foot-tall primate named Chewbacca (Peter Mayhew), the trio races to deliver the plans of a Death Star – a giant spaceship powerful enough to destroy a planet – to the leaders of the rebellion against the evil empire and its dreaded enforcer, Darth Vader (played in person by bodybuilder David Prowse and in voice by basso profundo James Earl Jones). Though several of the others in the series have gone on to surpass the original in box office receipts, this is still by far the best – and even when Lucas went back and attempted to update it by adding advanced computer graphics, he could not improve it. [Viewing note: *Star Wars*, as well as its first two sequels, suffers from the same condition that afflicted *Close Encounters of the Third Kind* for nearly three decades. Unless you're lucky enough to own one of the early VHS tape copies, you literally can't see *Star Wars* in its original form. Lucas eventually replaced it, and the middle trilogy's two sequels, with digitally remastered versions that include added effects. As a result, many fans (myself included) think the meddling only diminished the movies. In fact, there's a nifty 2010 documentary about the controversy, *The People vs. George Lucas*, which I'll cover in my second compilation] [Trivia note: As you watch and enjoy *Star Wars*, whether for the first time or the thirtieth, know that it was one of the most troubled productions in Hollywood history. The executives at Fox threatened to pull the plug several times, because they were aghast at how inept the dailies (the results on film of each day's shooting) looked, and how far behind schedule Lucas was falling. Lucas, meanwhile, developed a dangerous case of hypertension during his efforts to save the movie. Thank heaven he succeeded] **[W]**

The Empire Strikes Back
1980 – Irvin Kershner

I can't think of a more eagerly awaited movie sequel. The smashing debut of *Star Wars* three years earlier, and the news that more movies were in production, had created a buzz like no other anticipated screen reunion. Fans sat in long lines that in some cases began days before the movie was scheduled to open, on May 25, 1980, and producer George Lucas imposed tight security on the set to guard against premature leaks of plot surprises – including the big revelation about the relationship between Luke Skywalker and Darth Vader. Others might disagree – Gary Arnold, for example, thought this one surpassed *Star Wars* – but I don't think it matched the original. If it hadn't been such a huge summer hit, I would have placed it in the Flawed But Not Fatally category. The main reason is that it contains far less humor, and the acting (except for James Earl Jones as the voice of Vader, Alec Guinness as Obi-wan Kenobi and Frank Oz as the voice and animator of Yoda) is, to be kind, inadequate, as is most of the dialogue. Where it does exceed *Star Wars* is 1) in the John Williams score, which deepens and enriches his original suite. His new march for Darth Vader, and his themes for Yoda and Leia, are all unique and terrific, as are his revised orchestrations. And 2) the LucasFilm effects wizards created some unparalleled feats, including a thrilling battle on a snow-covered landscape (filmed in Norway) against giant land-walkers (actually highly detailed, stop-motion miniatures) and an escape by the Millennium Falcon through a teeming asteroid field. Lawrence Kasdan, not yet embarked on his own career as a director, wrote the screenplay along with Leigh Brackett, based on Lucas's original story. **[W]**

Raiders of the Lost Ark [100]
1981 – Steven Spielberg

Not since *The Crimson Pirate*, nearly 30 years earlier, has a movie offered such a rousing combination of thrills and humor. Spielberg had stumbled badly two years previously when he directed the disastrous *1941* (coming later), but he bounced back fully with this blockbuster adventure, written, like *The Empire Strikes Back*, by Lawrence Kasdan. The saga of Indiana Jones (Harrison Ford), part archaeologist and part soldier of fortune, begins with an action sequence that could qualify as the climax of many other movies. Somewhere in the Peruvian jungle in 1936, Jones is hot on the trail of a golden statue deemed sacred to the Hovito tribe. He finds it, after braving the (implausible) hazards of the treasure cave but then quickly loses it to rival treasure hunter Renee Belloq (Paul Freeman) before escaping from the angry natives. That's just prologue, however, because the rest of the movie involves Jones, on behalf of the U.S. government no less, attempting to track down the biggest find in archeological history: the lost Ark of the Covenant reputed to hold the original Ten Commandments. That effort results in several more hair-raising situations and pursuits – some of them shared with Marian Ravenwood (Karen Allen), an old and still-resentful flame – and though it's all comic-book adventure, conveyed by John Williams in his supremely popular score, there are nevertheless some intense scenes, so be careful about showing this one to young children. [Trivia notes: 1) In the crowd-pleasing bit when Indiana dispatches his sword-bearing attacker, the script had originally called for him to fight the larger man with his ever-present bullwhip. But the filming took place late in the day, and Ford was visibly tired, so he asked Spielberg, "Can't I just shoot him?" 2) Actor Vic Tablian holds a unique distinction here, playing two different characters in the same movie: the would-be treacherous Barranca in the opening sequence as well as the "Monkey Man" later on] [Caution: some intense and scary scenes] **[W]**

Ghostbusters
1984 – Ivan Reitman
"What a rollicking good time that was!" That's a line from the movie, but not the theatrical version. Reitman shot several scenes twice and included milder versions of the dialogue for the inevitable TV release. Nevertheless, it captures the spirit perfectly. The biggest hit of that summer, the story concerns

three languishing academics (Bill Murray, Dan Aykroyd and Harold Ramis – the latter two of whom collaborated on the screenplay) who attempt to make their fortune by capturing ghosts but unwittingly set the powers of darkness loose on New York City. It's all done entirely for fun, following Murray's lead as someone who cannot take the topic seriously. There's even a homage to the late John Belushi in the form of a gluttonous spirit; and the monstrous force that ultimately threatens the city is … well, you might call him the Pillsbury Doughboy's gigantic evil twin. Elmer Bernstein did the amusing score, including the title song sung by Ray Parker, which topped the year's charts. Sigourney Weaver is appealing as Murray's love interest, as is Rick Moranis as her dopey neighbor who becomes possessed by a demon. Go on – get slimed! The only (slightly) down note: portrayal of the chaos caused by ghosts running amok in the city recalls the real tragedy of the terror attacks on September 11, 2001. [Trivia notes: 1) Speaking of Belushi, he was cast as one of the Ghostbusters before his sudden and untimely death. So was Eddie Murphy, but he eventually opted to do *Trading Places* instead, teaming with Aykroyd. 2) The original version of that line of dialogue I mentioned above? "We came, we saw, we kicked its ass!"] [Caution: adult language and one sexual reference] [W]

Back to the Future
1985 – Robert Zemeckis
This entertaining and appealing time-travel comedy marks the first movie in which Zemeckis relied on special effects and elaborate staging, and he showed a masterful touch in both areas right out of the blocks. The biggest box-office hit of the year and the first of three episodes, the story concerns high school student Marty McFly (Michael J. Fox) and his friendship with the town's eccentric genius, "Doc" Emmett Brown (Christopher Lloyd). Asked to help Doc perform a secret experiment one night – it turns out he has invented a time machine installed in a De Lorean sports car – Marty suddenly finds himself pursued by murderous Libyan terrorists and is forced to seek refuge 30 years

in the past. There, in an attempt to seek a younger (but not younger-looking) Doc, Marty also meets his parents and possibly disrupts their meeting and eventual mating – meaning he has inadvertently threatened his own existence. The rest of the story involves the two friends attempting to set things right and get Marty … back to the future. Of course, that process is not without its hitches. Much of the humor derives from looking back at 1955 to see how different some things were and how Marty reacts to the changes. It's a consistently witty and clever movie, and the time-travel sequences are deceptively sophisticated. They involve a mix of live elements, old-fashioned hand-drawn animation in the form of electrical sparks and lightning strikes – enhanced in the film-printing process – which convey a sense that the forces of nature are being distorted by the time machine. The driving, orchestral score is by Alan Silvestri, but there's also a funny cameo appearance by Huey Lewis, and his rock band, The News, contributed two songs to the soundtrack, the main title theme and "Back in Time," performed over the end credits. [Trivia notes: 1) The producers also used time as an element of sorts in the movie's casting. The characters include Fox as Marty; Crispin Glover as his father, George; Lea Thompson as his mother, Lorraine; Marc McClure and Wendy Jo Sperber as his brother and sister, Dave and Linda; plus Thomas F. Wilson as Biff the bully. But in real life, all of the actors were in their twenties, with McClure the oldest at 28, followed by Sperber at 27, Wilson at 26, Fox and Thompson at 24, and Glover the youngest at 21. 2) Speaking of casting, all movies involve elements that have been changed or discarded (e.g., the original time machine resembled a refrigerator and rode on the back of a truck), but one created an exceptional challenge. Eric Stoltz had played Marty McFly for the first six weeks of shooting, until Zemeckis replaced him with Fox. That meant either reshooting everything or – which is what happened – skillfully and carefully inserting new shots of Fox where necessary but retaining original footage where possible. As a result, if you study the images closely you might notice some of the shots are of Stoltz] [Caution: language] **[W]**

Jurassic Park [100]
1993 – Steven Spielberg

Spielberg's career hit the doldrums after 1987, following the release of his masterful *Empire of the Sun*. He directed three lackluster attractions in a row – *Indiana Jones and the Last Crusade, Always* and *Hook* (none on this list) – but *Jurassic Park* immediately re-established his place at the top of popular American moviemaking. Based on Michael Crichton's bestselling novel, the story concerns an ambitious attempt by a visionary business tycoon (Sir Richard Attenborough) to create the ultimate amusement park, an island off the Central American coast where live dinosaurs roam. He almost pulls it off, but the whole scheme turns into a nightmare and a cautionary tale about trying to control nature. The cast includes Sam Neill as a bookish paleontologist, Laura Dern as his field partner and love interest, Jeff Goldblum as a skeptical and wisecracking mathematician, and Samuel L. Jackson and Wayne Knight (Newman on the TV series Seinfeld) as computer geeks. But the real stars are the computer-generated and robotic dinosaurs. They are totally believable and therefore totally terrifying, particularly the Tyrannosaurus rex and the velociraptors, who match the shark in *Jaws* as villainous movie creatures. Spielberg applied the same winning formula here, including a lofty score by John Williams, alternating periods of terror with emotion-releasing incidents of humor. He also directed the sequel in 1997 and produced a third movie in 2001, but neither matched the excitement and entertainment value of the original. [Trivia note: Most of the movie's exteriors were shot on the Hawai`ian island of Kaua`i – including the magnificent Napali cliffs. Near the end of production, Kaua`i was hit by a hurricane that trapped the entire 140-person crew on the island for several days. Spielberg said the hurricane, named Iniki, caused "the worst devastation I had ever personally witnessed," and he eventually worked a brief storm sequence into the script] [Caution: Even though the movie features children as characters, it contains intensely frightening scenes. That said; chances are the kids will love this story, and one way to dissipate the frightening aspects is to show them the

442

featurette on the DVD that describes how Spielberg and his crew created the dazzling dinos by computer animation and highly detailed, full-size models] **[W]**

Men in Black
1997 – Barry Sonnenfeld

We humans go about our business oblivious to the fact that, every day, some 1500 extraterrestrials inhabit our planet, most of them peaceful but some mortally threatening. To manage and sometimes combat the alien influx, we need a super-secret organization run independently of our government. That's the movie's premise, and it turns out to be thoroughly entertaining. Tommy Lee Jones, updating his Sam Girard character from *The Fugitive*, recruits a streetwise but rough-around-the-edges New York City cop (Will Smith in a terrific performance) to help track down a dangerous and seemingly invincible alien (Vincent D'Onofrio) walking around inside the skin of one of his victims, a brute of a farmer named Edgar. The "bug," as the alien is called, is after the "galaxy," a mysterious object that could spark an interstellar war and endanger Earth's existence. Along the way, Jones and Smith, as Agents "Kay" and "Jay," encounter a pawn broker (Tony Shalhoub) whose body parts instantly regenerate after being shot off, the pregnant wife of an alien giving birth, two normal-looking aliens who turn out to be not what they appear, and a beautiful pathologist (Linda Fiorentino) who runs the city morgue. Under Sonnenfeld's snappy direction and Ed Solomon's wiseacre script, you've got a couple of hours of great fun. Danny Elfman contributes the intricately hip score. [Trivia notes: 1) D'Onofrio developed Edgar the Bug's distinctive walk by wearing knee braces and taping his ankles. 2) The movie contains two connections to, of all things, *Dr. Strangelove* (coming in the next compilation). One, the titles – looking as though they were drawn with chalk by hand on a blackboard – were done by Pablo Ferro, who used the same style for the earlier movie. And two, D'Onofrio said he based his movements as Edgar on Peter Sellers in his portrayal of the eponymous doctor] [Caution: sexual references and slimy violence] **[W]**

47. Superior Sequels

If there is a reliable rule in choosing movies, it's that sequels almost always become pale renditions of their predecessors. I said "almost," because here are four examples that go against that overwhelming trend.

The Godfather Part II [100]
1974 – Francis Ford Coppola

It might be hard to believe the sequel to *The Godfather* could surpass its progenitor, but *Part II* does. As Pauline Kael wrote, the sequel both "enlarges the scope and deepens the meaning of the first film," and it "shows the consequences of the actions in the first." I think it does more. It actually punishes the audience for growing so comfortable with the fundamentally monstrous deeds of the primary characters. To be fair, *Part II* is not a standard sequel; it's really a seamless extension, in simultaneously opposite temporal directions, of the original story, combining both movies into one epic history of a particularly violent American family. It begins in Sicily at the turn of the 20th century, where young Vito Corleone's father and older brother have been murdered by Don Ciccio, the local warlord. We then follow Vito to America, where he grows to young manhood (portrayed by Robert De Niro in his first Oscar-winning role), and it depicts his transformation from quiet family man to avenger and then to Godfather. At the same time, intermittently, we follow Michael Corleone (Al Pacino, reprising his role) in his struggle to maintain control over his family despite an assassination attempt and a dangerous rivalry with Jewish mobster Hyman Roth (played by the legendary Lee Strasberg). Sequel or not, this is one of the truly great American movies. Approaching a half-century after its release, it stands as Coppola's masterpiece, a savage portrait of a family gone horribly wrong. In fact, it's so skillful that the final scene, which contains no violence, is probably the most shocking of all, because it confronts the audience with the magnitude of the tragic journey the Corleones have undertaken. Winner of six Oscars, including Best Picture, the movie is graced by Nino Rota's refined score based on the original. It won the composer an Oscar (he was nominated for *The Godfather* but did not win), which he shared with Carmine Coppola, the director's father. [Technical note: This was the last movie ever to be shot in the classic Technicolor process, and although its colors are subdued, they are unfaded by time. Today, digital processing can maintain and restore colors, but Technicolor was a glorious and unique resource, and anyone who saw movies in that format in theaters will never forget them] [Trivia notes: 1) Six of Strasberg's Actors Studio protégés appear in this movie. Along with Pacino (who was joined by Marlon Brando, the studio's most famous alumnus, in the first movie) and De Niro, there's Robert Duvall, playing Michael's foster brother and consigliere, Tom Hagen; Michael V. Gazzo as fellow mobster, Frankie Pentangeli; Bruno Kirby as the young Clemenza in De Niro's scenes; and Marianna Hill, a veteran of more than 80 movie and TV roles – and a drama teacher herself – as Fredo Corleone's gorgeous but slutty wife, Deanna. 2) Regarding Gazzo, he was a successful last-minute casting insert when Richard Castellano, who played Peter Clemenza in the original, bowed out of the sequel over creative differences with Coppola. 3) Pacino, John Cazale (who plays Michael's weak-willed brother Fredo) and Dominic Chianese (playing Hyman Roth's associate Johnny Ola) all worked together the following year in Sidney Lumet's shattering drama, *Dog Day Afternoon*. In that movie, Cazale played the more menacing character, and Chianese played Pacino's father. 4) Fifties teen heartthrob Troy Donahue, who plays a minor role as the erstwhile fiancé of Michael's sister Connie (Talia Shire, Coppola's real-life sister), was an old schoolmate of the director] [Caution: graphic violence, sexuality and rough language] **[W]**

Aliens [100]
1986 – James Cameron

Ridley Scott's original was all shock and terror, but Cameron's sequel is intense thrills, suspense and a surprising amount of humor. The title is appropriate; the original contained only one creature, while this one features dozens if not hundreds – including the big momma of the species. The movie's teaser line was "This time, it's personal," and that's what unfolds as Ripley (Sigourney Weaver), awakened after 57 years of hibernation, must return to the planet where she first encountered the monster to help save a bunch of presumably stranded colonists. Ripley is accompanied on the mission by a platoon of tough mercenaries called colonial marines, all colorful, appealing, incredibly courageous characters. The cast features Michael Biehn (Sarah Connor's rescuer in Cameron's *The Terminator*) and Bill Paxton (star of Cameron's *Titanic*) as lovable grunts, and Al Matthews as their cigar-chomping sergeant; Lance Henriksen as a most valuable android and Jenette Goldstein in a sensational performance as a fearless woman marine. Likewise, 10-year-old Carrie Henn makes an impressive debut as a young refugee. But the show belongs to Weaver, whose Ripley remains arguably the greatest movie heroine ever. Talk about getting "back on the horse," as she's advised early on. Driven by her maternal instinct, when she overcomes her fear Ripley is relentless no matter the threat. Cameron gives her several hairbreadth escapes plus two spectacular duels with the alien queen, including one going *mano a mano* with the creature via robotic limbs. Both are heart-stopping and represent the finest effort of Cameron's crew to create unprecedented illusions. Sci-fi thriller or not, Weaver and Goldstein are so good they both deserved acting Oscars. James Horner contributed the overpowering score. It's a great ride! [Caution: profanity and scenes of intense suspense] **[W]**

Back to the Future Part III
1990 – Robert Zemeckis

Part one of this trilogy was a lighthearted romp, and part two (not on this list) was a dud, but the third and last installment of the saga of Marty McFly (Michael J. Fox) and the time machine just soars. It's the most fun, cleverest and friendliest of the lot. In this unlikely but triumphant finale, Marty must travel back a hundred years to the Old West version of Hill Valley, his fictional hometown, to rescue "Doc" Emmett Brown (Christopher Lloyd) and see if they finally can put right what they threw out of whack at the beginning of the series. There they meet 1) Buford "Mad Dog" Tannen (Thomas F. Wilson), ancestor of Biff Tannen (also played by Wilson), the high-school bully in the original; and 2) Clara Clayton (Mary Steenburgen), a teacher who becomes the love of Doc's life. As in the first two installments, each time Marty revisits Hill Valley in a different timeframe we get to see specific elements of the town and how they appeared in that era – and the effect grows funnier as the trilogy progresses. What's different here, as mentioned, is a sweeter temperament, a strong bond between the two main characters and a genuinely thrilling climax involving an attempt to use a speeding locomotive to get Marty and Doc once again ... back to the future. It's a fine wrap-up to the comedy fantasy, with an updated score by Alan Silvestri that includes thrilling western themes. [Trivia notes: 1) Wilson, whose "Mad Dog" persona is truly menacing (this is his best performance of the three), is in real life a gentleman of religious faith and a hardworking TV actor with more than 100 appearances to his credit. Here, he also displays his horsemanship – and lassoing – skills as he does most of his riding and roping himself. 2) The story makes liberal use of the name "Clint Eastwood." Rather than get themselves in deep Dutch with the real guy, the producers asked his permission, which he immediately gave, along with his later compliments at how well the movie turned out. 3) Bit-player Hugh Gillan portrayed Hill Valley's mayor in 1885, but the original choice for the role was none other than Ronald Reagan. The former president and veteran screen actor reluctantly turned the part down, however, because at that point his health had begun to deteriorate. 4) Playing the three saloon regulars in the Old West sequences were Pat Buttram, Dub Taylor and Harry Carey Jr., whose combined appearances in real westerns, screen and TV, numbered in the hundreds] [Caution: language and mild violence] **[W]**

The Bourne Supremacy
2004 – Paul Greengrass
The first installment of the Jason Bourne saga introduced Matt Damon as a CIA-trained, invincible killing machine. It was as good as the genre gets – except that this one exceeds it on almost every level, including Damon's performance, which is excellent. Bourne, still on the run and still unsure of his identity, is now being hunted by a Russian assassin (Karl Urban as a murderous secret policeman) as well as the agency's operatives both overt and covert, and led by Pamela Landy (Joan Allen), who's genuinely trying to uncover what happened to Bourne and the whole fiasco that was the Treadstone program. The action, threats, thrills and escapes proceed from Goa, India, to Venice and then to Berlin, and finally to Moscow, where the suspense builds to an absolutely heart-pounding car chase through the city's crowded streets that dwarfs the chase through Paris in *The Bourne Identity*. It rivals even the immortal one in *The French Connection*. And like the sequel to *The Godfather*, this one deepens and enriches the whole story, borne – forgive the pun – by John Powell's sophisticated pulsing, moody score. Director Greengrass, taking over from Doug Liman in the original, shows skill and assurance galore. Suspense thrillers don't get any better. Franka Potente, Brian Cox and Julia Stiles reprise their roles. [Viewing note: Yes, this one was superior to its terrific predecessor, but from here on it was all downhill, even with Greengrass at the helm for *The Bourne Ultimatum* in 2007 and *Jason Bourne* in 2016 (neither here). Ditto Tony Gilroy's misbegotten *The Bourne Legacy* in 2012 (with Jeremy Renner stepping in, temporarily, for Matt Damon). The series just seemed to fall off the rails and grow increasingly wrongheaded] [Trivia note: Given the speed and intensity of the hand-to-hand combat scenes, accidents were bound to happen. In one case, Damon actually knocked fellow actor Tim Griffin unconscious during an interrogation scene] [Caution: violence] **[W]**

48. <u>Only</u> on the Big Screen!

Out of my entire list, trust me on these four titles. Avoid trying to watch them on your TV – and for heaven's sake don't even think about viewing them on your computer monitor or phone. Hold out for a theater experience wherever you might find it. You won't regret it.

Lawrence of Arabia [100]
1962 – David Lean
Two reasons why this movie should only be seen on theater-sized screens – and the largest of those, at that: 1) It is arguably the greatest movie ever made and therefore demands the effort and patience of viewing it in a theater, and 2) There are scenes where the landscape is so vast that the objects of attention literally shrink to invisibility unless the image is big enough. But those are technicalities. The main reason is if you don't see it large, you can't appreciate how visually overwhelming it is. This is not only David Lean's masterpiece, it's a moviemaking masterpiece for all time. In the entire history of the cinema, nothing else has ever matched its sweep and scope. If you have seen some of the computer-generated epics of the late 20th and early 21st centuries, and then see this, my guess is those later features will suddenly pale into insignificance, because every bit of scenery and panorama in *Lawrence of Arabia* (except for one, very brief shot) is real. As Orson Welles did with *Citizen Kane*, Lean launched the dreams and careers of a new generation of moviemakers with this monumental work. He and his crew spent *two years* in the deserts of Jordan, Morocco and elsewhere shooting *Lawrence*, and their patience and skills show magnificently. It's based on the true story of Thomas Edward

("T.E.") Lawrence, a well-educated commoner serving with the British Army in Cairo during World War I. Fluent in Arabic, he is sent to the Arabian Desert to assess the status of the Arab revolt against the Turks (who were allied with Germany in the war). There, through a series of twists, which are brilliantly dramatized by Lean and screenwriter Robert Bolt – and breathtakingly depicted by cinematographer Freddie Young – Lawrence conquers a Turkish stronghold at the Red Sea port of Aqaba. From that point on, he ascends into legend and, as some historians think, descends into madness. There are so many memorable scenes and stunning images it would be futile to try to list them all. Instead, be patient. Wait for the opportunity to view *Lawrence of Arabia* in a movie theater with a big, wide screen, a state-of-the-art sound system and preferably 70-millimeter projection. Then, you can appreciate shots where the desert's vastness swallows a caravan crossing it; where a gun belt dropped at the lower left corner of the screen is countered by its former wearer heading off at the upper right; where that individual, walking in the early morning, casts a shadow nearly a hundred feet long; where a man stands at the base of a cliff face so large you can barely see him; where a man on a camel approaches from a mile away on a desert path barely visible but unmistakable; and where an army of mounted Arabs heading off to battle is dwarfed by massive rocky cliffs. There are many more, equally dramatic moments. With Peter O'Toole in his incomparable debut in the title role – which represents yet another slight by the motion picture academy, because he did not win Best Actor – and Omar Sharif making a striking debut of his own (nominated for Best Supporting Actor but likewise not winning); Alec Guinness and Anthony Quinn as totally believable Arab sheikhs; Jack Hawkins as the gruff but pragmatic British general, Allenby; Claude Rains in a minor but witty turn as a crafty diplomat, and Arthur Kennedy standing in for real-life journalist Lowell Thomas as a world-weary reporter. Maurice Jarre's thunderous score – his first of four collaborations with Lean – brings the whole effort to perfection. [Trivia notes: 1) For the scene in which Omar Sharif seems to appear out of a mirage, approaching on a camel, Lean brought in truckload after truckload of sand of a slightly different color than the surrounding desert to draw the viewer's attention to the figure in the distance. 2) Many film buffs – me included – consider the scene where Lawrence blows out a lit match to be the greatest transitional device in all of cinema. It's breathtaking! 3) Soon after the movie's release, the geniuses at Columbia Pictures decided its 222-minute running time was too long, so they ordered two cut-downs for subsequent showings. As the years passed, some of the audio recordings of the dialogue were lost. So in 1987, for the movie's 25th anniversary, when film archivist Robert A. Harris restored *Lawrence* to its original length, the process required O'Toole, Guinness and others to re-record some of their performances. If you have a keen ear, you'll be able to tell where the new material was placed – and if your eye is keen as well you'll notice several places where film inserts could not be matched. 4) In the scene where the soldier on a motorcycle yells across the Suez Canal, "Who are you? Who are you?" the voice is Lean's. 5) For all of Lean's attention to detail, his brilliant portrait of T.E. Lawrence and the Arab revolt omitted one important historical figure who played a major role in the events – and she's a woman! Gertrude Bell was a British scholar who actually spent more time with the Arabs than did Lawrence, and she was even more of a fervent defender. She was highly instrumental in constructing the landscape of the new Middle East after the war. In fact, she's been called "The Woman Who Made Iraq." There's even a famous photo of her sitting between Lawrence and Winston Churchill at a postwar conference in Cairo] [Caution: shocking battle violence and some mild sexual innuendoes] [W]

Doctor Zhivago [100]
1965 – David Lean

Lean's follow-up to *Lawrence of Arabia* is a gorgeous visual extravaganza, an immense production and a sweeping story as well. The time frame is nearly the same – around World War I – but the location is Russia during the beginning of the Bolshevik revolution. Based on Boris Pasternak's novel – and told in flashback – it follows the life of Yuri Andreievich Zhivago (Omar Sharif), an orphaned young man of eastern Asian heritage who is taken in by an aristocratic Moscow couple, the Gromekos (Sir Ralph Richardson and Siobhan McKenna). He eventually marries his adopted sister, Tonya (Geraldine Chaplin; Charlie Chaplin's daughter – who radiates her father's face whenever she smiles) and becomes popular as a poet. Then, later on, he meets the love of his life, Lara (Julie Christie at her most beautiful), daughter of a seamstress who begins her young adulthood by becoming involved in two consecutive and disastrous relationships: one with a sophisticated but conniving raconteur (Rod Steiger, in the same year of his Oscar-nominated performance for *The Pawnbroker* – coming in a future compilation – and two years before winning the Best Actor Oscar for *In the Heat of the Night*), and the other with an idealistic but misguided revolutionary (Tom Courtney). Like the novel, the movie portrays one man's struggle to live an ordinary private life when historical events are driving an entire nation into chaos and desperation. Robert Bolt contributed a streamlined script that skillfully reduces complex situations to memorable single sentences, and Maurice Jarre's gorgeously romantic score is his most famous, including the title number, "Somewhere My Love." Like *Lawrence*, this movie is absolutely full of indelible images of seemingly endless vistas (once again shot by Freddie Young), which is why you must see it on the biggest screen possible – and boy, will you be glad you did! [Trivia notes: 1) Pasternak's dense, rambling novel took almost 50 years to complete. The finished version could not be published in the Soviet Union, so a manuscript was smuggled out, and the first edition appeared in Italy in 1957. Though the novel won the Nobel Prize for literature the following year, Pasternak was forced to decline the award. He died in 1960, before Doctor Zhivago became the worldwide sensation that inspired the movie. 2) Lean shot *Zhivago* in Finland and in Spain, where he actually recreated a full-sized Moscow street, which he re-dressed repeatedly to reflect the passage of years as the story progressed. 3) Though many of the snow scenes are real, some were simulated by using beeswax or soap chips, such as the haunting interior of the family's country home at Varykino, or the thrilling cavalry charge across a supposedly frozen lake, which actually was a field overlain with steel plates and covered with marble dust. 4) For Sharif, an Egyptian, to play the Russian Zhivago, he had to undergo a painful daily makeover involving a straight-haired wig and elastic bands pulling back the skin of his face to hide his Arabic features. 5) I admit this one is far fetched, Lean never mentioned it and, far as I know, no one else has ever raised the point. Julie Christie in *Doctor Zhivago* bears an uncanny resemblance in both face and facial expressions to Peter O'Toole in *Lawrence of Arabia*] [Caution: violence, sexual themes, and mild profanity] [W]

2001: A Space Odyssey [100]
1968 – Stanley Kubrick

Kubrick's science fiction masterpiece is so slow-paced that it takes over 25 minutes before someone utters the first line of dialogue, "Here we are, sir." In fact, dialogue in this movie is almost non-existent. There are long periods containing only music, or the breathing of astronauts in spacesuits, or sometimes no sound at all. As a result, many people who have seen *2001* only on television don't think much of it. That's because its impact can only be appreciated on a theater-sized screen where, paradoxically, the movie's periods of utter silence can be overwhelming. Likewise, the widescreen compositions are so detailed and dramatic that only the big screen can do them justice. Based on Sir Arthur C. Clarke's short story "The Sentinel," the movie involves the discovery and consequences of apparent alien involvement in the emergence of we humans and our eventual destiny. It presents an arresting vision of how far humans would have been developed by the beginning of the 21st century. Despite all of the improvements in special effects over the decades, this remains the one movie that really *does* seem to take place in outer space, and the space it portrays is, properly, a cold, lonely, alien and silent environment. The achievement is all the more impressive given that CGI was nowhere to be found when the *2001* team began production, in the mid-1960s. Even the supposed computer-graphic displays had to be created via animation and optical photo techniques. I liken the accomplishment to the SR-71, the fabled "Black Bird" reconnaissance aircraft developed earlier in the decade by aeronautical engineers who likewise lacked computers to design and test the plane. Nevertheless, they created an aircraft that set performance records unmatched to this day. The same with *2001*. Much has been made about the end sequence, in which the last surviving astronaut of a deep-space mission is taken on a journey by unknown hands across undetermined distances to an unidentifiable destination. Still mesmerizing, it is also perhaps the one part of the movie now showing its age – that and the hairstyles of the women. But it's a minor complaint. After half a century, *2001: A Space Odyssey* remains alone atop the genre. [Trivia notes: 1) *2001*'s slow pace was mirrored – and magnified – by the movie's production. Kubrick's meticulousness translated into extreme care in the preparation for every shot. For example, before the cameras rolled film, Kubrick would take as many as 50 Polaroid still photos of the set to make sure the lighting produced the desired exposure. The efforts paid off, because along with *Lawrence of Arabia*, *2001* is probably the most perfectly shot movie ever made. 2) For all its expansiveness, every scene (with one brief exception) in *2001* was shot on sound stages, including the early sequence that ostensibly takes place on the African savanna with humanoid apes. 3) Most people are shocked to learn that none of the indelibly haunting music in the movie's score was original, because it seemed to fit the mood of each scene perfectly. Along with the now-famous main title theme, "Thus Spake Zarathustra" by Richard Strauss, and "The Blue Danube" by Johann Strauss, Kubrick selected the music from existing compositions, including the "Gayane Ballet Suite" by Armenian composer Aram Khachaturian. It remains possibly the greatest musical interpretation of loneliness ever written. James Cameron used it for the opening sequence of *Aliens*. 4) Here's another surprising item. Despite the fact that 2001 focuses on only four major characters, the cast is almost shockingly large: more than 60 performers in various roles – and you'll understand why I used the term "performers" when you see it. 5) *2001* was portrayed as correct as 1960s science and technology could make it – except for one scene. Just before David Bowman attempts to reenter the Discovery spacecraft without his helmet, he takes a deep breath. The problem is that doing so before entering the vacuum of space could cause the air in your lungs to burst through your chest. If you're ever in a similar situation, scientists advise taking several deep breaths but then expelling the air from your lungs. [Caution: ape violence and a few mild utterances of profanity] [**W**]

Never Cry Wolf [100]
1983 – Carroll Ballard

Here's another one that can't be fully appreciated on the small screen. Many of its sequences are so visually striking, yet virtually silent, that only a theater-like experience can properly convey their majesty. This little-known feature from the director of *The Black Stallion* is one of the most haunting movies ever made – the Los Angeles Times critic called it "hypnotic," and I agree. Based on Farley Mowat's autobiographical novel, it relates the experiences of a biologist named Tyler (Charles Martin Smith, who played Terry the Toad in *American Graffiti*) investigating the behavior of wolves in the Canadian Arctic. Other than Brian Dennehy, who portrays Rosie, a colorful bush pilot, the only other significant characters are two Inuits, performed by two wonderful actors, Samson Jorah as Mike, a young man caught between two cultures; and Zachary Ittimangnaq as Ootek, an elder who serves as Tyler's *Deus ex machina* and who proves as wise as the Arctic summer days are long. As in Ballard's other great movie, the real stars are the land and the wild creatures – in this case the wolves. Ballard has an uncanny knack for giving them personalities without anthropomorphizing them. He also spent a very long time developing the sequences, shooting almost 750,000 feet of film with his skilled cinematographer Hiro Narita, and shooting every single day for a month to capture one brief but extremely complex scene. The results are spectacular. The movie's other delightful aspect is its surprising amount of humor, which actually serves to deepen the pathos you eventually feel for Tyler and for the creatures he is charged with studying, and whose fate his presence influences. <u>Example</u>: Tyler's mission is to determine how much effect the wolves are having on the size of the caribou herds. The problem is there are no caribou near the pack he is observing. The question, then, is what are the wolves eating? He thinks he knows, but there's no way to tell, unless he performs an experiment, and … well, let's just say the results would horrify a certain famous Walt Disney character, but they produce the movie's biggest laughs. Mark Isham wrote the deeply evocative, synthesized score. [<u>Trivia note</u>: By far the most complex and expensive part of the movie is the sequence where Tyler must run amid a stampeding herd of caribou. Lasting only a few minutes on screen, it took a full month of seven-days-a-week effort to shoot] [<u>Caution</u>: some intense scenes, both depicted and implied, involving animals, and two brief glimpses of non-sexual male nudity] **[W]**

49. Little Gems

We go from expansive panoramas to the cockles of the heart. Certain movies seem like delicate Christmas ornaments, bright and twinkly but so fragile that a sudden puff of air could blow them away. The three-dozen titles in this category – my second-largest – are just such ornaments. None is what you might call a great work, although quite a few have become classics. Yet all are easy to love and savor. You might see how a misplaced scene or even a line of dialogue could have caused any of them to fall apart, but I hope you'll agree they all hold together well enough to satisfy you. Each delivers a pleasant time and, here and there, a memorable experience, and each offers a welcome opportunity for you to while away a rainy afternoon or chilly evening. Incidentally, several of the earliest movies from in this category became inspirations for remakes in later years – alas, almost all of them inferior. I've noted those later titles where applicable.

Safety Last
1923 – <u>Produced</u> by Hal Roach
In the history of movies (yes, I know, I've repeated that phrase a lot, but sometimes it's the best way to describe a particular title's unique quality), nothing else, except perhaps *Jaws*, has delivered such a potent combination of laughs and screams. This one, wrapped in the gentle persona of enduring silent-screen star Harold Lloyd, begins with the simplest of plots. A country bumpkin arrives in the big city to make his fortune so he can marry his sweetheart, but he quickly gets bogged down in a nothing job with an obnoxious boss. His troubles worsen when he learns his sweetheart has arrived in town to see what she believes is his newfound success – because he has been disguising his true fate from her in his letters. Desperate to avoid humiliation, he concocts a spectacular publicity stunt meant to enhance his standing with his employer and win a handsome sum of cash. Naturally, it backfires, requiring him to attempt a

freestanding climb to the top of a 16-story building. That 18-minute climb, which Lloyd does largely for real, remains to this day one of the most unnerving sequences ever filmed – yet it's done with humor as well as thrills. Even more astounding, Lloyd had lost his right thumb and forefinger four years earlier in an accident, so he ascended the building with only three fingers on his right hand, wearing a prosthetic glove to hide his disability. This one's perfectly fine for kids – as long as they understand they should never try this at home. [Trivia note: Lloyd created much of the illusion that he was climbing up a building high above a city street – which he did entirely without a stunt double – by using clever camera angles. Nevertheless, the feat involved considerable risk and remains an impressive achievement, these 95 years later] **[B&W] [Silent]**

Love Me Tonight
1932 – Rouben Mamoulian
This early musical is amazingly delightful and a clear example of why Maurice Chevalier became such a big star in the early 1930s – and why the Production Code that governed movie content for so many years was so often silly. The opening number is unlike any other I can think of: It's a collection of ordinary sounds of a city awakening that quickly congeals into a rhythmic suite by the team of Richard Rodgers and Lorenz Hart called "That's the Song of Paree." The simple plot involves a Parisian tailor (Chevalier) who becomes smitten with the beautiful Princess Jeanette (Jeanette MacDonald – another major star of the period), except he calls her "Mimi," which allows him to launch into one of the songs that made him famous. There's also the classic "Isn't It Romantic?" which has lyrics that run from the sarcastic to the truly romantic – something I never understood until seeing it performed here. All in all, it's a lovely time. **[B&W]**

To Be or Not to Be
1942 – Ernst Lubitsch
In another nearly perfect little comedy from Lubitsch – the director of *Ninotchka* and *The Shop Around the Corner* – Jack

458

Benny stars as "that great, great Polish actor Joseph Tura," as he calls himself, and Carole Lombard co-stars as his gorgeous but not entirely faithful wife. The movie was a flop when released in 1942, because it poked fun at Adolph Hitler and his conquest of Poland, and because Lombard had been killed in a plane crash before its release. Now, in historical perspective, it's a gentle and delightfully witty satire, with comedian Benny in fine form. [Trivia note: Clark Gable, who had married Lombard in 1939 and by all accounts was devoted to her, became inconsolable after her death at age 33. He soon joined the U.S. Army Air Forces and flew combat missions as a gunner in a B-17 bomber over Germany] [Remake: The same title, released in 1983 and starring Mel Brooks and Ann Bancroft. It was a pale imitation – and not included here] **[B&W]**

Sitting Pretty
1948 – Walter Lang
Admittedly a trifle but amusing and charming, it's the movie that introduced the character of Mr. Belvedere, who appeared in two sequels and later a TV series, and who has been portrayed by several different actors over the years. Maureen O'Hara and Robert Young play Harry and Tacey (no misspelling) King, a young married couple living in the fictional suburb of Hummingbird Hill with their three little boys. And those boys present quite a challenge to their parade of nannies. Frustrated, Tacey takes out an ad in The Saturday Review magazine for a live-in household helper and is delighted when a seemingly perfect individual responds, one Lynn Belvedere. When Lynn turns out to be a man (played with relish by Clifton Webb), well, the laughs begin. How Mr. Belvedere manages to overcome gender bias, and the town gossips, led by chief gossip Clarence Appleton (played with matching relish by Richard Haydn), how he turns out to be a perfect caretaker of the boys (including one scene that should have any parent cheering who has ever been frustrated by the breakfast-table behavior of their toddler) and sets all of Hummingbird Hill atwitter is a treat to watch. **[B&W]**

It Happens Every Spring
1949 – Lloyd Bacon

The premise might seem completely silly: Ray Milland plays Vernon K. Simpson, a rather dull college professor and chemist who's trying to win the hand of his fiancée, Deborah (Jean Peters), straight-laced daughter of a straight-laced family. One day a baseball crashes through his lab window and wrecks an experiment he has been working on for months. Then, with the help of some brilliant and deceptively simple special effects, Simpson discovers that the baseball, which he finds lying in a tub of chemicals, repels wood. Let me restate that. It *really* repels wood! At the same time, he hears on the radio that the St. Louis baseball team is perhaps one good pitcher away from reaching the World Series. You can guess the rest. Simpson tries out for the Cardinals under the assumed name of Kelly and wows the coaching staff, so he begins pitching while trying to keep hidden both his chemical secret and his real identity – not wanting Deborah's family to discover he's sunk to becoming a sports professional. Yes, it's slight (and not really about baseball, which is why I didn't list it in the Men at Play category), but the pitching scenes are amusing, and the story is diverting. Reliable veteran character actor Paul Douglas plays Kelly's stalwart catcher. [Trivia notes: 1) To this day, I have no idea how the moviemakers accomplished the initial scene depicting the effect of the chemical on a baseball. The later scenes on the ballfield are obviously animated. 2) Because Simpson (aka Kelly) achieves fame and success essentially by using what would be an illegal substance and under an assumed name, Major League Baseball forbade 20th Century Fox from using the names of real teams or stadiums in the movie. Pity that same position wasn't applied to the use of steroids among the players in the 1990s and afterward] [B&W]

Angels in the Outfield
1951 – Clarence Brown

The second baseball-themed gem in a row, I reserve a special place in my heart for this slight but heartwarming fantasy. That's because they shot some of the scenes at Forbes Field, where the Pittsburgh Pirates once played, and where I spent some of the happiest moments of my youth – in the shadow of the "Cathedral of Learning," the tall building in the background that houses part of the University of Pittsburgh. The story follows some of the hardest-luck times of the Pirates and their fictional, foul-mouthed manager, Aloysius Xavier "Guffy" McGovern (once again, the always-excellent Paul Douglas), who receives unexpected help for his team's dismal performance in the form of a cadre of ball-playing angels. Guffy can't see his celestial reinforcements, however. That distinction belongs to a nine-year-old orphan (Donna Corcoran – part of the screen- and TV-acting Corcoran clan at the time). The character mix also includes a prissy but likable newspaper columnist (a young and appealing Janet Leigh). But there's no point giving the plot away, because it unfolds so pleasantly and easily – if predictably – that you'll enjoy it whether you know what's going to happen or not. Let's just say it ends happily and you'll be satisfied, surprisingly moved and more than a little entertained. [Trivia notes: 1) Bing Crosby appears briefly in the movie, because at the time he was part-owner of the Pirates. 2) You can see a reprise of the Cathedral of Learning, albeit computer generated, in the movie *42* (coming in the next compilation), about Jackie Robinson's first year in the Major Leagues] [Remake: in 1994 under the same title but dreadfully – and therefore not included here – but featuring my friend Sheldon Tromberg with his wife in one scene as extras] **[B&W]**

O. Henry's Full House
1952 – Five directors
You've probably noticed how I've sprinkled among all these titles some truly unique attractions, and this is another one. In his short life of 48 years, William Sydney Porter, known to the world by his pen name, O. Henry, wrote hundreds of short stories, all showing a keen sense of, and a rare compassion for, the human condition. They also were noted for their surprise endings – unexpected twists that made them particularly

461

memorable and often beloved. So in this movie, the producers tried to portray five of those stories using five different directors, an array of top screenwriters and a large cast of well-known actors – plus the one and only screen appearance of legendary novelist John Steinbeck. Despite this mix of talents and egos, the movie works surprisingly well. All five stories succeed to one degree or another as screen adaptations, and if you're not familiar with them, I guarantee you'll remember them afterward. In the first, "The Cop and the Anthem," the great Charles Laughton plays Soapy, a penniless bum whose aim is to get himself arrested before Christmas so he can spend the holidays in jail – indoors and warm and fed at public expense. In "The Clarion Call," a dark drama, detective Rory Calhoun is prevented from arresting an old acquaintance for murder (Richard Widmark at his creepy best – he's even menacing when dining on soup) because he owes the man a thousand dollars. In "The Last Leaf," the most moving and poignant of the quintet, starving artist Gregory Ratoff paints a most unexpected masterpiece. In "The Ransom of Red Chief," the funniest but weakest of the bunch, bungling kidnappers Fred Allen and Oscar Levant find their hands full with the child from hell. And in "The Gift of the Magi," the best and best-known tale … well, I'll leave that one for you to discover. All five in their own ways seem corny and simplistic by today's standards. Yet each displays a timelessness and keen sense of humanity – and two of the episodes pack an emotional punch that got to me, despite my best efforts to resist. [Trivia notes: 1) As I said, the movie is cast with many well-known actors of the time, but probably the best known has one of the smallest roles. It's Marilyn Monroe playing a … shall we say, lady of the evening. She's only onscreen for a couple of minutes, and her talent is still fairly raw, but even in this glimpse you can recognize her screen persona, particularly the distinctive way she shaped certain words with her mouth. 2) As I also noted, this movie had five directors, one for each episode, and three of them are named Henry (Henry King, Henry Koster and Henry Hathaway), which seems appropriate] [B&W]

Operation Mad Ball
1957 – Richard Quine

This lively component of the service comedy genre – World War II division – is often hilarious and thoroughly entertaining. Based on a play by Arthur Carter, and co-written by Blake Edwards (of the Pink Panther series), it concerns the antics of Private Hogan (Jack Lemmon), a wheeler-dealer who's intent on throwing his outfit, still stationed in France, one last great party before they get their orders to go home. Along the way he must outwit his nemesis, Captain Locke (Ernie Kovacs), woo a beautiful nurse (Kathryn Grant – who that same year became Mrs. Bing Crosby) and keep a bargain with an even bigger wheeler-dealer (Mickey Rooney, in an academy-ignored, knockout performance) who decides which ships leave the harbor in what order. It's a rollicking good time. [Trivia notes: 1) Lemmon and Kovacks co-starred the following year in another comedy based on a play, the delightfully romantic *Bell, Book and Candle*. 2) Sammy Davis, Jr. performs the movie's theme song, though he's uncredited. 3) On the wall of Skibo's (Rooney's) office is a pin-up of Ava Gardner, who was his first wife. 4) Rooney's date for the ball, Lieutenant Tweedy, is Marilyn Hanold, who went on to become a veteran TV actress and onetime Playboy magazine centerfold] **[B&W] [W]**

The Mating Game
1959 – George Marshall

In this stubbornly lighthearted story, Debbie Reynolds and Tony Randall – he in one of his rare romantic leads – play a young couple happily thrown together by circumstance. Randall is Lorenzo Charlton, an IRS agent assigned to investigate Pop Larkin (the great Paul Douglas in his last role), a Maryland farmer who apparently hasn't ever filed an income-tax return and shows no interest in the idea. Reynolds is Mariette Larkin, the ... um, farmer's daughter. But there's no overtly naughty connotation here; only bunches of subtle double entendres appropriate for the time. It's a breezy little, occasionally slapstick comedy with a happy though improbable ending. And

Reynolds, still only 27 at the time (though she had recently given birth to her second child), supplies enough playful energy to cover the whole production. She previews her force-of-nature performance five years later in *The Unsinkable Molly Brown* (coming in my next compilation). [Trivia notes: 1) IRS Inspector General Bigelow in the story is played by Charles Lane. He was one of Hollywood's most prolific character actors with more than 250 appearances, in both the movies and on television, in a career that spanned an astonishing 76 years. 2) Speaking of career longevity, director Marshall's lasted 60 years, beginning just as Hollywood was emerging and continuing into the 1970s. Unfamiliar to most movie buffs, his reputation for lowbrow comedies was legendary within the industry] **[W]**

Let's Make Love
1960 – George Cukor

It might sound strange, but at the time of its release the title of this innocuous, light-hearted and amusing musical did not mean what it means today. Back then, the phrase carried a far more reserved connotation. It meant making romance – wooing. Cukor directed *My Fair Lady* in 1964 (coming later), which won the Best Picture Oscar, but his work here is actually more assured – effortless, even. The libretto involves a news item mentioning that an off-Broadway play plans to satirize some famous celebrities, including fictional billionaire Jean-Marc Clément (Yves Montand). This annoys Clément to the point where he storms down to the theater to protest, only to be mistaken for an aspiring actor who looks like Clément. Insulted at first, he plays along as soon as he lays eyes on Amanda Dell (Marilyn Monroe, the year after she did *Some Like It Hot* and still at the peak of her charms), the show's leading lady. From then on he masquerades as the actor – he calls himself Alexander Dumas – and tries to win Amanda's heart. The songs are so-so, but the movie is harmless fun, featuring neat cameos by Milton Berle, Bing Crosby and Gene Kelly, all of whom Clément hires to help improve his onstage skills. Tony Randall is pretty good, too, as Clément's often incredulous assistant. **[W]**

The Little Shop of Horrors
1960 – Roger Corman
This is the low-budget inspiration of the big-budget stage musical and its subsequent movie version. Reportedly made in three days on a borrowed set, it's the story of Seymour Krelboyne (Jonathan Haze), a wimpy loser who works at Mushnick's, a flower shop on skid row. There, to impress his girlfriend, Audrey (Jackie Joseph), he accidentally breeds a plant with two unusual qualities: it can talk, and it craves human blood. It's funny and completely inoffensive – and the bit part by a then-unknown actor named Jack Nicholson is a must-see. [Remake: *Little Shop of Horrors* in 1986 starring Rick Moranis and Ellen Greene] [B&W] [W]

Bedtime Story
1964 – Ralph Levy
This is the original – and in some ways better – version of *Dirty Rotten Scoundrels*, with David Niven as Lawrence Jameson, a debonair con artist living on the French Riviera who charms wealthy ladies out of their clothes and their bankrolls. Marlon Brando is Freddie Benson, an American grifter who wouldn't hesitate to steal someone's last dime while pretending to be helping a sick relative. Jameson fancies himself sort of a Robin Hood, because he uses his gains to support artists and craftsmen and to preserve cultural treasures. But Benson holds no such pretexts; he's out for the money – and the conquests. Inevitably, they come into conflict as they vie for the attentions and the fortune of a beautiful American woman (Shirley Jones). The movie exhibits early '60s sensibilities, particularly where love, sex and marriage are concerned. But it's constantly amusing, and the locales are lavishly shot by special-effects veteran Clifford Stine. [Remake: *Dirty Rotten Scoundrels* (coming in the next compilation), released in 1988 and starring Michael Caine, Steve Martin and Glenne Headly as, respectively, Jameson, Benson and their quarry] [W]

Man's Favorite Sport?
1964 – Howard Hawks

I admit it; I'm a sucker for slick-but-lightweight early 1960s romantic comedies, more of which I'll be covering in a future compilation, and which describes this one to a tee. Here the subject is, of all things, fishing, though the plot is only pretext. Rock Hudson plays Roger Willoughby, author of books on expert fishing techniques. The problem is he's never been fishing in his life and actually hates the activity. Complications arise when he's forced by his boss to enter a fishing contest at a mountain lodge. The contest is the concoction of Abigail Page (Paula Prentiss), a woman who creates disaster anytime she goes near Roger, very much like Katharine Hepburn did to Cary Grant in *Bringing Up Baby* – which Hawks also directed. In fact, Hawks pays homage to that movie here in a scene involving a torn dress, and he even has Hudson speak the same line as Grant in that situation. It's entirely appealing, more than a little sexy and often quite funny and, despite Hudson's well-kept secret (he was gay, at a time when such a disclosure would have destroyed his career), he shows how good he was at playing romantic leads. Prentiss is delightful as the ditzy Abigail in the updated version of the Hepburn role. Henry Mancini composed the charmingly laid-back score. **[W]**

Play It Again, Sam
1972 – Herbert Ross

This most sweet-tempered of Woody Allen's movies also marks one of the few times he stars in but doesn't direct his own material. Based on his play of the same name, Allen creates a witty and endearing homage to the great romantic classic, *Casablanca*. He does so as Allan Felix, a nebbish, newly divorced San Franciscan who's desperate to recover his self-respect and find another love. He's helped by his friends David and Linda Christie (played by his frequent co-stars at the time, Tony Roberts and Diane Keaton), who arrange several prospective matches, all of which end disastrously but hilariously. Eventually, Allen realizes he's in love with Linda, and to win her heart he enlists a most unlikely ally, "Bogie" – Humphrey Bogart (wonderfully played by TV veteran, Jerry Lacy) in his *Casablanca* guise, who appears as a ghostly mentor giving Allan tough-guy advice. The rest of the plot is too clever to give away, so try it sometime and enjoy how it unfolds to a most memorable conclusion, one that includes a line often prompting movie-theater audiences to erupt in applause and cheers. [Viewing note: As many fans of *Casablanca* have discovered to their delight, this one makes a fun double bill with its inspiration] [Trivia note: The San Francisco setting fits the story well, but the reason the location isn't New York City – as in so many other Woody Allen movies – is a film workers strike there at the time forced the production to look elsewhere] [Caution: mild sexuality] [W]

The Goodbye Girl
1977 – Herbert Ross

Richard Dreyfuss won a Best Actor Oscar (at the time, the youngest ever to do so) for his all-stops-out performance of Neil Simon's screenplay – one of Simon's few works written directly for the screen – beating out some heavy-duty competitors, including Richard Burton. He's funny, quirky and, as the British say, indefatigable. Dreyfuss plays Elliot Garfield, a struggling Chicago actor who's forced to share a small Manhattan apartment with an ex-dancer and her daughter (Marsha Mason and 10-year-old Quinn Cummings, nominated for Best Actress and Best Supporting Actress, respectively). Directed by Broadway veteran Ross, the movie seems fairly ordinary for a while, until Dreyfuss stops the show with his declaration of rules for the apartment. Yes, it's a somewhat predictable story, but the lines are often laugh-out-loud funny, and Mason proves a fine foil for Dreyfuss. Along with his wiseacre shark expert Matt Hooper in *Jaws*, this remains his defining role. [Viewing note: As entertaining as it is, *The Goodbye Girl* suffers from an affliction I call plot fatigue. It rolls along at a sprightly pace for about three-quarters of its running time then loses much of its energy and interest going into the finale. In this respect, it resembles *Funny*

Girl and *A Star Is Born*. But those two movies eventually descend into painful sadness and depression. Here, it's fun to watch Elliot and Paula trading barbs; when they get together romantically, however, it's much less enjoyable. [Trivia note: Like many movies, this one almost didn't get made. It started out as a romantic comedy set in Los Angeles under the title "Bogart Slept Here" and was supposed to star Robert De Niro. But early in the production, just about everyone involved recognized it wasn't funny. So, Warner Brothers shelved it while Simon reworked the script and relocated the setting to New York, and the producers replaced De Niro with Dreyfuss. Good thing, too, because De Niro as Elliot would have been kinda creepy, particularly a year after he played the tormented Travis Bickle in *Taxi Driver* (not on this list)] [Caution: rough language (including some by Cummings) and brief, partial nudity] **[W]**

The Gods Must Be Crazy (and)
The Gods Must Be Crazy II
1985 and 1989 – South Africa – Jamie Uys

A comical fable told through the unique moviemaking eyes of South African director Uys (pronounced ACE). Someone tosses an empty bottle of Coca-Cola from the window of a small airplane flying over the Kalahari Desert of southwestern Africa. The bottle lands near a tiny village of Bush People, who have never seen such a mystical and wonderful "thing," as they call it. Immediately, however, it begins to change their lives for the worse, as it generates heretofore unknown emotions of jealousy and anger, and causes the tribe members to fight over its possession. Fearing a crisis, the elders designate Xi (KEE) to carry the troublesome object to the end of the Earth and throw it away. Xi is played by N!xau (not a misspelling, with the "!" pronounced by clicking your tongue), a real-life Bushman and an appealing presence on the screen. He sets off to dispose of the evil object, but along the way he experiences several adventures, including meeting white people for the first time, being thrown in jail, nearly being run over by a truck and getting caught in the middle of a civil war. Don't worry, though, most of it is all in fun and often very, very funny. [Trivia notes: 1) *The Gods Must Be Crazy* still holds the record for the biggest box office for a non-U.S. production. 2) Though the movie debuted in 1980, it didn't appear in the United States until 1985]

In the sequel, N!xau appears again, but with the name Xixo (KEE-ko). In this story he becomes separated from his two children, who are inadvertently kidnapped by a pair of game poachers. He sets off to find them and encounters a man and woman (Hans Strider and Lena Farugia] who are themselves stranded. From there the same kind of comic chaos ensues as in the first movie. Seen together, the two features make a delightful double bill. [Cautions: in the original, some nudity and near-nudity – though in innocent contexts – and scenes of violence. In the sequel, near nudity again, innocently presented, but more violence] **[W]**

My Favorite Year
1982 – Richard Benjamin
A funny and nostalgic look at the golden age of live television comedy, the story is a thinly disguised portrayal of a guest appearance by movie idol Errol Flynn on the Sid Caesar TV show, which was called Your Show of Shows. Here, the characters are Alan Swann (Peter O'Toole) appearing on The King Kaiser Show (Kaiser is played by Joseph Bologna). Mark Linn-Baker (who narrates intermittently) plays Benji Stone, a young writer on the show whose job becomes to chaperone Swann – who drinks to excess – and make sure he appears as scheduled on the live telecast. Everyone in the movie is delightful – particularly Bologna as the egotistical and neurotic King and Lainie Kazan as Benji's archetypical Jewish mother from Brooklyn. There's also a wonderful assortment of veteran character actors – including Cameron Mitchell playing a thinly veiled version of notorious Teamsters Union boss Jimmy Hoffa, and Selma Diamond as the show's wry seamstress – but O'Toole is sublime as Swann. Nominated for a Best Actor Oscar (and losing to Ben Kingsley as Mohandas Gandhi in a tough year that also featured Dustin Hoffman as Michael Dorsey/Dorothy

Michaels in *Tootsie*), this might be his best performance since *Lawrence of Arabia*. [Trivia note: The woman Swann dances with at The Stork Club is none other than Gloria Stuart, 15 years before her movie-stealing performance in *Titanic*] [Caution: mild sexuality] **[W]**

Max Dugan Returns
1983 – Herbert Ross
Another entertaining comedy from Ross and screenwriter Neil Simon, who had collaborated in 1977 on *The Goodbye Girl* and the following year on *California Suite* (not on the list). This is the story of Nora McPhee (Marsha Mason, Simon's real-life wife who starred in the title role in *The Goodbye Girl*), a widowed schoolteacher living in the Venice neighborhood of Los Angeles with her teenage son Michael (Matthew Broderick in his debut role). One night, she's visited by her long-estranged father, Max Dugan (Jason Robards). Max is on the lam from the Las Vegas mob because he's absconded with a sizable fortune from one of their enterprises. He also claims to be dying, and he wishes to make amends with Nora and spend his remaining days with Michael. Somewhat formulaic and predictable but always entertaining, and the three leads are eminently watchable, as is Donald Sutherland playing a police detective and Nora's love interest. The movie belongs to Robards, however, and he seems to be really enjoying himself. This isn't up to the caliber of his bravura performances in *A Thousand Clowns* or *All the President's Men*, the latter of which earned him a Best Supporting Actor Oscar. On the other hand, Robards went on to make nearly 50 more movies and TV dramas before his death in 2000, but none of those performances was quite as good as this one. David Shire composed the sprightly score, among his best. [Caution: language] **[W]**

WarGames
1983 – John Badham
The larger hit for Matthew Broderick that year was a big-budget, computer age/Cold War thriller about a kid from Seattle who

inadvertently connects with a super-secret Defense Department computer and almost – but not quite – starts a nuclear war with the Russians. It's a "What if?" fantasy, but big budget notwithstanding it's a lightweight story. Nevertheless, the young Broderick holds his own at the center of the story, opposite seasoned character actors such as Dabney Coleman, John Wood and Maury Chakin, and Ally Sheedy is pert and perky as his high school classmate and rescuing angel. A bit far-fetched and excessive – particularly the finale, which veers into wistfulness – but it's also completely engaging. Suspending your disbelief is painless. Arthur B. Rubinstein contributed the nifty electronic score. [Trivia notes: 1) The vast NORAD operations center portrayed in the movie – which is supposed to be able to withstand a direct hit by a nuclear missile – is a figment of the production team's imagination. The Defense Department permits no one without proper security clearance to enter the real facility at Cheyenne Mountain, near Colorado Springs, Colorado. Few details have ever leaked publicly about the place – though I did read a report once, which I've never seen verified, claiming it features an underground lake so large it can accommodate water-skiing. 2) Director Badham replaced Martin Brest as director when Brest was fired from the production over the usual "creative differences"] [Caution: language] **[W]**

Crocodile Dundee (and) Crocodile Dundee II
1986 and 1988 – Australia – Peter Faiman (and) John Cornell
Aussie personality Paul Hogan stars in the title role as Michael J. "Crocodile" Dundee, a bushman paid to lead a New York reporter/photographer Sue Charlton (Linda Kozlowsky, whom Hogan eventually married in real life) into the outback. When Mick, as he's affectionately known, saves Sue from the jaws of an enormous croc, she returns the favor by bringing him home with her to New York. So, it becomes a fish-out-of-water story but completely diverting. [Trivia note: David Gupilil, who plays Nev, is one of Australia's best-known Aborigines and has acted in nearly 40 movies, including *The Right Stuff* the previous year] [Caution: drug use, a Manhattan party scene, Kozlowsky's

bathing suit and other outfits might be a bit much for youngsters, and the croc attack scene is frightening] **[W]**

*   *   *

In *Crocodile Dundee II*, released two years later, Mick and Sue are living together happily in Manhattan – until her ex-husband unwittingly becomes the victim of an act of vengeance by a local drug kingpin. Then it's back to the Outback and the chase is on, with Dundee continually outwitting – and scaring the bejeebers out of – the bad guys. A bit harder-edged than the original, it still packs fun and thrills. Paul Hogan and Linda Kozlowsky reprise their roles from the original. [Caution: violence and mild sexuality – including Kozlowsky once again draped in some rather revealing outfits] **[W]**

Three Men and a Baby
1987 – Leonard Nimoy

As I've mentioned, Nimoy was the best thing about the Star Trek franchise, TV series and movies alike, including his turn as director, and here he reinforces that judgment. Based on a French title, *3 Hommes et un Couffin* (*Three Men and a Cradle* – not on this list), it's a constantly amusing and enjoyable story of three confirmed and financially successful New York bachelors (Tom Selleck, Ted Danson and Steve Gutenberg) who one day discover an infant – the product of Danson's character's indiscretion – on their doorstep and suddenly find their lives turned upside down with predictable comic consequences. Selleck is particularly good here as an easygoing architect who tries to balance responsibility for his newfound charge with his career and life as a single man. He's never been more appealing, and he gives the movie a bit more emotional weight than it would have achieved otherwise. [Trivia note: The moviemakers used a common device to portray Mary, the baby. They used infant twins Lisa and Michelle Blair in the role] [Mild caution: baby nudity and bodily functions, and implied sexuality] **[W]**

The Snapper
1993 – Ireland – Stephen Frears
A charming little tale about a working-class Irish family and their daughter's dilemma, and the second installment in Roddy Doyle's "Barrytown Trilogy," following 1991's sensational *The Commitments*, and preceding 1996's *The Van*, which I also liked but not enough to include among my top 500. The title refers to a slang term for a newborn baby of undetermined parentage. In this case, it's the baby of Sharon Curley (Tina Kellegher, in a sensational debut), eldest daughter of the Curley family. Kellegher has a great movie face; not that she's pretty, particularly, but she's amazingly expressive and appealing, and she portrays a maturity and screen presence well beyond her years. Her scenes with Colm Meaney, who plays Desmond "Dessie" Curley, her father, are precious and moving. He's no slouch, either, portraying a clueless male who's prone to quick temper but is no match for the fiery glance from his wife, Kay (Ruth McCabe). It's quite a dilemma for this Catholic family, having their daughter "in the family way" without the benefit of a husband. But it's touching to see how they all eventually rally 'round Sharon and welcome the newcomer into the clan. Their brief conga line to celebrate the birth while chanting "seven pounds, twelve ounces" is a kick. [Trivia note: For some unexplained reason, after the movie's original release the producers changed the music at the title sequence and beginning of the closing credits. Originally, both used a lovely version of the song, "Can't Help Falling in Love," which seemed much more appropriate] [Caution: plentiful rough language, albeit with a heavy Irish brogue] **[W]**

Don Juan DeMarco
1994 – Jeremy Levin
A thoroughly beguiling riff on the concept of sex and romance. Johnny Depp plays the title character, a young man of dubious background who attracts the attention of a sympathetic New York City psychiatrist (Marlon Brando) when he threatens to throw himself off a building. Therein begins a sensual tale of

intrigue and legendary lovemaking – or perhaps merely the delusions of a traumatized and disturbed young man. Whatever – and it's actually fairly clear which is the fantasy, and which is reality – Depp's performance is so captivating that it quickly matters not whether the narrative is taking place entirely inside his head. Likewise the beautiful women who grace the cast: Géraldine Pailhas, Rachel Ticotin, Talisa Soto and Marita Geraghty – and Faye Dunaway as Brando's wife. Love is in the air, the appreciation of womanhood pervades the atmosphere and, as Brando's character reminds us at the end, "Why not?" [Caution: sexuality abounds – exhilaratingly so – with occasional mild profanity] [W]

The Englishman Who Went Up a Hill But Came Down a Mountain
1995 – England – Christopher Monger

From the title, you might guess this is a goofy and trivial English comedy. Yes, it has comic moments, but the movie also shows a great deal of heart and poignancy. In 1917, two cartographers (Hugh Grant and Ian McNeice) drive into the little Welsh town of Ffynnon Garw (FER-non GARR-ow) to measure the elevation of the nearby mountain as part of a wartime topographical survey. They find, to the shock of villagers, that the beloved landmark falls 16 feet short of the minimum height necessary to be classified as a mountain. From then on, Ffynnon Garw would be designated as a hill – unless the good people can haul enough earth to the top to make up the shortfall and delay the survey team's departure until a second measurement can be conducted. Watching their struggle, you might find yourself ready to pitch in and carry a bucket of earth or square of sod to the top. This sweet tale, purporting to be based on a true story, is entirely fictional, but its emotions ring strong and valid. The charming cast includes Tara Fitzgerald as Grant's love interest and the always-reliable Colm Meaney as a character named Morgan the Goat for his ... um, preoccupation. Stephen Endelman did the folksy score. [W]

Looking for Richard
1996 – Al Pacino

Here's yet another unusual feature. For one thing it is, to date, the only movie Pacino ever directed. For another, despite its simplicity it took him several years to complete because he needed to do the filming in between his other (paid) screen and stage commitments. It's a highly personal rendition of Pacino's attempt, his struggle and the product of his effort to perform Shakespeare's "Richard III," often called the second-greatest play in the English language (after "Hamlet" – though I actually prefer "Henry V"). But it's more than that – it's probably the best movie about stage actors ever made, and though Pacino's indulgences and quirks show through the whole time, they're never so intrusive that they interfere with your fascination at this highly enlightening take on the craft – helped on by Pacino's friends and colleagues in the acting community – that so many practice but few ever master. [Caution: sporadic profanity] **[W]**

The Full Monty
1997 – England – Peter Cattaneo

This one gives hope to every man who's ever looked in the mirror and grimaced at his body (and as my years advance, it's an increasingly frequent occurrence – the grimacing, not the looking). The story of six working-class, unemployed Brits (Robert Carlyle, Tom Wilkinson and others) who hope to make a nice piece of desperately needed change by baring it all (frontally – hence the title) one night at a local pub filled with women looking for a visual thrill is more than a little funny, surprisingly touching and so appealing that it was adapted, successfully, in 2001 as a rousing Broadway musical – but which had the unfortunate fate of opening the same year as "The Producers," which swept the Tony Awards and became a Broadway phenomenon. [Caution: abundant sexual references – though the big reveal at the end is surprisingly demure] **[W]**

Waking Ned Devine
1998 – England – Kirk Jones

Another charmer from across the Pond involving working-class folk and the chance to strike it rich. This time the story involves a winning lottery ticket owned by a resident of a small town on the Irish coast, and how his fellow townspeople conspire to prevent the winnings from slipping away when the shock of the good fortune apparently gave the man a fatal heart attack. Ian Bannen, heading a fine cast of lesser-known but veteran actors in this gentle comedy of a morality play. It's to the movie's credit that how the dilemma is resolved ultimately seems less important than watching the residents work through some longstanding issues that had been dividing them – although an act of divine providence apparently allows the lottery ticket to avoid going unclaimed. Yes, a certified little gem. [Caution: geriatric nudity] **[W]**

Best in Show
2000 – Christopher Guest

Guest, who has done a fair amount of acting in other movies, specializes in making features that resemble documentaries but with fictional stories and his own brand of unique humor – and in playing roles that demonstrate his extreme versatility. Case in point: The story portrays some of the top contestants at the (fictional) 125th annual Mayflower Kennel Club dog show in Philadelphia, and Guest plays a redneck owner of a champion bloodhound. He's so good that it takes a few moments to recognize him. Yet this is the same man who played Count Rugen, the six-fingered, evil aristocrat in *The Princess Bride*. Among the rest of the cast, Eugene Levy shines as the awkward husband of a contestant (Kathleen O'Hara), and Fred Willard is hilariously clueless as a color commentator who sounds quite like former Vice President Joe Biden – though his part was based loosely on sports commentator and former Today Show host Joe Garagiola. [Caution: sexuality and occasional rough language] **[W]**

The Dish

2000 – Australia – Rob Sitch

For those of you too young to remember the night the whole world watched television, here's a most satisfying introduction to that event. The "dish" refers to the radio relay station in Parkes, New South Wales, Australia, which trained its antenna on the Moon on July 20, 1969, to receive the historic TV signal beamed at Earth from the Apollo 11 landing vehicle, while NASA astronauts Neil Armstrong and Buzz Aldrin became the first men to walk on the lunar surface. The task of relaying the signal would seem simple, but it turned out to be a heroic feat, because a fierce windstorm arose that day, threatening to tear the thousand-ton structure right off its moorings. But the operators – including Sam Neill as the radioastronomer in charge, and Patrick Warburton (better known as the lunkhead character David Puddy on the Seinfeld television series) as a straight-laced NASA engineer – refused to yield to the safety warnings and, as a result, gave something approaching a billion viewers worldwide a chance to see an unprecedented moment in history unfold live on their TV screens. Neill's character calls the mission "the greatest feat ever" and "science's chance to be daring." It truly was both. Much of the movie was shot on location at the actual dish, and it's funny, endearing, ultimately rousing and laced with popular music of the period – plus a hilarious misinterpretation of "The Star Spangled Banner." It's another great little movie! [Trivia notes: 1) As with many movies based on real events, this one takes a few dramatic liberties. The Parkes dish was actually one of three Australian facilities used to relay the Apollo 11 landing TV signal to the world. Though much of the time the lunar broadcast was carried by Parkes, a technical problem prevented it from receiving the signal from the landing and Armstrong's first steps. The Honeysuckle Creek dish, about 300 miles south of Parkes, handled those moments. 2) Along with being a great moment in history and science, the Moon landing was extremely risky. There's a reference in the movie to a terrifying moment during the landing sequence that only those in the know at the time appreciated. Still several

477

hundred feet above the surface and flying over a field of boulders, the spacecraft's computer issued a warning that only 30 seconds of fuel remained. Armstrong managed to bring the lander down safely with 17 seconds left, and everyone at NASA – and the guys at the dish – breathed a deep sigh of relief] [<u>Slight caution</u>: mild profanity] **[W]**

My Big Fat Greek Wedding
2002 – Joel Zwick

An update of the Cinderella story, but instead of the young but ethnically undetermined protagonist of the fairy tale, here we follow the life of a not-so-young Greek girl who's sliding through a boring and dead-end daily routine – until Mr. Right literally shines on her and changes everything. The script, by TV writer and bit player Nia Vardalos, was expanded from her one-woman stage show after Rita Wilson saw her performance in Toronto, and Wilson's husband Tom Hanks offered to help her turn it into a movie. Vardalos also plays the lead, Toula Portokalos, the plump and aging spinster daughter of a restaurant owner (TV veteran Michael Constantine) and his loving but cagey wife (the always delightful Lainie Kazan). Yes, it's somewhat contrived, and the setbacks Toula encounters in her romance with the handsome – but non-Greek – Ian Miller (John Corbett) get resolved a bit too easily. But the movie is far too appealing and good-humored for that to matter. My real complaint, as usual, is with the motion picture academy, which once again failed by not awarding the Best Supporting Actress Oscar to Kazan for her career-best performance. Kudos as well to Second City TV veteran comedienne Andrea Martin as Toula's wacky Aunt Voula; likewise to Bruce Gray and Fiona Reid as Ian's WASPish parents Rodney and "Harry." [<u>Caution</u>: mild sexuality] **[W]**

Little Miss Sunshine
2006 – Jonathan Dayton and Valerie Faris

Out of the hundreds of movies on this list, *Little Miss Sunshine* might need the most patience, because the way it starts out is likely to put you off. But if you stay with it, sooner or later you just might fall in love with this most dysfunctional of families. The title refers to a franchise beauty contest for preteens, the kind that achieved notoriety because of its connection to JonBenét Ramsey, the six-year-old girl from Boulder, Colorado, who was mysteriously murdered in 1996, and whose parents had been entering her in a number of these creepy contests – including one called Little Miss Sunburst – where parents dress up and make up their elementary-school-age daughters to look like temptresses. In this story, young Olive (Abigail Breslin), egged on by her extremely curmudgeonly grandfather (Alan Arkin, in an Oscar-winning role), is invited to participate in the pageant. So Olive and Grandpa are joined by her constantly bickering parents (Greg Kinnear and Toni Collette), her formerly suicidal uncle (Steve Carell) and her brother (Paul Dano), who has taken a vow of silence until he is accepted by the Air Force Academy. They all pile into an aging, hideous, VW Microbus for the drive from their home in Albuquerque to the event in Redondo Beach (actually Ventura), California, south of Los Angeles. From that point on, the movie grabs you, and despite its premise, you're probably going to find it difficult to let go. [Caution: language] [W]

Sunshine Cleaning
2008 – Christine Jeffs

You might think this is some sort of sequel to *Little Miss Sunshine*, and you'd be reasonable to make such a conclusion. Both movies were shot, entirely or in part, in Albuquerque – and not in the most scenic parts. Both also feature Alan Arkin, both deal with individuals struggling to hold their lives together, and of course both use "Sunshine" in their titles. But those similarities are coincidental. What really links them is their offbeat but affectionate portrayals of characters struggling at the fringes of legitimate society. In this case, it's the Lorkowski family, including Rose (Amy Adams), a single mother; Norah, her sister (Emily Blunt), an aimless soul; and their father, Joe (Arkin), who couldn't sell water to someone dying of thirst.

Their destinies change, in several unexpected ways, when Rose's lover, Mac (Steve Zahn), clues her in to the disgusting but well-paying task of cleaning up after crime scenes, suicides and sudden deaths. Despite the repulsiveness of the theme, the movie manages to keep all of its characters appealing and even maintains a surprising amount of humor. [Caution: sexuality and language] [W]

Julie &Julia
2009 – Nora Ephron
Julie and Julia represent the female halves of two couples – one of which you want to follow and enjoy, and the other you often wish would just butt out of the story. I might have placed Nora Ephron's last directorial effort (she died in 2012) in the Flawed But Not Fatally category if it were a serious movie. But it's such a lightweight comedy – and it's so often charming – that it more fittingly belongs here. Besides, I don't want to bash it because I really did enjoy watching. The Julie in the title is Julie Powell (Amy Adams again). She's soon to turn 30 and stuck in a dead-end job, assisting relatives of the victims of the September 11, 2001, terror attacks on the World Trade Center. What saves her is starting a daily blog, in which she attempts to prepare all 524 recipes in Julia Child's classic cookbook, Mastering the Art of French Cooking, beginning with her signature and most famous dish, boeuf bourguignon, and ending with her most complex, a deboned duck. Although Julie Powell is a real person who actually did start a blog about following Julia Child, that is the so-so part of the story. What lifts the movie above the ordinary is the portrayal of Child herself, during her days in Paris when she was learning how to cook, by the great Meryl Streep. And Streep is more than matched in charm by Stanley Tucci as Paul Child, Julia's husband. Together they're wonderful, and if nothing else *Julie & Julia* will strongly encourage you to reintroduce butter into your diet. The prolific and versatile Alexandre Desplat contributed the cheery, Françoise-sounding score. [Technical note: Streep, who stands 5 feet, 6 inches, playing Child, who towered at 6 feet, 2 inches, presented some physical and

photographic challenges for the actress and the production crew. They solved them via an assortment of tricks, including building special sets with doors and kitchen counters constructed at lower-than-normal heights, Streep wearing shoes with extra-thick soles and extremely high heels, and filming her specifically to disguise how tall she really was. In almost every case, it worked well] [Caution: sexuality and language] **[W]**

Stan & Ollie
2018 – England – Jon S. Baird
You should know those two names stand for the most beloved comedy team of all time, Laurel & Hardy. The duo had risen from their roots in vaudeville and silent films to become movie superstars in America during the 1930s (see *The Music Box*, *Way Out West* and *Block-Heads*, all from that era, elsewhere). But in the years that followed, their box-office appeal faded, to the point where, by the 1950s, Hollywood no longer wanted to produce their movies. *Stan & Ollie* covers the last couple of months of the pair's performing life, as they tour England doing stage appearances – at first to nearly empty theaters – while waiting for an appointment with a London producer to pitch their own screen version of the Robin Hood legend. All that is pretext, however, for arguably the most affectionate portrait of fading movie stars ever produced. As the title characters – though employing prosthetics and heavy makeup – Steve Coogan and John C. Reilly contribute absolutely dead-on portrayals of the real Stan Laurel and Oliver Hardy (I would swear Reilly's and Hardy's eyes are identical). But not merely their screen personas – though their meticulous re-creation of the soft-shoe dance scene from *Way Out West* is sublime. Both actors deeply humanize the men. By the movie's partly triumphant, partly melancholy fadeout, it's difficult to choke back tears at the memory of an onscreen partnership that brought so many delightful moviegoing memories to so many fans – including me – over nearly a century. [Trivia note: When Ollie died in 1957, a broken-hearted Stan resolved never to perform alone – a promise he kept for the rest of his life] **[W]**

50. Last But Not Least: My 100 Favorite Films

Maybe you noticed that I added "[100]" alongside some of the titles on this long list. That's because they also belong in this category. In his wonderful book (and one of my all-time favorites) <u>The Filmgoer's Companion,</u> British movie historian and commentator Leslie Halliwell once defined his "Hundred Favourite Films" as those he had "thoroughly enjoyed at several sittings, mostly over long periods of time," without applying any other criteria. Fair enough. Here, and in previous categories, are my own 100 favorites – including seven that I share with Halliwell in my top 100, and 18 more elsewhere in the book. I have adored them since the first time I discovered them, or I fell in love during subsequent screenings and they have never disappointed me since, no matter how many times I have seen them. That's *my* criterion.

By the way, repeatability is a key factor to consider if you ever decide to compile your own list of top titles. Often, seeing a movie the first time isn't what determines whether it will become one of your favorites; it's how you react to seeing it again – and again. That's when you discover if something has affected you enough to settle firmly into your psyche. It isn't an altogether predictable process. I didn't like a few of these movies the first time, some of which might surprise you. *The Godfather,* for example, took a second screening to change my mind. Most often, however, repeat viewings have provided the pure pleasure of revisiting cherished experiences. Alone or with friends or family, you can enjoy repeating your most treasured screen entertainments.

This last roster turned out to be a challenging exercise – culling the top 100. Some, I admit, aren't even that good, objectively speaking, and are outclassed by many of my other titles. Some are overly simple or sentimental and are easily outshone by better-known or more critically praised features, though some are acknowledged classics and stand among the finest movies ever made. Whatever their merits, I hold them all close, and I ache when they end because I hate to leave them – they've become like old, dear friends. I didn't give them specific rankings; such things are meaningless, and in any event with a few exceptions I'd be hard pressed to rank one above another. They all work for me, and I hope as the years go by you will get to see a lot of them and derive great pleasure as well.

The More the Merrier [100]
1943 – George Stevens
In the midst of World War II in Washington, D.C., there was a serious shortage of housing – and of eligible bachelors. To do her patriotic duty, Miss Connie Milligan (a most appealing if whiny Jean Arthur) advertises for someone to share her apartment at 1708 D Street N.W. (Let's not quibble that the location puts it in the middle of federal office buildings that existed even during the movie's timeframe) Along comes Mr. Benjamin Dingle (the great Charles Coburn in an Oscar-winning role), an elderly industrialist temporarily in need of housing. The problem is that Miss Milligan had intended to rent to a female, but Dingle will not be denied, so she relents. The very next day, Dingle meets Joe Carter (Joel McCrea), a handsome guy carrying around something that looks like an airplane propeller and being circumspect about his line of work. Carter also needs a place to stay, so Dingle offers him half of his room, and that's when the complications – logistic and romantic – begin. It's a funny story with sparkling dialogue from co-writers Robert Russell and Frank Ross. Coburn shows a mastery of physical comedy (there's a bit about a missing pair of trousers that's a real stitch), the romantic chemistry between McCrea and Arthur is sizzling, and the final scene is a delightful shock and surprise. [Remake: *Walk Don't Run* in 1966 starring Cary Grant, Jim Hutton and Samantha Egger] [B&W]

Adam's Rib [100]
1949 – George Cukor

A sly and sophisticated comedy of the sexes, with conservative prosecutor Adam Bonner (Spencer Tracy) pitted against his liberal defense attorney wife, Amanda (Katharine Hepburn). They battle in the courtroom by day and make up – demurely, because this was 1949, after all – in the bedroom at night. The case in question concerns a love triangle involving a husband (Tom Ewell), his wife (Judy Holliday) and the "other" woman (Jean Hagen). The dialogue, by husband–wife writing team Garson Kanin and Ruth Gordon (yes, that Ruth Gordon, who won an Oscar for her sly performance in *Rosemary's Baby*), is crisp and witty, the supporting cast is terrific (to see Holliday and Hagen in the same movie is a treat in itself), and the theme of the double standard applied to adultery is timeless. Except for *Miracle on 34th Street*, this might be the best courtroom comedy ever made. [Trivia notes: 1) Newcomer Holliday felt awed and nervous in the presence of Hepburn, and it shows in their early scenes together, particularly the first, where you can see her trembling. 2) Despite her case of nerves, Holliday apparently impressed Hepburn so much that she lobbied Harry Cohn, head of Columbia Pictures at the time, to hire Holliday to reprise her Broadway role in the film version of *Born Yesterday*. 3) That familiar-sounding voice singing "Farewell, Amanda" (written by Cole Porter, by the way) on the radio, and briefly on a record, is none other than Frank Sinatra] **[B&W]**

The Day the Earth Stood Still [100]
1951 – Robert Wise

This classic science-fiction tale (unlike the overblown and stupefying remake of 2008) was one of the first movies to express antiwar sentiments in the nuclear age. British actor Michael Rennie stars as Klaatu, a visitor from an unspecified neighboring world, whose flying saucer lands on the Ellipse in front of the White House in Washington, D.C. Promptly shot by a frightened young soldier but defended by Gort, his fearsome giant robot companion, the alien visitor eventually eludes the military and takes refuge in a boarding house in order to learn more about humans. There, he meets an attractive widow (Patricia Neal) and develops a friendship with her young son (Billy Gray, who played the son, Bud Anderson, in the 1950s TV series Father Knows Best), while forming an alliance with a sympathetic scientist (Sam Jaffe). Frustrated at the Earthlings' reactions to his arrival, Klaatu arranges for a demonstration of his civilization's awesome power, which results in a literal depiction of the movie's title. Intelligent, thoughtful and enduringly entertaining, it originated the cult phrase, "Klaatu, birada nicto," which became the title of an album by former Beatle, Ringo Starr. Bernard Herrmann's pioneering, part-synthesized score, much of which used a difficult-to-play electronic instrument called a Theremin, still gives chills. [Trivia notes: 1) Gort, the robot, was played by Lock Martin, who stood 7-feet, 7-inches tall and was working at the time as a doorman at Grauman's Chinese Theatre in Hollywood. 2) Gort's form consisted of two rubber suits, each with a zipper that could be kept out of view depending on the camera angle and with breathing holes under the chin (which can be seen in one brief shot). 3) The suit was so awkward and confining that Martin could not lift Neal as required in one scene, so the moviemakers faked it by having that action appear off-camera. 4) In the famous scene where Gort carries Neal up the ramp into the spaceship, the moviemakers substituted a life-sized but lightweight mannequin. 5) In the centerpiece scene, where the aliens neutralize the world's electricity, you can see vehicles moving in the first couple of shots, and in Times Square one of the theater marquees is flashing. 6) One of the best special effects in the movie is also the subtlest. Though set in Washington, all of the scenes involving the principal characters were shot either in studio sets or outdoors on the 20th Century-Fox backlot in Hollywood, which today is the site of the Century City complex in Los Angeles. All of the scenes where the characters appear against famous Washington landmarks were done either with doubles at a distance or the actors appearing against projected backgrounds] **[B&W]**

No Highway in the Sky [100]
1951 – Henry Koster

Based on a novel by Nevil Shute, the story is a bit dated, perhaps, but still quite engaging and appealing, and the script is subtle but exceptionally literate. James Stewart plays Theodore Honey, a rather absent-minded American research scientist working for the Royal Aircraft Establishment in postwar England. Absent-minded? Yes. He often walks into the wrong house or forgets he's already home. The trait is funny and endearing, but Mr. Honey's work isn't. He's been testing the tail segment of a new Reindeer aircraft – so named because the tail contains two sets of elevators and resembles a reindeer's antlers. Based on his mathematical formulas he thinks the tail design is flawed and dangerous, but he doesn't want to present his research to the establishment until he completes his testing, and he remains unconcerned that his findings could mean life or death to airline passengers. That rationale changes suddenly when one of the new planes crashes in Labrador, and the establishment dispatches Honey to investigate – aboard one of the suspect Reindeers. From there the story takes several dramatic turns and transforms Honey from a shy and eccentric boffin – as scientists of his ilk are called – to folk hero and even a person of romantic interest. Stewart plays his character a bit unevenly but with great charm, and his fine supporting cast includes Marlene Dietrich in her best role as a ripening movie star, Glynis Johns as a sympathetic flight attendant, Ronald Squire in a superb turn as the head of the establishment, and Jack Hawkins as a savvy executive and former pilot. [Trivia notes: 1) The fate of the fictional Reindeer in the movie presaged what happened a year later to the De Havilland Comet, the first British jet airliner, which suffered a series of crashes due to metal fatigue in its airframe and was quickly pulled from service, albeit temporarily. Redesigned versions ended up flying for the next 30 years. 2) Shute wrote several fine novels, including the classic *On the Beach*, but his training was as an aeronautical engineer] [B&W]

The Crimson Pirate (*encore*) [100]
1952 – Robert Siodmak

One of only two repeat titles in this list, I had to return to it in my most favorite category because I have adored it since I was a child – which is why I recommended it earlier for the kids and grandkids. If you didn't read my capsule then, here it is again. *The Crimson Pirate* is one of the most entertaining swashbucklers ever. Burt Lancaster, who despite his bleached hair never looked more dashing, plays Captain Vallo, leader of a fleetingly loyal pirate crew on a caper to rob both the English crown and the rebels on a fictional Caribbean island. But Vallo doesn't count on losing his heart to the daughter of the rebel leader (Eva Bartok), or on being betrayed by his men – one of whom reminds him that any pirate worth his salt would be willing to sell out his best friend or even his own mother. Robust, rousing and often laugh-out-loud funny, Lancaster and his boyhood pal and circus-acrobat sidekick Nick Cravat perform their own stunts, providing many surprises and delights. The violence is mostly of the comic book variety, so there's no problem introducing this classic to young kids. The great veteran British actor Torin Thatcher plays Vallo's second-in-command and sometime rival Mr. Humble Bellows. So, once again, "Gather 'round, lads and lasses, gather 'round," for a rollicking good time, all in glorious Technicolor! William Alwyn contributed the suitably rousing score. [Trivia notes: 1) Cravat plays his character Ojo (O-ho) as a mute because he couldn't disguise his Brooklyn accent. If you'd ever like to hear him speak, he plays a small part as a crewman in *Run Silent, Run Deep*. 2) The movie actually was shot in Mediterranean locales, where Lancaster and Siodmak were lying low during the investigations by the House Unamerican Activities Committee into possible communist influences in Hollywood – and both men at the time were suspected of being sympathizers. The "crimson" in the title was meant to satirize congressional hunting of communists – or reds, as they were called. 3) The first two hugely popular Disney *Pirates of the Caribbean* movies (none on this list) contain affectionate homages to *The Crimson Pirate*. 4) You can spot two future, well-known character actors among the bit players; Dana Wynter (who played Lancaster's wife in *Airport*, some 18 years later) as a senorita, and horror-movie regular Christopher Lee (who, coincidentally, also played a role in one of the *Airport* sequels – though it isn't on this list) as an aide to Vallo's enemy, the evil Baron Gruda (Leslie Bradley). 3) Speaking of Lee, before his death in 2015 at age 93 he was one of the most prolific actors in history, amassing an astounding 280 credits – including several on this list]

Bell, Book and Candle [100]
1958 – Richard Quine

This enchanting romantic fantasy features the second pairing of that year for James Stewart and Kim Novak, who also starred together in Alfred Hitchcock's gorgeous thriller *Vertigo*. Novak plays Gillian Holroyd, a witch who casts a spell to lure away her upstairs neighbor, Shepherd Henderson (Stewart), a book publisher, from his snobby fiancée (Janice Rule), Gil's former sorority sister and rival. Eventually, however, she falls for Shep's charms and in doing so loses her powers. Stewart, at 50, looks fit and sharp, and Novak (who was only 25 at the time) has never been more alluring. Her seduction of Shep is sure to interfere with the breathing of male viewers. There's also a "morning after" scene, in demure '50s style, that's about as romantic as cinema gets. It's topped off by the mother of all hat tosses, and I'd bet during the 30 seconds that follow you'd give anything to share such an experience. The excellent supporting cast includes Jack Lemmon as Gil's jaded brother, Elsa Lanchester as her spinster cousin, Ernie Kovacs as a witch-hunting author and Hermione Gingold as a spell-breaker. Based on John Van Druten's play, the movie's silvery exterior shots of New York in winter in the late 1950s remove any staginess and, along with a dreamy orchestral score that often turns delightfully jazzy by George Duning, create a sophisticated romantic mood. There's also a witty, clever and deceptively simple title sequence that draws you in right from the start. [Trivia notes: 1) Director Quine and Producer Julian Blaustein must have thought highly of Duning's score, because they placed his name in the credits immediately preceding their own. 2) Quine and Novak were linked romantically for several years, and they made two more movies together after this one, but they eventually married other people. 3) Kovacs and Lemmon had worked together the previous year as Army antagonists in *Operation Mad Ball*. 4) Speaking of working together, this was the second time Stewart did two roles with the same romantic co-star in the same year. He did it with Margaret Sullavan in 1940 in the classic comedy, *The Shop Around the Corner*, and in the dark drama, *The Mortal Storm* (coming in my second compilation). And, of course, along with *Bell, Book, and Candle*, he paired with Novak in 1958's aforementioned great Hitchcock mystery, *Vertigo*] **[W]**

The Music Man [100]
1962 – Morton DaCosta

DaCosta spent most of his career acting and directing on the New York stage, doing only two other movies. This one – his version of the Broadway hit – is as charming a screen musical as you are likely to see. It's great fun and a treat for all ages. Robert Preston stars as Professor Harold Hill, an alias the character uses as a traveling salesman and small-time hustler of band uniforms and instruments. Hill's trade brings him to the little town of River City, Iowa, where he meets his comeuppance but also finds love and happiness. And as Hill, Preston reprises to perfection the Tony Award-winning role he played for several years on Broadway. I considered placing Preston's performance in the Unforgettable category, but it isn't on the same level as some of the immortal portrayals listed there. Besides, the movie is more of an ensemble achievement, I wanted it here among my favorites, and the real stars are composer Meredith Willson's songs. They're wonderful, including the sweet ballad, "Goodnight, My Someone," the gorgeous "Till There Was You," and the grand finale, "76 Trombones," which gives the cast a rousing curtain call. Some of the songs are among the most unusual ever written, including "Rock Island," in which traveling salesmen aboard a train mimic its rhythm en route from one town to the next; "Piano Lesson," where the sung lyrics follow the notes of a keyboard exercise; the rapid-fire "Trouble;" the charming "Pick a Little, Talk a Little," sung by a chorus of the town's dowagers who flock together like barnyard hens; and the crisply choreographed "Marian the Librarian," as subtle a portrayal of romance and sexual awakening as ever presented on the screen. In a sense, *The Music Man* might be the most *musical* musical ever, because even the dialogue, or much of it, is spoken with a rhythmic cadence – and delightfully so. There's also the happiest of happy endings, one that is sure to leave you smiling and humming the theme song for days. Shirley Jones co-stars as "lovely Marian," the aforementioned librarian, and the great supporting cast includes Buddy Hackett as a pixie-ish fellow huckster, Paul Ford as the dotty mayor of River City, and eight-year-old Ron (Ronny in the credits) Howard at the beginning of his acting career as Marian's brother, Winthrop – a name that Howard proudly sprays whenever he repeats it. [Trivia notes: 1) The finale was filmed in Mason City, Iowa, which was Willson's real home town. 2) Jones once told the amusing story about how, three months into the production, she discovered she was pregnant, something that eventually demanded shooting from creative angles and placing objects strategically to hide her condition. By the time she and Preston were due to perform the scene where they kiss at the footbridge, she had become very pregnant, requiring them both to lean toward each other. During one take, Jones's yet-to-be-born son, Patrick, suddenly kicked, causing Preston to pull back and ask, "What the heck was that?" Then, years later, Patrick Cassidy went backstage to see Preston after a performance. As Patrick related the incident, after he had introduced himself, Preston immediately replied, "Oh yes, I've met you before." 3) About the ballad "Till There Was You," a young quartet of British musicians liked it so much when they heard it in 1962 that they performed it and added it as part of their second album. The group was The Beatles, and the royalties the song earned on the album "With the Beatles" ended up exceeding all revenues earned by Willson's estate for the entire play. 4) Along with his many stage roles, Preston enjoyed a

490

movie career that spanned nearly four decades, often playing villains. The year after *The Music Man*, he appeared on a Carol Burnett TV special and sang an amusing song about his many onscreen death scenes] **[W]**

A Thousand Clowns [100]
1965 – Fred Coe

Based on Herb Gardner's Tony Award-winning play, this bittersweet comedy about one man's conflict between his fight for individuality and his need to make a living became a cult classic in the late 1960s. Jason Robards plays Murray Burns, a TV writer who has burned out after enduring one too many episodes of the Chuckles the Chipmunk show. Now he idyls his days away in a one-room apartment or strolls Manhattan and Liberty Island with his nephew, Nick (the diminutive, 17-year-old Barry Gordon, playing considerably younger) – until two social workers show up to examine the boy's home environment. One of the social workers (William Daniels) is stern and straight-laced, but the other (the wonderful Barbara Harris, in her movie debut) immediately falls in love with Murray, and it turns out she's as conflicted as he is. The cast features actor-director Gene Saks as Chuckles, and Martin Balsam, who won the Best Supporting Actor Oscar for his role as Murray's brother, Arnold. The great Ralph Rosenblum edited the movie and provided several brilliant music montages. The plot line is too precious give away any more, except to say that the dialogue is sharp and hilarious (including one of the greatest telephone hang-up lines ever), and Robards as Murray is so appealing that you just might be seriously tempted to join him in his reveries. [Trivia notes: 1) Robards, Saks, Daniels and Gordon reprised their stage roles in the movie, while Harris replaced Sandy Dennis, and Balsam took over for A. Larry Haines. 2) Gordon was already a veteran of TV when he played Nick, even on the stage, having begun his acting career in 1955 at age seven. 3) Robards and Balsam made two more movies together; *Tora! Tora! Tora!* in 1970, where they never appeared in the same scene, and *All the President's Men* in 1976. In the latter title, Robards was the one who won Best

Supporting Actor. 4) John McMartin appears in a small role as a smarmy TV producer, and he also co-starred with Robards and Balsam in *All the President's Men*. 5) *A Thousand Clowns* holds the distinction of featuring two actors who would go on to become presidents of the Screen Actors Guild – but they're not the two you might guess. Barry Gordon presided from 1988 to 1995, and William Daniels followed from 1999 to 2001] **[B&W] [W]**

Barefoot in the Park [100]
1967 – Gene Saks

Make it a threesome (along with *Bell, Book and Candle* and *A Thousand Clowns*). I've always had a fondness for these romantic comedies, all based on stage plays and all filmed in Manhattan. Many young adults who saw this screen version of one of Neil Simon's early plays ended up longing to move into cramped, five-story walk-up apartments in Greenwich Village. Jane Fonda was never more appealing than here as Corie Bratter, co-starring with an equally appealing Robert Redford as Paul, playing newlyweds struggling through their period of adjustment. Charles Boyer appears as the mysterious Victor Velasco, the resident rake who lives in the building's attic, and Mildred Natwick plays Corie's dowdy widowed mother in an Oscar-nominated role. Neal Hefti's breezy score adds to the movie's romantic mood, and the opening carriage-ride scene alone is enough to get you thinking about booking your own suite at the Plaza. [Trivia notes: 1) Just one year earlier, Redford and Fonda were terribly miscast playing a pair of white-trash lovers in Arthur Penn's *The Chase*; in 1979 they reunited in the impossibly hokey *The Electric Horseman*, and in 2017 they co-starred again in the interesting but ordinary *Our Souls at Night* (none on this list). *Barefoot in the Park*, I would argue, was by far their most successful onscreen match. 2) Saks put aside his acting in movies temporarily to begin a successful run as a director, with this his first effort and following with *The Odd Couple*. He then continued doing both, as well as acting and directing on the stage, for two more decades. He died in 2015 at age 94] **[W]**

Bedazzled [100]
1967 – Stanley Donen
Not to be confused with the dull and predictable remake in 2000, this clever and astute telling of the Devil's dilemma features a British twist. It stars Peter Cook and Dudley Moore as, respectively, Satan – who in this story takes the name George Spiggott – and Stanley Moon, a schnook of a cook in a Wimpy's burger joint somewhere in London. Stanley pines for Margaret Spencer, the waitress (Eleanor Bron, who also acted in Donen's other movie of that year, *Two for the Road*). Spiggott is competing with the Almighty, whom George calls "Your Inevitable Hugeness," to see who can claim the first 100 billion souls – it's a fantasy, okay? When he rescues Stanley from the verge of suicide, he grants him seven wishes in exchange for his soul. Of course, the Devil somehow spoils each of Stanley's wishes, forcing him to use them up, and that battle of wits produces a great deal of side-splitting humor, particularly the last sequence, which is far too precious to divulge. This satisfying tale, co-written by Cook and Moore – with Moore also composing the music – is made even more interesting by Raquel Welch's ultra-seductive performance as one of the Seven Deadly Sins. Guess which one? [Caution: sexuality, including Raquel in a variety of skimpy attire] [Remake: In 2000, Brendan Fraser played Moore's role, and in a supposed twist Elizabeth Hurley donned the Devil's duds (not nearly good enough to be included here)] **[W]**

The Producers [100]
1968 – Mel Brooks
A number of years ago, the American Film Institute picked *Some Like It Hot* as the funniest movie of all time. I fully support that decision, but I think *The Producers* should run a close second. Brooks's first movie is still the best he ever made (he won an Oscar for the screenplay). It remains an American comedy classic and the justifiable inspiration for the huge Broadway hit of the same name, which Brooks premiered in 2001. Zero Mostel (listed only as "Zero" in the credits) and Gene Wilder play, respectively, Max Bialystock and Leo Bloom, would-be

Broadway impresarios who set out to produce the worst play ever so they will not have to repay their many investors. And what a rotten production they choose! It's a musical called "Springtime for Hitler," the creation of Franz Liebkin (Kenneth Mars), a Nazi loyalist living in seclusion in Manhattan. Max and Leo also pick the worst theatrical director imaginable, Roger De Bris (Christopher Hewitt), a let's-just-say flamboyant personality. And they select an equally wretched stage actor by the name of Lorenzo St. DuBois – or L.S.D. (Dick Shawn, in a performance that's so over-the-top it's amazing for its audacity). With these ingredients, you might ask, how could they miss? Well, you'll have to watch and enjoy the result. Just know that Mostel and Wilder make a perfect match as scheming producer who dares to dream, and his young partner who strives to break out of his nebbishness. Lee Meredith is stunning in 1960s fashion as Max's voluptuous Swedish secretary, Ulla. [Trivia note: Brooks himself is in the movie, sort of: He briefly dubs his own voice over one of the singers in the "Springtime" number] [Remake: Under the same title in 2005, with Nathan Lane and Matthew Broderick reprising their performances from the Broadway smash, but not matching the simplicity and appeal of the original, and therefore not included here] **[W]**

The Hot Rock [100]
1972 – Peter Yates

Five years after *Barefoot in the Park*, Robert Redford returned to New York, this time to play ex-con and expert thief John Dortmunder, a man who begins planning a daring jewel heist on the way home from his latest prison stint. He's pulled into the caper by his brother-in-law, Kelp (George Segal), a nervous locksmith. They're helped by a college gadabout and explosives expert (Paul Sand) and a smart-aleck stunt driver and semi-skilled helicopter pilot (Ron Liebman). The cast also includes Moses Gunn as a frustrated African diplomat and the great Zero Mostel as Sand's crafty lawyer father. Based on the Donald Westlake novel, William Goldman wrote the witty and wry script, which is full of tense sequences, hilarious miscues and deadpan humor. Plus, you'll learn why the phrase "Afghanistan banana stand" certainly can come in handy sometimes. Quincy Jones did the laid-back blues score, and watch for Christopher Guest in his quick movie debut. [Trivia note: *The Hot Rock* was shot in Manhattan while the twin World Trade Center towers were still under construction, and they figure prominently in the background in one scene – something that lends a melancholy note to an otherwise sparkling caper comedy] **[W]**

The Black Stallion [100]
1979 – Carroll Ballard

Sublime! Ballard's screen version of the Walter Farley classic novel is one of the most beautiful and captivating movies ever made – truly one for the ages. The story of Alec Ramsey, a young boy (12-year-old Kelly Reno, playing a little younger) who becomes shipwrecked on a desert island with a magnificent black horse, contains scenes of stunning beauty. *The Black Stallion* was easily the best movie of 1979, and it's a great, great title for kids, but I just couldn't separate it from my list of 100 favorites, because it's too dear to me for any other category. Ballard is a genius at filming animals, including in this case the eponymous horse, its stablemate and a menacing cobra. He's also very good at directing actors. Here, he gets probably the best performance of Mickey Rooney's long career, and it's yet one more shame on the motion picture academy members that they did not honor Rooney with an Oscar. They also shut out the movie except for sound editing. Everyone else is wonderful, too, including Hoyt Axton as Alec's father, Teri Garr as his mother, veteran movie actor and composer Clarence Muse as Rooney's wise friend, and the black stallion himself – played by Cass-Olé, who actually was dark brown with a couple of white spots concealed by dye. The superlatives continue with Carmine Coppola's beguiling score and what I consider the most wonderful end-credit sequence ever. Be sure to watch it all the way to that last, breathtaking shot. But the real stars are Ballard and his genius at staging and visualizing scenes, and the great cinematographer Caleb Deschanel, who paints with light the way the great masters used oils and watercolors. [Trivia note: After the movie's initial showing at the New York Film Festival in the fall of 1979, executives at United Artists, the distributor, weren't sure whether to release it nationally because they inexplicably thought it might be too unusual to attract mainstream audiences. Gary Arnold, who had seen the movie at a private screening, urged UA to give it a try in the D.C. area. They did, placing it at the Avalon Theater, and Gary's rave review in The Washington Post helped to draw sellout crowds during the Christmas season. The successful run apparently eased UA's doubts, because the distributor released *The Black Stallion* nationally the following spring] **[W]**

The Chosen [100]
1981 – Jeremy Paul Kagan
This charming, fascinating tale involves a friendship that builds out of initial antagonism between two young Jewish men in New York City in the 1940s. Reuven Malter (Barry Miller) is the son of a widowed father (Maximilian Schell, in perhaps the best role of his career), while Danny Saunders (Robbie Benson) is the son of an Orthodox rabbi (Rod Steiger, also in a fine performance and vastly different from his villainous Viktor Komarovski in *Doctor Zhivago* or his Oscar-winning redneck police chief Bill Gillespie in *In the Heat of the Night*). The contrasts between the two young men could not be more evident. Reuven and his father show genuine affection for each other, while Danny and Reb Saunders are almost entirely estranged. Reuven dresses normally, listens to popular music and likes girls; Danny studies the Torah and Talmud every day and shies away from outside contact. They seem destined to remain in different worlds, but after they meet during a street baseball game, and Danny hits a line drive directly at Reuven, shattering his glasses and injuring his eye, the boys begin developing a close and unusual friendship that eventually involves the entire Saunders family. Despite its slow pace, *The Chosen*, based on a short story by Chaim Potok, draws you in quickly. And its top-notch performances (Yet another Oscar travesty: Max Schell wasn't

even nominated), excellent script and assured direction by Kagan create a near-perfect little movie. The great Elmer Bernstein supplied the sentimental score. [Caution: some graphic newsreel footage of the Holocaust] **[W]**

Local Hero [100]
1983 – Bill Forsyth

This is Scottish writer-director Forsyth's most magical movie, a lovely, captivating tale of cultural conflict. A young Texas oil company executive with the given name MacIntyre (Peter Riegert) – whose heritage is actually Eastern European – is sent to northwestern Scotland to purchase a coastal village as the site for a refinery and tanker terminal. Little by little, however, he is seduced by the charm of the place, its quirky but lovable inhabitants and one strikingly appealing woman. Even those sketchy details might be too many, because if you simply give the movie half a chance, it will seduce and envelope you as it has millions of fans. With Peter Capaldi as Danny Oldsen, MacIntyre's geeky aide; Denis Lawson as Gordon, the village's jack of all trades; Jennifer Black as Stella, his comely wife; Fulton McCay as Ben, an eccentric but wise beachcomber; Jenny Seagrove as a sexy marine biologist – named Marina, who behaves suspiciously like a mermaid – and Burt Lancaster as Felix Happer, the oil company's CEO. Starting and ending in Houston, the movie offers one last shot that might provoke a longing in you that seems inconsolable – as though the village residents have won your heart and you are pleading with them to allow you to return. Mark Knopfler based his enchanting synthesized score on traditional Scottish tunes. [Trivia note: The movie's locale actually comprised several different and geographically separate sites in western Scotland, including Pennan for the village scenes, and Arisaig and Morar for the beach and other exteriors. The phone booth was installed only for the movie and, though at last report it remains in Pennan, it no longer operates] [Slight caution: just a wee bit o' rough language] **[W]**

American Flyers [100]
1985 – John Badham
Of all of my hundred favorites, this one might be closest to the border. It's probably the toughest to defend because in some ways it isn't a very good movie – it's contrived, unnecessarily melodramatic and predictable. Nevertheless, I'm quite fond of it because of its subject: bicycle racing. It was written by Steve Tesich, whose debut movie script was the delightful *Breaking Away*, which also deals with cycling. Here, two estranged brothers, Marcus and David Sommers (Kevin Costner and David Grant) attempt to renew their relationship while training for a grueling, three-stage, cross-country race in Colorado called the Hell of the West – a fictionalized version of the Coors Classic. Along the way they deal with longstanding family issues, Marcus's estrangement from his mother (versatile actress Janice Rule) and the specter of a fatal illness, while Rae Dawn Chong and Alexandra Paul provide the guys' respective love interests, Sarah and Becky. There's also a tense competition between the brothers and Marcus's former teammate and best friend, Barry "The Cannibal" Muzzin (Luca Bercovici). As I said, the plot is fairly standard and some of the editing is noticeably clumsy, but the racing scenes are terrific – electrifying, even – particularly the middle sequence, shot by Don Peterman and taking place among the breathtaking scenery of the Colorado National Monument. It's not for everyone, but maybe you'll warm to it, as I did. The movie's pulsing, catchy score is by Greg Mathieson and Lee Ritenour. [Trivia note: The high prairie landscape for the first stage of the race, shot near Boulder, today is almost entirely covered in urban sprawl] [Caution: language and sexuality] **[W]**

Lost in America [100]
1985 – Albert Brooks
Brooks is easily the most unique contemporary auteur in American cinema comedy, and though his list of attractions is relatively short his talent should not be minimized, particularly because he also stars in each of them. Here he plays David Howard, a highly paid executive at a Los Angeles advertising

agency. One day, he experiences sort of a breakdown during a meeting with his boss because he had thought he would be promoted, but instead he is ordered to pack quickly and move to New York City. As a result, he quits his job and, with his wife Linda (Julie Hagerty), decides to "drop out of society." So, they liquidate all of their assets and set out in a 35-foot recreational vehicle to find America. This grand plan lasts exactly one day, however, because the Howards make the terrible mistake of stopping in Las Vegas, and before it's over Linda has altered their lives drastically, possibly subconsciously and probably forever. The rest of the story deals with their coming to terms with their sudden crisis. It includes a stay in the sleepy town of Safford, Arizona, the dispatch of a cocky young fast food manager named Skippy (Joey Coleman), a desperate race across the country, and a Big Apple finale that wins applause and cheers. It's all very funny and all too plausible – except for the parking space (you'll see). [Trivia notes: 1) This was a lean production, with minimal crew and always using available scenery and building interiors. It truly is a road movie, in the tradition of – but not remotely resembling – David Howard's inspiration, *Easy Rider* (definitely not here). 2) The Mercedes-Benz salesman on the phone with David, billed as Hans Wagner in the credits, is actually Brooks with a German accent carrying on a conversation with himself] [Caution: language] **[W]**

Raising Arizona [100]
1985 – Joel and Ethan Coen
Full disclosure: I'm not a fan of the Coens. In fact, it continues to amaze me how well-regarded these moviemaking brothers remain in Hollywood despite producing a long series of self-indulgent and misconceived duds – even their hits are often repulsive. That said, *Raising Arizona* is their one exception. Though it also has its problems, it endeared itself to me right from the start and remains one of my hundred favorites. Usually I don't like portrayals of "simple folk" on the screen, because they tend to be patronizing and almost never convincing. And the folk here are particularly patronized. But for some

inexplicable reason it doesn't matter; all of the characters are funny and sympathetic. Particularly endearing is the protagonist and narrator H.I. "Hi" McDunnough (Nicolas Cage), a small-time crook who falls in love with Edwina (Holly Hunter in her breakthrough role), a police officer. They marry and proceed to work vigorously to start a family but soon learn that "Ed" can't conceive. About that time, they read a newspaper article about a famous Arizona husband and wife who have just been blessed with quintuplets and who tell the media they "have more than they can handle." So Hi and Ed plot to steal one of the babies for their own. Don't worry; it's all done for laughs, and at no time is anyone in real danger – even when they are pursued by a character who could be called the Biker from Hell. The whole cast, under the Coens' direction, hams it up big time – particularly John Goodman and William Forsythe as a pair of career criminals – but the movie works nevertheless because the Coens are so consistently clever visually, and their script is so witty. Here, the sight gags and wry one-liners reign supreme, and it's a great title to introduce to young people who dream of making movies. Carter Burwell wrote the twangy score. [Caution: a couple of errant swear words, some cartoon-like violence and a suggested bunny murder] **[W]**

Heavenly Pursuits (aka The Gospel According to Vic) [100]

1986 – Scotland – Charles Gormley

Here's another title that conveys the sense of this category perfectly: It captivates you while you're watching, leaves you with a sense of complete satisfaction, and beckons you to return again. The subject this time is miracles – or rather whether miracles are real or just coincidences enhanced by wishful thinking. Tom Conti plays Vic Mathews, a teacher at the Blessed Edith Semple School in Glasgow, Scotland, where the faculty and community are looking for a miracle to confirm that their namesake has achieved sainthood and should be canonized by Rome. That miracle seems to arrive when Vic tries to save the life of a careless student. Attempting to jump across a wide gap between two rooftops, he survives a fall of some 40 feet, suffering only cuts and bruises. But Vic, who's an agnostic, doesn't want the miracle-man distinction. He'd rather achieve miraculous progress with his troubled students the old-fashioned way: by working hard at it. And he'd like to romance the school's pretty music teacher, Ruth Chancellor (Helen Mirren at her most alluring). Vic grows angrier and more confused when additional unexplained events seem to find him, including what seems to be a genuine miracle. As Vic, Conti gives the best performance of his career, although I've never seen such a laconic protagonist. It's as though Vic decided to proceed through life in a permanently blissed-out state, and life has obliged him by doing no harm. Conti's facial expressions after Vic's brushes with mortality, and immortality, are priceless. The fine cast includes Jennifer Black of *Local Hero* (above) and David Hayman of *Hope and Glory* (below). [Trivia note: Ewen Bremner, playing the reticent student Stevie Deans, marked his movie debut here. He went on to appear in more than 90 titles, on TV as well as on the big screen, and he also became a producer] [Caution: language and sexuality] [**W**]

Hope and Glory [100]
1987 – John Boorman
Another example of my disliking every other movie by a director (or pair of directors in the case of the Coen brothers) but absolutely loving one title. Boorman's fanciful, autobiographical tale of a young boy growing up in England during the Blitz is a treasure, pleasing to look at and affectionately told. It's the story of the fictional Rowan family and their friends and neighbors, beginning on the day of the country's entry into World War II – Sunday, September 3, 1939 – and following them for a calendar year of wartime experiences. The movie is full of rich and sometimes raunchy humor but also genuine pathos, and it features a wonderful cast – at the center of which is Sebastian Rice Edwards, only 10 years old at the time, playing Bill, the son of Clive and Grace Rowan (David Hayman and Sarah Miles). He's feisty and quite mature for his age. In fact, sometimes he's

501

more level-headed than anyone else, particularly his precocious older sister Dawn (Sammi Davis) and his dotty grandfather (Ian Bannen, age 59 at the time but slightly made up to look 73). The movie contains two distinct parts, and they're both hugely appealing. The first unfolds in the family's row house in London, where you grow attached to everyone. The second takes place in the gorgeous English countryside (in Middlesex and Sussex), which seems more idyllic and appealing than anywhere else on Earth, a place you'll most likely love. There's a sequence that becomes a humorous take on the Biblical miracle of the fishes that will leave you in stitches, and the fadeout line often brings cheers. As Gary Arnold said when he first screened *Hope and Glory*, and highly recommended it to me, it's a movie that cries out for a sequel – or several sequels. You just don't want to leave this wacky family. Peter Martin contributed the oh-so-British score. [Trivia note: Boorman eventually did do a sequel, *Queen and Country* in 2014 (not on this list). It has its moments but ends up a pale imitation of the original] [Caution: sexuality and rough language (mostly by the kids, not the adults!)] **[W]**

Moonstruck [100]

1987 – Norman Jewison

This lighthearted modern romance about Italian-Americans, which doesn't involve the Mafia and for the most part actually stars Italian-Americans, is quite dear. Set in New York City, though much of it was shot in Toronto, it involves Loretta Castorini (Cher, in an Oscar-winning role), widowed after a brief marriage and now engaged again to the wimpy and dull Johnny Cammareri (Danny Aiello). Cosmo, her father (Vincent Gardenia), isn't pleased, but Rose, her mother (Olympia Dukakis, also winning an Oscar), doesn't mind because Loretta is not really in love with Johnny, although she likes him. "When you love 'em they drive you crazy because they know they can," Rose advises. As Loretta begins making her wedding plans, Johnny flies off to Sicily to visit his dying mother. Before he leaves, he asks Rose to visit his estranged brother Ronnie to invite him to the wedding. She agrees but quickly discovers that

Ronnie (Nicolas Cage) is far different from his older brother. Ronnie is a hothead who bears a grudge, and Loretta is immediately attracted to him. Before either of them knows what has happened, they have fallen into bed and in love. That can't be allowed, given Loretta's engagement, so in a famous scene she slaps Ronnie and orders him to, "Snap out of it!" But you know, and she knows, things will never be the same. The versatile Jewison gave his actors lots of freedom, and they made the most of John Patrick Shanley's Oscar-winning script. Every character is vivid, particularly Ronnie and Loretta, whom you just know will end up together. [Trivia notes: 1) Olympia is the cousin of Michael Dukakis, the former governor of Massachusetts who unsuccessfully ran for president against George H.W. Bush in 1988. Dukakis cheered him on during her Oscar acceptance speech. 2) Many of the scenes required multiple takes because Jewison's indulgent, on-set laughter at the actors' antics often brought the shooting to a halt] [Caution: mild sexuality] **[W]**

The Princess Bride [100]
1987 – Rob Reiner
You could classify this as a fairy tale for adults, although there's nothing off-color about it – it would deserve a "G" rating except for one utterance of a religious epithet by a 10-year-old, and a profane declaration by an angry, wounded man. Based on the William Goldman novel, it's a story within a story. An elderly man (Peter Falk) visits his beloved grandson (Fred Savage), who's home in bed with a cold, and he insists on reading to him from a favorite book of his own childhood, The Princess Bride, by S. Morgenstern. Despite the boy's initial indifference, the grandfather presses on, and from there the movie very cleverly bounces back and forth between the story and the reading of the story. In the imaginary world, a beautiful young woman named Buttercup (Robin Wright, in a fine debut) falls in love with a poor farm boy named Westley (Cary Elwes, in a superb debut). He leaves her to seek his fortune but later is thought to have been killed by the Dread Pirate Roberts (who appears, sort of,

further into the story). Deeply grieved and no longer caring what happens, Buttercup agrees to marry Prince Humperdinck (the versatile Chris Sarandon), who seems noble and gallant but is revealed to be treacherous. Humperdinck conspires with his evil henchman Count Rugen (the even more versatile Christopher Guest, in impeccable aristocratic guise) to kidnap Buttercup and blame her abduction on Florin's enemy, Guilder. (Or is it Guilder's enemy, Florin? I keep confusing the two) To accomplish this, he hires the cunning and evil Vizzini (Wallace Shawn), assisted by Inigo Montoya (Mandy Patinkin), the greatest swordsman in the land; and Fezzik, a giant (professional wrestler Andre the Giant, who stood 7 feet tall and weighed 450 pounds). Their plans run awry when … well, that's enough exposition. Better for you to discover and enjoy the Screaming Eels, the Cliffs of Insanity, the R.O.U.S.'s, the Pit of Despair and other wonders. The movie is unfailingly clever, and Reiner directs with the surest of hands. It's a great one to introduce to kids when they begin to appreciate adult humor, and you all can enjoy the beautiful English and Irish scenery, Mark Knopfler's charming score, one of the greatest sword fights ever filmed, and the terrific cameo performances (in heavy makeup) by Billy Crystal and Carol Kane as Miracle Max and his hectoring wife, Valerie. [A note about the book: In Goldman's novel, he purports to have abridged the Morgenstern classic, taking out the long and boring parts the way his own father did when he read the tale to him in his boyhood. I'm not saying the novel isn't extremely clever and enjoyable in its own right; it is. But when Goldman wrote the screenplay, he mercifully abridged and rearranged his book (at least, a lot of the dialogue), leaving only the best parts and thereby doing onscreen what he had purported to do with the novel. The rest of the story he leaves for you to discover within the book's pages] [Trivia note: Despite Andre's great size and strength, he was a remarkably fragile man at the time of the shoot. Wrestling injuries had weakened his back severely, to the point where he could barely lift even the lightweight Robin Wright, who had to be assisted by unseen cables] **[W]**

Midnight Run [100]
1988 – Martin Brest

This gritty and extremely clever chase caper pits a bounty hunter against his prey, his competitor and the Chicago mob. Jack Walsh, the bounty hunter (Robert De Niro) has five days to find mob accountant, star witness and bail-jumper Jonathan "the Duke" Mardukas (Charles Grodin) and return him to Los Angeles to stand trial. Walsh quickly unearths Mardukas, who has been hiding in New York. But when Jack captures him, Mardukas claims to be terrified of flying, so Jack must find an alternate means of getting him across the country. That complication eventually requires several modes of transportation, but to say any more would give away too much of the fun and surprises. The cast just brims with colorful character actors, particularly Joe Pantoliano as a bail bondsman, Yaphet Kotto as an FBI agent, John Ashton as a rival bounty hunter, Robert Miranda as a dim-witted hood, and especially Dennis Farina as a calmly murderous Las Vegas mob boss. Danny Elman wrote the wry, punchy score, and George Gallo supplied the sharp and witty – if profanity-laden – script. [Trivia notes: 1) The scene where Jack and Mardukas struggle to survive a plunge into a river with heavy rapids was shot in New Zealand, though the action was supposedly taking place in Arizona. The reason? The stream water in New Zealand was much warmer and more comfortable for the actors. 2) Brest appears in a witty cameo as a ticket clerk at McCarron Airport in Las Vegas. 3) Though Dennis Farina's character is supposed to be a former Chicago mob boss, and De Niro's is a former Chicago policeman, in reality Farina had served on the Chicago police force for nearly two decades. 4) As a testament to De Niro's prowess and versatility as an actor, he began shooting *Midnight Run* and playing the gruff but altogether likable and honest Jack Walsh immediately after he had finished his role as the murderous Al Capone in *The Untouchables*] [Caution: The term "profanity-laden" is not exaggerated here. With well more than 100 uses of the "f" word in the dialogue, the movie is not for delicate ears] [W]

Let It Ride [100]

1989 – Joe Pytka

A thoroughly lovable fantasy about a loser's fabulous day at the horse races in Miami, graced by an unerring ability not to take itself too seriously. Richard Dreyfuss plays Jay Trotter, a track regular who drives a cab at night to stay solvent and whose estranged wife Pam (Teri Garr) has agreed to take him back on the condition that he abandon his gambling compulsion. That is Jay's intention at the beginning, but he soon discards it when he hears a tape, secretly recorded by his friend and fellow driver, Looney (musician David Johansen), of a conversation between two passengers. One is a horse trainer who tells an associate that he has been deliberately holding back a thoroughbred in several races so he can make a big score. Trotter decides to bet on what he sees as a sure thing so he can return to Pam with a little more cash in his pocket. That action seems to unleash the fates, which propel Jay through an incredible winning streak, to his great delight and increasing self-confidence. But the good fortune also creates frustration among his friends and fellow tracksters, all of whom begin to dissociate themselves from him – as if his good luck is bad for everyone else. The rich assortment of fine supporting players and veteran character actors provides the movie's heart and charm, particularly Robbie Coltrane as a jaded ticket seller, Richard Dimitri as an outlandishly dressed track lizard named Tony Cheeseburger, Richard Edson as a loan shark's slimy enforcer, Jennifer Tilly as an irresistible bimbo and Ed Walsh as the wizened proprietor of a trackside bar. They and everyone else in the movie seem demented in some way, but endearingly so – except Pam, whom Garr endows with enough common sense and real concern for Jay that she keeps the whole thing balanced. Shot at the gorgeous Hialeah Park racetrack by Curtis Wehr, with a lively, tongue-in-cheek score by Giorgio Moroder, the movie feels as comfortable and familiar as an old shoe. [Trivia notes: 1) This is the second time Dreyfuss and Garr teamed as husband and wife onscreen. The first was in 1977 in *Close Encounters of the Third Kind*. 2) Screenwriter Nancy Dowd (*Slap Shot*) objected so much to how director Pytka changed the ending that she withdrew her name from the credits, surrendering authorship to the fictional Ernest Morton] [Caution: language and some sexuality] **[W]**

The Commitments [100]
1991 – Alan Parker

A terrifically energetic musical comedy set amid the working-class families of Dublin, Ireland, and representing all youngsters who dream of breaking out of the drabness of their lives into the bright lights of stardom. Robert Arkins is Jimmy Rabbitte, one of the dreamers, a hustler who fancies himself an impresario. He decides to put together a band that performs his favorite music, Soul, featuring the songs that arose out of Detroit (known as MoTown) in the 1960s and immortalized by artists such as Wilson Pickett, Otis Redding and Joe Tex; and by Aretha Franklin, Mary Wells and the Marvelettes. So, Jimmy begins auditioning talent, and the audition sequence alone is priceless and hysterically funny. From those tryouts, and some other decisions and recommendations, he chooses the 10 members of the band eventually named The Commitments, including six musicians, three backup singers and a soloist – every one of them a distinctive character. For example, there's Joey "The Lips" Fagan (Johnny Murphy), the itinerant trumpeter whose background might or might not be imaginary. There's Mikah Wallace (Dave Finnegan), the fearsome drummer who doubles as the band's most effective bodyguard. There are the Commitmentettes, the band's backup singers, including Bernie (Bronagh Gallagher), Imelda (Angeline Ball) and Natalie (Maria Doyle Kennedy), each of whom can belt out a song as electrifyingly as any Motown artist ever did. And there's Deco, the lead singer, played stunningly well by Andrew Strong. Only 16 years old when Parker cast him but looking and performing far beyond his years, Strong's voice gives the band its strength – its soul. All the while, Jimmy provides an unusual and amusing narration, as he pretends to be interviewed after becoming famous. Whether he and the band will succeed, given the mercurial personalities involved, is questionable. But that's almost immaterial. What makes the movie so special is watching these appealing characters grow together into a genuinely talented group, short-lived though it might be. Funny, profane and always entertaining, *The Commitments* is Parker's love letter to Dublin, and it will leave you satisfied and feeling that you've also got soul. So say it once, and say it loud, "I'm black and I'm proud!" [Trivia notes: 1) The movie's slang is so alien to non-Irish audiences that during the original promotional campaign the distributors provided critics and journalists with a handbook called "A Tosser's Glossary." Speaking of which, don't be a tosser; see the movie! 2) As I have cautioned below, the movie is chock-full of profanity, because Dubliners are naturally profane – to the point where the cast even interjected harsher words not in the script to make their lines sound more natural to them. 3) Parker insisted that all of the cast's vocals be recorded live during their performances to capture their energy and spirit, a most challenging task for the audio technicians. But the effort paid off; some of the group's renditions of Motown classics are sensational. 4) Possibly the most accomplished musician of the group was Arkins, whom Parker cast as the band's manager because of his acting qualities. He sings one number over the opening credits and another as audio background, but he doesn't play or sing on-camera. 5) The only non-musician in the cast is Murphy, whom Parker also chose for his acting ability. 6) It's the stuff of casting legend. Strong came to Parker's attention when he attended an early production session with his father, Rob Strong, a noted singer in Ireland – aka the "Father of Irish Soul" – with whom Parker was consulting about the movie's soundtrack. At his dad's invitation, Andrew performed some of the songs under consideration and, despite his considerable youth, blew everyone away] [Caution: Yes, there's plenty of profanity in this movie – even senior citizens toss around the "f" word the way other people say "darn it" – but the Dublin accents are so heavy it probably will take you a while to begin to understand the dialogue, even the cussing] [Viewing note: Although the movie is in English, it really could use subtitles for American audiences] **[W]**

Groundhog Day [100]
1993 – Harold Ramis

This one must have been a pip to shoot, because it's difficult enough keeping track of things just watching it unfold on the screen. Bill Murray, in his best role, plays Phil Connors, a frustrated weatherman for a television station in Pittsburgh assigned to do what they call in the TV biz a puff piece, a stand-up report from Punxsutawney, Pennsylvania, on February 2nd – Groundhog Day. He's accompanied there by his attractive new producer, Rita (Andie MacDowell, in the first of three consecutive titles), and a dorky cameraman (Chris Elliott). As Phil expects, everything proceeds duly and dully according to plan – until an unexpected blizzard traps the crew for an extra night. That's when things go seriously haywire. The next morning, instead of February 3rd, somehow Phil has become trapped in a perpetual Groundhog Day. It occurs over and over and over again, so many times that you can't even count, but the excruciating process serves to transform Phil as a human being and, possibly, find him true love. As with many of my favorite movies, this one combines lots of laughs with truly touching moments, and though it's a fantasy it accumulates a reservoir of real emotion. Murray is perfect as Phil, who runs through the classic gamut of emotions for people who are trapped in their destiny: shock, denial, anger, bargaining and finally acceptance. Everyone else in the cast is fine, too, including Steven Tobolowsky as Ned Ryerson, perhaps the world's biggest nerd, and Rick Ducommun and Rick Overton as two colorful locals. Like many of the others in this category, *Groundhog Day* is a little movie – but it's a great little movie. [Trivia note: The movie exteriors weren't shot in Punxsutawney. Instead, the producers chose Woodstock, Illinois, which they thought looked more like Punxsutawney … than Punxsutawney! Actually, the producers rejected the real town because 1) it doesn't have an attractive central square (I know – I've been there), 2) Gobbler's Knob is a real hilltop in a wooded area, and 3) Woodstock is close enough to Chicago that it made transportation during the shoot much easier for cast and crew] [Caution: mild sexuality] **[W]**

509

Michael [100]
1996 – Nora Ephron
A love story but an unconventional one, because it's about unbridled enjoyment of the human experience in all of its forms. This whimsical fantasy is a lightweight take on the German movie *Wings of Desire* (poorly remade by Hollywood as *City of Angels* – and neither on this list). It's much closer to the portrayal of angels in the endearing classics, *It's a Wonderful Life* and *The Bishop's Wife*, but with an updated twist. John Travolta plays the title role, Michael the Archangel, who has descended to Earth, perhaps for the last time, first to help a widow (Jean Stapleton) keep a bank from seizing her property, and then to bring two lost souls (William Hurt and Andie MacDowell) together. Not as lyrical as *Local Hero*, but in some ways it's just as captivating, due entirely to Travolta, who's as self-assured here as he was in *Get Shorty* but in a different context. He seems to be having a thoroughly wonderful time, and his enthusiasm is infectious, connecting with fellow cast members and audiences alike. There are several fine scenes, but Travolta's effortless number on the dance floor while flanked by a gaggle of females is the best physical work he's done since *Saturday Night Fever* (coming in the next compilation), and MacDowell's impromptu ballad about a flat tire is the most endearing number since Diane Keaton crooned "Seems Like Old Times" in *Annie Hall*. Michael sums it all up by declaring, rightly, "you can never eat too much sugar" – or pie! Randy Newman composed the distinctly American score. [A slight caution: mild profanity and harm (albeit temporary) to an adorable dog] [W]

The Muse [100]
1999 – Albert Brooks
The second in this category by Brooks, who over the years has produced some of the most enjoyable and unusual comedies in Hollywood, and this one qualifies on both counts. Here he plays Steven Phillips, an Oscar-winning screenwriter whose star is beginning to fade – he's "lost his edge," as friends, family and studio executives put it. Becoming increasingly worried about

510

maintaining his family's comfortable lifestyle, he turns to his still-successful friend Jack Warrick (Jeff Bridges), who in turn refers him to the secret of that success, Sarah Little (Sharon Stone, in her best role). Sarah, Jack explains to Steven, is a Muse, in the classical Greek sense. She's an immortal who can inspire humans to do their best – *if* she decides to help them. When she accepts Steven as her latest project, his life will never be the same, particularly where his marriage to Laura (Andie MacDowell, in yet another appealing role) is concerned. That's enough of the plot. You'll have to discover the rest for yourself – but you won't be disappointed. [Trivia note: The movie's music, which resembles classical pieces, was composed by none other than Sir Elton John – and he sings the movie's pop theme over the end credits] [Caution: brief nudity and a touch of rough language] **[W]**

Catch Me If You Can [100]
2002 – Steven Spielberg

The best screenwriters will take a simple theme and work it over and over again in as many variations as possible, in as many clever ways as possible, until the audience appreciates every new and nuanced version. The interesting thing about Jeff Nathanson, however, is that he's definitely not one of the best screenwriters. In fact, other than this title, I can't think of another movie he's written I found appealing. I'd place him in the same league with John Boorman, Alan Parker and the Coen brothers, one of whose titles each you'll find elsewhere in this category, but the entirety of their other work I could not abide. Yet in *Catch Me if You Can*, Nathanson took the theme of misdirection and elevated it to perfection – even better than David Ward did in *The Sting*. You'll find it in almost every scene, and the genius is how subtly or quickly it can be presented. That's fitting, because this is Spielberg's gossamer movie. It's light as a feather, and though its running time is over 2 hours it skips along ever so briskly. Based on the true story of Frank Abagnale, Jr. (Leonardo DiCaprio), a most unusual prodigy who, during his teen years in the mid-1960s (he's two weeks older than I am), ran away from his divorcing parents (Christopher Walken and Valerie Bey) and managed to defraud banks and corporations alike out of millions of dollars. The story follows the attempts of FBI agent Carl Hanratty (Tom Hanks), who specializes in tracking down check forgers, to catch Frank – if he can. Told mainly in flashback, it details how Abagnale began his career as a teenage criminal, how Hanratty eventually brought him to justice, and what happened after that. Spielberg uses the 1960s period to his advantage, featuring an amusing title sequence in the tradition of *The Pink Panther* (coming in the next compilation), and a crisp, sophisticated score by John Williams that evokes the best of Henry Mancini – who did *The Pink Panther*). Thoroughly absorbing and surprisingly affecting, it also features a nice turn by Amy Adams in her first major role. [Trivia notes: 1) Spielberg shot *Catch Me If You Can* at nearly 50 locations across the United States and Canada, more than any other of his movies, but the shoot took only 52 days. Must've been a whirlwind production. 2) His music here marks the second time Williams imitated Mancini. The first was in one of his earliest credits, *How to Steal a Million* (coming in my second compilation)] [Caution: language and sexuality] [W]

Step Into Liquid [100]
2003 – Dana Brown

In 1966, Bruce Brown, father of the director here, made a simple, 16-millimeter documentary called *The Endless Summer* (coming in the next compilation). It followed two surfers around the world in search of "the perfect wave." Produced on a tiny budget, it became a cult classic, and *Step into Liquid* is its successor. A far more technically dazzling look at the world's surfing scene at the beginning of the 21st century, like the first movie this one is episodic, following the exploits of surfing enthusiasts all over the world and in some seemingly unlikely places – such as Ireland, Vietnam, the Houston Ship Channel and, that magnet for surfing enthusiasts, Sheboygan, Wisconsin! No matter the location, it's a captivating exploration of one of humanity's most ethereal activities, populated by a host of characters whose unique take on living (Their slogan is, "Surfing is not a matter of life and death – it's much more important than that!) might just encourage you to grab a board and shoot a curl, all against a background of a memorable theme and a host of cool songs composed and compiled by Richard Gibbs. The finale, where surfers travel 100 miles off the Southern California coast to a location called the Cortes Bank, where wind and currents converge to produce some of the most monstrous waves on Earth, is awesome and terrifying. But be the waves giant or tepid, this movie, as its participants would describe it, will leave you "stoked!" **[W]**

Secretariat [100]
2010 – Randall Wallace

In the summer of 1973, horse-racing fans across the country glued themselves to their TV screens to watch the 99th running of the Belmont Stakes and see whether Secretariat, who had been named Horse of the Year in 1972, could do what had not been done in a quarter century – win the anchor leg of racing's Triple Crown. Secretariat had already won the Kentucky Derby and the Preakness, both in record times (which stand to this day). But the Belmont, at a length of a mile and a half, was known as the "graveyard of speed horses." If you're old enough to remember what happened, I don't need to go on. If you're too young to remember, you should watch to find out, because it's electrifying, and I don't exaggerate. What I can tell you is this is a compelling, well-told story about the people involved with the horse – people who dared to reach higher than they had ever reached before and risked, literally, everything in the process. Though the movie skirts over a lot of personal details about the real characters, it doesn't gloss over them, either, and Diane Lane, John Malkovich and the diminutive Otto Thorwarth (playing, respectively, owner Penny Chenery Tweedy, trainer Lucien Laurin and jockey Ron Turcotte) give terrific performances. But the real glory of the movie belongs to the production team, which not only recreated the Derby and Belmont in precise detail but also seamlessly melded the five different thoroughbreds that collectively played the greatest racing horse of all time. [Trivia note: This is an unusual one, because I don't want to spoil anything. After you've watched the movie, look up the details of Secretariat's unprecedented performances in the Kentucky Derby, the Preakness and the Belmont Stakes then search for the horse's highly unusual physical attribute. I guarantee you'll find the information astonishing] **[W]**

Chef [100]
2014 – written, produced and directed by John Favreau
Ostensibly a movie about the skillful preparation of food, it's also one of the nicest stories about father–son bonding I've ever seen – but the food and food-prep scenes are terrific as well. Favreau stars as Carl Casper, a rising-star chef at a popular L.A. restaurant who becomes involved in a public war of words with a trendy restaurant critic (Oliver Platt). When the war escalates, via a storm of angry exchanges on Twitter, and the restaurant's owner (Dustin Hoffman, in a wry performance) inserts himself, Carl decides he must quit – something that ignites the real story. It seems Carl's devotion to his work has damaged his relationship with his son Percy (11-year-old Emjay Anthony, who's hugely appealing). But with the help of his ex-wife Inez (Colombian supermodel Sofia Vergara), and an unexpected trip to Miami – including a brief encounter with Inez's other ex-husband (Robert Downey Jr.) – Carl's life is transformed in a great way, involving a coast-to-coast road trip in a food truck. A happy ending, yes. And some of it seems too easy and improbable. But that trip from Miami back to L.A. is almost heavenly – it makes you wish you could have accompanied Carl, Percy and Carl's buddy and co-chef, Tony (Bobby Cannavale), to savor some of the mouth-watering gourmet delights they serve, and encounter, along the way. [Trivia notes: 1) Favreau spent weeks under the tutelage of Chef Roy Choi, learning the culinary basics, and it shows. 2) Favreau had directed and co-starred with Downey six years earlier in *Iron Man* (coming in a future compilation)] [Caution: rough language and mild sexuality] **[W]**

Postscript – Roll Your Own

Now that you've browsed through my list and, I hope, found more than a few new-to-you titles to explore, maybe you should start thinking about your own all-time favorites. The hundreds of titles I've presented here represent the hard work of many, many talented people who, in the immortal words of *Singin' in the Rain*'s Lina Lamont, labored to bring "a little joy into your humdrum lives." They've certainly done so for me and, as I've said, I hope many will work their way onto your favorites list as well. But I'll let you in on a little secret, in case you haven't discovered it for yourself. The best way to tell how well you like a movie is how you react to it when it's available to be seen. I have enjoyed many movies at first viewing, but somehow they haven't managed to hold up for a second screening. Others, however, have intensified with repetition, and some have never failed to satisfy, no matter how many times I've sat through them. Figuring out which ones do the same for you – which is not an easy task, because you'll find that your tastes change over time – will help you begin to compile your own list of favorites. I think you'll find it a rewarding experience.

Why do it? Because, as I wrote at the beginning, digital technology is bringing us more and more movies on a permanent basis, which means you can introduce your children and grandchildren to your favorites. And even if you're not around to show them, someday they might enjoy a laugh or a sigh or a gasp they might not have discovered except for your recommendation, and in doing so they'll achieve a connection to their past and to someone who thought enough to pass on a potentially memorable experience.

Movies might not be eternal, but for the time being they offer a way to bond the generations. As long as that's possible, I want to bequeath some of the most enjoyable moments of my life to my loved ones, and their loved ones, and so on.

I hope you'll do the same.

Recommended Books

We're doubly fortunate to live in the digital age. Not only can we preserve and prolong many of the classic products of cinema indefinitely, but the Internet also allows us to seek and find the best movie books – whether or not they're still in print. If you're deeply interested in movies, here are 22 of my favorite titles – plus one ancillary source – to get you started. They include some of the best backgrounders and volumes of critiques ever written, plus a couple of source novels, all of which I think will greatly add to your moviegoing pleasure.

The Making of Kubrick's 2001
Edited by Jerome Agel

An expensive, coffee-table volume about the movie's production was published in 2015, but I haven't yet seen it, and in any event this mass-market paperback compilation, published in 1970, managed to cram a huge amount of production details between its covers – including nearly 100 pages of photographs and drawings, all culled from other sources. It's a little gem of cinema history.

David O. Selznick's Hollywood
Ron Haver

This is one of the most gloriously detailed, beautiful accounts about movie production imaginable, though the title is currently out of print. The probable reason: It must have been hugely expensive to produce. Haver devotes the centerpiece of his book – including 75 lavishly illustrated pages – to Selznick's masterpiece, *Gone with the Wind*. But there's plenty of other eye-popping material to keep you interested from cover to cover.

The Filmgoer's Companion
Leslie Halliwell

At the risk of seeming immodest, Halliwell's classic text is like a print version of this ebook. He writes capsules about notable movies, actors and actresses, directors, producers and even themes. But unlike him, I've only published five editions – he has published 12, each much more expansive, and each a highly informative, magnificent love letter to cinema.

The Godfather
Mario Puzo

The first two filmed versions of Puzo's 1969 bestseller, *The Godfather* in 1972 and *The Godfather Part II* in 1974 – both of them Best Picture winners – sensationalized and popularized the nature and operations of Italian-American organized crime in the United States. Both movies stand on their own as towering cinematic achievements. If you ever want to gain more background about this topic, however, albeit fictionalized and a bit fanciful but in an eminently readable form, consider going back to the source.

The Hunt for Red October
Tom Clancy

Ever since I first read Clancy's tale that originated the fabled character of CIA analyst Jack Ryan and made him a publishing star, I've considered it the quintessential page-turner – a lengthy book that, once started, is difficult to put down. Originally released by the relatively unknown Naval Institute Press, The Hunt for Red October quickly became a phenomenon. It's easy to understand why. Whether based on real research or his own imagination, Clancy weaves an intensely gripping story about the high stakes played by the men involved in modern submarine warfare. The 1989 movie was well-crafted for general audiences, but the novel (excuse the pun) dives much deeper and in a satisfying way.

Into Thin Air
John Krakauer

The ill-fated expedition in May 1996 to the summit of Mount Everest, and chronicled in the movie, *Everest*, was based on this personal account by Krakauer, who had decided to participate in the climb in order to do an article for Outside magazine. A former climber himself, Krakauer knew all about the growing worries surrounding the proliferation of Everest expeditions; likewise the casual attitudes expressed by some of the clients happily paying large sums for such a dangerous undertaking. But little did he know the scope of the tragedy that would unfold those two fateful and tragic days on the mountain. His clear-headed and sobering account stands as a warning to anyone who would ever again dare to take for granted the power and indifference of Nature.

The Jaws Log
Carl Gottlieb

Jaws became the first summer movie blockbuster and, temporarily, the biggest box-office hit of all time. But before the smashing success came the excruciating production, which dragged on for months beyond its original deadline and created often-agonizing but not-altogether-negative experiences for its cast, its crew and its 27-year-old director, Steven Spielberg. Gottlieb's eminently readable chronicle of those months on Martha's Vineyard, Massachusetts, during the shoot makes for fascinating reading. It isn't so much a technical description of the production as an engaging tale about the personalities involved and the seemingly insurmountable obstacles they faced. All-in-all, it's a fun read.

The Princess Bride
William Goldman

Most moviegoers know Rob Reiner's version of Goldman's novel as a delightful, funny, whimsical tale of "true love." But the book's full title is The Princess Bride: An Illustrated Edition of S. Morgenstern's Classic Tale of True Love and High Adventure. Within its pages is a richer story, a much subtler one, and one that has grown even more enjoyable as the years – and the subsequent editions – have gone by. You could call Goldman's work a book within a book within a wonderful contrivance. Essentially, Goldman claims that his father told him the story of The Princess Bride during his serious illness as a child, and ever since then he resolved to research S. Morgenstern, the elusive author, and introduce him to an appreciative world. The joke, however, is that the text flowed wholecloth from Goldman's imagination. If you love the movie, read the novel, and you'll likely enjoy them both immensely – though for different reasons.

The Right Stuff
Tom Wolfe
As good as Philip Kaufman's 1983 movie is, Wolfe's book is even better. He takes nonfiction prose to an ethereal level in his description of the men who risked their lives to advance American aviation, from the early days of the jet age in 1947 to the end of Project Mercury in 1965, the first stage of the country's manned space program. And full credit goes to Wolfe for giving the saga of the test pilots' and astronauts' wives equal footing with the story of their husbands. In doing so, he has created a unique American history destined to remain a classic. It's an engrossing chronicle and not to be missed.

When the Shooting Stops ... the Cutting Begins: A Film Editor's Story
Ralph Rosenblum and Robert Karen
It isn't much of a coincidence that some of the best films of the 1960s and '70s featured Ralph Rosenblum as their editor. From *FAIL-SAFE* to *A Thousand Clowns* to *Annie Hall*, Rosenblum's brilliant touch is evident. And here, in this well-written chronicle, with the help of co-author Karen he describes the filmmaking process from the editor's standpoint. He includes descriptions of how he managed to create the illusion of an entire squadron of bombers taking off in *FAIL-SAFE*, when the U.S. Defense Department refused to provide more than one film clip of a single plane; how he livened up *A Thousand Clowns*, which was a Broadway play set in a one-room apartment; and how he turned *Annie Hall* from a vague and unfocused collection of scenes shot-by-shot into an Oscar-winning love story.

The reviews of Pauline Kael

If you grew up in the 1960s and loved and screened movies with any intensity or seriousness, and if you continued your cinephilia through the '70s and '80s, then more likely than not you read Kael regularly in The New Yorker magazine. Probably the most popular film critic of all time, Kael started life on a chicken farm in Petaluma, California, in 1919. She dropped out of college just before World War II, bounced around without distinction for a couple more decades, and then emerged from practically nowhere to take movie fans by storm with her unique wit, insights and ability to craft a phrase, either in ecstatic praise or savage ridicule. There were many fine critics before her – James Agee comes immediately to mind – and there have been many since. But no one has ever matched her combination of popularity, erudition and stature. To get an idea of how much celebrity she commanded, here's what journalist Sam Staggs wrote about doing a 1983 telephone interview with Kael for a magazine called Mandate. You can find the full text of his article, titled "Did She Lose It at the Movies?" in the 1996 anthology **Conversations with Pauline Kael**.

> "I had expected a brassy, metallic voice to crackle over the [telephone] wire: the press had portrayed her as a scold. Instead, she sounded like Marilyn Monroe, if Marilyn hadn't been shy and insecure. A breathy voice, sweet but firm, sexy, cultured, with more than a little show biz and perfect California enunciation … After a ten-minute chat I felt frightfully excited, as though I had talked to a star: as indeed I had."

Kael herself once described her captivating prose this way.
> "I worked to loosen my style – to get away from the term-paper pomposity that we learn at college. I wanted the sentences to breathe, to have the sound of a human voice."

Even if you're just starting – or even considering starting – a study of the movies as an art form, I can't think of a better introduction than the essays and reviews of Pauline Kael. Here are the 12 compilations of her work:

I Lost It at the Movies (1965)
This volume, published three years before she began her New Yorker gig, is her first compilation. It includes Kael's takes on some of the classics of the screen, and some fans consider her intensely personal review of *Shoeshine* (not on this list), a film by Italian director Vittorio De Sica, to be perhaps the greatest ever written. Though it's her most famous title, you might want to wait before reading it. Maybe start with Reeling (see below), which covers many familiar movies; or even 5001 Nights at the Movies (also below), which presents hundreds of her reviews encapsulated, and see how much you enjoy her writing. Then backtrack with as many of the earlier works as you like.

Kiss Kiss, Bang Bang (1968)
Another compilation containing Kael's reviews before she joined The New Yorker, this one includes brief takes on over 250 movies released from 1965 through 1967. She writes that she derived the book's title from an Italian movie poster, which she thought embodied the appeal of movies in the briefest possible language. The phrase has also been associated with the James Bond series.

Going Steady (1969)
Covering her first New Yorker reviews, which appeared under the blanket headline "The Current Cinema," Going Steady spans 1968 through 1970, including essays on movies that have faded from memory. I mention this because reading a Kael review of an obscure or even unknown title can show you why so many cinephiles love her. She is one of the few film critics who can engage your interest and arouse your delight even if you've never heard of the subject of her praise – or her scorn.

Deeper into Movies (1973)

Moving on to reviews from 1969 through 1972, some of Kael's essays here achieved legendary status, such as her gushing over Robert Altman's *McCabe and Mrs. Miller* and her savage pan of *Ryan's Daughter* (both coming in the next compilation), which as I mentioned earlier hurt director David Lean's feeling so much it was one of the reasons he stopped making movies for 15 years.

Reeling (1976)

In her fifth compilation, Kael moves into her prime, to the point where these reviews influenced audiences perhaps more than any other national critic. When she praised *The Godfather Part II* and *Nashville* in her inimitable way, for example, she ensured their commercial successes. And when she gave her blessing to Bernardo Bertolucci's notorious *Last Tango in Paris* (not here), which featured Marlon Brando shouting an unprintable opening line, she legitimized a movie that American audiences might otherwise have considered borderline pornographic.

When the Lights Go Down (1980)

This one covers the mid-to-late 1970s and features her notable reviews of *Jaws* and *Close Encounters of the Third Kind*, among dozens of others, plus what became one of her two most famous essays, "The Man from Dream City," about Cary Grant.

5001 Nights at the Movies (1982)

You might call this one "Pauline Kael Lite," because it features hundreds and hundreds of capsule reviews – yes, I know, like what I've done – but none of her full-length essays. Still, as I mentioned above, this might be the best way for you to gain an introduction to her style.

Taking It All In (1984)

The volume includes about 150 titles covering her reviews from 1980 through 1983. By this time, Kael had firmly reached the pinnacle of American film criticism, to the point where she felt no reluctance to pan the works of some of the country's most prominent directors – Francis Ford Coppola, for example, whose *Cotton Club* she thoroughly trashed.

State of the Art (1987)
Covering 1983 through 1985, Kael shocked her readership with an essay called "Why Are Movies So Bad?" which reflected her sabbatical spent in Hollywood during that period and which savaged the movie industry's shift from the studio system to risk-averse corporate management. Reviews of titles I've mentioned include raves for *Diner*, *Fanny and Alexander*, *Local Hero* and *Tootsie*.

Hooked (1989)
This one, including her reviews from 1985 through 1988, tested my patience with her pans of two titles I hold in high regard, both from Steven Spielberg: *The Color Purple* and *Empire of the Sun*. On the other hand, she shared my deep admiration for *The Unbearable Lightness of Being*.

Movie Love (1991)
Kael's eleventh compilation covers her reviews from 1988 through her retirement from The New Yorker in 1991. Movie Love is distinctive, for me at least, because it features very few titles of true distinction – a comment aimed more at the movie industry than at Kael. Plus, to my frustration, she lambastes one of my favorites: Kevin Costner's Oscar-winning *Dances with Wolves*.

For Keeps: 30 Years at the Movies (1994)
Published several years after her retirement, For Keeps features Kael's favorite reviews; her magnificent essay on Cary Grant and a wonderful bonus: her most famous essay, "Raising Kane," about the making of *Citizen Kane*. If you choose to buy only one book by Pauline Kael, I'd recommend this one – though it's currently out of print and available only from resellers.

Alphabetical List of Titles

C

D

G

I

J

K

L

M

N

O

P

Y

Z

Once Again ... My 100 Favorites
(in alphabetical order)

For Your Additional Consideration

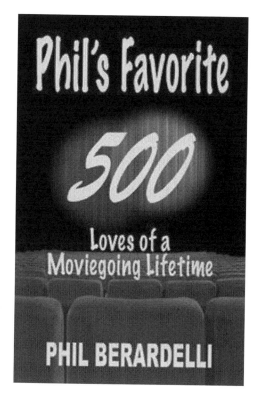

If you have enjoyed browsing through this compilation, please consider buying the ebook edition as well. Along with all of the content within these pages, I've included hundreds of links to movie clips and featurettes plus other references related to the capsule reviews. It's an inexpensive ($6.99) but fascinating and valuable addition to your moviegoing library.

Made in the USA
Columbia, SC
23 February 2023

12768268R00296